Communicating
Professionally

Communicating Professionally

A How-To-Do-It Manual®

Catherine Sheldrick Ross & Kirsti Nilsen

An imprint of the American Library Association

Chicago   2013

DR. CATHERINE SHELDRICK ROSS is Professor Emerita at The University of Western Ontario. She has taught graduate courses in reference services, readers' advisory work, and research methods in the MLIS and PhD programs at Western. She has presented more than 50 workshops to library professionals in the United States and Canada. Together with Patricia Dewdney, she has written two previous editions of *Communicating Professionally* and is a four-time winner of the Reference Services Press Award. She has published extensively in the areas of reference services, readers' advisory, and the ethnography of reading for pleasure. With co-authors Lynn (E. F.) McKechnie and Paulette M. Rothbauer, she has published *Reading Matters: What the Research Reveals about Reading, Libraries, and Community.*

DR. KIRSTI NILSEN is currently an independent researcher and writer. She taught introductory and advanced courses in reference, government information, collection development, special libraries, and information policy in the MLIS programs at both The University of Western Ontario and the University of Toronto. She was the co-author with Catherine Ross of the first and second editions of *Conducting the Reference Interview.* In addition, she is the author of *The Impact of Information Policy* and co-author of *Constraining Public Libraries: The World Trade Organization's General Agreement on Trade in Services.*

© 2013 by the American Library Association. Any claim of copyright is subject to applicable limitations and exceptions, such as rights of fair use and library copying pursuant to Sections 107 and 108 of the U.S. Copyright Act. No copyright is claimed for content in the public domain, such as works of the U.S. government.

Printed in the United States of America
17 16 15 14 13   5 4 3 2 1

Extensive effort has gone into ensuring the reliability of the information in this book; however, the publisher makes no warranty, express or implied, with respect to the material contained herein.

ISBNs: 978-1-55570-908-2 (paper); 978-1-55570-928-0 (PDF); 978-1-55570-929-7 (ePub); 978-1-55570-930-3 (Kindle).

Library of Congress Cataloging-in-Publication Data
Ross, Catherine Sheldrick.
    Communicating professionally : a how-to-do-it manual for librarians /
Catherine Sheldrick Ross and Kirsti Nilsen. — Third edition.
        pages   cm
    Includes bibliographical references and index.
    ISBN 978-1-55570-908-2 (alk. paper)
    1. Communication in library administration—United States. 2. Communication in library science—United States. 3. Library records—United States. 4. Library science—United States—Authorship. I. Nilsen, Kirsti. II. Title.
    Z678.R65 2013
    020.1'4—dc23   2013011593

Cover images © Shutterstock, Inc. Text composed in Minion Pro and Interstate typefaces.

∞ This paper meets the requirements of ANSI/NISO Z39.48-1992 (Permanence of Paper).

To Patricia Dewdney

Contents

Preface

In this third edition of *Communicating Professionally*, our goal
remains the same as it was in the first two editions: to provide a handy
source for library professionals that covers all aspects of professional
communication in one convenient book. The first edition began as a
response by Catherine Ross and Patricia Dewdney to the many librarians, educators, and students who attended our continuing education
workshops and graduate library and information science courses
and who asked us, "Where can we read about these communication
skills?" or "Can we use your handouts to develop our own staff training?" From the outset, we have tried both to compile some of our
most useful training materials and to provide a broader framework
for thinking about the communication skills needed in our field. And
now in the third edition, Kirsti Nilsen brings her expertise as a teacher
and a researcher in reference, library and information policy, and bibliography. Since the previous edition of *Communicating Professionally*,
new developments in technology have expanded the range of tools
available for professional communication. In this revision we have
updated all references and added new sections to take into account
the opportunities offered by new communication media. However,
the basics of human communication have not changed. The goal of
this new edition continues to be to translate these basic principles
into practical guidelines and exercises that can be used for training.
We also include current research-based material on communication
in general as well as findings of recent research on communication
conducted within the field of library and information science itself.

Effective communication is not a gift innate in the lucky few
but consists of skills that can be learned and practiced and taught
to others. Library professionals need to understand the principles

underlying effective communication, and they also need to learn and intentionally use specific communication skills in situations that arise on the job. Therefore, we have retained the microskills training approach, developed by Allen E. Ivey, but adapted it here for the library context.

This preface explains how the book is organized first to teach specific communication skills and second to show how individual skills can be combined effectively in specific library applications. We also suggest ways you may wish to use the book, and we describe features that are new in this expanded edition.

Underlying Assumptions

You will probably get better results from this manual if you share some of our fundamental beliefs:

- The primary mission of a library or information center is to serve its community by linking users, or potential users, with resources that meet their diverse and ever-changing information needs. (This may seem self-evident, but it's the premise on which all our other assumptions are based.)
- Communication skills are central to our jobs. Anyone in any kind of helping profession needs to be able to listen effectively, to ask productive questions, to speak in public, to write clearly, and to help groups function efficiently. The success of our mission and the survival of our institutions depend on the ability of library staff members to communicate with the public.
- Communication skills are learned rather than innate. Even those people who seem to be naturally good at interpersonal communication have learned these skills early in their lives, often from modeling others. And we know from research studies that those people who do not seem at first to be very good at interpersonal communication show after training the most immediate and lasting improvement in their communication behavior.
- Tools that are specifically designed for library staff training now exist. The methodology and resources for successfully

identifying, teaching, learning, applying, and evaluating human communication skills have been available for many years in other helping professions—social work, teaching, counseling, and health services. Now that we have an established body of research on communication skills within library and information science itself, we are able to draw on this work to teach skills to library practitioners in ways that address specific library contexts and applications.

Communicating Professionally takes a people-oriented rather than a system-oriented approach to information service. If you believe that people can change, and that they really do want to learn how to give better service, then this book will provide you with some tools for helping yourself and others. Through systematic observation of behavioral changes and through feedback from our trainees, we know that these skills *can* be learned and *do* work in actual on-the-job situations.

Frameworks for Thinking and Learning

Communicating Professionally is, above all, intended to be a practical guide. Believing that there is nothing so practical as a good theory, we have based this book on two major frameworks for thinking and learning about human communication: *microtraining* and *sensemaking*. We explain these approaches in more detail in Chapter 5.

Briefly, *microtraining* is based on the idea that complex communication behavior can be broken down into its constituent parts or small (micro) skills and that these skills can be taught, one at a time, in a systematic way that involves the following steps:

1. Defining the skill and identifying its function
2. Observing the skill modeled
3. Reading about the skill and the concepts behind it
4. Practicing the skill in a context that provides feedback (e.g., audiorecording or videorecording)
5. Using the skill in a "real world" context and observing the consequences
6. Teaching the skill to others

Microtraining, a model developed by Allen E. Ivey for teaching interview skills to counselors, is an excellent way to teach basic speaking skills to prospective librarians and information service workers. Following Ivey's basic hierarchy of microskills (see Chapter 5), we have concentrated on those skills most appropriate for information service—particularly the basic listening sequence, questioning techniques, and other skills that library staff can use in their everyday contacts with clients and staff.

We found at the same time that we could extend the microtraining method to written communication and group work. For written communication, the components that make for effectiveness can be identified (unity, coherence, clarity, brevity, variety, force, correctness, etc.), modeled, practiced, and taught just as oral communication skills can be taught. Many microskills that contribute to an effective interview are identifiable in group work, as psychologist Robert F. Bales demonstrated many years ago in his work on group interaction. There is no reason, then, why group skills cannot be taught as part of a microtraining program.

The second major framework for *Communicating Professionally* is *sense-making*, an approach that gives rise to user-centered strategies and techniques for interpersonal communication. Following the work of Brenda Dervin, we have used sense-making to focus on how people "make sense" of their world, leading us to reject the traditional way of thinking about information as existing objectively, a self-contained construct, some kind of commodity to be bought, stored, and transferred. Instead, sense-making holds to a view of information as constructed by the individual within situational and perspectival constraints. This concept of information is dynamic and requires us as information providers to ask, "How does information help individuals deal with particular problems or situations that arise in their lives?" Library staff will be more effective in their communications with the public and with other staff if they focus on the situations that generate information needs, the questions people have about these situations, and the ways in which people hope to use the information as a way of responding to these situations ("uses").

Similarly, sense-making can help us to write more effectively. Writers are helped, for example, if they think of a piece of writing not as a self-contained object but as part of a transaction with a reader. To write a useful report, the writer should consider the situation that has made the report necessary, the questions that readers might have in their minds, and the ways in which readers might expect to use the report.

Sense-making operates at two levels in *Communicating Professionally*. The first level is the interaction between you, the practitioner who provides information service, and the people who seek your help in the library. The other is the interaction between us, the authors, and you, the reader. We have tried to present our ideas in a way that will help you make sense of our ideas so that you can take what you need from this book to help you through situations that arise in your work. Each reader comes to this book with unique experiences and perspectives, each has different needs, and each of you will be looking for different ways in which to use the help that we offer.

How This Book Is Organized

In order to combine the theory of sense-making with the technique of microtraining, we have organized *Communicating Professionally* by presenting first a set of communication skills, then a chapter that explains the theoretical underpinnings of communication skills training, then a set of applications within which these skills can be applied, and finally a chapter on teaching others.

Specifically, the book includes the following four elements:

- **Single skills.** Chapters 1–4 focus on single nonverbal, listening, speaking, and writing skills. For each we give a definition, examples, exercises, and a brief discussion of the functions or effects of the skill.
- **Integration: Putting it all together.** Chapter 5 outlines our approach to communication theory, especially sense-making theory and microtraining. Here we elaborate on the concept of intentionality, discuss the skills of integration, and provide some practical tips for practicing.
- **Applications.** In Chapters 6–9 we discuss common situations in libraries that require the use of nonverbal, listening, speaking, or writing skills. For example, in these chapters you'll find applications such as conducting the reference interview, managing the employment interview, handling complaints and other problematic situations, leading or participating in a group discussion, introducing a speaker, making a presentation yourself, writing

instructions, writing a winning proposal, and creating web content.

- **Training others.** Finally, Chapter 10 covers using the techniques provided in *Communicating Professionally* for staff training.

We have designed this book in a modular format so that you can begin anywhere and move through the book following your own path. The single skills are a good place to start, but you may prefer to begin with the theoretical aspects presented in Chapter 5 and then work through the earlier chapters. If you start with any of the specific applications in Chapters 6–9, you will find referrals to the appropriate earlier sections that describe the particular skills required.

Because learning is an active process centered in the learner, we want to involve you as much as possible in the process of discovery. This book presents a series of starting points for your own further exploration. The sidebars labeled **Did You Know?** include interesting research findings or pertinent examples. The **Quick Tips** sidebars are practical hints that we've found useful or at least worth trying. We also include **Exercise** sidebars because it is not sufficient to read about a skill. To learn and really master the skill, you have to try it out yourself. We stress this because learners have repeatedly told us that something that seemed simpleminded and trivially easy when they read about it proved unexpectedly rich, complex, and tricky when they tried it themselves. All of the exercises are indexed by content under "Exercises" in the index.

Each chapter ends with an extensive section called **Annotated Bibliography**, divided by topic and consisting of books, articles, websites, and multimedia that we have used or that we recommend. The treatment of each topic in this comprehensive book must necessarily be concise, but you can use the annotated bibliographies as starting points for a more thorough and detailed exploration of any topic that particularly interests you. All authors cited in the text and/or in the annotated bibliographies are listed in the index.

What's New?

This third edition of *Communicating Professionally* features four kinds of changes and additions:

- **More and newer resources.** We have checked all references for the latest editions of key resources that we have retained from the second edition of our own book. Throughout we have replaced older material with material that reflects new research, evolving understandings, and emerging issues. The sidebars for all the chapters include some new exercises, examples, and quick tips.

- **More emphasis on cross-cultural communication.** As the research literature on cross-cultural communication continues to expand, we have been able, in each successive edition, to put more emphasis on the effects of different ethnic, cultural, national, and linguistic backgrounds on the daily communication activities in libraries. In addition to a specific section on this topic in Chapter 6, we have also tried to integrate an awareness of cross-cultural communication throughout the book in our treatment of individual skills, common library situations, research facts, examples, and exercises.

- **New applications.** We have added some sections on topics not addressed in previous editions. Specifically there are new sections on applications that have been scantily addressed within the library literature itself but are nevertheless important to library practitioners. Examples include the following: the employment interview (both conducting the interview and being interviewed) in Chapter 6 on speaking one-to-one; the focus group and self-directed work teams in Chapter 7 on working in groups; the poster presentation in Chapter 8 on making presentations; an expanded section on contributing to the professional literature in Chapter 9 on producing texts; and of course new sections throughout, described next, that address applications of new communication technology.

- **Communicating electronically.** When we started thinking about the revisions needed for this third edition, we planned at first to add a new self-contained chapter focusing exclusively on new electronic media. That plan was abandoned when it became clear that no area of communication—written communication, communicating one-to-one, working in groups, or making presentations—is unaffected by new communication technology. New technology has transformed the ways in which people communicate in every area of library service, changing how users interact with the library staff and with library resources and changing how library staff communicate with each other and with users.

We have therefore integrated throughout the book material that addresses issues raised by technological change. In addition, we have added new material on the virtual reference interview and writing digitally, and we have introduced new sections on these and other topics: virtual teams, virtual conferencing, and virtual discussion sites in a new section on virtual groups in Chapter 7; presentation software in Chapter 8 on making presentations; and forms of electronic writing, such as instant messaging and online chat, virtual discussion sites, Facebook, and blogs in Chapter 9 on producing texts. Throughout the book, we have also introduced new examples to help library staff improve their electronic communication, both oral and written.

Who Can Use This Book?

Anybody. Anyone (professional or not) who has been taught helping skills can be a helper. Anyone who is in need of skills can be helped to acquire them. We see this book as useful not only to librarians and other library staff but also to library volunteers, staff trainers, clerical assistants, board members, and information and referral counselors. In short, the book is for anyone who wants to improve communication skills in the library context or help others do so. An experienced trainer can pass on the skills not only to staff but also to library users, for example, by teaching the skills needed for volunteer leadership of book discussion groups.

Having said that anyone can use this book, we must add a few cautionary notes. Individuals who use this book for independent study may initially feel awkward or frustrated in practicing the individual skills or in trying to integrate the skills into their everyday behavior. This is normal! When you have a communication accident, try the tips for recovering in Chapter 5. In a group training situation, the best results will come with an experienced, supportive leader (which you can all become, eventually—but begin training on a small scale first).

Use the ideas and materials in this book, but develop your own style. If something doesn't work, try it again. Examine what happens carefully, and reflect on it. If you try again and it still doesn't work, try something different. Take from this book what works for you in your own situation. Perhaps you'll just copy a page for a presentation slide or a handout. Maybe you'll use this book to develop a course outline or as a source of a reading for a course curriculum. Or you might find one or two tips that help you improve the way you handle a problem situation.

Learn, Do, Teach . . . and Give Feedback

Please try out the communication skills, and then give us feedback. Allen E. Ivey advises his trainees to "learn, do, and teach." Learning a skill requires being able to demonstrate the skill yourself, not just reading about it. The first step is to practice the skill immediately, right in the training group, where you will be supported when you risk trying out something new. The second step is to practice or use the skill in real-life, on-the-job situations. In this second stage, you will be integrating the skill into everyday behavior and experimenting with specific behavioral contexts or situations. The final step of skill mastery is to teach another person. When you are able to teach someone else, you have truly mastered the skill. Make a commitment to the process by contracting with yourself to "learn, do, and teach" as you work through this book, whether you use it as an individual self-study manual or as a guide to group training. Then we would like to hear from you. You can reach us by e-mailing ross@uwo.ca. Let us know what works for you, how you adapt the material, and what new ideas or exercises you develop. We hope that you will not only make a "learn, do, and teach" contract but will also provide us with feedback so that we too can go through that cycle again.

Acknowledgments

To the attendees in our workshops, students in our graduate courses, and readers of earlier editions who have tried out the exercises and have given us feedback, suggestions, and fresh examples of what works and what doesn't. We have drawn upon your experience and advice.

PART 1
Skills

Nonverbal Behavior

1.1. Introduction to Nonverbal Behavior

You convey nonverbal messages to other people all the time—it's impossible not to. The real question is: What kind of message are you sending by such behavior as your use of eye contact, tone of voice, facial expression, posture, gestures, positioning of arms and legs, style of dress, and the distance you stand from other people? The ideal, of course, is to be aware of all these elements of nonverbal behavior and make sure that the message you send is one of professionalism and your desire to help library users.

Researchers have distinguished various dimensions of nonverbal behavior:

- **Kinesics**—the way we use our bodies, head, arms, and legs, as well as facial expression, posture, and movement
- **Proxemics**—the way we use interpersonal space; the distance we stand from another person
- **Paralanguage or vocalics**—how we say something: the pitch, rate, loudness, and inflection of our speech
- **Chronemics**—the way we time our verbal exchanges; waiting time and punctuality; duration and urgency
- **Physical appearance**—the way we look: body type; clothing; hair and skin color; grooming; accessories and cosmetics
- **Gesture**—the way we use our body to express meaning: hand and arm movements; head and eye movements (nodding or shaking head, rolling eyes, winking)

These nonverbal cues convey nuances of meaning and emotion that reinforce, or sometimes contradict, the spoken words. When interpreting the meaning of any communication, people rely on both verbal and nonverbal cues. However, under many circumstances, and especially when there is a discrepancy between the verbal and nonverbal messages, people tend to give more weight to the nonverbal cues. Compare the following examples:

> "That's interesting." (Said as the speaker smiles and looks encouragingly at the other person.)
> "That's interesting." (Said in a flat tone as the speaker shrugs and looks away from the other person.)

In the second example, the verbal message, or *what* was said, is contradicted by the paralanguage, the *way* it was said. When we interpret nonverbal behavior, we pay attention to a cluster of cues all at the same time—tone of voice, posture, facial expressions, and so on—to figure out emotions or attitudes. Verbal cues take precedence for factual, abstract, and persuasive communication. Nonverbal cues are given more weight for messages about attitudes or feelings.

It is important to understand that much nonverbal behavior is culture specific (see also 6.6.3 on cross-cultural communication). We learn what is appropriate within our own culture, and we take our own culture as the norm. Variations are interpreted as too much or too little of something, too close or too far away, too loud or too restrained, too pushy or too standoffish. At an early age, we begin to learn how far away to stand from another person, how much physical touching is acceptable, what kind of eye contact is appropriate, and how long to look.

These lessons are never taught formally, but they are learned. For example, a scolding parent or teacher might say to a child, "Stand up straight and look at me when I'm talking to you." From the middle-class Anglo-American perspective, this looking is understood as an appropriate and respectful listening pose. Children who won't look us in the eye are considered shifty, guilty, or otherwise lacking in openness and integrity. In contrast, direct eye contact may be considered inappropriate among many African Americans, Native Americans, or Hispanic Americans, who believe that lowering the eyes is a sign of respect.

Misunderstandings often occur because of the differing communication styles used by people in "high-context" versus "low-context" cultures. According to Edward T. Hall (1976), high-context cultures differ from low-context cultures in how much they rely on cues other than words to convey and interpret meanings. Hall has argued that in any given communication situation there is far more going on than we can possibly pay attention to. Therefore, we filter out those signals that our culture considers less important. Low-context cultures pay attention to direct messages and the explicit meanings of the words themselves and downplay the context—the *way* in which the words are said. High-context cultures, which are group oriented with a strong sense of tradition, place importance on ambiance, rapport, and trust building and rely more on nonverbal cues such as eye movements, tone of voice, gestures, and facial expressions (Berlanga-Cortéz, 2000).

To complicate matters, appropriate communication style varies with other factors, such as status, gender, age, generational differences, and the formality of the situation. So it is not a simple matter of learning the "right" cultural behavior but rather attuning ourselves to these factors as they pertain in any given situation and with any given individual. We may not always be communicating what we think we are communicating to a person whose culture is different from our own. McGuigan (2002) points out that we overlook cultural differences at our peril. We might be violating deeply held cultural values and be perceived as arrogant or rude. The following sections on individual skills describe some of the common meanings of nonverbal behavior in mainstream North America, with notes on alternative interpretations.

1.2. Eye Contact

Making eye contact is one of a cluster of skills known as *attending skills*. By using attending skills, many of which are nonverbal, we show our interest in others by paying attention. Attending skills are the anchors in Allen E. Ivey's microskills hierarchy, the most basic skills that we must learn before we move on to other skills such as active listening, questioning, summarizing, or confronting (Ivey, Ivey, and Zalaquett, 2010). Eye contact is an attending skill that we all recognize. The appropriate use of eye contact is one of the most powerful cues we have for opening and maintaining communication. It has been described as a visual handshake that connects you nonverbally with the other person.

Exercise

Soundless TV
Develop your awareness of body language. Watch a television drama, soap opera, or reality TV show online with the sound turned off. Try to interpret what the characters are doing and feeling, using no cues but the actions. What emotions are being displayed? What is the relationship between the characters? How do you know? Later check your interpretations by replaying the sequence a second time, this time with the sound turned on. Which nonverbal cues did you use most during the soundless TV?

Did You Know?

Gender differences are really cultural differences. Regardless of ethnic background, boys and girls grow up in essentially different cultures. For example, boys tend to play outside, in large groups that are hierarchically structured, whereas girls play in small groups or pairs, often with their best friends. For an interesting discussion of how this pattern results in communication accidents between women and men, read the books by Deborah Tannen (1990, 1994).

Did You Know?   **?**

Researchers have found that verbal content and some facial expressions can be highly controlled by the individual but that certain body movements and tone of voice are less susceptible to conscious control. These latter cues are therefore harder to fake. In novels, characters are sometimes described as having a smile that "doesn't reach the eyes." In an authentic smile (called the "Duchenne smile"), involuntary muscles around the eye contract, producing a crinkly-eyed effect that doesn't happen in the fake smile. Nonverbal behaviors not under conscious control are more likely to reveal real thoughts and feelings than are the words themselves (Puccinelli, 2010: 276-277).

Exercise

Attending Skills

Find a partner with whom you can role-play a conversation. Ask your partner to talk about a topic in which he or she is personally interested. Your role is to listen and to encourage your partner to say more by using the attending skills of eye contact, smiling, and nodding along with verbal encouragements such as "That's interesting," "What happened next?" and "uh-huh." Which of these skills do you feel comfortable doing? Which ones need more practice? Change roles. How does your partner's use of attending skills affect the way you talk about your topic?

Middle-class Anglo-Americans communicate that they are listening by looking at the other person, and they may feel that without eye contact no communication is taking place. For middle-class Anglo-Americans, looking at the person talking to you usually indicates warmth, interest, and a desire to communicate. We can powerfully influence how much another person talks by our use of eye contact. Frequent breaks in eye contact are usually interpreted as inattention, lack of interest, embarrassment, or even dislike. Therefore, looking down at the floor, up at the ceiling, or over at a file will cause the other person to stop talking. Maintaining appropriate eye contact indicates interest and encourages the other person to continue talking.

But what is appropriate eye contact? Too much can be as bad as too little. A prolonged and unwavering stare can seem hostile, rude, intrusive, or even threatening. Appropriate eye contact involves neither staring nor avoiding. Unless the context is a courtship, the time spent looking directly into the other person's eyes is actually very brief. Your eyes will move from the speaker's eyes to chin, hairline, mouth, and back to the eyes. Listeners and speakers tend to adopt an alternate pattern of looking and looking away. Moreover, the looking times of speaker and listener are not symmetrical. In mainstream North American culture, listeners spend twice as much time looking as do speakers.

1.3. Smiling and Nodding

Smiling and occasional nodding function as minimal encouragers (see 3.3) in conversation, reassuring the other person that you are friendly, interested, and listening. Smiling is a sign of warmth in most cultures, but in some places—in Japan, for example—smiling may indicate discomfort or even hostility. Nodding the head up and down is usually a positive signal and is understood to mean agreement. But in many cultures, a head nod means that the other person is listening politely or following what you are saying, not necessarily agreeing with it. To complicate matters, in some cultures the side-to-side nod means agreement and the vertical nod means disagreement. If you usually listen impassively, try nodding occasionally. Don't overdo it. An occasional single nod of the head encourages people to say more; successive nods get them to stop.

1.4. Pausing

The effective use of pauses, or silence, is really a kind of nonverbal behavior, although it is often combined with speaking and listening skills. A well-placed pause can substitute for a conversational turn. Pausing is intentional silence, either as a delay before you speak or used instead of speaking. For example, when it is your turn to speak, you wait before speaking, or say nothing, until the other person speaks again.

The effect of pausing varies according to culture. In some cultures, lengthy and frequent pauses are a sign of inattention. In others, such as some Native American cultures, they are a sign of attention and respect, an indication that the listener is taking the speaker's last statement seriously and considering a worthy answer. It is important to know what effect your pauses may have in different situations. The intentional use of pauses can be helpful in many communication contexts, but is especially valuable during an interview, such as the reference interview (6.4.1), the employment interview (6.5), or an interview between a supervisor and a supervisee. In mainstream North American culture, effective pausing sharpens an interviewer's listening skills and conveys attentiveness to the interviewee. A pause may function as an encourager or a probe. It says to the interviewee, "I'm listening" and "Go on." Because the interviewer relinquishes her turn at the conversation, the interviewee is likely to expand on what he has previously said. Consider these examples:

> **Librarian:** Please tell me about your research.
> **User:** Well, this is in the area of applied microbiology.
> **Librarian:** . . . (pause, combined with encouraging body language)
> **User:** I'm studying the action of lactic acid bacteria in cheese.

> **Supervisor:** How is the self-study report coming along?
> **Staff member:** Fine.
> **Supervisor:** . . . (pause, combined with encouraging body language)
> **Staff member:** Well, actually it's taken a while for some people to get their sections done, and some parts need extra editing. But I think we'll have the final draft by next week.

Exercise

Practice Pausing

For a timed session of half an hour, make a conscious effort to use pauses while speaking to someone at home or at work. Ask a question and then—just wait. One or two seconds of blank time might seem endless to you, but it will give the other person a chance to think before responding. Note what happens after the pauses. Did pausing improve communication? Were there any negative outcomes? Try this exercise at various times with different people.

A Quick Tip

Consider the Context

Don't misread nonverbal behavior. Each individual nonverbal signal should be considered in context and interpreted as part of a cluster of behaviors. You might think that a firm handshake indicates confidence while a weak handshake shows a lack of gumption. But maybe not. A limp handshake may indicate something else entirely, such as arthritis. Kendra Cherry (2011) advises that you interpret a particular signal in the context of all the other nonverbal behaviors: "A person's overall demeanor is far more telling than a single gesture viewed in isolation."

Did You Know?

Pauses serve various purposes: they are used for cognitive processing, as a control mechanism, to indicate acceptance or refusal, or simply for turn taking (Goodwin, 1981).

Pauses are also important as a listening skill when they follow a statement or a question. A common difficulty for librarians who are learning to ask effective questions (see 3.4) is remembering to pause after the question while the other person formulates an answer. It's too easy to ask a question and then rush to answer it yourself, for example, "What would help you? Do you want X?"

Effective pausing is more difficult to learn than one might think and requires practice. Pauses longer than ten seconds may confuse the user, who becomes unsure whether the other person is still listening. Very short pauses tend to be unnoticeable. Some librarians habitually pause while considering what the user has said or deciding what to do next. But pausing too often or too long can be awkward, especially over the telephone. Used correctly, however, pausing is a skill that helps reduce the common mistakes of talking too much, cutting the other person off, and interrupting. The skills that supplement pausing are restatement, encouragers, and nonverbal skills that show attentiveness.

Steps to Using Pauses Effectively

1. Observe your own behavior. Under which circumstances do you normally pause? Under which circumstances do you *not* pause, but perhaps should?
2. Consciously attempt to vary the lengths of your pauses. Pause for a longer or shorter time than usual, and observe the effect. Experiment by substituting short pauses for questions or statements.
3. Use appropriate body language. When you pause, make eye contact, and use other body language that says, "I'm listening—go on."
4. Train yourself to wait. When asking a question, practice stopping at the end of the question until the other person answers.

1.5. Posture

Your posture, or the way you hold your body, signals your mood and attitude to others, including library users. Slumping signals fatigue, boredom, or discouragement. Rigidity suggests nervousness or disagreement. Closed postures, such as crossed arms or orienting yourself away from the other person, often convey detachment or disagreement, no matter what your words say. When you give out mixed messages, other people trust the nonverbal cues.

1.6. Physical Appearance

How you look and what you wear can be considered as nonverbal communication, especially those aspects that are within your control. For example, we have limited control over weight and height. In North America, however, we have a great deal of choice about what we wear and how we decorate ourselves. Despite the phasing out of explicit dress codes, appearance *does* matter in service organizations.

The standards for an "acceptable" appearance vary according to the immediate task, our status in the organization, and whether or not we work with the public. For example, when you are giving a public presentation, you are generally expected to be dressed more formally than you might be for your everyday activities. For an event such as a media interview (8.7), you want to appear professional and to avoid distracting elements such as noisy jewelry. In special libraries you will be explicitly or implicitly encouraged to fit in with the corporate image.

In the absence of clear-cut dress regulations, consider how various aspects of appearance may be read by others. You will then be able to take steps to avoid unintended interpretations, some of which are culturally determined by the expectations and assumptions of the interpreter. You may think that a particular outfit is cool, but you may be sending unintended messages about your professional status or role within the organization. Clothing chosen to express individuality, for example, may not be seen as professionally appropriate by people whose culture does not place a high value on individuality.

One reason to adopt a professional appearance is that it helps library users identify you as an employee whom they can ask for help. From an unobtrusive study conducted in various types of libraries, Durrance (1989: 33) concluded:

> Appearance of the staff member (including age and dress) plays
> an important role in helping observers make decisions, especially
> when the environment fails to send a clear message; 56% used

A Quick Tip 🕐

Trunk Lean
To convey relaxed attentiveness during a conversation, stand or sit so that you are leaning slightly toward the other person. This is called "trunk lean."

environmental clues to decide if they had been working with a librarian. Well-dressed, older individuals were assumed to be librarians while casually dressed younger people were thought to be students.

One of Durrance's students approached a young man seated behind the reference desk, who said that he was not the librarian, but rather a friend of the librarian. When "the librarian emerged from the stacks, the observer concluded from her age, her casual clothing, and her bright pink hair that she was not a librarian either" (Durrance, 1989: 33).

This example raises the much-debated issue of whether library staff who serve the public should wear identification tags. Some research indicates that library users feel they have been better served if they know the name of the staff member helping them, in much the same way as they like to know the name of the doctor who treats them in an emergency ward. For those employees who are concerned about privacy and security, however, the purpose is served by tags that indicate their function or position. Some libraries give employees the option of using an "alias" on tags. The key consideration in the name-tag debate, and indeed in the entire issue of appearance, is really accessibility. Can people identify you as someone who is able to help them, and do they feel comfortable in approaching you?

> ### Exercise 🔧
>
> **Does a Name Tag Help?**
>
> If you don't normally wear an identification tag, make one and wear it for an hour while you stand near your public access catalog. Do you find that more people tend to ask you questions? If people still do not ask you for help, try asking them if they found what they wanted. The results may be surprising.

> ### Exercise 🔧
>
> **Get Out of My Face**
>
> In an article (Celik, 2005: 38) on the difference between Turkish and American senses of personal space, the author, who is from Turkey, describes an encounter in the Chicago O'Hare International Airport on his first visit to the United States:
>
> > I anxiously approach the lady at the information desk of the airline company for help. Although I am nervous and upset, I try to tell her about the situation as I ask if she can put me in the first available flight to my destination. Although I thought I spoke to her in a calm, polite way, she says: "Get your face out of mine first of all." I have no idea what is going on and why she reacted the way she did. She acts intimidated and upset even though I thought I was being polite.
>
> Using the framework of the zones of personal space, explain what happened in this encounter. Why did the lady at the information desk behave as she did? What could she have done differently?

1.7. Personal Space

The distance we stand from another person and our body orientation, such as leaning forward or turning aside, can send powerful nonverbal messages. The dimension of nonverbal behavior called "proxemics" is the way we use space in interpersonal communication. As is the case with other nonverbal behaviors, our sense of the appropriate use of personal space is culturally determined. Anthropologist Edward T. Hall (1974: 2), who coined the term *proxemics*, has described it as "the study of man's transactions as he perceives and uses intimate, personal, social and public space in various settings while following out-of-awareness dictates of cultural paradigms."

Hall (1963) explains how personal space works, using four zones expanding outward in concentric circles with the individual at the center. Imagine an invisible bubble that surrounds your entire body

6 to 18 inches away from your skin. Only people with whom you have a very close relationship would be welcome at this *intimate distance*. Next, at a distance away from you of 1.5 to 4 feet, is *personal distance*, a space into which you would feel comfortable admitting family members and personal friends. Next, from 4 to 12 feet away, is *social distance*. This is the physical distance you would leave between yourself and an acquaintance when having a conversation. It is used in formal social interactions, including business and professional encounters. And finally there is *public distance* of 12 to 25 feet away, which is used for public speeches and the like. This conceptual framework is useful in explaining why you may feel uncomfortable when talking to someone from another culture. His or her culturally learned sense of appropriate distance may differ from yours (Berlanga-Cortéz, 2000). For example, someone from the United Kingdom or Norway may perceive a personal distance of 2 feet as too close (pushy), whereas someone from Latin America or the Mediterranean is apt to find it too distant (unfriendly).

Be aware of your own sense of personal space and the distance that you like to keep in the following situations: (1) during a conversation between yourself and a close friend and (2) during a conversation between yourself and someone you have just met in a professional context. Do you ever find yourself backing up? Or, contrarily, do you find yourself trying to close the gap? Knowing that feelings of discomfort may be caused by differing concepts of personal space makes it easier not to feel invaded or, alternatively, to feel that you are getting the cold shoulder.

> **Did You Know? ?**
>
> Sociologist Dane Archer (*Personal Space: Exploring Human Proxemics*; video, 28 min) describes what happens in a proxemics experiment in which the personal space of experimental subjects is invaded by three people who approach too closely. The most common response for the "invaded" person is to leave, usually without saying anything. Only 2 percent say something to their invader.

1.8. Vocal Qualities

Vocal qualities, sometimes called "paralanguage," are what get lost between the recording of a voice and the transcript of the words. These vocal cues include volume (loud or soft), pitch (high or low), rate of speech (fast or slow), rhythm, emphasis, use of speech fillers, and fluency. After you have become accustomed to hearing your own recorded voice, evaluate your speaking style using the following checklist of questions. Try to be objective as you listen to your voice. Ask yourself whether there are any features of your speaking style that prevent you from sounding as effective as you would like.

> **Did You Know? ?**
>
> Spanish-speaking people use silence to indicate agreement, whereas Native Americans use silence to indicate disagreement (Evans et al., 2010: 39).

Exercise 🔧

On Emphasis
Say each of these sentences in as many different ways as you can. In each case, how does the change in emphasis affect the meaning of the sentence?

- Maria gave that disk to John.
- Who do you think you are?
- I didn't say that I think he is good at teaching.

Vocal Qualities: A Checklist

❑ Does every word and every sentence sound like every other? Or do you vary the pitch and emphasis depending on the sense?

❑ Do you sound tired and bored? Or energetic and interested?

❑ Is your tone tight? Nasal? Breathy?

❑ Do you mumble? Or can your consonants be distinctly heard?

❑ Do you speak so softly that people often can't hear you?

❑ Do you have a machine-gun delivery so rapid that people sometimes miss what you say?

❑ Do you speak so slowly that people have trouble waiting for you to finish your sentences?

❑ Do all your sentences, even declarative ones, have an upward intonation as if you are asking a question? Do you sound hesitant and unsure? Or do you sound confident in what you are saying?

The way you speak sends a message. Is it the message you intend? If not, you may want to work on correcting problems that you have identified. Following are exercises related to six aspects of voice: emphasis, variety, voice quality, articulation, projection, and inflection.

Emphasis

Dull speakers tend to give equal emphasis to every word, overlooking the importance of emphasis to reinforce meaning. See the difference it makes to the meaning when you vary the emphasis. Read aloud the following sentence, putting the emphasis on a different word each time:

> *Would* you like me to help you?
> Would *you* like me to help you?
> Would you *like* me to help you?
> Would you like *me* to help you?
> Would you like me to *help* you?
> Would you like me to help *you*?

Variety

There are four main ways to achieve variety. Change the pitch and inflection; change the pace; change the volume; and use pauses. Read aloud the passage below, making it sound as flat and inexpressive as you can. To increase the monotony, you can use a singsong rhythm in which the predictable pattern of rising and falling tone bears no relation to the sense of the passage. Then read it with great variety, using pauses and exaggerating the variations in pitch, pacing, and loudness to emphasize the meaning of the passage. To get a better sense of the differences in the way a listener hears these two versions, record the two readings and then replay them. You may be surprised that what you thought was a greatly exaggerated reading was not really exaggerated, just more interesting.

> A fearful man, all in coarse grey, with a great iron on his leg. A man with no hat, and with broken shoes, and with an old rag tied around his head. A man who had been soaked in water, and smothered in mud, and lamed by stones, and cut by flints, and stung by nettles, and torn by briars; who limped, and shivered, and glared and growled; and whose teeth chattered in his head as he seized me by the chin. "Oh! Don't cut my throat, sir," I pleaded in terror. "Pray don't do it, sir."
>
> "Tell us your name!" said the man. "Quick."
>
> —From Charles Dickens's *Great Expectations*

Voice Quality

The quality of your voice depends on the way you form vowel sounds and use the resonators of your upper throat, mouth, and nose. Because the vowel carries the weight of the tone, the way to improve tonal quality is to work on vowels. The muscles in the jaw and throat play an important role here. If the jaw and throat are tense and closed, the vowel cannot be open and the tone will sound tight or harsh.

Read aloud the following passages, prolonging and exaggerating the vowel sounds. Repeat, paying attention to lip action.

> The Rainbow comes and goes
> And lovely is the Rose
> > —From Wordsworth's "Ode: Imitations of Immortality"

> Far and few, far and few,
> Are the lands where the Jumblies live;
> Their heads are green, and their hands are blue,
> And they went to sea in a Sieve.
> > —From Edward Lear's "The Jumblies"

Exercise

Evaluate Your Own Voice
Record yourself in an informal conversation. Then record yourself reading aloud. Your first thought as you replay your recorded voice might be, "But that doesn't sound like me." However, the voice that you hear recorded is the voice that other people hear.

A Quick Tip

Wait a Day
After recording your voice, don't listen to it immediately. You will be better able to evaluate it dispassionately if you allow some time to separate yourself from what you've recorded.

Exercise

A Test for Nasal Twang
Hold your nose as you say "ee-ah-oo." Your nose shouldn't vibrate. If it does, then you have some nasality. The only sounds in English that should be nasal are *m*, *n*, and *ng*.

Articulation

While the vowels carry the tone of the voice, the consonants are what distinguish one word from another. Read the following words: *hit, bit, mitt, hill, his, big*. The vowel is the same. Only the consonants differ. Distinct pronunciation of the consonants requires the energetic use of the articulators—the lips, tongue, and palate. Mumblers are lazy pronouncers of consonants.

Read aloud the following passage. Record yourself as you emphasize the consonants, especially the ones at the ends of the words. Pay attention to lip movement and tongue action. You will be surprised that what felt to you like an extravagant exaggeration of consonants comes through on the recording as good clear articulation.

> Andrew Airpump asked his aunt her ailment;
> Did Andrew Airpump ask his aunt her ailment?
> If Andrew Airpump asked his aunt her ailment,
> Where was the ailment of Andrew Airpump's aunt.
> —From "Peter Piper's Practical Principles
> of Plain and Perfect Pronunciation"

As you practice this next selection, emphasize the consonants. You should be able to feel the muscles of your tongue and lips working energetically. Because this is a patter song from Gilbert and Sullivan's *The Pirates of Penzance*, you might want to emphasize the rhythm, too.

> I am the very model of a modern Major-General,
> I've information vegetable, animal, and mineral,
> I know the kings of England, and I quote the fights historical,
> From Marathon to Waterloo, in order categorical;
> I'm very well acquainted too with matters mathematical,
> I understand equations, both the simple and quadratical,
> About binomial theorem I'm teeming with a lot o' news
> With many cheerful facts about the square of the hypotenuse.
> —From Gilbert and Sullivan's *The Pirates of Penzance*

Projection

Children have no trouble with projection. Newborn babies can cry for hours and do. It's all a question of proper breathing. If your breath is shallow and irregular, your voice will be thin and weak. What is needed is an efficient and regular use of breath—not breathiness for the first few words and running out of breath by the end. The way to increase loudness is to increase the pressure of breath below the larynx, not to tense up the muscles of the upper chest and throat. Tensing the throat raises the pitch and produces a harsh, strident tone. Keep the throat relaxed. Good projection depends on an adequate breath supply, resonance, and some prolongation of the vowel sounds. Of course, because you want to be understood as well as heard, you also have to articulate the consonants distinctly. Practice outside or in a large room by reading a prose passage (pick any paragraph from this book), using three different levels of projection:

- As if in conversation with several other people
- As if in a staff meeting with 20 other people
- As if in a large auditorium (imagine bouncing your voice off the back wall)

Inflection

English speakers indicate questions by ending sentences with a rising inflection: "You do?" However, some speakers use this same pattern of rising inflection when they intend to make a declarative statement so that their statements sound like questions. Among linguists, this speech pattern has been called "high rising terminals" (HRT) or sometimes "recurrent intonational rises." But more popularly it is known as "uptalk" or "upspeak." Uptalking has become a common speech pattern, particularly among young women, though it is by no means limited to them. George W. Bush used it too—listen to a speech sample at http://itre.cis.upenn.edu/~myl/languagelog/archives/002708.html.

Why has uptalk become so pervasive? Some communication experts claim that, for teens and children, peer identity plays a role, because people want to sound like their peers. Others claim that uptalk is used by generally confident speakers to invite a response or to invite agreement from another person (Liberman, 2006). Whatever its causes and whatever its origin, whether valley girl speak or something else, it is generally agreed that uptalking sounds uncertain and lacking in confidence to non-uptalkers. They are likely to conclude, correctly or not, that you are asking for approval rather than making a confident statement. Uptalk can easily become an habitual speech pattern.

Exercise

Voice Makeover
Find out whether or not you use uptalk. Many people are unaware of the inflection of their own voice. Record yourself during a conversation with a friend. Talk naturally the way you normally would. Replay the conversation and listen for a rising inflection. Ask your friend to listen too and help you identify uptalk, if any.

Exercise

Up and Down
Try reading the following sentences. First read them with a rising inflection. Then read them as if you really believed them.

My name is Barbara.
This is a good project.
It gives me great pleasure to introduce you to this afternoon's speaker: Mary Entwhistle.
The library will be closing in 15 minutes.
This is a very interesting book.

Research suggests that discourse markers can be any of these:

- Little fillers that give the speaker a moment to decide which words should come next
- A means to connect the speaker and the hearer
- A connection between one part of an utterance and the next
- An insertion that means "I'm quoting"

Speech Fillers

Using speech fillers is not, strictly speaking, a quality of voice, but we are including it anyway as a coda to this section because this behavior sends a message to others. Interspersing your speech with phrases such as "like," "you know," "I mean," and "Do you know what I mean?" can be distracting and sound unprofessional. Technically a type of "discourse marker," these speech fillers are often an unconscious habit that people fall into without being aware of it. However, not all discourse markers are annoying or distracting. Some, such as "well," "now," "actually," and "okay" perform an important function in conversation beyond being fillers. These expressions make the language livelier and more personal and can be used to indicate acknowledgment, agreement, or involvement.

Assess your own use of discourse markers to see whether you overuse certain expressions that function only as fillers. How can you do this? Listen to yourself. Observe *when* you use these fillers. Ask yourself: What purpose do they serve? Which ones seem to have no purpose? Which ones do you overuse that you would now like to eliminate from your speech?

1.9. Annotated Bibliography

General

Adler, Ronald B., and Jeanne Marquardt Elmhorst. 2010. *Communicating at Work: Principles and Practices for Business and the Professions*. 10th ed. New York: McGraw-Hill. This frequently revised text considers intercultural communication and cultural diversity in Chapter 2. Chapter 3 deals with nonverbal communication, including personal space and distance, appearance, and the physical environment in addition to body language.

Birdwhistell, Raymond L. 1970. *Kinesics and Context: Essays on Body Motion Communication*. Philadelphia: University of Pennsylvania Press. A classic work on body language, originally published in 1940.

Burgoon, Judee K., Laura K. Guerrero, and Valerie Manusov. 2011. "Nonverbal Signals." In *The Sage Handbook of Interpersonal Communication*, 4th ed., edited by Mark L. Knapp and John A. Daly, 239–280. Thousand Oaks, CA: Sage. An updated overview of scholarly research, with an extensive bibliography.

Cherry, Kendra. 2011. "Top Ten Nonverbal Communication Tips." About.com.Psychology. http://psychology.about.com/od/nonverbalcommunication/tp/nonverbaltips.htm.

Dodd, Carley H. 2012. *Managing Professional and Business Communication.* 3rd ed. Boston: Allyn and Bacon. This is a lively general book on all aspects of communication in the workplace. Among the many areas covered are managing nonverbal communication, communication conflict, and intercultural communication.

Durrance, Joan C. 1989. "Reference Success: Does the 55% Rule Tell the Whole Story?" *Library Journal* 114, no. 7: 31–36. Reports on an unobtrusive study of the reference desk.

Evans, David R., Margaret T. Hearn, Max R. Uhlemann, and Alan E. Ivey. 2010. *Essential Interviewing: A Programmed Approach to Effective Communication.* Belmont, CA: Brooks/Cole. Chapter 2 in this workbook deals with attending behavior.

Goodwin, Charles. 1981. *Conversational Organization: Interaction between Speakers and Hearers.* New York: Academic Press. A useful classic.

Grassian, Esther, and Joan R. Kaplowitz. 2005. *Learning to Lead and Manage Information Literacy Instruction.* New York: Neal-Schuman. Discusses nonverbal behavior of instructors.

Hargie, Owen, and David Dickson. 2004. *Skilled Interpersonal Communication: Research, Theory and Practice.* 4th ed. New York: Routledge. Earlier editions were titled *Social Skills in Interpersonal Communication.* This book includes chapters on the importance of interpersonal communication and provides a skill-based approach to nonverbal communication, listening, and speaking. See also *The Handbook of Communication Skills,* 3rd ed., edited by Owen Hargie (New York: Routledge, 2006), which covers research, theory, and practice in communication skills.

Hunt, Gary T. 1985. *Effective Communication.* Englewood Cliffs, NJ: Prentice-Hall. Chapter 5 on nonverbal communication includes exercises and questions for discussion.

Ivey, Allen E., Mary Bradford Ivey, and Carlos P. Zalaquett. 2010. *Intentional Interviewing and Counseling: Facilitating Client Development in a Multicultural Society.* 7th ed. Pacific Grove, CA: Brooks/Cole, Cengage Learning. This classic textbook provides a structured approach for learning the hierarchy of microskills. This latest edition is particularly good on how culture and gender affect nonverbal behavior.

Knapp, Mark L., and John A. Daly, eds. 2011. *The Sage Handbook of Interpersonal Communication*. 4th ed. Thousand Oaks, CA: Sage. Comprehensive coverage of research on nonverbal communication. Includes a section covering the consequences of nonverbal communication in various contexts, including computer-mediated communication and intercultural and workplace perspectives.

Manusov, Valerie, and Miles Patterson, eds. 2006. *Sage Handbook of Nonverbal Communication*. Thousand Oaks, CA: Sage. An informative collection of articles covering research on the communication aspects of nonverbal behavior.

Perkins, Pamela S. 2008. *The Art and Science of Communication: Tools for Effective Communication in the Workplace*. Hoboken, NJ: John Wiley. A lively book with lots of hints and suggestions for improving workplace communication.

Puccinelli, Nancy M. 2010. "Nonverbal Communicative Competence." In *APA Handbook of Interpersonal Communication*, edited by David Matsumoto, 273–288. Washington, DC: American Psychological Association. Covers research on the intersection of psychology and nonverbal communication.

Remland, Martin S. 2006. "Uses and Consequences of Nonverbal Communication in the Context of Organizational Life." In *Sage Handbook of Nonverbal Communication*, edited by Valerie Manusov and Miles Patterson, 501–519. Thousand Oaks, CA: Sage. Discusses the functions of nonverbal communication.

Tannen, Deborah. 1990. *You Just Don't Understand: Women and Men in Conversation*. New York: William Morrow. A popular, easy-to-read book by an expert on gender differences in communication.

———. 1994. *Talking from 9 to 5: How Women's and Men's Conversational Styles Affect Who Gets Heard, Who Gets Credit, and What Gets Done at Work*. New York: William Morrow. Popular follow-up to *You Just Don't Understand*.

———. 2007. *Talking Voices: Repetition, Dialogue, and Imagery in Conversational Discourse*. 2nd ed. Cambridge: Cambridge University Press. A readable introduction to the scholarly research that underlies Tannen's popular books.

Todaro, Julie, and Mark L. Smith. 2006. *Training Library Staff and Volunteers to Provide Extraordinary Customer Service*. New York: Neal-Schuman. Identifies body language, proxemics, and positive communication as crucial factors underlying excellent customer service in libraries. Provides compact lists of ideal communication strategies as well as behaviors and phrases to avoid.

Intercultural Nonverbal Communication

Berlanga-Cortéz, Graciela. 2000. "Cross-Cultural Communication: Identifying Barriers to Information Retrieval with Culturally and Linguistically Different Library Patrons." In *Library Services to Latinos: An Anthology*, edited by Salvador Güereña, 51–60. Jefferson, NC: McFarland. Provides a good discussion of the impact of nonverbal communication on cross-cultural communication.

Celik, Servet. 2005. "'Get Your Face Out of Mine': Culture-Oriented Distance in EFL Context. A Helpful Guide for Turkish EFL Teachers." *TÖMER Language Journal* 128: 37–50. http://www.tomer.ankara.edu.tr/dildergileri/128/37-50.pdf. Well worth reading for its examples of cultural differences in nonverbal behavior.

Hall, Edward T. 1959, 1973. *The Silent Language*. Garden City, NY: Doubleday. A classic work on cross-cultural communication.

———. 1963. "A System for the Notation of Proxemic Behaviour." *American Anthropologist* 65, 5: 1003–1026. Although aimed primarily at researchers, this article is a good introduction to the history and value of this kind of research, particularly for understanding intercultural relations.

———. 1966. *The Hidden Dimension*. New York: Doubleday. A pioneering work on the cultural use of space and proxemics written from the perspective of an anthropologist.

———. 1974. *Handbook for Proxemic Research*. American Anthropological Association. Washington, DC: Society for the Anthropology of Visual Communication.

———. 1976. *Beyond Culture*. New York: Doubleday. Provides a framework for comparing cultures based on the way they communicate, introducing the terms *high-context* and *low-context* to characterize differences.

McGuigan, Glenn S. 2002. "When in Rome: A Rationale and Selection of Resources in International Business Etiquette and Intercultural Communication." *Reference and User Services Quarterly* 41, no. 3 (Spring): 220–227. Describes the problems for business of intercultural miscommunication and provides an annotated list of helpful books and websites.

Vocal Qualities

Crannell, Kenneth C. 2012. *Voice and Articulation*. 5th ed. Belmont, CA: Wadsworth. This highly recommended text explains how the vocal apparatus works, provides an overview of the variety of speech patterns, and includes many varied exercises that can help you improve your speaking voice.

Liberman, Mark. 2006. "Uptalk Is Not HRT." *Language Log* (blog), March 28. http://itre.cis.upenn.edu/~myl/languagelog/archives/2006_03 .html. An interesting discussion of the attempt to understand uptalking, with links to related blog posts and ongoing discussion.

List-Handley, Carla. 2008. "Teaching as Performance." In *Information Literacy Instruction Handbook*, edited by Christopher N. Cox and Elizabeth Blakesley Lindsay, 65–73. Chicago: Association of College and Research Libraries. An information literacy specialist discusses how to improve teaching.

Videos

Dane Archer, a professor of sociology at the University of California, Santa Cruz, has produced a series of videotapes and trainer's guides on nonverbal communication. We recommend these for training library staff:

- *The Human Face: Emotions, Identities and Masks* (1995; 31 min)
- *The Human Voice: Exploring Vocal Paralanguage* (1993; 30 min)
- *Personal Space: Exploring Human Proxemics* (1999; 28 min)
- *A World of Differences: Understanding Cross-Cultural Communication* (1997; 30 min)
- *A World of Gestures: Culture and Nonverbal Communication* (1991; 28 min)

These and other videos are available from Berkeley Media LLC, Saul Zaentz Film Center, 2600 Tenth Street, Suite 626, Berkeley, California 94710; phone: (510) 486-9900; e-mail: info@berkeleymedia.com; fax: (510) 486-9944. For more information or to order videos, see http://www.berkeleymedia.com/.

Listening

2.1. Goals of Effective Listening

Good listening is the foundation of all oral communication among people. This is so because communication is not a one-way process of a speaker's sending a message to a passive receiver. Communication is a two-way transaction in which the listener and the speaker are actively involved. A good listener is always engaged in selecting, interpreting, remembering, making guesses and trying to confirm them, coming to conclusions, and checking out the conclusions by playing them back to the speaker.

Effective listening involves two things:

1. You have to be actually listening. Listening is not the same thing as not talking. Instead of really listening, people who are not talking may be daydreaming, waiting for their turn to talk, or thinking of what they will say next.
2. You have to let the other person *know* that you are listening by using verbal and nonverbal attending skills.

Listening is hard work. Some authorities on listening imply that you have to be actively listening and remembering *all* the time. On the contrary, this goal of full-time active listening is not only impossible; it is undesirable. There may be times when it is sensible and energy conserving to ration your attention and choose *not* to listen. However, in this section, we are talking about those other times when it is your job to listen. In libraries, the duties of supervisors and of reference librarians in particular require excellent listening skills.

A good listener, who is actually listening (as opposed to just pretending to listen), has the goal of understanding the other person's point of view. Good listening will help you on the job in these ways:

- Finding out what someone wants so that you can satisfy needs (reference librarians do this, as do salespeople and lawyers)
- Understanding someone's point of view, attitude, feelings, or concerns so that, as a supervisor, you have the information you need to plan effectively, anticipate problems, and resolve conflicts
- Receiving information to form an opinion or reach a decision
- Maximizing your learning during training sessions
- Getting feedback about your own performance so that you can correct problems before they become crises

2.2. Active Listening

Active listening is a concept that emerged from the client-centered work of psychologist Carl Rogers. According to Rogers, the key is to listen for the total meaning of what the other person is saying and then to let the other person know you have understood (Rogers and Farson, 1973). First developed in the context of nondirectional counseling, active listening has since been adopted as a useful skill in many other fields, including management, the health-care professions, and librarianship.

The goal of the active listener is to try to understand the whole message—the content, emotions, and attitudes expressed—and then respond verbally and/or nonverbally to show that understanding (e.g., "So you're worried that . . ." or "It sounds as if you feel . . ."). The listener doesn't have to agree with the speaker—only show an understanding of what was said (Rothwell, 2012). Active listening involves the use of three different kinds of skills:

- Attentive body language: eye contact (1.2) and smiling and nodding (1.3)

- Following skills: minimal encouragers (3.3) and attentive pauses (1.4)
- Reflecting skills (3.8 and 3.9)

See 2.4 for more on how these clusters of skills work together in the service of active listening.

Active listening is a particularly useful technique for dealing with problematic situations (6.7), whether they involve co-workers or library users. Consider the following scenario.

Example

The Case of the Grumpy User
A user wants a particular business book for an important project he is working on for the next day, but the book is on loan and not available. He says:

> "What a crummy library! I don't know why I bother to come here. You never have what I want and you seem to be wasting all your money on junk like teen vampire novels."

Here are some possible responses. Which one shows active listening? For each of these seven responses, what do you think the user is likely to say or do next?

1. We do our best to make the best materials available. But if you have a complaint, you can go to the director's office.

2. We do unfortunately have a limited book budget, and recently it has been cut. So we can't have multiple copies of everything.

3. Did you know that the Business Library at the University of X [in a nearby city] has a really good collection of business books?

4. If I were you, next time I would start earlier on an important project.

5. The popular fiction collection is a very important part of our mandate.

6. It's hard to respond to these last minute requests, but if you had contacted us earlier we could have recalled the book or got a copy from one of our branches.

7. It sounds like you are really frustrated that you can't get this book. Perhaps I can help you today find some other material that would help you with your project.

(Adapted from Turner, 2004: 37)

Exercise

Don't Listen
With a partner, role-play a conversation in which you play the part of the *worst* listener you can possibly be. For this exercise, your partner is trying to tell you about a recent event or situation that matters to the teller. Ask a third person to observe and to write down the ways in which you were not listening. Here are some possibilities: interrupting; changing the topic; fidgeting with your pen or drumming your fingers; looking away; remaining impassive and showing no response at all to what was said. What other characteristics of a poor listener were you demonstrating? Ask your partner how these behaviors affected the conversation.

Exercise 🔧

Active Listening

Having role-played the worst possible listener, now become the best. Have your partner tell you again about a recent event that matters, but this time be the best listener you can. Sit face-to-face with your partner in a quiet location. Lean forward slightly so that you are really focused on the other person. First observe your partner's facial expression, mood, and gaze. Then ask your partner to tell you about the event.

Listen attentively and use minimal encouragers such as "uh-huh" or "that's interesting." Think about what is being said and not said.

Then summarize key elements, using your own words. Ask your partner if you got it right–did you get the feelings and mood right as well as the factual content? Ask your partner to tell you whether he or she felt listened to and *really* understood. Which particular behaviors that you used in this exercise, but not in the **Don't Listen** exercise, made the difference (People Communicating, 2009-2010)?

2.3. Barriers to Listening

Active listening requires concentration—that's why it's called "active." But there are real obstacles to developing active listening habits. Ellis (2009: 32–35) lists a number of them: lack of motivation, diminishing attention span, familiarity with the material, attitudes that make for unreceptivity, and environmental considerations. Motivation to listen can drop off when listening is a constant and unremitting part of the job. Because of limitations in the human attention span, people find it hard to concentrate fully for more than 15–20 minutes without a break. Familiarity with the material tends to make us hear what we expect to hear. Our attitudes can filter out what gets through to us—if we disapprove of the person or the message we might resist hearing what they say. Finally, an uncomfortable physical environment (e.g., too hot, too cold, too noisy) makes it harder to listen actively.

Unfortunately, in exactly those situations in which good listening is most crucial—in situations of conflict or disagreement—it is the hardest to do. There are strong reasons why so few of us listen well, even when we think we are listening.

The following are seven specific behavioral barriers to effective listening:

1. **Perceiving selectively.** We may hear only those messages that fit into our model of the world, and we may filter out other contradictory messages.
2. **Making assumptions.** Instead of listening, people often assume. But it's dangerous to assume we know what other people feel or may mean in a given situation. One person may feel quite differently from the way another person—you—would feel in the same situation. Instead of assuming, ask.
3. **Giving unsolicited advice.** Advice given before we have listened carefully to the problem is usually both inappropriate and unproductive. People usually are unprepared to accept unasked-for advice and sometimes find it offensive.
4. **Offering facile reassurance.** Saying "Don't worry, it's probably nothing" before you have heard the complete account is a way of cutting someone off.

5. **Being judgmental or critical.** When we are judgmental, we are not trying to understand another person's point of view. We are distancing ourselves from that point of view, often to repudiate it, to argue against it, or change it. We are saying, in effect, "You are wrong (silly, selfish, shortsighted) to think or feel that way. It would be better if you looked at the situation the way I do."

6. **Being defensive or arguing.** If we feel threatened by the other person's point of view, we tend to defend our own positions instead of listening in order to understand.

7. **Failing to understand cultural differences.** We may allow ourselves to be unnecessarily distracted by differences in language patterns, such as the dialect of the speaker. More important, we sometimes miscommunicate if we do not understand the role that silence plays in cross-cultural communication. Or we may misinterpret people because we do not have the same sense of timing in speech (see Cross-Cultural Communication, 6.6.3).

Be aware of these behavioral barriers to listening. Monitor your own listening style. Which of these barriers are problems in your own listening?

2.4. Improving Listening Skills

There are some specific things that you can do to improve your listening skills, by really paying attention to what the other person is saying and showing that you are listening.

Really Listen!

Don't interrupt. Be patient. Let people (even painfully slow talkers) finish their own sentences. And don't give any clues that you are ready to respond—don't open your mouth or otherwise signal that you want to jump in. You may be itching to say something, but relax and make a conscious effort to refocus on what the speaker is saying.

Exercise

How Do Other People Listen?
Observe a conversation between two people who are doing more than exchanging small talk. What do you notice? Consider the following questions:

1. What did their body language tell you? Did they use eye contact appropriately? Did their postures suggest attentiveness?
2. Did you notice anyone interrupting? Changing the topic? Jumping to conclusions? Being judgmental? Signaling disagreement by eye rolling, sighing, or head shaking?
3. Did you notice any particularly good examples of attending skills or of reflective listening skills?

Did You Know?

In a conversation between people of different status, the person with the higher status is much more likely to interrupt than vice versa. Interrupting is a way of exercising power.

Thinking about what you yourself want to say is not listening! Monitor your own responses to check how often you interrupt or think of interrupting.

Don't do all the talking yourself. Don't be afraid of staying silent and simply listening. Often people think that they are listening when they are really doing one of the following:

> Giving advice ("If I were you, I would . . .")
> Providing unasked-for information ("Did you know . . . ?")
> Describing their own similar experience ("That's nothing compared to what happened to me. Let me tell you . . .")
> Moralizing ("You should really be more careful. . . .")
> Evaluating or judging ("You're wrong to pay any attention to that. . . .")
> Interpreting ("I know why you are saying that. It's because you really think . . .")
> Arguing for a contrary position ("That's not true. It's really not X at all but Y. . . .")

Wait for an answer. If you have asked a question, wait for an answer. Don't fill in the pauses while the other person is thinking by answering your own question. Again, don't be afraid of silence (see 1.4 on pausing).

Don't change the topic. If you change the topic, you convey the message that you are not interested in hearing what the other person is talking about, that you want to talk instead about what *you* think is interesting. Changing the topic is a way of asserting power.

Listen for the whole message. Listening for cognitive content is only part of the job. You also want to listen for feelings. Perceiving feelings is essential in understanding another person's point of view.

Listen between the words. Take into account gestures, facial expression, pauses, emphasis, tone of voice, changes in pitch, and so on (see Chapter 1 on the significance of nonverbal behavior). A library user's hidden message may be, for example, "I would like help, but I don't like to ask for it." Listen for what is *not* said as well as for what is said.

A Quick Tip 🕐

Listen More; Talk Less
President Lyndon Johnson had a sign in his office that said, "You ain't learning nothing when you are talking" (Boyd, 2009).

Did You Know? ?

March is Listening Awareness Month, according to the International Listening Association (http://www.listen.org/). This Association sponsors a journal and conferences on listening, which it defines as "the process of receiving, constructing meaning from and responding to spoken and/or nonverbal messages."

Show That You Are Listening

Listening is not enough, however. You also have to *show* that you are listening. Therefore, the second part of effective listening involves a cluster of skills that reassure the other person of your attention. The first two are *attending skills*; the second two are *reflective listening skills*:

> **Use eye contact.** It conveys that you are attentive and interested (see 1.2).
>
> **Use minimal encouragers.** Nodding, smiling, and making short responses like "uh-huh," "oh, yes," and "that's interesting" (see 3.3) express interest and encourage the other person to continue talking. (Be sure that you are not just pretending to be attentive; you *are* being attentive and are using eye contact and encouragers to communicate genuine attention.)
>
> **Check your understanding.** Paraphrasing or restatement of content (see 3.8) is a useful skill that allows you to check whether or not you understand the intellectual content of what has been said. Reflecting feelings (3.9) allows you to check your understanding of how the other person feels.
>
> **Ask questions.** Two kinds of questions are particularly useful. Open questions (see 3.4) act as invitations to tell you more, such as, "What are your feelings about this?" Probes clarify what you don't understand, such as, "Can you give me an example of what you mean?"

2.5. Annotated Bibliography

Adler, Ronald B., and Jeanne Marquardt Elmhorst. 2010. *Communicating at Work: Principles and Practices for Business and the Professions.* 10th ed. New York: McGraw-Hill. Chapter 4 provides excellent tips on listening effectively.

Blicq, Ron S. 2005. *Communicating at Work: Creating Messages That Get Results.* 4th ed. Toronto: Prentice Hall Canada. See especially his guidelines for listening.

Boyd, Stephen. 2009. "Improve Your Listening Skills Today!" Public Speaking Tips: Listening Skills. http://www.speaking-tips.com/

A Quick Tip

Pay Attention
Don't fiddle with your mobile phone or stare at computer screens. Don't check your e-mail or text while someone is talking to you.

Did You Know?

Two stumbling blocks to effective listening are (1) evaluating what is being said before the speaker is finished and (2) comparing the speaker's situation with something that happened to you. Stay open-minded, and try to understand the speaker's point of view. Don't sidetrack the conversation by talking about yourself (Blicq, 2005: 282-283).

Did You Know?

Failure to "listen" occurs in virtual environments as well. One older chat user interviewed by Connaway and Radford (2011: 48) complained, "I needed information on the West for a book a student was reading. The person did not listen to the question and gave the wrong information. The person did not listen to my needs and did not answer the question."

Listening-Skills/. This website includes a dozen short articles written between 2003 and 2011 on various ways to improve listening skills.

Connaway, Lynn Silipigni, and Marie L Radford. 2011. *Seeking Synchronicity: Revelations and Recommendations for Virtual Reference.* Dublin, OH: OCLC Online Computer Library Center. http://www .oclc.org/reports/synchronicity/full.pdf. An accessible summary of a major research study of virtual reference (VR), this report emphasizes the importance of relationships and relationship building when providing VR service.

Dodd, Carley H. 2012. *Managing Professional and Business Communication.* 3rd ed. Boston: Allyn and Bacon. Chapter 4 covers the significance of listening in organizations, with many cases and examples.

Ellis, Richard. 2009. *Communication Skills: Stepladders to Success for the Professional.* Chicago: University of Chicago Press. Chapter 5 provides suggestions for improving listening skills.

Hargie, Owen, and David Dickson. 2004. *Skilled Interpersonal Communication: Research, Theory and Practice.* 4th ed. New York: Routledge. Chapter 7 (pp. 169–195) covers theoretical and practical approaches to listening as a social skill.

Jaffe, Clella Iles. 2010. *Public Speaking: Concepts and Skills for a Diverse Society.* 6th ed. Belmont, CA: Wadsworth. Chapter 4 is on effective listening.

Korpijaakko-Huuhka, Anna-Maija, and Anu Klippi. 2010. "Language and Discourse Skills of Elderly People." In *APA Handbook of Interpersonal Communication*, edited by David Matsumoto, 253–272. Washington, DC: American Psychological Association. The authors examine the effect of variables such as education and lifestyle choices on elderly communication, seeking to "enhance our understanding of both group-level and individual changes in healthy aging" (p. 268).

Nichols, Ralph G., and Leonard A. Stevens. 1957. *Are You Listening?* New York: McGraw-Hill. This pioneering book in the field of listening still commands attention.

People Communicating. 2009–2010. "Listening Exercises to Help You Become a Better Communicator." Tips and Tools for More Effective Communication with People in the Workplace. http://www.people -communicating.com/listening-exercises.html. This site includes many exercises and additional information on listening skills.

Purdy, Michael, and Deborah Borisoff, eds. 1997. *Listening in Everyday Life: A Personal and Professional Approach.* 2nd ed. Lanham, MD: University Press of America. This work includes chapters on gender issues, intercultural listening, listening skills in the helping professions, and listening online.

Rogers, Carl, and Richard Farson. 1973. "Active Listening." In *Readings in Interpersonal and Organizational Communication*, 2nd ed., edited by Richard C. Huseman, Cal M. Logue, and Dwight L. Freshley, 541–557. Boston: Holbrook Press. This much-cited article introduced the term *active listening*. Originally published in 1957 (Chicago: University of Chicago Industrial Relations Center), it is often included in edited collections. An excerpt of the main points is available from Gordon Training International at http://www.gordontraining.com/wp-content/uploads/ActiveListening_RogersFarson.pdf.

Rothwell, J. Dan. 2012. *In the Company of Others: An Introduction to Communication*. 4th ed. New York: Oxford University Press. This book further applies active listening techniques with current examples.

Smith, Kitty. 1994. *Serving the Difficult Customer*. New York: Neal-Schuman. This text includes a chapter on active listening skills for problem situations.

Tannen, Deborah. 1990. *You Just Don't Understand: Women and Men in Conversation*. New York: William Morrow. The author provides an excellent and readable overview of research on gender differences in talking and listening patterns and also shows how misunderstandings commonly arise.

Todaro, Julie, and Mark L. Smith. 2006. *Training Library Staff and Volunteers to Provide Extraordinary Customer Service*. New York: Neal-Schuman. This work provides suggestions for listening to customer complaints (pp. 72–75).

Turner, Anne M. 2004. *It Comes with the Territory: Handling Problem Situations in Libraries*. Rev. ed. Jefferson, NC: McFarland. The author discusses how active listening can be used when dealing with problematic situations.

Wolvin, Andrew D., ed. 2009. *Listening and Human Communication in the 21st Century*. Chichester, UK: Wiley-Blackwell. This work reviews scholarly research on listening.

Speaking

3.1. Introduction to Speaking Skills

For maximum effectiveness, the skills covered in this chapter should be learned and practiced one at a time. Think of the downhill skier at the Olympics. The downhill run seems to be effortless, because the skier has practiced over and over again the separate motions needed to get down the hill without wiping out. These perfected movements are then combined for a flawless race. Similarly, you will find it helpful to work on each skill separately although your ultimate goal is to integrate the skills. Become familiar with the function of each skill so that you can use an appropriate one in particular situations. To use Allen E. Ivey's term, you will be using the skill "intentionally."

3.2. Acknowledgment

Acknowledgment, or restatement, is a skill that involves restating or "playing back" the content of what the other person has just said. You restate a key part of the previous statement, using either the same words or a paraphrase. This restatement encourages the other person to confirm, correct, or explain further. Acknowledgment and minimal encouragers (3.3) are both "attending behavior" skills. That is, they are behaviors that show that you are paying attention. Attending behavior forms the foundation of the microskills hierarchy developed by Allen E. Ivey (Ivey, Ivey, and Zalaquett, 2010) (see 5.4), because they establish a good climate for further conversation.

Examples

User 1: I need some information on how the financial industry is regulated.

Librarian: We have quite a bit of information on financial regulation (or simply, "Financial regulation, uh-huh").

User 2: Have you anything on whales?

Librarian: Wales, the place? (Paraphrasing to ensure a shared understanding. This gives the user a chance to correct, if you got it wrong.)

User 3: I'm doing a paper on the effects of stress on heart disease, and I need to find out the kinds of stress tests that can be used with people with a heart condition. I'm also interested in recent articles on the Jenkins Activity Survey and whether it has any validity.

Librarian: Uh-huh. You're doing a paper on the effects of stress on heart disease and you want to find out . . . ? (With complicated statements, the librarian may catch only part of what's been said. That's okay. The procedure is to repeat what you can and ask for repetition on what you missed: "You wanted articles on—what was that again?")

Restatement is an excellent quick way to indicate that you have been listening (see 2.4) and helps to establish a good climate of communication. In acknowledging, follow these guidelines:

- Be brief. Restating a phrase or even just one word is often enough. You don't want to parrot back everything that's been said.
- Use a matter-of-fact, accepting tone. Responding with an upward intonation ("Financial regulation?") may convey disapproval or even incredulity about what has just been said.

Most people already use acknowledgment in certain situations such as repeating a phone number. So it is not a question of learning an entirely new skill but of using consciously a skill already employed in other contexts.

Exercise

Acknowledgment

What could you say to acknowledge a user who asks the following?

1. Where is your medical section?
2. I need to find *Time* [the magazine].
3. I need something on China. (Check your own mastery of the skill of acknowledgment. Was your response useful in clarifying what kind of china is wanted? If not, what could you say instead? Look again at the whales/Wales example.)

A Quick Tip

Avoid Implied Questions

When using acknowledgment, be careful to avoid using an upward intonation unless you are truly asking a question. Saying "financial regulation?" may suggest that you are skeptical, incredulous, or disapproving. In general, try to avoid nonverbal behavior that makes implied comments about users' requests.

3.3. Minimal Encouragers

Examples of useful minimal encouragers are short phrases such as:

- Uh-huh.
- I see.
- Go on.
- That's interesting.
- Tell me more.
- Anything else?
- Can you give me an example?

These phrases, which encourage the other person to say more, are nonjudgmental and free of content. There is a tacit rule in conversation that people should take turns speaking, but a very brief remark such as "uh-huh" counts as a turn. You don't need to respond at length to every statement made. Let the other person describe the problem, while you use encouragers, along with appropriate body language, to show that you are interested and are listening.

Example

> **User:** I'm trying to find some books for my neighbor.
> **Librarian:** Yes, uh-huh (in an interested tone).
> **User:** You see, she's in her eighties and can't get out much. But she does like to read.
> **Librarian:** I see.
> **User:** She likes mysteries, but she's read all the Agatha Christies and all the Marjorie Allinghams and Josephine Teys.
> **Librarian:** Anything else?
> **User:** Well, she likes the older style cozy mysteries—you know, the kind set in English country houses or small villages. She's not keen on a lot of sex and violence. Also not any of those forensic mysteries.

A Quick Tip

Encouragers
Minimal encouragers are especially effective when the speaker:

- has something to say that he or she is very eager to tell,
- wants to express some intense feeling, or
- has a grievance.

3.4. Open Questions versus Closed Questions

You can ask questions in different ways. The form in which you ask the question determines the sort of answer you will get. This section will help you do four things:

- Distinguish between open and closed questions when you hear them.
- Formulate your own open questions.
- Understand how open and closed questions function in conversations and in interviews.
- Recognize when it is appropriate, for your purposes, to ask an open question or to ask a closed question.

So what's the difference between open and closed questions? A closed question requires a Yes/No, This/That response. The question itself specifies several possible answers and requires the other person to choose from the options provided. "Which do you want on this topic—an article or a book?" is an example of a closed question.

An open question allows people to respond in their own terms. A handy way of recognizing whether a question is open or not is to look at the way it begins. If it begins with Who, What, Why, Where, When, or How, the question is probably open. "What format do you want the information in?" is an example of an open question.

Open and closed questions differ in both function and effect. Asking closed questions can be a way of assuming control, because the questioner takes the initiative in selecting the aspects of the topic to be considered and what can be said about it. For this reason, closed questions are used in courtroom cross-examinations ("Did you or did you not hear the defendant say X at 8:00 p.m., Friday, May 15?"). For librarians, closed questions can be useful to confirm a fact ("So you wanted to know just the name of the archaeologist who discovered the Crystal Skull?"). Closed questions invite brief factual answers and may be useful when only brief answers are wanted.

The less restrictive structure of open questions invites elaboration and longer answers. When you ask open questions, you give up some control over what gets talked about. Instead of specifying the aspect of the topic to be discussed, you ask the other person what aspect of the topic concerns him or her ("What did you want to know about the

Crystal Skull?"). Closed questions usually involve making assumptions. Open questions make no assumptions.

Some Useful Open Questions

To find out what a person wants in order to supply the need:
What sort of thing are you looking for?
What information would you like on this?
What sort of material do you have in mind?
What requirements do you have (for the project, design, etc.)?

To get a description of a problem or event:
What was the first thing that happened?
And then what happened?
Who have you talked to about this?
What have you done about this so far?

To encourage the person to elaborate:
What aspect of X concerns you?
What else can you tell me about X?
Perhaps if you tell me more about this problem [project], I could make some suggestions.

To get clarification:
What do you mean by X?
What would be an example of that? Can you give me an example?
Can you help me to understand X?

Did You Know? **?**

Some questions that look closed actually function as open questions. For example, "Can you tell me . . . ?" or "Would you mind telling me . . . ?" may seem to be closed questions that could be answered with a Yes or No. But in English, prefaces such as "Can you/would you" are understood as politeness mechanisms, or softeners, that really mean, "If you are able, please tell me . . ." or "If you are willing, please tell me . . ."

Examples

CLOSED QUESTION

"I've noticed that you have come late three times this week. Are you having a problem with your car?" This closed question will probably be answered by, "Well, no, not really."

OPEN QUESTION

"I've noticed that you have come late three times this week. What is the problem that is keeping you from getting here on time?" This open question invites the staff member to describe the problem but makes no assumptions about what the problem may be. Guessing "Is it this? Is it that?" can be risky and sometimes offensive. Moreover, it's not very efficient in situations like this one when the problem may be any number of things: an unreliable car, a sick child, a health problem, or, sometimes, a low priority assigned for promptness.

Did You Know? **?**

In some cultures, direct questions (either open or closed) may be interpreted as too direct and therefore impolite. You may want to rephrase an open question as a statement: "I may be able to help you better if you could tell me more about X."

Use open questions when you want:

- to hear in the other person's own words the nature of a problem or situation,
- to encourage the other person to talk, or
- to avoid guessing or making assumptions.

Sample Handout for the Following Exercise on Asking Open and Closed Questions

Before you begin, pick a recorder who writes down the group's suggestions. Take ten minutes to fill out this form. At the end of ten minutes, a spokesperson for each group will read out your user question, your open and closed questions, and your best question of all.

Library User: There are so many books on World War II here that I can't find what I want.

Write down three possible *closed* questions that you could ask.
1. _____
2. _____
3. _____

Write down three possible *open* questions that you could ask.
1. _____
2. _____
3. _____

When you have finished writing down your open and closed questions, examine them to see that your closed questions are really closed and your open questions are really open. Remember: a closed question limits the response to a Yes/No/I don't know or a This/That answer.

Which of your six questions do you think would work best?

_____

Exercise: Asking Open and Closed Questions

This activity works well as a small group exercise. It gives people a chance to clarify the differences between open and closed questions by generating their own examples. It also demonstrates that closed questions always contain assumptions. For each small group of about five people, produce a handout with a different user question. You can think of your own user questions, but here are some that work well:

Where do you keep your medical books?
I'm looking for something on writing.

I have to give a speech at a wedding on Saturday and don't
   know where to start.

I'm having trouble with this index.

Do you have any materials on literacy?

3.5. Avoiding Premature Diagnosis

Premature diagnosis is another term for jumping to conclusions.
These are some examples of premature diagnosis:

> A young adult, who is wearing running shoes, jeans, and a tee
> shirt, asks for some material on bees. The librarian asks, "Is
> this for a school project?"
>
> A woman in her thirties asks for pictures of Scandinavian
> costumes. The librarian asks, "Is this for your child—a
> costume to make for your child?"
>
> An elderly man asks for books on entomology. The librarian
> asks, "Are you trying to get rid of ants?"

In each case, the librarian assumed something about the user's situation and asked a closed question that made the assumption explicit
to the user. Sometimes the librarian is right (the elderly man *did* want
to get rid of carpenter ants), but that was just good luck. When the
librarian is wrong, the user may find the assumption offensive (the
woman who was asked if the Scandinavian costume was for her child
responded angrily and demanded, "Do I look like I had a child?").

Premature diagnosis is one of the most common causes of communication accidents in libraries—try to avoid it. You can't help making
assumptions, but you can avoid making these assumptions explicit to
the user. Instead of guessing and asking a closed question based on
your guess, ask an open question that makes no assumptions.

Compare the following ways of handling the same question:

> Version 1
>
> **User:** Do you have an elementary math book?
> **Librarian:** Is this book for a child?
> **User:** No, I want it for myself.
> **Librarian:** So you're teaching the adult basic education
>   program?
> **User:** No, I'm not a teacher.

Librarian: Oh, I thought you were. A lot of teachers come in asking for basic books for their courses.
User: Is that so?

Version 2

User: Do you have an elementary math book?
Librarian: We have books of that sort in both the children's and the adults' sections. How do you plan to use this book?
User: It's for myself. To brush up.
Librarian: What sort of things do you want this book to cover?
User: Charts and graphs. I'm writing a report for work, and I'm not sure which graphs to use.

3.6. Sense-Making Questions

Open questions are effective at getting people talking. But when someone needs help and it's your job to provide that help, you may want to use a form of open question called "sense-making questions," so called because they represent techniques derived from Dr. Brenda Dervin's sense-making theory. Sense-making questions provide more structure than open questions but are less likely to lead to premature diagnosis than closed questions.

The strategy of sense-making grew out of Brenda Dervin's research on how people seek and use information (see 5.3). Dervin uses the term *sense-making* to refer to her model of information seeking—which really deals with how people "make sense" of the world. According to this model, information needs arise from specific situations in a person's life. Individuals go through their everyday lives, trying to make sense out of what is happening, seeking certain outcomes, while trying to avoid others. Sometimes people can't achieve particular goals by themselves and so they turn to others for help. For example, they have to fill out their income tax forms but don't understand the difference between an expense and a capital cost. So they go to an accountant. They are looking for a job and need tips on how to write a résumé. So they go to the public library for a book on writing a résumé.

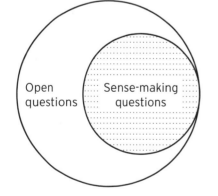

FIGURE 3.1. A Special Form of Open Question

In general, then, people often have some gap in understanding that must be filled in before they can achieve a goal. If it is your job to provide help, you need to know three things:

- The situation the person is in
- The gaps in his or her understanding
- The uses or helps—what the person would like to do as a result of bridging this gap

How do you find out these three things? Ask sense-making questions. A *sense-making question* is a special kind of open question that asks specifically about situations, or gaps, or helps.

Some Sense-Making Questions

Here are some examples of good sense-making questions to ask when you need to determine the precise nature of the help needed.

To encourage the person to describe the situation:
What are you working on?
How did this question arise?
What happened that you need to know this?

To find out how the person sees his or her situation:
What problem are you having in this situation?
Where would you like to begin?
Where do you see yourself going with this?

To assess the gaps:
What kind of help would you like?
What are you trying to understand?
What would you like to know about X?
Where did you get stuck in this project?

To identify the kind of help wanted (uses):
What would help you?
How do you plan to use this information?
What would you like to see happen in this situation?
What are you trying to do in this situation?
If you could have exactly the help you want, what would it be?

Exercise: Practice, Practice, Practice

As a way to start using sense-making questions, pick one question from the list **Some Sense-Making Questions** and use it during a reference

---

Exercise

Sense-Making Questions

Try this exercise in pairs. One person, who plays the role of the user, is given one of the scenarios provided. The other person, who plays the role of a librarian, has the job of asking sense-making questions to find out what the user really wants to know. The user answers questions asked but doesn't volunteer information freely or spill the whole story all at once. The librarian should continue to ask sense-making questions until the user is satisfied that the real question is completely understood.

Scenario 1: User is a student who has to write an English essay, which is to be "a close analysis of the text" of a short twentieth-century poem written in English. He doesn't have a particular author or poem in mind, and his first problem is that he doesn't know what is meant by "a close analysis of the text." He asks, "Where is the section on poetry?"

Scenario 2: User is worried that genetically modified (GM) foods could be harmful to her health. She wants to find articles that will tell her whether GM foods can ever be harmful and if so which ones. She says, "I'm having trouble with this catalog."

Scenario 3: User has a neighbor who is building an addition to his house that will raise the roof one and a half stories above every other house in the neighborhood. She wants to find out whether there are any building codes that would prevent this addition from going up. She asks, "Where is your law section?"

transaction. "What would you like to know about X?" is an easy one to start with. Whenever it seems to apply, use your chosen question until you feel comfortable asking it. Then try another question, perhaps, "How do you plan to use this information?" Observe what happens when you ask these questions. This experience in real situations will help you understand the function of sense-making questions.

Be prepared to ask more than one question. If the first one you ask doesn't produce the information you need, follow it up with a different one.

3.7. Follow-Up Questions

Always (well, almost always) ask a follow-up question at the end of any reference interview. There are two kinds of follow-up questions: (1) those that allow users to tell you whether you gave the kind of help they were really hoping to get and (2) those that invite the user to ask for additional help if needed.

A Quick Tip 🕐

Follow-Up Questions
Unless they are invited to return for further help, many people will ask their question only once. Therefore, follow-up questions are especially useful when you are too busy to provide further help right away. When you can spend only 30 seconds directing a library user, always say, "If you don't find what you are looking for, please come back to this desk for more help."

Some Follow-Up Questions

To invite the user to ask for additional help:
If you don't find what you are looking for, please come back and ask again.
Is there anything else I can help you with today?

To discover if the need has been met:
Does this completely answer your question?
Is that the kind of help (information, material, direction) you were hoping to get?
Will this help you?

Often, a follow-up question allows you to discover—and repair—communication accidents before the user leaves the library. A word of warning, however: in some cultures, it is considered a lack of respect to answer a follow-up question by indicating that the service was not helpful. In addition, some users may be reluctant to say that they did not find what they were looking for because they are afraid of "losing face." For example, when you ask some international students if the material you provided was helpful, they may say "Yes" out of politeness and to show respect even if the material was not at all helpful. To interpret the response, first watch for nonverbal signs of hesitancy or dissatisfaction, and then try another way of finding out what is needed, perhaps

---

Did You Know? ?

Research has shown that asking follow-up questions is one of the most important skills you can use in the reference interview. Describing a Maryland reference training program, Lillie Seward Dyson (1992) provided statistically significant evidence that asking follow-up questions enhances your chances of giving a correct answer.

---

avoiding direct questioning. (For example, "If that is not exactly what you are looking for, I would be glad to look for some more material.")

3.8. Reflecting Content

Reflecting content (or, to use Allen E. Ivey's term, "reflecting meaning") is a way of communicating that you have been really listening and have understood. Moreover, like acknowledgment (3.2), this skill gives you a chance to check that your understanding is accurate. When you reflect content, you focus on the cognitive aspects of what has been said. Use this skill in situations when it really matters that you have heard and understood correctly. When you reflect content, you are not supplying any new information of your own. You are mirroring back to the speaker what you have understood from her verbal and nonverbal behavior. If you have misunderstood, the other person will be able to correct you. The two major ways to reflect content are *paraphrasing* and *summarizing*.

Paraphrasing

Paraphrasing feeds back what has just been said in the previous comment. A common structure to use for paraphrasing is to start with an introductory clause, such as:

> It sounds like . . .
> So you think . . .
> You're saying . . .
> You mean . . .
> As you see it . . .
> As I understand you . . .

When you are paraphrasing, conclude with a concise summary giving the essence of what you think was meant. Here are some tips for paraphrasing:

- Be concise. Usually a short, pithy sentence is enough.
- Feed back the essence by restating what you understand to be the main idea of what was just said.
- Don't add to or change the meaning of what you have heard.

A Quick Tip 🕐

Paraphrasing

A warning: don't use this skill of reflection for small talk, or the exchange may go something like this:

User: Looks like we're in for a spell of stormy weather.
Librarian: Sounds like you think there's going to be a storm?
User: Yes, that's what I just said.

- Avoid sounding like a parrot. Use your own words as well as some of the keywords you have heard.
- You may want to use a checkout such as, "Is that how you see it?" or "Did I get that right?"

EXAMPLE OF PARAPHRASING

Librarian 1: Dave has applied for the senior position in the children's library, but I don't think he'd be a good choice.

Librarian 2: You don't think we should choose him?

Librarian 1: No. He's excellent with children and knows a lot about children's books, but he doesn't have the management skills to keep things running.

Librarian 2: So the only problem is with his management ability?

Librarian 1: Right. I've never seen anyone less organized. He can't organize his own desk. He's late for everything. So you can see what would happen if he were responsible for a whole branch.

Summarizing

Summarizing covers a larger span of conversation. It may be used as a summary of a complex discussion, as a transition to a new topic, or as a good conclusion to an interview. Here are some tips for summarizing:

- Synthesize the gist of what was said over the course of a number of previous statements.
- Condense.
- Go for the big picture.

EXAMPLE OF SUMMARIZING

Librarian 2: So what you're saying is that Dave knows children's work but doesn't have the organizational skills needed for a management position.

3.9. Reflecting Feeling

A statement may have cognitive content, emotional content, or both. If the content is primarily cognitive, an appropriate response is to reflect content (3.8). But if the content is primarily emotional, it is important to acknowledge that you have heard and understood the feelings that have been expressed. An appropriate response is to use the skill of reflecting feeling. Reflecting feeling is like reflecting content except that you are focusing on the emotions expressed rather than on the cognitive content. In assessing the emotional content, take into account not only the other person's words but also the body language (see Chapter 1).

Reflecting feeling can be a suitable response to all types of emotion: positive, negative, or ambivalent (including emotion directed toward yourself). Trying to ignore negative emotions or denying them simply doesn't work. A common structure useful to reflect feeling is to start with an introductory clause, such as:

> It sounds as if you feel . . .
> Maybe you feel . . .
> I sense that you are feeling a bit . . .

Follow the introductory clause with an adjective that captures the emotion, such as discouraged, hopeful, pleased, concerned, frustrated, undecided, angry, or excited. End with "about" or "that" and a keyword or clause.

Another way of structuring this skill is to use an introductory clause, such as "It sounds as if you" followed by a verb (resent, fear, mistrust, hope for, appreciate) followed by a keyword or clause. You can vary this structure to get a form that you feel comfortable using. For example:

> It sounds like these layoffs have left you feeling a bit insecure
>   and worried about your own job.
> I get the feeling you're sorry we ever started this project.
> Perhaps you feel that you are left doing all the work and you
>   resent it.

Some Tips for Reflecting Feeling

- Take body language into account when you are assessing the feeling being expressed.
- Use your own words to sum up the key emotion(s) rather than simply repeating the words you have heard.
- Be tentative. Instead of saying, "You must be . . ." you could say, "You seem to be . . ." Give the other person a chance to

---

Exercise

Role-Playing Reflecting Feeling

Imagine that you are talking to a colleague in the staff room who is telling you about her supervisor. She says, "This morning I was ready to quit. You remember all that fuss that Cheryl made about doing a needs assessment. She made me drop everything to work on it. I spent hours getting it done. Now she says she doesn't think we need one after all and that we should just forget about it."

Consider the following responses:

- You shouldn't let Cheryl get to you this way. [Giving advice]
- Something way worse happened to me when I was working with Cheryl. [Sympathy seeking]
- Doing a needs assessment is very important. I have a good book on it. [Providing unasked-for information]

What could you say instead that would reflect feeling?

You can do this exercise in a group. Write on a card the situation outlined above. A volunteer plays the role of the frustrated staff member by reading her lines, "This morning I was ready . . ." The rest of the group responds by reflecting feeling. Make up more situations to be role-played.

correct you, if you got the feeling wrong. You may want to use a checkout, such as, "Is that how you see it?" or "Did I get that right?"

- Avoid making statements that seem to imply judgments or evaluations of the person's ability, such as, "You sound like you are having a lot of trouble handling that."

EXAMPLE OF REFLECTING FEELING

Library User: I want to talk to somebody about this book [Stephanie Meyer's *Twilight*]. My daughter is only 11, and she got this book from your YA section. Do you think this kind of story about sex with a vampire is a good model for someone her age?

Librarian: You seem to be pretty upset about this.

User: Of course I'm upset! Who wouldn't be upset when public libraries circulate books to children that are filled with explicit sex about demonic vampires and I don't know what all.

Librarian: I can see that this situation has really caused you concern.

This is not the time to explain the library's collection policy or to get into a discussion of the literary merits of popular fantasy fiction or to explain that actually *Twilight* has been called by some people "abstinence porn" for the way it shows that abstinence can be really hot. First, the user needs a chance to express her feelings and have them recognized and acknowledged. The librarian, in reflecting these feelings, is letting the other person know that the feelings are heard and understood. The librarian is not evaluating the feelings or sharing them or agreeing with them or saying that the user is right or wrong to feel this way.

3.10. Inclusion

Many communication accidents can be avoided simply by telling the other person what you are doing. For example, you could explain to a user that you are going to look for an index, that you are checking a special database, or that you are looking for other subject headings. Inclusion means providing a description of what you are doing or an

---

A Quick Tip 🕐

Reflecting Feeling Accurately
Remember that there are two aspects to accurate reflection of feeling. You have to capture the correct feeling, and you have to get the intensity of the feeling right. Consider these possibilities to convey different degrees of intensity: exasperated, irritated, nettled, sore, mad, angry, fuming, furious, infuriated. You would have to decide, in a given situation, which, if any, of these accurately reflected the feeling. Another way to suit your response to the intensity of the emotion expressed is to use an appropriate qualifying adverb:

- somewhat angry
- very angry
- extremely angry

explanation when the reasons for what you are doing are not readily apparent.

Inclusion is an attending skill. It maintains the communication process between two people when one person must perform a task that does not, in itself, require interpersonal communication or when one person must do something that might otherwise signal an interruption or termination of the conversation. Inclusion helps to answer unspoken questions: Are you still there? Are you still working on my problem? Why are you doing something that doesn't seem related to my problem? Inclusion reassures the person you are helping (e.g., "I'm going to check the shelves for you and will return in a minute"). In addition, inclusion often has an instructive function. Describing and explaining your behavior helps the observer learn how to replicate that behavior. For example, when the librarian says, "What I am doing now is looking for other headings we could use," the user learns that an index may include alternate terms.

Inclusion is a skill that is particularly useful in these situations:

- When the other person cannot see what you are doing. On the telephone or in chat communications, always describe behavior that interrupts normal conversation (e.g., "I'm going to put you on hold. Please wait a moment," or "I'm writing this down as you speak," or "I'm looking for some websites on your topic that I can send you"). Use inclusion with anyone who can't see what you are doing, such as a person who is blind or a person with whom you are communicating online: "I'm looking in an index now."
- When the relationship between your behavior and the problem is not immediately apparent to a layperson. For example, a library user may expect you to answer his question off the top of your head, but you need to check a reference source to be sure. Say, "I want to be sure so I'm verifying this in the current directory."
- When you want to instruct the user (and the user wants to be instructed). Explaining precisely what you are doing helps the user learn the procedure. "I'm going to look in a database called Medline. Here it is . . . and I'm looking under the heading Alzheimer's Disease . . . I see two items . . . one called 'Researchers Study Causes of Alzheimer's Disease.' "
- When you ask a question or make a request that may seem unrelated or inappropriate to a library user. Users

Did You Know? ?

Users often do not know why a librarian suddenly leaves them, when they have asked for a particular journal or book. If you don't tell the user that you are going downstairs to the stacks to get the requested journal, he may think:

- You've gone on a coffee break or to lunch.
- You're working on something else.
- You didn't hear him.

sometimes do not understand that it is necessary for you to determine the scope of their query and may think you are prying. Instead of asking, "Why do you need this information?" you can use inclusion to introduce your question: "The library has a great deal of material on this topic, and we'll have a better chance of finding the best sources if you can tell me something about how you plan to use the information."

- When you want to draw attention to something that could easily be overlooked. For example, although you wouldn't necessarily explain to a regular user that you're charging out the books for 21 days (the normal borrowing period), you might point out that the videos are due back in one week, not three.

- When the other person will have to wait because the task takes a few minutes, you need to concentrate on the task without talking, or you are going to be out of sight. People usually do not mind waiting as long as they know what to expect. If there's a line-up, people become less impatient when you acknowledge them, even if you can't immediately help them. Eye contact is important here, especially if you can't say anything at the moment. When you can explain, you could say, "I'm going to help this man, and I have a telephone call waiting, and then I will be right with you," or "I'm going to my office and will be back in about three minutes," or "This will take me some time to check because I have to call the university library. Would you like to wait while I do that?"

Inclusion involves four basic steps:

1. **Acknowledge.** Restate the problem or otherwise indicate that you are listening so that your next action will be seen to be related: "So you want to see if we have anything on salamanders."
2. **Describe briefly** what you are doing (or have done or are just about to do): "I'm looking under 'salamanders' in our catalog to see if we have books." If you want to instruct the user, provide more detail.
3. **Explain briefly** why you are doing it. State the reason for your behavior, or summarize the advantages: "This could be in the biology section or it could be in the pet

books. The catalog will tell us all the places we should look and it might also tell us what else to look under."

4. **Indicate the time required** for the task, if appropriate. Be specific. Say, "I should be able to call you back this afternoon" rather than "I won't be able to call back right away" or "This may take a while."

3.11. Closure

Closure is the art of the tactful ending. It really consists of a cluster of skills that are used to signal leave-taking. We are all familiar with some of the ritualistic nonverbal skills that signal the end of any conversation—changes in body orientation, such as moving away from the other person, or changes in eye contact, such as looking toward an exit or a watch. Sometimes, however, these nonverbal cues give the other person a feeling of being suddenly cut off. To wrap up a conversation smoothly, you may want to use the verbal skill of closure.

Some functions of closure are:

- to indicate that discussion of a topic has been completed, at least for the moment;
- to focus the participants' attention on what has been achieved in the discussion; and
- to establish a good communication climate so that the other person looks forward to the next encounter (Hargie and Dickson, 2004: 280–289).

First, closure can be used effectively during an interaction when the conversation is wandering. Don't make the mistake of cutting off the other person midsentence or of changing the subject abruptly. Not only will you be perceived as impolite but also the other person may, despite appearances, actually be telling you something relevant. However, when it is apparent that the conversation is clearly off-track, you can get back to the point tactfully by first acknowledging what the other person is saying and then by returning quickly (not pausing) to the main purpose of the conversation. You might say, "Yes, the arrangements you have worked out for daycare sound great. But tell me, now, about the dates you want for these census records" or "It's really a shame about that fender-bender in the parking lot.

> **A Quick Tip** 🕐
>
> **Closure**
> Closure can also be used when you realize you're going to have to refer the user to someone else. For example, "This sounds like a pretty technical topic, so what I'd like to do is locate our science and technology librarian."

Exercise 🔧

Being Explicit
Practice making instructions and directions more explicit by rewording or expanding on each of the following:

1. Look for articles about the last election using the library's catalog.
2. If you want the printed back issues, you can find them in the stacks.
3. Try the music library for that.
4. You'll need to get a card from the circulation department.
5. Go to the fiction section on the third floor.

But, to get back to these pathfinders, what do you think we should do for the graphics?" Knowing the effect of the questions you ask enables you to choose an appropriate questioning style. You can ask open questions (3.4) to encourage the reticent person to provide more details about the task at hand but practice closure to focus digressers.

The second way to use closure is to signal the end of an interaction. If the conversation has been brief, perhaps all that is necessary is a one-phrase summary or a comment to suggest future steps, such as, "So now you know how to download an e-book to your e-reader at home" or "Next time you'll know that we have other material that's not in the catalog." In almost all reference transactions, it's a good idea to use a follow-up question (see 3.7) that will provide you with both a chance to confirm that the user has received what she or he wanted and the opportunity to close the conversation, for example, "If that database doesn't have what you are looking for, please come back and ask again."

If the interaction has been longer, which sometimes occurs in reference interviews but more often occurs in group situations such as a meeting, summarize (see summary as a skill involved in reflecting content, 3.8). In your summary, you close by drawing attention to the main accomplishments of the interaction, for example, "We've been able to get through all our agenda items today, and I'm particularly pleased that we came to a consensus on the Sunday opening issue."

3.12. Giving Instructions and Directions

People who work in libraries increasingly are called on to give instructions or directions. For example, you may need to instruct a library user in the use of the catalog or teach someone how to get access to electronic books. You may need to give someone directions for finding a book or for going to another library. Information literacy programs involve complex sequences of instructions. Instructions and directions are basically descriptions of procedures or steps that another person must take. Giving effective instructions and directions is a skill that can be learned and improved. Instructions and directions are often misinterpreted or ignored because they are too complicated or detailed or because they are not understood.

Tips for Giving Instructions or Directions:

- **Use appropriate body language.** Show that you are attentive through eye contact, posture, gestures, and voice. To ensure that the person is ready to hear your instructions, be assertive. Use more eye contact, make your voice stronger (but not louder), and lean forward (see Chapter 1).

- **Be clear and specific.** Give explicit directions. Avoid general statements or requests. "Ask the fiction librarian" is too vague. Instead, say, "Go over to that desk (gesturing) where the sign says Fiction. Tell the person sitting there that you want help in finding books by George Orwell."

- **Avoid jargon and abbreviations.** It's okay to use ILL, OPAC, ISSN, VLE, and URL among staff, but users find these abbreviations confusing and may hesitate to ask what they mean. Use plain language.

- **Check to make sure that your instructions were heard and understood.** Remember that cultural differences may affect the response. Some users may think that to admit not understanding what you said is a failure in showing respect. Observe the user's reaction—a puzzled look may tell you that your directions were not clear, even though they seemed clear enough to you. Verify that the user has in fact seen the sign you pointed to or knows where the stairs are. For example, "Go over to that desk where the sign says Fiction. Do you see it?"

- **Ensure that the person can carry out the directions.** Watch where the user goes and intervene if necessary. In the case of using a library resource or piece of equipment, watch while the user carries out each step. It is not enough for the user to watch the librarian demonstrate. What looks simple often turns out to be hard for a first-time user. You could say, "Now, you look for the first article while I watch" or "Show me how you are going to combine these two terms."

3.13. Confrontation

Confrontation uses an important cluster of skills derived from assertiveness training. The two main kinds of assertiveness skills are positive (which help people to express themselves confidently in situations such as giving or accepting a compliment) and negative (which help people to deal constructively and honestly with conflict). In this section we focus on the latter skills as used in confrontation, sometimes called "conflict assertiveness." Confrontation is appropriate when you want to persuade others to change their behavior or when you want to refuse an unreasonable request. Using assertiveness skills is one way to replace less productive ways of dealing with conflict, such as the nonassertive or the aggressive behavior illustrated in the following examples:

- Saying nothing about the problem and bottling up your feelings until one day you can't stand it anymore and you explode. However, the other person may never have realized that her behavior bothered you and now thinks you are overreacting. Assertiveness skills would let her know in a timely way how you feel and why so that she has the option of changing.
- Attacking the other person's character or motives. But an approach that makes other people feel guilty, put down, or maligned doesn't motivate them to change. Instead, it makes them defensive so that they stop listening and start arguing ("No, I'm not/No, I didn't/What about last week when you did X?").
- Simply giving in to every request so that eventually you are not only overloaded with work, having agreed to do things you can't possibly do, but you also feel resentful and badly treated.

Conflict assertiveness is important for dealing with clients, co-workers, supervisees, and employers. Of the many techniques commonly used in assertiveness training, we will describe two of the most useful skills: DESC and the broken record.

DESC

DESC is a technique for asking other people to change their behavior. The acronym represents four steps: **D**escribing the situation; **E**xpressing feelings; **S**pecifying changes; and pointing out **C**onsequences. Here's how to use DESC:

Describe the unacceptable behavior in factual and unemotional terms. Simply describe the behavior. Do not attribute blame. Do not suggest reasons why the situation has occurred (such as that the other person has been selfish, thoughtless, careless, malicious, etc.): "Mary, we have noticed that for the past three meetings of our committee, you have been 15 minutes late each time."

Express how this makes you feel and why (or **Explain** why the behavior is unsuitable). If you can't express/explain why, the other person is not likely to feel motivated to change: "When we have to wait for you, we feel frustrated because we are wasting our time when we are all very busy."

Specify what changes you would like to see happen. Often it is best not to specify exactly how to implement the change but to involve the other person in thinking through how best to achieve the desired outcome: "We would like to schedule the next meeting at a time when everyone can be on time." (This gives Mary a chance to say, "I can't seem to get to 3:30 p.m. meetings on time because that's when I'm busiest. But if we could reschedule the meeting for 9:00 a.m., I could be on time.")

Consequences: Explain the good consequences of the proposed change or the bad consequences that the change will prevent: "If you could come on time, we could be more efficient and finish the meetings more quickly."

In situations in which expressing feelings may not be appropriate or useful, substitute explaining for the second step. That is, instead of expressing how the behavior makes you feel, explain why the behavior is unsuitable or unacceptable. See 6.7.1 for examples of situations in which you might use DESC.

This skill is not guaranteed to work every time. The other person is always free to listen to your explanation about how the unacceptable behavior makes you feel and then say, "So what? That's your problem."

Exercise

Using DESC

You are a librarian in charge of an information center in the head office of a large petrochemical company. Your clientele are the 200 scientists and researchers who work for the company. The company has decided to expand the space available for offices. When you look at the plans, you see no provision to expand the space for the library. This is disheartening to you, especially because you have often pointed out to your management committee that overcrowding limits your ability to provide information. Furthermore, you see that space is being wasted: the large hallway that bisects the library space is unnecessary and takes up space that you need. What do you say to decision makers?

D _____

E _____

S _____

C _____

A Quick Tip ⏱

"I," "You," and "We" Messages

Beginning your assertive statement with "you" tends to put the other person on the defensive. Try starting with "I." Instead of saying, "You make me feel annoyed because you are always late for your shift" say, "I feel annoyed because I often have to wait for you after I end my shift." Use "we" instead of "you" or "I" to communicate the idea of a shared problem. For example, "We will both feel a lot better if we can work out a new schedule."

But DESC usually works better than most other styles of dealing with conflict.

It is important to remember that assertiveness skills tend to be situation specific and culture specific. In some cultural groups, where indirectness is valued in face-to-face communication, assertive behavior may actually exacerbate the situation because it is so direct. It may cause people to feel they have "lost face." Cultures differ in the values that they place on individualism, rationality, competition, and personal control. For a good discussion of the role of gender and culture in assertiveness, see Richard F. Rakos (2006).

SOME QUICK TIPS FOR USING DESC

- Describe clearly what the behavior is and why it is a problem. Being indirect and nonspecific usually doesn't work, because the message won't get through. For example, it is not effective to say, "Mary, we hope that next week our committee can be more efficient." Mary may heartily agree, interpreting this comment as a criticism of certain digressers who sidetrack the committee's discussions.
- Involve the other person in the solution. People are more apt to make changes if they feel that they have participated in the decision.
- Practice the DESC script in your own mind before you use it.
- DESC is a two-way street. Listen to other people when they tell you about a problem they would like you to change. DESC depends on good will and trust.

The Broken Record

The broken record technique can be used as part of the DESC strategy. It simply means repeating a phrase and, if necessary, repeating it again to get your point across. By not introducing any new content into the conversation, you prevent the other person from seizing on a new point to argue with you. For example, when you say, "I'm sorry, we don't offer free photocopying here, but you can get a copy card at the information desk to use with the public photocopiers," the library user might say, "Yes, but I just need a few pages." Now would be the time to use the broken record and say again, "We don't provide free photocopying here." If the user says, "Couldn't you do it for me just this once?" you could repeat, "I'm very sorry, we don't provide photocopying here, but you can get a copy card at the information desk."

If instead you engage with the details of what the user says, you may get into a nonproductive discussion about whether breaking the rules for one person "just this once" is fair to others who abide by the rules or you may end up arguing about what "a few pages" means. When you stick to the broken record, the user eventually gets the point that no one is going to do his photocopying for him.

To use the broken record effectively, it's important to remain calm, not raise your voice, and not look anxious. Smile pleasantly and say, "I'm very sorry, but we just don't provide photocopying service here."

3.14. Giving Feedback

"Feedback" is a term we all use a lot. In this section, it is used to describe the process in which a listener or reader provides information to a speaker or writer about the effectiveness of a particular communication event. Feedback provides evaluative information on both the content and the process—on both the what and the how. You may be called on to provide feedback in many situations that arise in libraries. For example:

- You are a supervisor doing a performance appraisal.
- You are teaching a skill in a staff training session and have to evaluate a learner's performance.
- Your colleague has asked you to listen to her booktalk and offer suggestions for improvement before she presents it to an audience.
- Your friend has asked you to criticize the design of his website.
- Your colleague has asked you to read over his grant application and suggest specific ways to improve it.

Some Guidelines for Giving Feedback

- Immediate feedback is best. If possible, provide the feedback right away.
- Start with one or two positive comments. Even when the performance is not generally very good, find something that you can praise sincerely. You could say to the booktalker, "You chose an excellent book to talk about" or "I liked your enthusiasm." Feedback that is entirely negative undermines

---

Did You Know? ❓

"Feedback" is a term that was developed initially in the context of self-correcting biological systems as well as control systems in the fields of engineering and mathematics. When adapted by communication theory, the term *feedback* has been used to refer to the information that closes the circuit between source (speaker/sender) and receiver (listener/viewer/reader). Feedback allows the source to evaluate what sense the receiver has made of the message. Feedback can take the form of a spoken comment, a sigh, a smile, a long silence, a written message, a citation in a paper, a changing attitude, or many other actions (De Castro, 2009: 5–6).

A Quick Tip 🕐

Written Feedback
The guidelines for giving oral feedback also work with written feedback. In some situations, such as performance appraisals or training assessments, it's a good idea to follow up oral feedback with a written memo (see 9.4 on memos).

A Quick Tip 🕐

Show Appreciation
In a busy environment, it's often easy to forget to say thank you to colleagues. Try, "I really appreciated your help with . . ." or "I'm so grateful for . . ." (People Communicating, 2009-2010).

the receiver's self-respect and discourages further effort. The person getting the entirely negative feedback may think, "So-and-so is out to get me" or "I'll never be able to do this."

- Leave the other person in control. If you are a supervisor doing a performance appraisal, it is your job to provide both positive and negative feedback. But if a friend or colleague asks you for feedback, leave that person in control of the kind and amount of feedback wanted. Feedback is more likely to be useful when it is solicited rather than imposed. For example, someone who says, "Please read my research proposal and point out all the places where it seems unclear or weak" is likely to act on suggestions given.

- Be specific. Instead of saying, "Your presentation slides need improvement," it is better to say, "I can't read your slides from the back of the room. Perhaps you could cut some of the text and use a larger font." Focus on concrete examples.

- Be descriptive rather than simply evaluative. Don't say, "You kept the discussion going well," but rather, "When you led the group discussion, you asked several open questions that generated a lot of response, especially your question about X." When you give negative feedback, it is especially important to stick to observable facts and behaviors. Not, "You didn't do very well with that last reference interview" or even, "When you were negotiating that interview, you seemed bored." It is better to say, "When the user was talking to you, you were looking away and tapping your pencil."

- Be realistic. Suggest improvements you think the person is actually capable of making.

- Limit your suggestions to two or three. If you ask for ten changes all at once, your suggestions will be discouraging rather than helpful.

- Suggest rather than prescribe. In most situations, it works best to suggest a change tentatively as something the other person may want to consider, accept, modify, or set aside.

- Consider the needs of the receiver of your feedback. Provide the amount of information that the receiver can use rather than everything that can be said. When someone asks for feedback without being specific, your first question should be, "What kind of feedback would help you?"

- Seek out opportunities to offer sincere praise. People will recognize and resent insincerity.

- Create a climate that is positive and encouraging—that's the key to giving feedback.

3.15. Receiving Feedback

Receiving feedback is a skill, just as much as giving feedback is, and similarly requires practice. We need to learn how to listen to feedback and use it constructively. Here are some guidelines for receiving feedback:

- Specify what kind of feedback you want. If you are chiefly interested in how someone else understands the basic points in your draft speech, say so. Otherwise, you may be disappointed when the other person comments only on your presentation style.
- Let the other person know your special concerns. When you ask for feedback, say what particularly concerns you so that the other person can address this. When you ask someone to listen to your speech, for example, you might say, "I am worried that my voice is not strong enough to be heard at the back of the room, so I'd appreciate it if you could raise your hand whenever my voice sounds faint."
- Listen carefully to the feedback. Observe the rules for being a good listener (see Chapter 2) by paying full attention, not letting your mind wander or race ahead, and not obsessing on one particular comment. To show that you are paying attention, use appropriate eye contact and body language.
- Don't be defensive. Avoid explaining or arguing why you were right all along. Instead of saying, "Well, I thought that was a pretty good joke to start my speech with, even if some people can't take that kind of humor," try saying, "So you felt the joke didn't go over well." After all, you asked for feedback, and the other person is being honest in his reactions.
- Summarize and paraphrase (3.8) key points of the feedback to make sure that you've understood it. Say something like, "So, with the exception of the initial joke, you felt the tone of this speech was all right, and there weren't any major problems with my delivery. But I should try to make the

> **Exercise**
>
> **Receiving Feedback**
> Think of a recent work situation in which you did not receive any feedback and would have liked some. This might have been a situation that you felt you handled well or one that you fear you handled badly. It could be a presentation that you gave, a new procedure that you taught to the staff, or an interaction with a library user. How did you feel when there was no feedback? It's possible to ask for feedback—whom could you have asked in this particular situation? How would you phrase your request? Remember to identify specific aspects of your performance on which you would like feedback.

speech a bit shorter and cut back on the number of slides."
Then use a checkout: "Is that what you're saying?"

3.16. Offering Opinions and Suggestions

Librarians are often asked to offer their opinions and suggestions: recommendations for reference sources or search procedures, feelings about an issue, opinions about preferred options. Even when opinions or suggestions are not requested, the librarian may find it helpful to bring new facts, skills, or points of view to the discussion. Offering opinions and suggestions involves many of the same skills as giving directions (see 3.12): using appropriate attending behavior, making clear and specific statements, and asking for feedback. Unlike directions, opinions involve evaluative statements—judgments based on experience, personal perspectives, or individual attitudes and beliefs that may not be shared by the other person. Suggestions about what to do or how to solve a problem are a matter of personal judgment and are best offered tentatively.

The first step in offering opinions and suggestions effectively is to assess the situation. Has your opinion been sought? Have you been asked for suggestions? If not, consider the possibility that the other person may not be receptive. A common communication accident is to offer opinions and suggestions prematurely. (The user says, "I have to do a project on information overload" and the librarian jumps in with some suggested sources. But the user wants the number of English-language Internet sites). Avoid premature diagnosis (3.5) by delaying suggestions until it is clear what kind of help the person wants.

Sometimes, the other person does not ask for your opinion or suggestions, but it seems to you that a new point of view might help. If so, first assess the other person's willingness and readiness to hear what you have to say: "Would it help you if I told you about my experience with this?" or "Would you like some suggestions about options and possible next steps?" Or indicate how your opinions and suggestions could help: "It might help you to decide if I suggested some options." Watch the response carefully; if you sense the person is not ready to listen to suggestions, do not offer them.

Even when someone does ask for your thoughts, there are times when it's not appropriate to offer either opinions or suggestions. In some cases, the other person is looking for support or reassurance rather than a true opinion ("How do you like the picture I just bought for my office wall?"). In other cases, it's unwise to offer an opinion that may be interpreted as expert advice or fact, especially when the topic is not within your expertise—when, for example, a library user wants to know if you think he should sue someone or change doctors. Or someone may ask whether you personally agree with the library's book selection policy when she really wants to find an ally for her crusade to remove *And Tango Makes Three* from the children's library. In these cases, exercise intentionality by taking into account the consequences of your offering an opinion or suggestion. If you're not sure when or if you should offer an opinion, ask yourself, "How would my opinion help (or harm) in this situation? What might the consequences be? What is this person trying to do?"

Offer suggestions or opinions in cases where they will help to solve a problem, but only when the other person is receptive. Follow these three steps:

1. Make sure that the other person is ready to hear your suggestions or opinions. Use your active listening skills (2.2). Make eye contact, and use appropriate body language (see Chapter 1). Observe the other person's reaction.

2. Be brief and specific, as in giving directions (3.12). State the suggestions clearly, and be specific without giving unnecessary detail. Do not let your opinions become a vehicle for excessive self-disclosure or long stories justifying the opinion.

3. Ask for feedback. Make sure the suggestions have been understood (or that the opinions have been correctly interpreted). For example: "Do any of these suggestions seem useful?" "Does this seem reasonable to you?" "Does this give you any new ideas?"

Some Tips for Giving Opinions and Suggestions

- Identify your opinions as opinions rather than general truths; for example, "My personal feeling is . . ." or "I tend to think that . . ." or "This is my opinion of this book, but others may disagree."

- Avoid saying, "You should . . ." or "What you ought to do is . . ." Most people dislike being told what they ought to do. Say, "Let's think about options—one might be to change your topic" rather than "You ought to change your topic."

- Don't make suggestions in the form, "If I were you, I would do X" because, of course, you are not the other person. "If I were you" is the preamble for a great deal of unsolicited and not very useful advice.

- Express suggestions tentatively as options: "You can go three ways with this. You can place a hold on the book, and we will contact you when it is available—this may take about three weeks. Or you could try the music library. Or perhaps we could look for a similar book that would help you right away."

- Try using acknowledgment (3.2) or reflection of feeling (3.9) instead of giving unsolicited, irrelevant opinions or suggestions: "It's certainly a problem when you're not sure what the teacher wants" works better than "Oh, those teachers never explain the assignment. It drives us crazy trying to figure out these assignments. You ought to complain."

- Distinguish between professional and personal opinions. Know when to express your professional opinion and when to express your personal opinion: "Some people have told us they found the violence in this book hard to take" is better than "Oh, don't read that—it's full of violence. You won't like it. I hated it." In this example, offering factual information is better than offering a personal opinion that may not be shared.

3.17. Annotated Bibliography

General Works

De Castro, Paola. 2009. *Librarians of Babel: A Toolkit for Effective Communication.* London: Chandos. This little book focuses on written communication; however, Chapter 1 has a succinct explanation of the communication process in general.

Dewdney, Patricia, and Catherine Sheldrick Ross. 1994. "Flying a Light Aircraft: Reference Service Evaluation from a User's Viewpoint." *RQ* 34, no. 2 (Winter): 217–230. This article describes user reactions toward librarians' use of acknowledgment, questioning skills, inclusion, giving instructions, and making referrals.

Evans, David R., Margaret T. Hearn, Max R. Uhlemann, and Allen Ivey. 2008. *Essential Interviewing: A Programmed Approach to Effective Communication*. 7th ed. Monterey, CA: Brooks/Cole. This workbook covers attending skills (Chapter 2), effective questioning (Chapter 3), and reflecting content and feeling (Chapters 4 and 5).

Hargie, Owen, ed. 2006. *The Handbook of Communication Skills*. 3rd ed. New York: Routledge. This is a thorough review of verbal and nonverbal behaviors. See especially "Explaining" by George Brown, pp. 195–228; "Reflecting" by David Dickson, pp. 165–194; "Reinforcement," by Len Cairns, pp. 47–165; and "Questioning" by David Dickson and Owen Hargie, pp. 121–145. Also covers self-disclosure and persuasion.

Hargie, Owen, and David Dickson. 2004. *Skilled Interpersonal Communication: Research, Theory, and Practice*. 4th ed. New York: Routledge. This work covers 14 skill areas: nonverbal communication; reinforcement; questioning; reflecting; listening; explaining; self-disclosure; set induction; closure; assertiveness; influencing; negotiating; and participating in as well as leading group discussions.

Isenstein, Laura. 1992. "Get Your Reference Staff on the STAR Track." *Library Journal* 117, no. 7 (April 15): 34–37. This article describes a program for training reference staff to use open questions, paraphrase, and follow-up.

Ivey, Allen E., Mary Bradford Ivey, and Carlos P. Zalaquett. 2010. *Intentional Interviewing and Counseling: Facilitating Client Development in a Multicultural Society*. 7th ed. Belmont, CA: Brooks/Cole, Cengage Learning. Chapter 3 covers attending behavior, and other chapters cover listening, paraphrasing, reflecting feeling, confrontation, and influencing skills.

Reference and User Services Association. 2004. "Guidelines for Behavioral Performance of Reference and Information Service Professionals." http://www.ala.org/rusa/resources/guidelines/guidelinesbehavioral. This resource includes specific guidelines for listening and inquiring.

Rentz, Kathryn, Marie Flatley, and Paula Lentz. 2011. *Lesikar's Business Communication: Connecting in a Digital World*. 12th ed. New York: McGraw-Hill. This frequently revised text (formerly *Lesikar's Basic Business Communication*) provides methodological analyses of the main forms of business communication and includes useful sections on speaking skills.

Questioning Skills

Dervin, Brenda, and Patricia Dewdney. 1986. "Neutral Questioning: A New Approach to the Reference Interview." *RQ* 25, no. 4: 506–513. This is the primary source on the theory and practice of sense-making questions in the context of the reference interview.

Dickson, David, and Owen Hargie. 2006. "Questioning." In *The Handbook of Communication Skills*, 3rd ed., edited by Owen Hargie, 121–145. New York: Routledge. This chapter discusses the function of questions in many contexts, including their role in professional discourse. It provides a thorough discussion of all types of questions.

Dyson, Lillie Seward. 1992. "Improving Reference Services: A Maryland Training Program Brings Positive Results." *Public Libraries* 31, no. 5: 284–289. This frequently cited study found that training in questioning skills can improve reference success.

Ross, Catherine Sheldrick. 1986. "How to Find Out What People Really Want to Know." *The Reference Librarian* 16 (Winter): 19–30. Theory and practice of open and sense-making questions.

Reflecting Content and Feeling; Inclusion; Confrontation and Assertiveness; Offering Opinions and Suggestions; Closure

Bower, Sharon Anthony, and Gordon H. Bower. 2004. *Asserting Yourself: A Practical Guide for Positive Change*. Updated edition. Cambridge, MA: Da Capo Press. This book explains the technique of DESC and how to use it, with many exercises.

Caputo, Janette S. 1984. *The Assertive Librarian*. Phoenix, AZ: Oryx Press. Chapter 5 on "Verbal Assertion" includes an excellent discussion of DESC, the broken record, and several other very practical techniques for handling conflict.

Michell, Gillian, and Roma M. Harris. 1987. "Evaluating the Competence of Information Providers." *RQ* 27, no. 1 (Fall): 95–105. This article reports on an experiment in which the level of inclusion was varied.

People Communicating. 2009–2010. "Thank You Phrases for the Workplace." http://www.people-communicating.com/thank-you-phrases.html. It's just what the title says.

Rakos, Richard F. 2006. "Asserting and Confronting." In *The Handbook of Communication Skills*, 3rd ed., edited by Owen Hargie, 345–382. New York: Routledge. This chapter provides a scholarly review of assertiveness behavior.

Writing

4.1. Analyzing the Audience

This chapter covers the general writing skills that should become second nature so that you can use them in various professional applications. See Chapter 9 for details on writing forms that you are likely to need in your work. There we cover soup to nuts—messages and memos, letters and reports, instructions and manuals, and newsletters and signs. We also cover written communications for groups, writing publicity and promotion, writing about books (e.g., booklists, annotations and reviews), and contributions to professional literature.

Whatever type of written communication you are doing, your first step should be to analyze your intended audience. A written text (in either print or electronic form) is an intermediary in the process of communication between two active parties: the writer and the reader. As a writer, you expect to spend a lot of energy thinking about how to express your message in words. But you should also spend some time thinking about what your readers will do with the words you have written.

Good professional writing is writing that communicates to its intended audience. It should not be an exercise of self-expression or of looking into one's heart and writing unless you are writing a lyric poem. Instead, consider how readers read. For example, on webpages readers normally don't read every word carefully. They scan. Therefore a well-written webpage is optimized so that scanners can easily find the most important information.

Your readers will have to interpret your text, and their interpretation will be colored by many factors, including their relationship to you, their roles, their skill at reading, their knowledge of the topic at hand, their previous experiences, expectations, and biases, and their goals in reading the text. Some of these constraints may be barriers preventing certain readers from interpreting your words as you intended. Unfortunately you won't hear from your readers about the difficulties they are having. They can't provide you with the sort of feedback that is possible in a face-to-face conversation. Therefore, you should try to anticipate problems.

Before starting to write, ask yourself these questions about your readers:

- Is a written document the **best way to communicate** in this instance? Or would a face-to-face meeting or some combination of written and in-person communication be best?
- What is your **purpose**? What effect do you hope to have on your readers? Here are some common reasons for writing: to amuse; instruct; explain; generate interest; foster goodwill; ask for or give information; persuade to act; make a request; turn down a request; recommend; thank or congratulate someone; report some activity. Write with your effect in mind. Use a style suited to your purpose.
- Who is the **target audience**? Are your readers a homogenous group who will understand a specialized vocabulary and professional jargon and acronyms? If not, you will have to translate the specialized insider language into language that can be understood by a general readership.
- What do your **readers want to know** about this topic? Consider the needs, interests, and experiences of your readers, and slant your writing to take these needs into account.
- What **gaps** are there in your readers' understanding of your topic? What do your readers not know that you must tell them?
- What do your **readers already know** that you won't need to tell them?
- What **format, organization, and style of presentation** will best help your reader understand your text?
- What **biases** of your readers should you take into account?
- Is your intended audience **internal or external** to your organization?

- Will your writing have **more than one audience**? If it will go up a chain of approval through the hierarchy of the library, library board, or university senate—or out into cyberspace—you need to take into account all of your audiences and not just the first one. Given the ease of mass copying and forwarding of electronic text, assume that your writing may reach unintended readers.

4.2. Choosing an Appropriate Style

A good writer doesn't use the same style all the time but suits the style to the occasion. As Cicero put it in *De Oratore*, "no single kind of style can be adapted to every cause, or every audience, or every person, or every occasion." Here are some elements to consider when choosing a style.

Formality

Choose an appropriate degree of formality. The range goes from slang to a style that is very formal. Avoid the extremes: slangy familiarity is unsuitable for business writing; equally unsuitable is the formal legalistic style that used to be recommended. Avoid phrases like *incumbent upon, aforementioned, heretofore, herewith, as per, letter of the 14th inst., please be advised, deem it advisable, the subject of your request, in accordance with your instructions,* and so on.

Views on writing style are embedded in their historical period and change through time. Thus Almonte C. Howell advised readers in *Military Correspondence and Reports* (New York: McGraw-Hill, 1943: 2), "The writer should . . . not use the first person pronoun . . . not even the second should be used." Such formality now seems decidedly quaint. A moderately informal style is best for most kinds of writing done in a library setting. For e-mail messages, letters, memos, and internal reports, aim for a conversational style. Make your memo sound as if a real person has written it, not an impersonal bureaucracy. It's okay to use contractions such as *it's* and *can't* rather than *it is* and *cannot*. Use personal pronouns such as *we, you,* or *I think* rather than *one thinks* or *it is thought* or *this writer thinks*. For formal reports, you may want to achieve a more formal style by avoiding contractions and the overuse of personal pronouns. But even here a

> ### A Quick Tip 🕐
>
> #### Take the Shortcut
> E-mail and texting abbreviations are quick, informal ways of indicating a ritual phrase or a qualifying remark. Texting and Twitter have greatly expanded the number of abbreviations because they save keystrokes. Many (such as fyi and asap) are familiar and long-established, while others have emerged more recently as texting shortcuts—for example, the use of numbers (2, 4, and 8) to indicate sounds. Some familiar abbreviations such as bfn (bye for now) or f-t-f (face-to-face) often appear as b4n and f2f. The word *later* shows up as l8r. With the proviso about considering your audience and purpose, use abbreviations if you are comfortable doing so. But keep up: lol means "laughing out loud," not "lots of love." Our advice is dodi (Don't overdo it). See the list of chat abbreviations at Techdictionary.com (http://www.techdictionary.com/index.html).

plain style is best. There is no excuse for sounding stuffy, pompous, or bureaucratic. For the informal short formats of text messages and tweets, use abbreviations if you have reason to believe the reader will understand them.

EXAMPLE

> **Stilted and overly formal:** This is to advise you that your request of the 18th inst. has been approved.
>
> **Conversational:** You will be pleased to know that you have permission to use the rare book materials that you asked about in your May 18th e-mail.

Tone

Tone is the emotion or attitude that is conveyed by your writing. The basic rule of good professional writing is to adopt a courteous tone that respects the feelings of your readers. You may want to convey other tones as well: enthusiasm for a particular book in a book review; pride in institutional accomplishments in a report; regret in a letter that turns down a request; pleasure in a message of congratulation. The following tones, however, are never appropriate: tones that are sarcastic, contemptuous, belittling, indifferent to the reader, or threatening. In online discussion forums and chat rooms, an angry, abusive message is called "flaming," a metaphor that conveys the corrosive power of this negative tone. After you have written something, ask yourself how the intended reader is likely to understand the particular passage, whether in a report, letter, memo, or text message. If in doubt, revise. Often you can improve the tone by recasting a negative message into a positive form.

EXAMPLES

> **Negative:** Unless you pay these fines within two weeks, the library will cancel borrowing privileges and turn your account over to a collection agency.
>
> **Positive:** Please pay these fines within two weeks so that we can settle your account promptly and maintain your borrowing privileges. (Admittedly you may have to adjust the tone in "final notices.")

> **Negative:** No exceptions can be made to this policy.
>
> **Positive:** This policy applies equally to everyone.

Negative: I don't want to read any more personal rantings and ravings in this discussion group.

Positive: Does anyone out there have some constructive ideas for how to solve this problem?

Readability

Some writing is harder to read and understand than is other writing. The harder the text, the fewer the readers who will be able to understand what you have written. If you want your writing to be intelligible to the general population, don't write something requiring a college reading level or specialized background knowledge. Jakob Nielsen (2005) recommends that when writing web content that can be read by everyone and not just high literacy readers, you should aim at a grade six level for the homepage and a grade eight level at deeper levels.

The following six factors affect the readability of a text:

- **Vocabulary.** Long, abstract, uncommon words are harder to understand than short, concrete, familiar ones (the number of syllables alone does not tell the whole story—watermelon is easier than chthonic). Specialized jargon and acronyms are often unintelligible to the nonspecialist. Consider the following: ALA, CIP, DDC, ILL, LC, MARC, OCLC, OPAC, SL, VR. Unless you are sure that your readers will understand the shortened form, spell it out when you mention it first: interlibrary loan (ILL).
- **Sentence structure.** Long, complex sentences with several subordinate clauses are harder to understand than short, simple ones. Inverted word order is harder to understand than the normal English word order of subject/verb/object. To make the text easier for readers, give preference to short, simple sentences written in normal order. On the other hand, using too many short, regular sentences can be deadly. Remember: "See Sally jump. See Spot run."
- **Conceptual difficulty.** Some texts may be hard to read because the concepts being discussed are unavoidably complex and difficult. You won't be able to simplify the concepts, but you can help the reader out by making your text as readable as possible in other respects: vocabulary, sentence structure, active voice (see 4.3), word order, organization, and so forth.

Exercise

Study Readability
Select a paragraph or two from something that you have written recently as part of your work.
Examine the passage in terms of the six factors listed that affect readability.
How readable is the passage?
Is its level of difficulty appropriate for the intended audience?
If not, revise the passage to make it easier to read.

A Quick Tip

Checking Readability
Readability studies have shown that writing intended to communicate with the middle-level adult reader should average about 16 to 18 words per sentence. Your word processing software can tell you how many words there are in the document, the average number in each sentence, the number of words per paragraph, as well as the percentage of passive verb constructions and your score on readability scales. For one example, see Redshaw (2003) for guidance on using MS Word readability statistics.

- **Background knowledge required.** Sometimes readers need certain background knowledge before they can make sense of a text. You can help them by putting this necessary background information first or by referring them to some other source such as an appendix where they can find out the necessary background.
- **Organization of the text.** Texts are easier to read when they are organized with the needs and expectations of the reader in mind. A method of organization that works well for many kinds of writing is to consider the order of importance to the reader. Ask yourself, "What is the one thing that the reader most wants to know?" and put this first. For reports of more than a few pages, use an executive summary. For other patterns of organization, see 4.5.
- **Motivation of the reader.** If you can motivate your readers by showing that your text can help them, they will be more willing to cope with its difficulties.

A reminder: People commonly talk about readability as if it were a property of the text alone. It's not. Readability depends on the interaction of the reader with the text. Simple texts are readable by almost every reader. The more complex the text, the fewer people will find it readable. The whole trick is to match the demands of the text to the capacities of the intended readers.

4.3. Writing with Impact

Here are some suggestions for giving your writing more punch:

- **Try reading aloud** your sentence or paragraph. If you can't read it without stumbling, there is probably something wrong with the rhythm. Usually it helps to revise it so as to make its rhythm closer to the cadences of the spoken language.
- **Use personal pronouns.** If you want to involve your audience, don't be afraid to address the reader directly or to say *you*, *we*, and *I*.

    Change: When the report was read, it was considered convincing by this reader.
    To: When I read your report, I found it convincing.

- **Be concrete and specific.** Use concrete words. You will convey a more precise image to the reader if, for example, you change *for some time* to a specific time period, such as *for three years*.

  > Change: The event did not take place due to poor conditions.
  > To: The director cancelled the literacy class because of the blizzard.

- **Prefer verbs to noun phrases.** Verbs convey more energy than nouns. Compare:

He had the expectation of	He expected
She had knowledge about	She knew about
He made arrangements for	He arranged for

  Watch for nouns formed from verb stems that end in *-ation* and *-ization*. Using too many will bloat your sentences and spoil their rhythm.

- **Use the passive voice sparingly.** Some styles of writing, such as research papers written to match the style requirements of certain journals, require the passive voice. However, in most cases, you can improve your writing and give it more energy by systematically replacing passive verbs (e.g., *X was done*) with active ones (e.g., *I did X/Mary did X*). Using the passive voice is usually undesirable because it is vague about agency, leaving the actor unidentified. Passive constructions have the added disadvantage of leading often to other writing problems: dangling constructions and misplaced modifiers (see 4.8). However, passive verbs can be used appropriately in the following instances:

  > When you want to avoid shifting gears in midsentence: "When the water started dripping through the ceiling onto the books, it was first noticed by the security guard."
  > When you want to emphasize the object of the sentence rather than the actors: "A new system was installed in June."

Exercise ⚒

Writing for Impact
Rewrite the following sentences using verbs instead of noun phrases to convey the action:

1. She brought to a conclusion her examination of the problem.
2. Vincent undertook an evaluation of the system software.
3. The trainer was in a questioning mode.
4. The director gave information to the effect that . . .

Exercise ⚒

Active Verbs
Rewrite the following sentences to make the verb active:

1. In this book, step-by-step directions are provided on how to build a sauna.
2. An initiative was taken by the committee to survey the YA community.

In the following case, does it make any difference to the meaning which variant you use? Explain.

1. The new employees were taught how to use the catalog by the librarian.
2. The librarian taught the new employees how to use the catalog.
3. The use of the catalog was taught to the new employees by the librarian.

When the actors in the sentence are unknown: "Two art books were defaced."

When you know the actors but, for reasons of tact, don't want to identify them: "The file was misplaced."

- If your sentence is not among these exceptions, use the active voice. (You may find that avoiding overuse of passive verbs takes a conscious effort on your part. So much bureaucratic writing uses passive constructions routinely that the passive voice may seem to be the norm).

> Change: After discussing options, the policy was developed by the committee. [Note the dangling construction here. See 4.8.]
> To: After discussing options, the committee developed the policy.

> Change: It was noted by the Director . . .
> To: The Director noted . . .

> Change: The method of making a piñata was demonstrated by Carol to the children.
> To: Carol showed the children how to make a piñata.

4.4. Writing Clearly and Briefly

Writing clearly and briefly is the key to keeping your readers' attention. Redshaw (2003) explains that clarity is what your *readers* think is clear. She advises against assuming that what's clear to you is also clear to your readers. Here are two relatively easy ways to make your writing tighter and more economical.

Omit Unnecessary Words

If you can leave out a word or phrase without changing the meaning, then cut. Go through your text after you have written it, looking for clutter. Replace wordy constructions. Brevity is a virtue in all writing, but it is essential when writing texts that will be read on screens rather than on printed paper. See Blicq (2005) for more examples.

Change:	To:
due to the fact that	because
in the event that	if
at this point in time	now
it is clear that	clearly
as a means of	for, to
end result	result
there are some librarians who	some librarians
twenty in number	twenty
in the majority of cases	usually
it is interesting to note that books	books
it is probable that	probably

Prefer Short, Simple, and Concrete Words

Change:	To:
discontinue	stop
utilize	use
commence	start
terminate	end
optimum	best
remuneration	pay

EXAMPLES

Wordy: Due to the fact that Peggy lacks the necessary expertise to utilize social media for communicating with users to the required extent needed, she is ineligible to obtain a promotion to a position with higher remuneration at this point in time. (41 words)

Better: Because Peggy doesn't yet know how to use social media effectively, she can't be promoted now. (16 words)

Wordy: It is important to note that in the majority of cases where the introduction of new technology is initiated in an organizational setting, there is an increase in anxiety on the part of workers with respect to the continuance of their employment. (42 words)

Exercise

Before-and-After

This exercise in plain language writing can be done individually or as a group. On the Plain Language Guidelines website (http://www.plainlanguage.gov/examples/index.cfm), look at some examples of text *before* the plain-language makeover. Pick one example, and use your editing skills to make it better. If you are doing this exercise in a group, when you finish the edit after an agreed-upon time period, share your edited text with other group members. As a group, discuss the suggested changes and decide which ones you like and why. Then compare your edited version with the *after* version provided on the website. Does the *after* version give you any ideas for additional improvements you could make?

Better: When new technology is brought into the workplace, workers often feel that their jobs are threatened. (16 words)

4.5. Organizing

There is no "one best way" to organize. Everything depends. It depends on the subject matter, on your purpose, on the reader, and on the medium used for reading—paper or a screen. Choose the style of organization that will save your readers time. Remember that what works and what doesn't may change when you are writing online (see 4.11). Here are some tips that generally work for longer documents, whether the format is print or electronic.

Be clear about your purpose. Don't leave your readers guessing what your main point is. Tell them right away unless there is some good reason not to. Subtle indirection and obliqueness, which are often virtues in literary writing, are usually faults in business writing. Here are four things you can do to clarify your purpose:

1. State your purpose clearly at the beginning, especially if the document is lengthy. Tell your readers (1) why you are writing and (2) what, if anything, you want them to do. This rule is particularly important in e-mail messages and other electronic documents. Readers often don't scroll through multiple screens to find some request for action hidden at the end. Consider these examples of textual beginnings:

   [A report] This report summarizes the results of a six-month study of staff training programs for reference librarians and ends with three suggestions for improving the staff training in our own system.
   [A memo] Please look at the attached proposal for reorganizing the children's department and let me know if you agree with the recommendations.

2. For each paragraph, write a first sentence that indicates what the paragraph is about and how the paragraph is related to your overall purpose. This topic sentence

---

A Quick Tip 🕒

Six Hidden Words
Can't think of a good opening sentence for your memo or report? Blicq and Moretto suggest using the six hidden words technique, which newspaper reporters often use.

First, write "I want to tell you that . . ." and then write what you want to tell your reader. After you have written it, delete the words "I want to tell you that . . ." You will probably be left with a good opening statement (Blicq and Moretto, 2001: 8-10).

provides a generalized statement, which the rest of the paragraph supports with specific details and examples. For example:

Topic sentence
Last year, in planning our conference, we paid too little attention to timing.

Supporting details
Three of the talks didn't start on time, and several speakers went over their allotted time.
Participants had no time to ask questions.
Presenters giving talks at the end of the day ran out of time.

3. Summarize the overarching argument at the end, repeating the key ideas. For example:

In summary, the three reasons to revise the conference planning procedures are A, B, and C.
In a nutshell, the applicant that best matches what we need in this job is Maria Lopez, who possesses in spades the key competencies of X, Y, and Z.

4. Use formatting to help your reader see the overall structure of long or complex passages. Break up a long block of text into coherent units. Use informative titles, headings, and subheadings to let the reader know what the section is about. Commonly used headings for various kinds of reports and memos include Statement of the Problem, Background Information, Scope, What Happened, Findings, Results of the Study, Recommendations, Further Considerations, Points for Further Study, Possible Problems, Implications, Action Requested, and Implementation. For less formal documents, opt for headings that are both informative and interesting.

Include only necessary details. If any of your examples, statistics, or quotations fails the "So what?" test, cut it out. Be selective and discriminating. If you overwhelm your readers with facts they don't need to know, it's harder for them to see the pattern, design, or organization of the piece.

Choose an appropriate order. The following are common methods of organization:

- **Order of importance:** With this form of organization, you start with the most important points first and proceed in decreasing order of importance. Information and arguments presented early in a piece of writing have more impact than information and arguments presented later. The details at the end are least important and can be cut by an editor who is short of space. (When in doubt, arrange the points in order of importance to the reader, not in the order of importance to the writer.)
- **Topical:** This method is useful when a topic has some obvious subdivisions (management and union; writers, publishers, and distributors; three ways to improve readers' advisory service). This is a good organization for web writing, where the linear demands of a logical sequence (cause and effect) are harder for the reader to follow.
- **Chronological:** Use this method when the time sequence is important, as when giving instructions (first do this, second do this, and so on), explaining a process, narrating an event, reporting information about trends over time, or describing historical development (beginnings, expansion, flowering, decay).
- **Spatial:** Use this method to indicate spatial relationships, as when presenting information on geographical regions or when describing the physical layout of a building (the east wing of the library; the local history room on the second floor; the reading garden). Pick one spatial sequence and stick to it: left to right, top to bottom, north to south, the first room reached on the tour to the last room.
- **Comparison:** When you want to compare two or more items, you may find it best to select relevant attributes and discuss each of the items with respect to these attributes. For example, if you were evaluating which jobber to use, you might organize your findings like this:

Turnaround time:	Jobber A; Jobber B
Cost:	Jobber A; Jobber B
Coverage:	Jobber A; Jobber B

- **Pro and con:** When you are evaluating something, you can cluster into two sets all the arguments for a proposal and all the arguments against a proposal.
- **Logical sequence:** Two kinds of logical arrangements are problem/solution and cause/effect (or effect/cause).

4.6. Using Inclusive and Nondiscriminatory Language

Avoid language that excludes people. This means that you should inform your language use with an understanding of cultural differences that arise from racial, ethnic, or national background or from gender, sexual orientation, belief system, or age.

One obvious area that requires sensitivity is nomenclature. Because language is dynamic, there is no universally accepted practice for referring to particular racial or ethnic groups. For the 2000 census, for example, the U.S. government used the following terms: White, Black or African American, American Indian or Alaska Native, Asian, Native Hawaiian or other Pacific Islanders, Hispanic or Latino. Categories were expanded for the 2010 census, which included alternate and broadened terms, such as Black, African American, or Negro; Hispanic, Latino, or Spanish origin; Asian Indian, Chinese, Korean, and so forth. People were encouraged to self-identify, because individuals often prefer to categorize themselves more narrowly than the broad categories of the 2000 census.

A good rule of thumb is to use the terms preferred by the particular group members themselves. But be aware that these terms change over time and may be different for in-group members and nongroup members. Also be aware of subtle political differences as well as cultural traditions. You may encounter difficulty when you use one term to refer to several groups who may share a language but not other cultural attributes (e.g., Arabic or Spanish speaking).

A problem for English speakers can arise in forms of address. For example, in Chinese and Korean families, the family name comes first and the generational and given names next. The latter two are sometimes hyphenated in English. In some cases, people may feel offended if they are addressed by their first names. To show respect, use formal titles until you are invited to do otherwise (Adler and Elmhorst, 2010: 436).

Titles pose problems of their own unless you know the gender of the person to whom you are writing. To solve the problem of salutations in letters, try "Dear Board Members," "To the Selection Committee," or "Greetings," or omit the salutation altogether and begin with a subject line, such as "Reference for Linda Lomez."

Just as it is no longer appropriate to assume that all letter recipients are honorary males ("Dear Sirs"), so it is now inappropriate to use the generic pronoun "he" to refer to people in general. Pluralizing "to each his own" into "to each their own" solves the problem of inclusiveness but introduces a grammatical error (see discussion of faulty pronoun references in 4.8). But "to each his or her own" sounds awkward. So what to do? In this book, we have chosen to refer to individuals sometimes as "he" and sometimes as "she." Rosalie Maggio (1991: 16–19) provides 13 strategies for avoiding what she calls the "pseudogeneric 'he.'" Here are three:

- **Pluralize.** Instead of writing "The circulation clerk must be attentive. He or she should look up from his or her work," write "Circulation clerks must be attentive. They should look up from their work."
- **Use the first or second person.** Instead of writing "The librarian must use his or her knowledge of communication skills," write "As librarians, we must use our knowledge of" or "As a librarian, you must use your knowledge of."
- **Use a definite or indefinite article.** Instead of writing "A library director usually gives her or his report to the board," write "A library director usually gives the report to the board."

4.7. Checking Spelling

Even in the informal world of tweets and texting, it's a good idea to pay attention to correct punctuation, correct grammar, and correct spelling. No one is offended by correctness, but a lot of people are put off by errors and judge the offending writer as lacking in credibility.

The spell checker on your word processing software can do a lot to eliminate typographical errors, but it can't do everything. It works by matching the words in your text against the words in its own dictionary. Therefore, it catches misspelled words and typographical errors like *alot* or *errors*. But be aware of what it won't do. It won't catch mistakes like *it's* used as a possessive or *stationery* used to mean motionless. It won't recognize that you have written *batch* instead of *match*, *or* instead of *of*, or *wards* instead of *words*. A spelling checker matches patterns of letters. It doesn't analyze meanings of words to determine whether a word is correct in its context.

Spelling checkers catch only about three-quarters of your errors. Some common mix-ups that the spell checker won't correct are these:

its/it's	to/too/two
their/there/they're	who's/whose
your/you're	accept/except
a while/awhile	then/than

Additionally a spell checker won't correct grammatical misusage of I/me/myself (e.g., the faulty case of "for Jane and I") or less/fewer. See Judy Rose (2006) for a discussion of some of these problem words.

4.8. Avoiding Common Grammatical Errors

Hundreds of excellent books are available on grammar and correct usage. Use them by all means. However, because 20 percent of writing errors account for about 80 percent of actual writing problems, you should pay most attention to the 20 percent. Eliminate from your writing the following most common errors.

Dangling Constructions

A participial phrase, infinitive, or modifier at the beginning of a sentence must refer to the grammatical subject. A rule of thumb is to look at the noun directly after the comma. Is this noun in fact the person or the thing that the modifier is really supposed to refer to? If not, revise. Consider this sentence:

Exercise

Dangling Constructions

How would you correct the following dangling constructions?

1. Being in a damaged condition, I was able to buy the book very cheap. (What was in a damaged condition—the buyer or the book?)
2. To find something quickly, the book must be indexed.
3. Lifting the heavy stack of encyclopedias, her face turned quite red from exertion.
4. As the Project Director, several of Bill's initiatives for getting funding were successful.
5. Being open on Sunday, the circulation staff was very busy.
6. Driving through Banff National Park, bears were seen eating blueberries.

Worried about the job layoffs, even the houses on the street seemed threatening to Sally. (Who was worried—the houses?)

It should be revised as follows:

Worried about the job layoffs, Sally found even the houses on the street threatening.

Ambiguous or Faulty Pronoun References

Make sure that your pronouns agree with their antecedents and that each pronoun has a clear antecedent. Consider:

Anna had hoped to go with May to the conference, but she couldn't afford the registration fee. (Who couldn't afford the fee—Anna or May?)

The advisory group recommended a national survey of libraries to assess bibliographic control of official publications, but the committee thought it unfeasible. (What does the *it* refer to—the use of a national survey or the entire recommendation?)

A writer must first analyze their audience. (This construction is becoming increasingly common because it avoids the inclusive but awkward *his* or *her*—see 4.6). However, the sentence is still wrong because the plural pronoun *their* does not agree with the singular antecedent *writer*. Try instead: "Writers must first analyze their audiences." Or "As a writer, you should first analyze your audience."

Comma Errors

Do not use a comma to separate two independent clauses.

Change: Chris was on time, however, many others were late.
To: Chris was on time. However, many others were late.
Or: Although Chris was on time, many others were late.

Enclose a parenthetic expression between commas. Use either two commas or none at all.

Change: Many people however, like stories of zombies, vampires, and werewolves.

To: Many people, however, like stories of zombies, vampires, and werewolves.

Faulty Parallelism

Present parallel ideas in a parallel form.

Change: She has the necessary writing skills, background knowledge, and can organize effectively.

To: She has the necessary writing skills, background knowledge, and ability to organize.

Or: She writes well, knows the background, and can organize effectively.

When you use the construction *not only X but also Y*, remember that X and Y should be grammatically equivalent. If X is an infinitive, then Y must be an infinitive; if X is a verb plus adverb, then Y should be a verb plus adverb.

Change: Mario not only liked to fish but also paddling his canoe.

To: Mario not only liked fishing but also enjoyed paddling his canoe.

Or: Mario liked not only fishing but also paddling his canoe.

Problems with Possessives

Add an apostrophe and *s* to form the possessive of all nouns, both plural and singular, unless the plural already ends in an *s*. If the plural already ends in an *s*, add an apostrophe only. Hence: a year's work; three years' experience; this library's staff; all the libraries' staff; woman's work; women's work. There is some flexibility with proper names. It's *Morris's Disappearing Bag*, but both Dickens's book and Dickens' book are used. Whichever you choose, be consistent.

With regard to pronouns, only indefinite pronouns use an apostrophe to form the possessive. Hence: anybody's guess; someone's mistake. But note that there is no apostrophe used to form the possessive of definite pronouns: hers, theirs, its. Remember that *it's* is not a proper form of the possessive but rather a contraction for *it is*.

Did You Know? ?

Some word processors include writing tools that help you check your grammar and style. Such programs check sentence length for overly long sentences and may highlight problems such as passive constructions, clichés, faulty subject-verb agreement, and faulty capitalization and punctuation. Like spelling checkers, style checkers work by matching patterns and do not take meanings into account. They are useful because they highlight for your attention suspected stylistic faults that you may have overlooked. But they don't relieve you of the final responsibility of exercising your own judgment.

Using Words Incorrectly

We could write a whole chapter solely on the subject of incorrect usage. Fortunately, other people have done this for us (see the Annotated Bibliography in 4.14 and especially Ron Blicq's 2005 text, *Communicating at Work*, which includes a handy glossary of words and phrases that often cause trouble). Here are a few examples of misused words and phrases that appear in library reports, letters, memos, and even books:

- *affect* (the verb) versus *effect* (the noun)
- *principal* (which can be an adjective, meaning "main," or can be a noun, meaning either "director" or a sum of money on which interest is paid) versus *principle*, which is always a noun and means a basic source or rule
- *fewer*, which refers to discrete units (things that can be counted), versus *less*, which is used to describe general amounts (hence fewer people, less water)

Language changes with use: when a sufficiently large number of people "misuse" a word, that misuse becomes an acceptable variant. On April 17, 2012, the American Press (AP) announced via Twitter that the *AP Stylebook* had given up the fight over *hopefully*: "We now support the modern usage of hopefully: 'It's hoped, we hope.'" Previously, the only accepted meaning for "hopefully" was "in a hopeful manner," as in "'The lost book may be found,' the librarian said hopefully."

These troublesome words are used correctly in the following example:

> The budget cut affects the number of books we can purchase. Our principal said to us hopefully, "We'll have to try to do more with less," but of course the immediate effect of the budget cut was that we had to make do with fewer books. Hopefully library service will not be adversely affected if we buy extra books using the interest from the Mudge Foundation money (without, of course, touching the principal).

4.9. Using Tables, Charts, and Graphs

A writing task often involves summarizing quantitative data. You may present quantitative data in words, in tables, or in graphs or charts, and each method has its own advantages. A presentation in words can explain, interpret, and evaluate. But a sentence is a poor way to show the relationships among a lot of numbers. Consider this sentence: "In a survey of library use of Web 2.0 and Social Media Tools, 85 percent of libraries reported using Facebook, 49 percent reported using Twitter, and 42 percent reported using blogging tools." The comparison is clearer when the data are presented in a table. Use tables to draw the reader's attention to specific data, not to trends of data. De Castro (2009) points out that tables capture information concisely and display it efficiently, at any desired level of detail.

Charts and graphs provide additional ways to present a mass of numeric data in a visual form that readers can take in at a glance. Use graphs to show relationships or to promote understanding of the meaning of results (De Castro, 2009: 46). Appropriately used, charts and graphs:

- show the data in a way that clarifies relationships,
- present many numbers in a small space,
- make the data easier to understand,
- provide visual impact, and
- save the reader's time.

The most commonly used charts are pie charts, bar charts, and line graphs. Most computer software can automatically construct these for you. However, you still need to make your own judgment about when to use each type and how to present it.

Pie charts show how the whole of something is divided into its parts. The circle or pie always represents 100 percent. Pie segments are drawn in proportion to the size of the parts making up the whole. Proportions are therefore very easy to see at a glance, which is why pie charts are so popular for showing how a sum of money is spent.

Pie charts work best with six or fewer segments. With more segments, they become confusing, hard to interpret, and lose their effectiveness. However, if the data you are reporting have more than six categories, you can reduce the number of segments in your pie chart by collapsing some of the categories. For example, suppose that you wanted to show the percentage of public libraries in each province in Canada. Instead of using ten segments, you could collapse the ten Canadian provinces into five regions: Atlantic provinces, Quebec, Ontario, Prairie provinces, and British Columbia.

The problem with pie charts is that it can be hard for the reader to compare small variations in the size of the segments. This is why pie

Top Social Media Tools
Used by Libraries

Facebook	85% reporting use
Twitter	49% reporting use
Blogging tools	42% reporting use

TABLE

2013 Library Budget

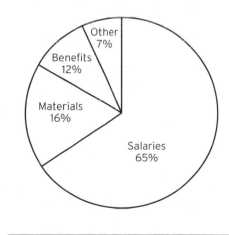

PIE CHART

What percentage of readers read
these genres of fiction regularly?

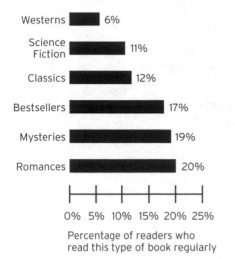

Percentage of readers who
read this type of book regularly

BAR CHART

2010 Book Circulation
in Lincoln Branch

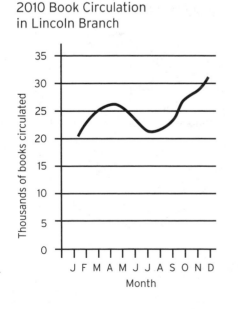

LINE CHART

charts are not highly esteemed by statisticians. However, pie charts can be a very effective way of illustrating the relative size of the parts to the whole, for example, the library's annual budget according to type of expense.

Because not all graphics software packages make readable charts, make sure that you follow basic principles of good pie chart design. All lettering should be horizontal so that the reader won't have to turn the page sideways to read the label. You need a title over the chart that explains the factor being analyzed (expenditures, age, ethnic origin), the time period referred to, and the unit of measurement (number, percent). And you need a label for each segment: children x percent, young adults y percent, adults z percent.

Two or more pie charts can be used to illustrate comparisons—one pie chart to represent the sources of income and another pie chart to represent expenditures. (But make sure that you make the circles the same size.)

Bar charts use the length of bars to represent values such as frequency, amount, weight, cost, and participation rate. Because each bar is separate from its neighbor, the bar chart is suited to representing information about separate units, as in the example showing the percentage of readers who read different genres of fiction. Bar charts can be used to show percentages or to show absolute numbers.

The length of the bar is determined by the value or amount of each variable, measured on a scale that should begin at zero. The bars should be arranged systematically in a form appropriate to the chart's purpose. An arrangement by size from largest to smallest is common, but other possibilities include an arrangement by time, by alphabetical order, or by geographical location.

Bar and column charts differ only in the placement of the oblong boxes: when the oblong box is placed horizontally, it is called a "bar chart"; when it is placed vertically, it is called a "column chart." Deciding which way the bars should run is a matter of convenience and common sense. The labels on horizontal bars are easier to read, but vertical columns seem to some people a more appropriate representation of growth factors such as weight or height or units produced.

Line graphs or line charts are made by plotting a series of values along two scales (the line is the result of connecting the dots that represent the plotted values). Line graphs show how changes in one factor are related to changes in another. Familiar examples include circulation statistics over several years or graphs showing fluctuation in annual revenue.

Whereas bar charts present information in a limited number of discrete steps, line graphs present continuous information spread over many data points.

The most commonly used line graph is the time series, which plots the occurrence of something over time, measured in seconds, hours, months, years, decades, centuries, and so forth. The time series is a succinct way of showing trends, patterns, or changes over time, such as the number of times that library users accessed the public terminals for the Internet each month or the number of Master of Library and Information Science degrees granted each year. Line graphs can also be used to link two variables that are not in a time series, such as the relationship between the number of school years completed and the amount of income earned.

The essential elements in a line graph are the horizontal or X-axis, the vertical or Y-axis, the plotted line, the scale or grid lines, and the plotted points. In a time chart, you should use the horizontal axis to represent time, expressed in units such as days, months, years, and so forth. Use the vertical axis to represent the amount of the variable being measured, such as price or circulation figures. When your line graph is not a time series, use the horizontal axis to represent the variable that changes regularly in a series of equal divisions, such as the number of school years completed. Use the vertical axis to represent the variable that changes irregularly, such as amount of income earned.

Sometimes line graphs can convey a distorted impression of the data. When you are using a software package to display data, ensure that the distances representing units of measurement are appropriate. If the vertical axis is compressed owing to a large number of data points, the graph tends to flatten out the line and minimize differences. If the vertical axis is lengthened by spacing out the grid markings, differences may be exaggerated. To avoid these distortions in scale, follow the three-quarter rule. Make the height of the vertical axis about three quarters the length of the horizontal axis. Distortion can also occur if quantitative scales are not made to start at zero. If a large part of the scale is left out, small changes appear exaggerated and are hard for the reader to keep in proportion.

Some Quick Tips for Using Charts and Graphs

Before you decide on the form of visual display to use, ask yourself, "What am I trying to show?" Choose the form that will best convey your intended point.

- Make the data stand out clearly.
- Eliminate clutter. Too much detail can be confusing. Limit the number of curves on a line graph to three if the lines cross, four if they don't.
- Avoid what Tufte (2001: 107) calls "chartjunk"—all that ink that doesn't convey information, such as "overbusy grid lines and excess ticks, redundant representations of the simplest data, the debris of computer plotting, and many of the devices generating design variation."
- On line graphs, don't use grid marks that interfere with the presentation of the data. Small tick marks are usually preferable.
- Be careful with colors. What looks clear and distinct on screen may not be so evident on paper.
- Label all the parts of the graphic clearly. Whenever possible, put labels on the graphic itself to eliminate for the reader the extra step of consulting a legend. Give your chart a descriptive label so that the reader can easily tell what the graphic is supposed to demonstrate.
- Design the graphic with the reader's convenience in mind. Don't use cryptic abbreviations or coding involving cross-hatching that make reading the graph into an exercise in code breaking. Avoid using all uppercase for labels. Keep the lettering horizontal. Vertical lettering is hard to read, and words running in several different directions look cluttered.
- Proofread. Double-check the accuracy of the numeric data.
- Finally, remember that computer-generated graphics may not meet high standards for presenting data visually. You may have to modify your output.

4.10. Formatting the Page

Writing, in both print and digital form, conveys nonverbal messages too. Consider the message that is conveyed by the following when found in a letter from a job applicant: spelling mistakes, a letter crowded onto the top half of the page, poor quality paper, and a *cursive* or *fantasy* font.

Appearance counts. At worst, a cramped, cluttered page design may discourage readers from reading the text at all (this is especially true of publicity materials, where the reader has no obligation to look at what you have written). At best, a good design can enhance, reinforce, or clarify the text's significance. Design elements should be not simply decorative. They should be functional, helping to make the text intelligible or to draw attention to something of importance.

With respect to texts that you will write in a professional context, most readers have a purpose in mind—they are trying to get something done. Format the page in the way that will most help readers achieve their purpose by saving their time. (See p. 87 for more formatting tips.)

4.11. Writing Digitally

These days most texts, except maybe shopping lists and Post-It notes, are composed digitally. We write documents using word processing software, and then we either print the documents or distribute them in electronic form. We send these files or PDF documents as e-mail attachments, and we mount them on websites, blogs, or various social media sites. We also compose directly in e-mail, chat, and instant messaging as well as in social media sites. Computer-mediated communication has catalyzed a huge growth in the kinds and amount of writing that people do.

Despite worried talk (Birkerts, 2006) about how digital writing—all that e-mailing, blogging, tweeting, and texting—is ruining genuine reading and writing, it would be more useful to acknowledge that different kinds of literacies are developing along with new technologies for disseminating text. And it is still the case that the basic rules for good writing apply to all kinds of writing, digital or not. There are, however, some extra things to consider when writing in the digital text universe.

There are two kinds of digital documents, each with its own features and special considerations. Some documents, such as letters, reports, booklists, proposals, meeting agendas, and sometimes memos are written, and often distributed, online, but they are intended eventually to be printed for reading. These documents are amphibious with two kinds of life: an online life and a printed life. But the printed life takes precedence. Other texts, such as hyperlinked webpages, blogs, Facebook postings, e-mail messages, short message service (SMS) messages, tweets, and the like may sometimes be printed but live predominantly a digital life.

The first category of documents follows rules of writing that haven't changed much since the days of the typewriter. Your written text is expected to be interesting, concise, logically structured, clearly written, organized in a linear way, and free from typographical errors and mistakes in punctuation and spelling. Putting your document into PDF format makes it more like a print document—a static text that can be distributed electronically but cannot be changed by the reader.

The second category of texts is a whole new ball of wax. You still have to make the text interesting, logically organized, clear, and free from errors. But other factors take on far more importance than they ever did in the composed-for-print world, namely, brevity, speediness in getting to the point, informality of tone, and user interactivity. In addition, in forms such as webpages and blogs, not just the words but also graphical elements, color, and pictures are important. The key is to make the page easy to scan visually. And remember that readers may be reading your text on the small screens of mobile devices—tablets and phones—as well as on desktop screens. (See 9.3 for suggestions on writing messages.)

In web documents, organization is even more important than it is for printed documents. Because readers move through the information using hypertext links, it is essential to define carefully each hierarchical level and the links within and outside of the text (De Castro, 2009: 39). A poor structure is a stumbling block that may keep a reader from ever seeing important sections. (See 9.13.4 for suggestions on organization of webpages.)

An overarching rule when writing texts that will be read on screens is to be aware of how readers actually read online (Liu, 2005). They don't read every word. They scan text looking for information that serves their immediate purpose. Jakob Nielsen (2006) has used eye-tracking software to find out how readers' eyes move around a webpage. He reports that readers' eyes move very, very fast, typically

Some Quick Tips to Make Your Format More Reader Friendly

- Keep the design simple and uncluttered.
- Learn from others. Get help from professional designers. Take a look at what other libraries are doing.
- Break up long paragraphs and long chunks of text into smaller units. People find shorter passages of text more inviting and less intimidating to read.
- Make your text easy to scan visually—especially web documents—by using headings and subheads.
- Use vertical lists to speed up the reader's grasp of information. Numbered lists are best when order is important, such as in step-by-step directions, and bulleted points should be used when order is not so important.
- Give emphasis to a heading, phrase, or word by using **boldface**, *italic*, or color, but use restraint. If you emphasize a few keywords, you help the reader scan. But if you highlight whole sentences or sections, your page looks cluttered and confusing. In highlighting, as in everything, there is a point of diminishing returns.
- Use white space deliberately. Think of the blank page as space to be organized into an intelligible design of black and white (or on webpages black, color, and white). Remember that the white space is not the accidental area left over but an active part of the design of the page. Use white space to frame the text and highlight important divisions. For letters and reports, leave generous margins of at least 1.25 inches (3 cm). Break up long blocks of text by leaving space between the sections. For newsletters, fliers, and publicity materials, use empty spaces boldly as a deliberate contrast to the full spaces.
- Consider legibility in selecting typefaces, or fonts, and font sizes. For most printed materials, it is best to pick one family of type and stick to it throughout. Mixing fonts can produce a cluttered, amateurish appearance.
- Pay attention to other factors that affect the legibility of type in printed documents. These include the number of characters per line, the amount of space between the letters and between the words (called "letter spacing" and "word spacing"), and the amount of space between the lines (called "leading" and pronounced to rhyme with "sledding"). More space results in more legibility, up to a point.
- Be consistent. Decide on the width of margins and the size, style, and placement of headlines, and then stick to the same design throughout.
- Use tables, charts, and graphs to summarize numeric information (see 4.9).
- Use graphics but only when they are useful and informative. If you yourself aren't skilled at artwork, you can often find appropriate public domain images that can be used. But practice restraint: lackluster, generic images unrelated to the text too often clutter up PowerPoint slides and turn webpages into an obstacle course.

Did You Know? ?

The font size used for most of this book is 12 point, but readers who are either under 10 or over 65 often prefer something larger (and no one likes to read anything as small as this 6 point type).

Did You Know? ?

A basic design choice is between serif and sans-serif fonts. Serifs are the small counterstrokes at the ends of the main strokes. Serifs increase readability when texts are printed on paper but look blurry when read on screens, especially on the small screens of smart phones and tablets. For high-resolution print documents, the standard advice is to use sans serif for headings and serif for body text. When it comes to long blocks of text printed on paper, readability studies have shown that serif fonts such as Times New Roman, Garamond, and Georgia are easier to read and easier on the eyes than sans-serif fonts such as Arial, Helvetica, Geneva, and Verdana. However, everything changes for texts written for online reading. Sans-serif type is preferred on websites for the text body, while serif is often used for headings, which are usually in a larger font size. (But use serif fonts for print-friendly versions of your website).

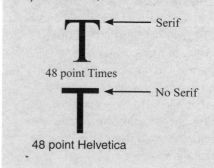

← Serif

48 point Times

← No Serif

48 point Helvetica

following an F-pattern down the page. First they read in a horizontal movement across the top of the content, then they skip down the page a bit and read horizontally for a shorter area (the longer and the shorter cross bars of the F), and finally they scan the content's left margin in a downward vertical movement (the stem of the F). On the basis of this empirical research, Nielsen makes three key recommendations:

- Don't expect readers to read your web content thoroughly, word by word.
- Put the most important information in the first two paragraphs.
- Start your "subheads, paragraphs, and bullet points with information-carrying words." Why? Because readers scanning vertically read the first two words more than the third or subsequent words.

4.12. Editing Your Work

Whether your document is to be printed on paper or read on a screen, edit it carefully before sending it out. This caveat applies to *any* message written in a professional context, whether it is a quick e-mail to a colleague or a report intended for wide distribution and archiving. Because you probably will compose it using word processing software, your first reading of it will be on-screen. Unless it's a *very* short message, you may want to print it out and read it on paper. Likely you have distributed something only to find that it contains an embarrassing error that makes you groan, "How did I miss that?" It's easy to miss mistakes, even when you are looking for them, because you see what you expect to see. That's why it helps to change things up. Changing the medium—whether by reading a text aloud for the ear or by printing out an electronic document—often makes it easier to identify a problem that needs fixing. If the document is very important, ask a colleague to read it and provide feedback.

Some Editing Tips

Check the technical content:
Is it coherent and consistent in all parts?

Are all cited items included, and are they accurate?

Are tables and figures clear, correct, and readable?

Do the copyediting:

Check the language, grammar, format, and style.

Look for typos and spelling errors.

Look for garbled passages, dropped lines and words, and the like.

Read the text over and over again from beginning to end:

Read it silently and then aloud.

Ask a colleague or friend to read it and give you feedback.

4.13. Postscript: Keeping Your Reader in Mind

Consider the three elements that enter into any piece of writing:

WRITER   TEXT   READER

Throughout this chapter, we have emphasized the importance of the reader, the invisible partner in the enterprise. Try to make your writing reader centered rather than writer centered. Writer-centered texts are organized in ways that are convenient for the writer and contain information that the writer wants to convey. Reader-centered texts are organized in ways that help the reader make sense of the text and that contain information that answers questions in the reader's mind.

Some Quick Tips for Writing Reader-Centered Texts

- Write the first draft in whatever order is easiest for you. But organize (or reorganize) the final draft so that it serves the needs of your intended readers.
- Write from the reader's point of view. Your reader approaches the text with tacit questions in mind: How does this text help me? How does it answer my questions? Why should I care about this? So what? What does the writer want me to do? Why is it in my interest to do what the writer wants me to do? What are the implications of this information for me? Your writing should answer these questions.
- Write texts intended for the general public in plain language that ordinary people can understand. Your language should

not be a barrier between the public and what the public wants to know.

4.14. Annotated Bibliography

General Texts on Writing

Adler, Ronald B., and Jeanne Marquardt Elmhorst. 2010. *Communicating at Work: Principles and Practices for Business and the Professions.* 10th ed. New York: McGraw-Hill. This frequently revised text covers business writing in Appendix II. See also discussion on culture and communication in Chapter 2.

Blicq, Ron S. 2005. *Communicating at Work: Creating Messages That Get Results.* 4th ed. Toronto: Prentice Hall Canada. This comprehensive guide to written (and oral) business communication includes excellent guidelines for writing many sorts of print and electronic documents. It emphasizes the writing process and ultimate objective of communication rather than grammar or mechanics. The text includes an extensive section of exercises for each chapter.

Blicq, Ron S., and Lisa A. Moretto. 2001. *Writing Reports to Get Results: Quick, Effective Results Using the Pyramid Method.* 3rd ed. New York: John Wiley for IEEE. One of the best little books we've seen on report writing, this text includes basic guidelines for writing clearly and concisely at a computer terminal.

Canavor, Natalie. 2012. *Business Writing in the Digital Age.* Thousand Oaks, CA: Sage. Written for business students, this text provides instruction on writing clearly and concisely. Chapters cover writing skills and editing for all types of traditional and digital media.

De Castro, Paola. 2009. *Librarians of Babel: A Toolkit for Effective Communication.* London: Chandos. This work focuses on writing in various contexts.

Plotnik, Arthur. 2006. *The Elements of Expression: Putting Thoughts into Words.* New York: Barnes and Noble. This witty and humorous book is for people who care about language and want to write and speak effectively and expressively.

Williams, Joseph M. 2007. *Style: Ten Lessons in Clarity and Grace.* 9th ed. New York: Pearson Longman. This best seller is said to teach skills better than any other style book.

Two peer-reviewed quarterly journals that regularly publish articles on aspects of business writing:

> *IEEE Transactions on Professional Communication* (for more
> information, see http://ewh.ieee.org/soc/pcs/?q=node/24)
> *The Journal of Business Communication* (current and back
> issues available at http://job.sagepub.com/)

Style and Organization

Corbett, Edward P. 1998. *Classical Rhetoric for the Modern Student*. 4th ed. New York: Oxford University Press. Valuable for its discussion of the figures, tropes, arrangements of words, and other stylistic resources available to the writer, this book covers aspects of writing style that are not covered in *Communicating Professionally* and that are usually short-changed in books on business and technical writing. It is available as a free download at http://www.filestube.com/c/classical+rhetoric.

Hacker, Diana, and Nancy Sommers. 2009. *The Bedford Handbook*. 8th ed. Boston: Bedford/St. Martin's. This compact handbook provides basic information on the writing process, sentence construction, word choice, and grammar as well as examples, tips, and exercises. Designed for students, but useful to all writers, this work can be used in conjunction with the website http://bcs.bedfordstmartins.com/bedhandbook8e/#t_518572.

Lamb, Sandra E. 2011. *How to Write It: A Complete Guide to Everything You'll Ever Write*. 3rd ed. New York: Ten Speed Press/Random House. This popular work explains how to write both personal and professional materials confidently and clearly. It covers all kinds of employment-related communications and includes many examples.

Maggio, Rosalie. 2009. *How to Say It: Choice Words, Phrases, Sentences, and Paragraphs for Every Situation*. 3rd ed. New York: Penguin. This text is valuable for advice on writing both work-related and personal letters.

PlainLanguage.gov. 2011. "Federal Plain Language Guidelines." PlainLanguage.gov: Improving Communication from the Federal Government to the Public. http://www.plainlanguage.gov/index.cfm. The guidelines provide a range of advice, examples, tips, and resources.

Rose, Judy. 2006. "Ten Common Mistakes Your Spell Checker Won't Find." http://writingenglish.wordpress.com/2006/09/18/ten

-common-writing-mistakes-your-spell-checker-won%E2%80%99t
-find/. This work includes a continuing discussion on her blog.

Stevens, Kevin T., Kathleen C. Stevens, and William P. Stevens. 1992.
"Measuring the Readability of Business Writing: The Cloze Procedure
versus Readability Formulas." *The Journal of Business Communication*
29, no. 4: 367–381. This article discusses the flaws of readability
formulas and recommends the cloze procedure for testing readability
for a specific audience.

Strunk, William Jr., and E. B. White. 1999. *The Elements of Style*. 4th ed.
Boston: Allyn and Bacon. Concise and elegant—a classic—this fourth
edition was republished in 2009 as the fiftieth anniversary edition
(New York: Pearson Longman).

Zinsser, William. 2006. *On Writing Well: The Classic Guide to Writing
Nonfiction*. 7th ed. New York: Harper Collins. Full of practical
wisdom, this book is highly recommended.

Layout and Graphics

Blicq, Ron S., and Lisa A. Moretto. 2000. *Guidelines for Report Writing*.
4th ed. Englewood Cliffs, NJ: Prentice Hall. Chapter 12 provides
concise guidelines for creating illustrations, charts, and graphs, with
excellent examples.

Gray, Bill, and Scott Wills. 1998. *Tips on Type*. Rev. ed. New York: Norton.
This book covers type classification and the principles of layout and
legibility.

Parker, Roger C. 2006. *Looking Good in Print: A Guide to Basic Design
for Desktop Publishing*. 6th ed. Sebastopol, CA: Paraglyph Press/
O'Reilly Media. This text provides lots of examples and a list of
common design pitfalls. It includes a section on creating documents,
newsletters, and forms for use on the web.

Rentz, Kathryn, Marie Flatley, and Paula Lentz. 2010. *Lesikar's Business
Communication: Connecting in a Digital World*. 12th ed. New York:
McGraw-Hill. Chapter 12 provides color examples of bar charts, pie
charts, statistical maps, and pictograms.

Tufte, Edward R. 2001. *The Visual Display of Quantitative Information*. 2nd
ed. Cheshire, CT: Graphics Press. Tufte elegantly sets forth the theory
and practice of designing statistical graphics, charts, maps, and tables.
See also his other books on the visual display of information published
by Graphics Press, including *Envisioning Information* (1990), *Visual
Explanations: Images and Quantities, Evidence, and Narrative* (1997),
and *Beautiful Evidence* (2nd ed., 2006).

Tukey, John W. 1977. *Exploratory Data Analysis*. Reading, MA: Addison-Wesley. Tufte (2001: 53) notes that it was John Tukey who first used graphics as instruments for reasoning about quantitative information, making statistical graphics respectable.

Inclusive Language

Maggio, Rosalie. 1991. *Dictionary of Bias Free Usage: A Guide to Nondiscriminatory Language*. Phoenix, AZ: Oryx Press. This work provides an excellent rationale for eliminating biased language and suggests 15,000 substitutions for 5,000 discriminatory words and phrases.

Miller, Casey, and Kate Swift. 1988. *The Handbook of Nonsexist Writing for Writers, Editors, and Speakers*. 2nd ed. New York: Harper and Row. This book includes a whole chapter on the pronoun problem.

Schwartz, Marilyn, and the Task Force on Bias-Free Language, Association of American University Presses. 1996. *Guidelines for Bias-Free Writing*. Bloomington: Indiana University Press. This well-respected handbook includes chapters on gender, race, nationality and religion, disabilities and medical conditions, sexual orientation, and age.

Writing Digitally

Angell, David, and Brent Heslop. 1994. *The Elements of E-mail Style: Communicate Effectively via Electronic Mail*. Reading, MA: Addison-Wesley. This is an excellent manual in the tradition of Strunk and White. In addition to the principles of good writing, the authors deal specifically with writing e-mail messages.

Birkerts, Sven. 2006. *The Gutenberg Elegies: The Fate of Reading in an Electronic Age*. Boston: Faber and Faber. This work is an elegy for a lost era of intensive, deep reading, long engagement, and entrance into the private imagined worlds of fiction.

Canavor, Natalie. 2012. *Business Writing in the Digital Age*. Thousand Oaks, CA: Sage. Written for business students, this text provides instruction on writing clearly and concisely. Chapters cover writing skills and editing for all types of traditional and digital media.

Canavor, Natalie, and Claire Meirowitz. 2010. *The Truth about the New Rules of Business Writing*. Upper Saddle River, NJ: FT Press. This highly recommended compact book provides 52 well-organized and readable sections on all kinds of analog and digital business writing.

Eden, Sigal, and Yorham Eshet-Alkalai. 2012. "Print versus Digital: The Effect of Format on Performance in Editing Text." Paper presented at *Chais Conference on Instructional Technologies Research 2012: Learning in the Technological Era*, edited by Y. Eshet-Alkalai et al., 13–21. Raanana: The Open University of Israel. http://www.openu.ac .il/innovation/chais2012/downloads/c-Eden-Eshet-Alkalai-63_eng .pdf. This study found no significant difference between editing text in print and editing in digital format. Also useful is the literature review of previous studies of print versus digital reading that did find significant differences.

Liu, Ziming. 2005. "Reading Behavior in the Digital Environment: Changes in Reading Behavior over the Past Ten Years." *Journal of Documentation* 61, no. 6: 700–712. The author argues for the emergence of a new screen-based reading behavior "characterized by more time spent on browsing and scanning, keyword spotting, one-time reading, non-linear reading, and reading more selectively," with less time spent on "in-depth reading, and concentrated reading."

Nielsen, Jakob. 2000. *Designing Web Usability*. Berkeley, CA: New Riders Press. This influential and still-relevant book provides good advice on creating readable content and clean, uncluttered page design.

———. 2005. "Lower-Literacy Users: Writing for a Broad Consumer Audience." *Alertbox* (blog). March 14. http://www.useit.com/ alertbox/20050314.html. This article reports that, unlike accomplished readers, low literacy readers read slowly and laboriously, word by word, and are not able to scan for information. When reading gets tough, they skip completely over whole chunks.

———. 2006. "F-Shaped Pattern for Reading Web Content." *Alertbox* (blog). April 17. http://www.useit.com/alertbox/reading_pattern. html. Eye-tracking studies show that readers' eyes follow an F-shaped pattern when reading webpages, tracking two horizontal bars across the top of the page and then a vertical scan down the page.

Nielsen, Jakob, and Kara Pernice. 2010. *Eyetracking Web Usability*. Berkeley, CA: New Riders Press. Based on a huge eye-tracking usability study of human eyes looking at websites, this book shows why some designs work and others don't. Provides tips for page layout, site elements, navigation menus, and the use of images.

Redshaw, Kerry. 2003. "Web Writing: Writing for a New Medium." *KerryR.net*. http://www.kerryr.net/webwriting/index.htm. This excellent site includes suggestions on writing, FAQs, gender-neutral language, repurposing print documents for the web, and grammar, punctuation, and word usage.

Ross, Catherine Sheldrick. 2002. "Reading in a Digital Age." In *The Digital Factor in Library and Information Services*, edited by G. E. Gorman, 91–111. International Yearbook of Library and Information Management 2002/2003. London: Facet Publishing. This work considers similarities and differences in the ways in which readers engage with print text and digital text.

Integration

Putting It All Together

5.1. How to Use This Chapter

The strategy of this book so far has been to provide you with a lot of separate pieces. Moreover, we have recommended that initially you focus on these separate pieces, or skills, one at a time. But it is a simplification to think of these skills as separate—a fiction used to make the initial learning easier. When used in the library workplace, the skills are combined. You may learn open questioning in your training workshop by practicing asking open questions and nothing else. But the ultimate goal is to use the individual skill of open questioning as appropriate, along with some other appropriate skills, in the service of a larger purpose.

So, like the king's horses and the king's men, you have the job of putting Humpty together again. The real test of the skills presented in Chapters 1–4 is how they fit together in the applications presented in Chapters 6–10. In fact, one approach to using this book is to start with some application, such as making a presentation (8.3), and then work backward to the skills involved. See Chapter 1 for nonverbal skills, including vocal quality, and Chapter 4 for writing skills. We are giving you pieces and suggesting in the applications sections how these pieces might fit together. But we hope that you will make a lot of the connections yourself to suit your own needs.

Use this chapter to help in the process of putting things together. The organization goes from general to specific. We start with a rapid survey of some of the theoretical underpinnings of the book, go on to discuss a theory of communication that is particularly suited to information work, describe Ivey's concept of intentionality as a prerequisite for learning how to integrate skills and everyday behavior, and end with some very specific suggestions for learning and integrating new skills.

5.2. Theory and Paradigms

In writing this book, we have been fairly eclectic, passing on a variety of ideas and suggestions that we have found helpful and that have worked for us. Much of the advice we pass on is absolutely standard (every book on writing will tell you to write concisely and to avoid the passive voice). However, a source of unity in this book is our theoretical orientation (or paradigm or set of mental maps about the world).

Anyone writing about communication/reading/information has some mental model, however unexamined, of what is involved in these processes. One model, let's call it Paradigm A, is based on the following assumptions:

Paradigm A

1. Knowledge is objective. The way to know about the world is to stand outside it somehow and observe it objectively.
2. Information consists of objective observations about the world.
3. Information is a commodity, valuable in itself, regardless of its use. Information is made up of a lot of separate little bits. The more bits of information one has, the better.
4. Communication is a one-way process of sources sending messages to receivers.
5. Giving information requires the creation of structures in which messages travel top-down, from expert to layperson (e.g., doctor-to-patient or advertiser-to-television viewer).
6. The receiver of messages is passive, expected to hear or read the message accurately and in its entirety, and to incorporate its content in unaltered form.
7. Meaning is in the message itself, fixed in the text.
8. Evaluating information service consists of recording the frequency with which the information is ex-

changed and measuring the extent to which people receive messages accurately and completely.

9. Information is context-free.

This book has been written within the framework of an alternative model, Paradigm B, which is based on different assumptions:

Paradigm B

1. We are part of the reality that we study. We can't stand outside the world to view it as it really is, because our instruments, experiments, culture, language, and worldview affect what we perceive. Where we stand and look from affects what we see. Knowledge depends on perspective.

2. Information consists of observations about the world that are affected by the contexts in which the observations are made.

3. Information is valuable only in relation to the context in which it is used.

4. Communication is an interactive process between speakers and listeners, writers and readers.

5. The receiver of the message participates actively in making meaning.

6. The meaning that is created depends on previously learned cultural codes, previous life experience, the present situation, and individual perspectives of the listener or reader.

7. The ultimate test of the value of an information service is the helpfulness of the information to the user in terms of what that user is trying to do or know at a particular time and place.

8. Information is situationally based, and its meaning depends on context.

Arguments in support of the assumptions of Paradigm B have all been elaborated at length elsewhere (see the Annotated Bibliography at the end of this chapter for a sampling). It is enough to say here that this second paradigm, along with its implications, lies behind three recurrent themes in this book:

- Communication is an interactive process involving feedback.
- Any good theory of communication (including reading, writing, and teaching as well as one-to-one interactions) must give a starring role to the reader/message-receiver/ learner, who is an active participant in constructing the sense of what is said or written.
- To understand the meaning of something, you have to know its context.

5.3. Sense-Making: A Theory of Information as Communication

Many books on communication for librarians and others begin with a theory of the communication of information derived from electrical engineering—a model developed by Claude Shannon and Warren Weaver and usually presented something like this:

CHANNEL

SOURCE → SIGNAL → RECEIVER

This model is useful for solving the problem for which it was originally developed: determining the most economical way to send and receive electronic signals along channels that are noisy with random electrical interference. The original theory was concerned not with meaning but with electronic pulses. It doesn't matter what you send over the wires, including nonsense, because information is anything that reduces uncertainty for the decoder. When we transpose this model from the engineering context to the context of human communication, we really are using a metaphor. The metaphor highlights certain areas of similarity between decoding electronic messages and decoding human messages, but it obscures an important difference. With human communication, meaning is of primary importance. Meaning, moreover, is not so much *there* in the message as constructed by the receiver (listener or reader).

Dr. Brenda Dervin is a communications researcher who works from within Paradigm B. We have found her work especially fruitful for the field of librarianship, because it focuses on what she calls "the human side of information." Dervin argues that most prevailing models of communication, including the Shannon-Weaver model, assume that information is a commodity that can be generated, stored, accessed, and transferred. That is, information is understood to be an autonomous object with meaning and value in itself, apart from any user.

Following others who have argued for the social construction of reality, Dervin maintains that information is a construct of the user. In her theory of information, human beings are not seen as passive receptacles but as actively involved in constructing their own reality. This theory allows us to explain some of the puzzling problems of research into information-seeking behavior: Why does the same message mean different things to different people at different times? Why do people not always follow directions? And why do people sometimes reject as useless information that experts judge as high quality?

Dervin and her colleagues developed their alternative theory of information in the course of extensive research, beginning in the early 1970s, that examined actual citizen information-seeking behavior. She was interested in the kinds of situations that people see as problematic, the kinds of questions they have in these situations, where they go for help, the kinds of answers they get to their questions, and how the answers help them cope with their situations. From this research, Dervin developed "Turning Public Libraries Around," a series of workshops for California librarians in which she introduced the theory she calls "sense-making" as well as the technique of neutral questioning (which she later renamed "sense-making questions")

Here at last was a systematic basis for developing dynamic interviewing strategies, a framework that was consistent with Allen E. Ivey's microtraining model but took into account the nature of information service. "Information," in Dervin's terms, is the process of making new sense or getting a new picture of the world in order to move ahead.

Dervin called this theory "sense-making" to emphasize information seeking as a primary human activity. It is what people are trying to do as they work through situations in their lives—going on quests, meeting barriers, facing dilemmas, running into contradictions, asking questions, and seeking happiness. When people become stymied—when, as Dervin puts it, their own knowledge or sense has run out with respect to a particular situation or when they are unable to progress without forming some kind of new sense—then they seek outside help. They ask their mothers or the taxi driver. They call up their accountant or doctor. Or they visit some institutional system, such as the library. This visit is a detour from their usual life path made in order to get help not otherwise available. The information need, we should note, is not context-free but has arisen from a specific situation unique to the individual.

Given this uniqueness, the problem that the sense-making approach tries to address is this:

> *How can institutions meet information needs when those needs are overwhelmingly unique, having arisen from unique situations?*
>
> *Human individuality seems too complex to handle. How can we deal with people on their own terms and do it systematically?*

The answer is that although the situations themselves are unique, there are some repeated patterns in the ways that people need, seek out, and use information. We can use these similarities to develop a systematic approach to understanding people's information needs. Three kinds of significant questions can be used as keys to understand people's sense-making journeys. These are questions about:

- the *situation* and how the individual sees it;
- the *gap* in the individual's understanding of the situation—what seems to be missing; and
- the intended *uses* for the information—how the individual hopes the information will help.

These dimensions—the crucial elements in the sense-making process—form the situation/gap/uses triangle that is also addressed in 3.6 in the discussion of sense-making questions.

The direct, practical relevance of the sense-making approach is clearest in library work involving finding out people's needs for information, especially reference service. But there are others: research into community needs, program evaluation, readers' advisory work, and even collection development and organization. Consider, for example, that we can improve public access to our collections by creating displays according to the situation/gap/uses model. You can start with an everyday-life situation and make that situation the subject of a display featuring library materials in different formats drawn from fiction and nonfiction and from different subject areas. Situation-based library displays might focus on

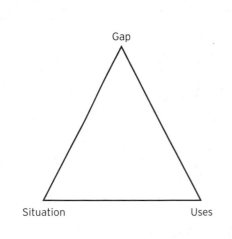

FIGURE 5.1. Sense-Making Triangle

topics such as these: job-hunting; moving to a new city and finding out about services available; making the decision about whether or not to retire; figuring out how to help aging parents stay in their home or move; dealing with a chronic health problem; adopting a dog. In each situation, there are many possibilities for gaps that people may have in their understanding and many different kinds of help they may want. The job hunter may want to get some ideas about career options or learn résumé-writing skills or get some help preparing for the job interview or locate career counseling services. Library displays can benefit from a way of thinking about information that focuses on the situation that the person is in, the gaps in the person's understanding, and the way the person hopes to use the information.

The sense-making approach also offers a vantage point from which to think about writing and working in groups. Readers receiving written texts and participants at group meetings are all sense-makers, valuing information to the extent that it helps them fill in gaps in their understanding and make progress toward their goals. Therefore, a writer drafting memos, reports, or public service announcements may do a better job by remembering that readers are in unique situations, have gaps in their understanding, and want certain kinds of help. The writing should address these situations, gaps, and sorts of help wanted.

5.4. Microcounseling and Microtraining

As we explained in the preface, Allen E. Ivey's theory of microcounseling and microtraining has been extremely influential in the way we have chosen to organize this book. Ivey developed the microskills approach in the early 1960s as a way of teaching new counselors to use the basic communication skills necessary in any interview. The smallest component of an effective interview he called a "microskill," beginning with the basic listening sequence that includes attending behavior such as eye contact and body language as well as verbal tracking skills such as acknowledgment. These formed the basis of his hierarchy of microskills, from the basic listening sequence through influencing skills and culminating in skill integration.

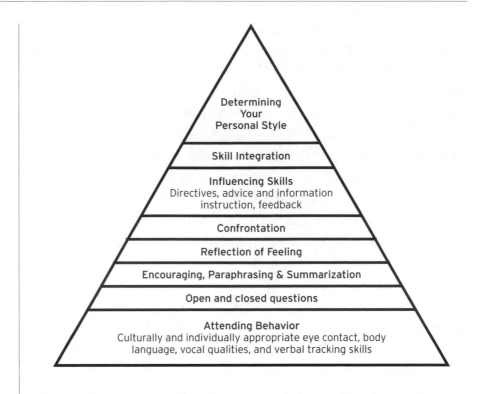

Determining
Your
Personal Style

Skill Integration

Influencing Skills
Directives, advice and information
instruction, feedback

Confrontation

Reflection of Feeling

Encouraging, Paraphrasing & Summarization

Open and closed questions

Attending Behavior
Culturally and individually appropriate eye contact, body
language, vocal qualities, and verbal tracking skills

(Adapted with permission from Allen E. Ivey, Mary Bradford Ivey, and Carlos P. Zalaquett. 2009. *Intentional Interviewing and Counseling: Facilitating Client Development in a Multicultural Society*. 7th ed. Pacific Grove, CA: Brooks/Cole, 15.)

FIGURE 5.2. The Microskills Hierarchy

The microtraining approach refers to the way in which microskills are taught. Skills are introduced one at a time in a sequence of four steps. For each skill, the trainee first learns to identify or recognize the skill by observing others' behavior in performing the skill or by picking out the skill from a transcript, videotape, or some other exercise. (For example, see the exercise on open and closed questions in 3.4.) At the second level of training, learners are given exercises in which they demonstrate the skill, for example, by asking open questions in a mock interview. Third, students learn active mastery of the skill by intentionally using the skill in a real-life situation. In the library context, demonstrating active mastery might mean recognizing the need to encourage a library user to talk more about the information problem and using some open questions to elicit details about the type of help needed. The final level of skill mastery is the ability to teach a skill to someone else—perhaps a colleague or a library user.

Although initially designed to aid counselors toward their goal of helping clients and enhancing their developmental growth, the

Four Levels of Skill Mastery

1. Identification
2. Basic mastery
3. Active mastery
4. Teaching mastery

(Ivey, Ivey, and Zalaquett, 2009: 7-8)

microskills system has been enormously successful in many contexts, including physician–patient communication, management and business situations, and librarianship. Elaine Z. Jennerich (1974) was perhaps the first to recognize the value of microskills training for librarians and conducted a major research study to evaluate the effect of teaching library school students the microskills most useful for public service.

In our information services and professional communication courses in the Master of Library and Information Science program at The University of Western Ontario, we have emphasized listening and questioning skills for communicating with library users. Following the essential steps in the microtraining method, we focus on one skill at a time, defining the skill, modeling it, and involving students in role-playing interviews, using the exercises that we include in *Communicating Professionally*. Our experience suggests that the most effective method for teaching the skills involves the learner in a combination of activities:

- Hearing short presentations in lecture format
- Reading independently the sections in *Communicating Professionally* and other relevant materials
- Getting actual experience practicing the skill in role-played or real-life situations
- Receiving feedback
- Discussing the experience afterward in a small group setting

When students encountered the normal problems in learning these skills, we found it was essential to emphasize two things: the concept of intentionality or choice and the difference between learning the skill in the first place and using it with mastery later. Once articulated, these interconnected ideas seem familiar, even self-evident. They have been pointed out in a variety of fields. The first edition of *The Chicago Manual of Style*, for example, introduces its rules by saying that there is no rule that can't be broken if the writer's purpose requires it. E. H. Gombrich (1979: 11) in *The Sense of Order: A Study in the Psychology of Decorative Art* says this:

> Whether we use a typewriter, ride a bicycle or play the piano, we first learn to "master" the basic movements without attending to them all the time, so that our conscious mind is left free to plan and direct the over-arching structures. . . . There is no craft

Did You Know? ?

"If you don't use it, you lose it," according to research on training in basic communication skills. Trainees who do not practice or use their new skills during the year following training lose the skills, although retraining may bring them up to post-training levels again.

which does not demand this breakdown of the skill into elements which are steered by the larger movement; mastery of plaiting, weaving, stitching or carving demands this structure of routines collectively guided by the conscious mind.

The early stages of learning require concentrated attention on the small units until those units become automatic. At this point the units become part of our repertoire of responses, to be used when appropriate, and the mind is free to concentrate on the larger purpose. The problem with the store clerk who says, "Have a nice day. Thank you for shopping at X" is that the response is automatic (too automatic), but it is not used with intentionality: the response has become mechanical because it is divorced from genuine feeling or purpose.

5.5. Intentionality

Through all this, we found it useful to keep reminding ourselves of Ivey's concept of intentionality, possibly the most important concept in microtraining. Intentionality has to do with choice: once the trainee has acquired the ability to use individual skills and to integrate them, he or she needs to be able to judge when these skills are appropriate, what effect they are likely to have, and what is the range of potentially helpful responses to a particular situation. Ivey defines intentionality as follows:

> Intentionality is acting with a sense of capability and deciding from among a range of alternative actions. The intentional individual has more than one action, thought or behavior to choose from in responding to changing life situations. The intentional individual can generate alternatives in a given situation and approach a problem from different vantage points, using a variety of skills and personal qualities, adapting styles to suit different individuals and cultures. (Ivey, Ivey, and Zalaquett, 2009: 21)

Skills must be learned individually, but together they form a repertoire from which the helper can draw spontaneously, selecting one skill in a certain situation, adapting another skill to supplement, trying yet another skill if the first one doesn't work. Intentionality means flexibility—the ability to use a range of skills and to improvise. It means not depending on one skill or always using the same skill in similar situations. Intentionality in the microtraining model goes hand-in-hand with the sense-making model. Both theories are based on a view of human beings as actively pursuing goals and making choices to reach those goals.

In each new edition of his text, Ivey has placed increasing emphasis on "cultural intentionality" or the ability to recognize situations in which microskills such as direct eye contact might not be culturally appropriate and to adapt one's behavior accordingly. "Culture" is presented by Ivey as a broad concept that includes not only religion, class, and ethnicity but also gender, sexual orientation, lifestyle differences, and other individual differences. What is required is an awareness of this diversity and a repertoire of communication behavior that can be used effectively in any given situation.

In the seventh edition (2009), Ivey and co-authors reiterate that being multiculturally competent requires knowledge, awareness, and skills and recognition that "the same skills may have different effects on people from varying cultural backgrounds" (p. 21). We need to become aware that cultural differences exist and develop skills that can be used with intentionality with individuals from diverse cultures. This means that "you face a lifetime of multicultural learning" (p. 43).

Intentionality is not limited to verbal skills. The intentional helper becomes adept at using nonverbal skills or writing skills, as the need dictates. Much of the rest of this book illustrates how various skills can be used to supplement each other, how one skill can be substituted for another, and how several skills can be integrated to achieve specific purposes in the process of communication.

5.6. The Problem of Manipulation versus Genuineness

When library staff first learn new communication skills, they may react by saying that they're being taught to manipulate their own behavior in order to manipulate others. Some trainees say that they feel deceptive when they try to make the transition from practicing a skill in a training setting to using the skill in a real-life setting. Suppose, they say, that it's not natural to me to use encouragers or ask open questions to get people to talk. But I learn these skills and use

> **Exercise** 🔧
>
> **Genuineness**
> This exercise can be done in a small group. The group leader asks each person to identify a skill or behavior that is felt to be both "manipulative" and alien to that person's normal behavior. Meanwhile a group member is recruited to list on a blackboard or flip chart each skill mentioned. When everyone in the group has had a turn, the group leader asks about each skill mentioned, "To what extent does everyone share this feeling that this skill seems manipulative?" Those not sharing this feeling are asked for some suggestions on decreasing the feeling of lack of genuineness.

them, and hey presto, people open up and tell me things. Isn't there something deceptive and manipulative about this?

Well, there might be, depending on motives. In the service of base motives, these skills can be abused. In the service of shared goals, these skills facilitate communication and allow you to be more helpful. To communicate more effectively with others, we may need to change our own behavior—to learn new skills such as different ways of asking questions or of organizing a report. In fact, although the same complaint of manipulativeness could be leveled at writing skills, few people feel that changing their writing style to make it clearer and more forceful makes their style less genuine.

This issue of genuineness is not simply a matter of motivation, however. When we first learn a new skill, it may seem awkward and alien to our normal behavior—not genuine, we say. However, the skill becomes more natural with practice (see 5.7). When we find that we can make the skill work for us in a variety of situations, it becomes part of our normal behavior. Then it is perceived as genuine. In the meantime, our genuineness consists of our sincere desire to help, even if helping more effectively means behaving a little awkwardly at first.

5.7. Tips for Practicing

Remember the old joke about how to get to Carnegie Hall? (Practice, practice, practice.)

5.7.1. Practicing Verbal Skills

Changing your communication behavior is hard work. It's not easy to break old patterns of response. But unless you practice your new skills, you'll lose them. Here are ten tips to help you through the learning process.

1. **Make a commitment.** Promise yourself that for a specified period of time—the next hour or on Thursday afternoons—you will consciously use one of your new skills.
2. **Start immediately.** Begin practicing the skill right away. Remind yourself by taping to your desk a photocopy from this book outlining the skill or by putting an

elastic band on your wrist. At first, you may feel awkward, but practice anyway. Most library users respond positively when they see that you are trying hard to help.

3. **Practice one skill at a time.** Best results come from practicing one skill over and over until you have become comfortable with it. Don't try to use all the skills at once. A good skill to start with is acknowledgment or restatement (3.2). An easy sense-making question (3.6) to use is, "What kind of help would you like?"

4. **Use support groups.** Practice with a co-worker who has made the same commitment. Give each other feedback and share experiences. Or set aside time at regular staff meetings to discuss your progress.

5. **Learn from missed opportunities.** Each time you do *not* use one of these skills, think about the situation afterward. Was there an open question you might have used? How could you have used the DESC sequence to influence the outcome of the conversation (see 3.13)?

6. **Develop your own style.** There is no magic list of open questions and no perfect sequence in which to use your skills. Adapt your behavior in a way that is comfortable for you in the situation at hand. Use words that function in the same way as those in the examples, even if the exact words differ.

7. **Learn from communication accidents.** When you are first learning these skills, you may find that they do not always work. If the user seems puzzled, you may have had a communication accident. Recover by explaining to the user what you are trying to do. For example, "I asked you that question because I can help you more if I know a little bit about what you plan to do with the information" or "I want to make sure I understand what you're looking for." Users hardly ever become angry in such situations, but, if it happens, recover simply by saying "I'm sorry" and explaining.

8. **Practice off the job.** Microskills work in any situation where your help is being sought—by family, friends, even strangers asking directions. Practice these skills in your daily life—you may be surprised at how much everyday communication improves.

9. **Observe others.** Notice how others use microskills—the salesperson who restates your request, the talk show host who asks open questions, the physician who encourages you to describe your problem, the museum guide who gives directions well. Pay particular attention to those people you like dealing with—chances are they are using microskills.

10. **Teach someone else.** After you have learned a skill and practiced it, pass it on to someone else. Teach a co-worker one skill that you have found to be particularly effective. Your ability to teach someone else demonstrates that you have really mastered the skill.

5.7.2. Practicing Writing Skills

Improving writing skills requires a conscious choice to pay attention to the "how" as well as to the "what" of writing. Here are some tips to help you practice new writing skills:

1. **Make a commitment.** Be prepared to work hard.
2. **Take stock.** Analyze something that you have written recently, when the quality of the writing mattered. Consider this written work in terms of the skills discussed in Chapter 4—choosing an appropriate style, writing with impact, writing clearly and briefly, and so on. Which writing skills did you use well? Which ones need more work?
3. **Focus on one skill at a time.** You can't do everything at once. Pick one area in which you feel your writing needs to be improved. In everything that you write for the next week, scrutinize each paragraph with this skill in mind. If you were focusing on writing briefly, you could ask yourself: Do I need every word? Could I convey the same idea more succinctly? Which words/sentences/whole paragraphs or sections can I cut out?
4. **Revise.** Don't be content with your first draft. Good writers edit their work and revise and revise and revise.
5. **Don't worry** that your first draft falls short with respect to the skill you are working on. Get something

written down first. Then you have something to revise. It's the final draft, not the first draft, that counts.

6. **Leave enough time.** Let an important piece of writing sit for a day or so. When you come back to it, you will see things to improve that you didn't see at the time of writing.

7. **Read out loud** your piece of writing. If it's hard to read out loud without stumbling over it, there is probably something wrong with the rhythm that you should fix.

8. **Ask for feedback.** Show an important piece of writing to someone whose opinion about writing you respect, and ask for suggestions for improvement. Let it be known that you are not fishing for compliments but really do want to hear about parts that the reader found confusing or too vague or too wordy.

9. **Sharpen your critical awareness.** Examine other people's writing. What is there about a particular letter, memo, or report that makes it good (or not so good)?

5.8. Skill Integration

In any communication process, the participants have certain goals. In some situations (e.g., giving information to the public about a new service), the goals are explicit, limited, and planned in advance. In other situations, such as reference transactions, the goals may be developed on the fly during the transaction itself. Hidden goals may become apparent, and goals may change.

Achieving a goal usually requires the use and combination of several skills. Although the process of learning a new skill requires you to focus on one skill at a time, the effective use of new skills depends on your ability to draw on a range of skills for the purpose of achieving a specific goal. You may even overlap skills. Let's say the user has asked for "information on wind turbines." One of your goals is to obtain a more complete description of the information need. At the same time, you want to establish a good communication climate by showing the user that you are attentive. Two goals, and at least three possible skills, come into play here: nonverbal attending skills (Chapter 1), acknowledgment or restatement (3.2), and open questions (3.4).

When you practiced restatement, you focused on simply repeating or paraphrasing what the user had said: "You're looking for something on wind turbines?" When you practiced asking open questions, you learned to ask, "What would you like to know?" A simple example of skill integration might be: "What would you like to know about wind turbines?" or "What kind of information on wind turbines would help you most?" Of course, the interview goes on. Pursuing your goal of finding out what the user really wants to know, you might use encouragers, more open questions, a sense-making question, and a closed question to confirm your understanding. If the user gets sidetracked, you might use the skill of closure (3.11). Once you understand what's needed, your goal may change. You might need to give directions or instructions (3.12) and, at the end, elicit feedback (3.15). Being able to use any or all of these skills appropriately to further the goals of the interview is evidence of skill integration.

On a larger scale, skill integration may mean combining different forms of communication (each of which involves several skills) to achieve a goal. Let's say your goal is to persuade your staff to attend a meeting. Related objectives involve giving information about the time, location, and purpose of the meeting, getting information about how many people are coming, persuading people to come, and asking for suggestions of additional topics to be discussed at the meeting. To achieve your goal, you might send a written invitation or e-mail requesting confirmation of attendance. If you get 100 percent confirmation, you've probably achieved all your objectives. If not, perhaps there were writing skills that could have improved the response. Or you might supplement the invitation with some personal telephone calls, during which you use appropriate verbal and nonverbal skills.

The subsequent sections of this book present situations in which more than one skill and perhaps more than one form of communication can be used, with examples of how skills can be integrated to achieve particular purposes.

5.9. Annotated Bibliography

Theory, Paradigms, and Research Approaches

Bateson, Gregory. 2000. *Steps to an Ecology of Mind: Collected Essays in Anthropology, Psychiatry, Evolution, and Epistemology*. Chicago:

University of Chicago Press. Originally published in 1972 (San Francisco: Chandler Publishing). This book includes Bateson's essays that focus on problems of epistemology: what knowledge we have, how we get it, and how it is organized.

Berger, Peter L., and Thomas Luckmann. 1966. *The Social Construction of Reality: A Treatise in the Sociology of Knowledge*. New York: Doubleday. This much-cited book introduced the concept of "social construction" of reality—that what people think and believe is the case becomes the case.

Burr, Vivien. 1995. *An Introduction to Social Constructionism*. New York: Routledge. This introductory text shows how the study of language can be used as a focus for our understanding of human behavior and experience. See especially Chapter 2, "Does Language Affect the Way We Think?"

Khoo, Michael, Lily Rozaklis, and Catherine Hall. 2012. "A Survey of the Use of Ethnographic Methods in the Study of Libraries and Library Users." *Library and Information Science Research* 34: 82–91. This article identifies 81 studies that have used ethnographic methods to study the culture of libraries or library users from an insider perspective.

Nahl, Diane, and Dania Bilal. 2007. *Information and Emotion: The Emergent Affective Paradigm in Information Behavior Research and Theory*. ASIST Monograph Series. Medford, NJ: Information Today. Seventeen chapters examine the role of emotion and the affective dimension in different information contexts and different user groups, including pleasure-readers, critical care nurses, undergraduate students, international LIS doctoral students, and stay-at-home mothers.

Powell, Ron. 1999. "Recent Trends in Research: A Methodological Essay." *Library and Information Science Research* 21, no. 1: 91–119. Powell reviews some newer approaches that have gained ground in LIS research, including ethnography, grounded theory, phenomenology and hermeneutics, symbolic interactionism, and discourse analysis, with an emphasis on the use of these methods in LIS research.

The Nature of Information and Sense-Making

Dervin, Brenda. 1983. "Information as a User Construct: The Relevance of Perceived Information Needs to Synthesis and Interpretation." In *Knowledge Structure and Use: Implications for Synthesis and Interpretation*, edited by S. A. Ward, and L. J. Reed, 155–183.

Philadelphia: Temple University Press. This is a useful early statement of the user-centered approach to information.

Dervin, Brenda, and Patricia Dewdney. 1986. "Neutral Questioning: A New Approach to the Reference Interview." *RQ* 25, no. 4: 506–513. This article explains the theory and practice of sense-making questions and is still the best starting point for the topic.

Dervin, Brenda, Lois Foreman-Wernet, with Eric Lautervach, eds. 2003. *Sense-Making Methodology Reader: Selected Writings of Brenda Dervin*. Cresskill, NJ: Hampton Press. This text brings together 17 articles, authored or co-authored by Dervin between 1980 and 2002, that together track the development of sense-making as a theoretical framework and methodology for conducting user-centered research.

Skill Integration

Gombrich, E. H. 1979. *The Sense of Order: A Study in the Psychology of Decorative Art*. Ithaca, NY: Cornell University Press.

Ivey, Allen E., Mary Bradford Ivey, and Carlos P. Zalaquett. 2009. *Intentional Interviewing and Counseling: Facilitating Client Development in a Multicultural Society*. 7th ed. Pacific Grove, CA: Brooks/Cole. See Chapter 1, "Towards Intentional Interviewing and Counseling," and Chapter 13, "Skill Integration: Putting It All Together."

Jennerich, Elaine Z. 1974. "Microcounseling in Library Education." Unpublished doctoral dissertation. Pittsburgh, PA: University of Pittsburgh Graduate School of Library and Information Sciences.

Jennerich, Elaine Z., and Edward J. Jennerich. 1997. *The Reference Interview as a Creative Art*. 2nd ed. Littleton, CO: Libraries Unlimited. This book builds on the pioneering work in Elaine Jennerich's University of Pittsburgh dissertation, "Microcounseling in Library Education."

PART 2
Applications

Speaking One-to-One

6

6.1. Introduction to Speaking One-to-One

This chapter considers the application of speaking skills in commonly occurring situations involving two people: initiating the communication process (the first 60 seconds); using the telephone and voice mail; conducting interviews, including employment and reference interviews; coping with special situations; dealing with problem behaviors; and communicating with colleagues, employees, and volunteers.

6.1.1. Communicating Face-to-Face: The First 60 Seconds

When you are speaking one-to-one you need to incorporate all of the skills we've covered in Chapters 1–4 and put it all together as discussed in Chapter 5. Being approachable is the first step both in giving good customer service and in communicating successfully with your co-workers. Regular library users often hesitate to ask for help. To be approachable, you have to be available physically, and you must appear willing to help. Being available means being where the users are and not behind a high desk where users can't see you. Looking approachable involves using nonverbal skills, such as a welcoming posture, smiling, eye contact, and wearing an identification tag (see 1.6), and being constantly on the alert for users who need help. Even if you have other work to do, scan the area every few minutes so that you don't miss people who look as if they could use some help.

Approachability can be successfully conveyed on the phone as well through tone of voice (see 1.8 on vocal qualities).

6.2. Using the Telephone and Voice Mail

This section covers general use of telephone and voice mail in libraries. For suggestions on the telephone reference interview, see 6.4.4.

6.2.1. Answering the Telephone

Because your caller cannot see you nodding and smiling over the telephone, you should pay special attention to vocal qualities and verbal skills. For the caller at the other end, your voice represents the whole library. You are literally the frontline. Here are some suggestions.

Develop a pleasant speaking voice. Monitor how you sound over the phone. Is your tone interested and courteous? Do you speak slowly and clearly enough to be easily understood? Do you sound as if you welcome the call? (See 1.8 for exercises to improve variety and articulation).

Identify yourself. When you answer the phone, your greeting should clearly identify your library and your role or name, but above all it should indicate your willingness to provide service. Instead of saying "Yes" or "Hello," try something like this:

> Hamilton Public Library. How may I direct your call?
> Reference Department. Rose Lapointe speaking. How can I help you?
> Good morning. The Legal Information Center. This is Frances Lopez.

Acknowledge (see 3.2). Be sure to acknowledge the caller's question promptly by restating at least part of it. If you didn't quite catch the question, repeat what you did understand and let the caller fill you in on the rest:

> Yes, I'd be happy to check that for you in WorldCat.

Uh-huh, the new Margaret Atwood book.

Beerbohm. And that's spelled B-E-E-R-B . . . ?

Use minimal encouragers (see 3.3). Minimal encouragers like "Uh-huh," "Go on," "That's interesting," and "Anything else?" are especially important over the phone as cues that you are listening. Without these encouragers, the caller is apt to wonder if you are still there.

Volunteer your help. Don't force the caller to pry help out of you. If the caller asks, "Is Ms. Lapointe there?" don't just say, "No, she's not here." Say, "Ms. Lapointe will be back at one o'clock. If you'd like to leave a message, I'll make sure she gets it when she returns" or "Ms. Lapointe is not here at the moment. Can anyone else help you?" If the caller asks, "Do you have a storyhour Saturday morning?" don't say, "No, I'm sorry, we don't." Volunteer to tell the caller the times when you *do* have a storyhour.

Clarify the question or request. Use open questions (see 3.4) to find out what kind of help the caller wants. For example:

How may I help you?

What information would you like on that?

What aspect of X are you interested in?

What kind of help would you like?

Explain. Because the caller cannot see you, it is often a good idea to explain what you are doing (see 3.10). If you are going to ask people to wait, don't just say "Hang on" or "Okay, I'll look" and then go away. The caller won't know what you are doing or how long to expect to wait. Studies show that people can cope better with frustrating experiences if they are told ahead of time what to expect. Therefore, explain what you are doing and how long you expect to be. If more time is passing than you anticipated, give your waiting caller a progress report. Say, "I haven't forgotten you." Offer to take the number and call back if you think it will be more than another minute or two.

Refer. If you can't answer the question yourself, don't say, "No, I don't know anything about that program" or "That's not our department." Instead, you could say something like, "We have a term paper clinic on campus; here is the phone number. The clinic is open from 9:00 to 5:00, Monday to Friday. Would you like me to transfer you?" or "If

> **A Quick Tip** 🕐
>
> **Smile!**
> Smile when you're on the phone. Smiling conveys warmth in your voice (Walters, 1994).

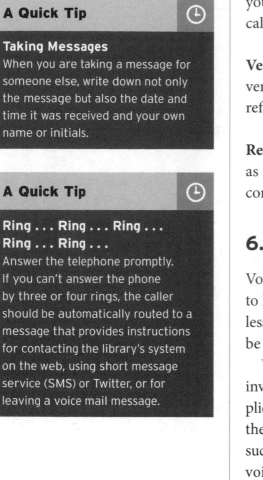

you would leave your number, I'll find out about that program and call you back within half an hour."

Verify. If the caller has asked for some particular help, repeat and verify the key facts before you rush off to find the answer (see 3.8 on reflecting content).

Record messages accurately. Restate names and telephone numbers as you write them down (see 3.2). This gives the caller a chance to correct errors. Standard message forms are helpful and save time.

6.2.2. Voice Mail

Voice mail is one of many options that libraries provide to allow users to leave messages. Some of the options such as SMS and Twitter are less cumbersome than voice mail systems, but voice mail is likely to be in use for many years to come.

Voice mail systems can be as simple as the recorded message that invites the caller to leave a name and number to call back or as complicated as a multilevel menu of choices that connect the caller with the right department or enable the caller to perform certain actions, such as confirming a flight on an airline phone system. Well-designed voice mail systems offer convenience and efficiency to the caller. Although voice mail has certain disadvantages for the caller and the library—some users are put off, are impatient to get through to a real person, and refuse to leave a message—there are real advantages of convenience and efficiency both to the caller and to the library.

Fortunately you can reduce or even eliminate many disadvantages of voice mail system by setting it up properly. To create an effective automated greeting or menu:

- Keep routine announcements short and simple. Avoid nonessential statements such as "Thank you for calling. The reference desk is not staffed in the evening . . ." and get to the point: "You've reached the reference desk. Please leave a message or call back. Our hours are . . ."
- Reduce the time callers have to spend listening to menu options by explaining how to skip the items that are not relevant.
- Simplify actions required of the caller. Break down instructions into manageable steps. Avoid complicated or

confusing directions, for example, "Enter the first three letters of your last name, press the number sign, and then choose one of the following seven options."

- When possible, give callers the option, early in the message, to transfer to a real person if that is their preference.

Answering your messages promptly is an important part of effective voice mail. You should have a policy that calls are returned within a certain period of time, for example, within three working hours.

When You Are the Caller

Getting the most out of voice mail requires that the caller leave a clear message. Here are some tips for callers:

- Think about your message before you pick up the phone. No one likes long rambling messages like, "Gee, I was hoping you'd be in your office but I guess this is lunch-time . . . let's see, maybe it would be best if you called me—no, I won't be here so I will call you maybe tomorrow . . . blah blah . . ."
- Begin with the name of the person you want to reach. Some voice mail numbers are shared among several people (or you may have the wrong number).
- Identify yourself clearly, spelling your name if it is likely to be unfamiliar to the person you're calling; for example, "Mr. Milstead, this is Esther Mendez calling back from the Central Library."
- Give your phone number twice, speaking slowly.
- When you are leaving a message, announce yourself (name and phone number), and then immediately state why you are calling.
- Continue with details that expand on your initial statement, ending with a closing statement of what you would like the listener to do in response, for example, "I'm calling to see if you can attend the meeting on Tuesday at 9 a.m. Please call me back by Monday to let me know. My number again is . . ."
- Remember that tone of voice matters (see 1.8).

Exercise

Annoying Voice Mail
Have you had a recent experience with a voice mail system that left you feeling anxious, frustrated, or annoyed? Collect as many examples as you can (ask colleagues and friends to describe their experiences), and identify the features of the system that created problems. Suggest ways in which the system, message, or menu could be improved.

6.3. Interviewing

When librarians think of interviewing, the reference interview is probably the first thing that comes to mind. However, there are many other kinds of interviews that are commonly used in library settings—for example, interviews for purposes of selecting or evaluating employees, counseling interviews, interviews to gather information or solve problems, and research interviews. We begin with a discussion of the generic interview and generic interviewing skills that apply in a broad range of types of interviews. Next we focus on reference interviews of various kinds, including those resulting from imposed queries; research interviews; telephone and virtual reference interviews; and readers' advisory interviews. Then we discuss the employment interview from the perspectives both of the interviewer and of the interviewee. Some other types of interviews are covered in other chapters. Because media interviews are a form of presentation, we cover them in Chapter 8 (see 8.7). For information on moderating a focus group, which is a form of group interview, see 7.5.3. An interview might occur as part of a conference or workshop when you interview a speaker in front of an audience or include an interview with a visiting author into a book group presentation. See 8.2 on arranging for other people to speak and the related readings in 8.8. See also the Annotated Bibliography for this chapter (6.8).

6.3.1. What Is an Interview?

An interview is a conversation directed intentionally to some purpose. It usually involves the asking and answering of questions. People who work in libraries and information centers participate in different kinds of interviews with different purposes. Consider personnel interviews conducted to select or terminate an employee, conduct a performance appraisal, hear a grievance, or counsel a troubled employee. Public service staff may conduct reference interviews with researchers or adult independent learners, readers' advisory interviews, and problem-solving interviews. Research interviews comprise another category of directed conversation: the interview is a primary way of collecting data for oral history projects, user surveys, needs assessment, and evaluation research.

Whatever the purpose of the interview, the interviewer should have a clear idea, before the interview starts, of why she is conducting the

---

A Quick Tip 🕐

It's Not a Social Occasion
Remember that an interview is not a social event but a directed conversation to a purpose. Just listen. Don't talk about yourself even when you have had a similar experience.

interview and what she hopes to have accomplished by the end. Two common purposes for an interview are giving information or getting information. Usually one of these purposes predominates. When the primary purpose of an interview is to give information or instruction, the interviewer is justified in doing much of the talking. However, if the primary purpose is to get information, the interviewer should spend most of her time asking questions and listening. Other purposes of the interview may include problem solving and counseling.

An important factor in any interview is the extent to which the interviewer and interviewee share a common purpose. At one end of the scale, both parties share a common purpose and know that they do. At the other end, each party has a separate and opposed purpose. Consider the case in which a supervisor wants a staff member to realize that her work is inadequate, but the employee feels she is doing the best she can under poor working conditions and wants to defend her performance. Sometimes an interviewer makes an erroneous assumption about the interviewee's purpose, as in the case of a library user who asks for "a book about a classic novel," hoping to find a brief plot summary for a book report due today. He wants the minimum possible to get through the assignment and is not really interested in reading the book. In such cases, the interviewer must be aware that the interviewee may be working on a "hidden agenda" or the interview will be ineffective.

6.3.2. Dimensions of the Interview

Interviews may differ greatly, one from another, in terms of the five dimensions discussed here. An interviewer who is aware of the range of possible variations can select the style of interview that best suits the occasion and purpose.

Control

Who is in charge? At one end of the scale are interviews in which the interviewer controls everything: which topics to discuss and which aspects of the topics to consider. This style of interviewing, sometimes called the "directed interview," relies to a large extent on closed questioning (see 3.4) and can be useful when certain, specific facts are wanted. At the other end are those interviews in which both parties are equal partners. The interviewer asks open questions, encourages the interviewee to introduce topics of importance, and allows the

Did You Know? ?

Body language in the interview situation often expresses perceptions of status and power. In an interview between people of different cultures, it's important to pay attention to body language.

interviewee to ask questions of his own. This style of interviewing, sometimes called the "nondirected interview," is effective in finding out the interviewee's attitudes and perceptions or in exploring a problem for the first time.

The dimension of control is also related to the roles assumed by the participants. For example, if the interviewer is perceived as having a much higher status or more power than the interviewee (such as in the employment interview—see 6.5), the interviewee is likely to expect a directed interview. If the interviewer wants to conduct a less directed interview, she'll have to use particular skills to reduce the effect of perceived roles. Conversely, if the interviewer is perceived as having a lower status (say, a student interviewing a library director for a school project), the interviewee may attempt to direct the interview, possibly reframing some of the questions or asking questions of his own.

Trust

How much trust is there between the interviewer and the interviewee? The range goes from the hostile interview, in which neither side trusts the other, to the mutual trust interview, in which both participants respect and trust the other. The hostile interview, exemplified in an extreme form by the police interrogation, provides the poorest possible climate for either giving or receiving information. Again, this dimension is often affected by the participants' perceptions of roles and status. When interviewers spend time at the beginning of an interview to establish rapport, they are increasing the level of trust.

Duration

How long does the interview last? The typical reference interview lasts three minutes or less, but a reference interview with a scientist in a special library who wants the librarian to find relevant research for an ongoing research project may last for 20 minutes or longer. Interviews for hiring, performance appraisal, and counseling typically last up to an hour. Research interviews (e.g., oral history) may be even longer or may extend over a series of one- or two-hour sessions. The length of the interview may be within the interviewer's control, or it may be constrained by other factors including the time that either the interviewer or interviewee can devote to the interview.

Structure

Unlike ordinary conversation, an interview (directed or nondirected) has a structure that must reflect its purpose. The stages of an interview usually are:

1. establishing rapport;
2. general information gathering or getting the big picture;
3. specific information gathering;
4. intervention, such as giving information, advice, or instructions; and
5. ending, including feedback or summary.

These stages can be iterative, occurring in loops throughout the interview, as, for example, when the interviewer needs to reestablish rapport or do some more general information gathering before the interview ends. Three patterns for the structure of the interview are recognizable:

The funnel sequence. The interview begins with open conversation and moves toward closed questioning and specific information gathering or information giving at the end.

The inverse funnel sequence. The interview begins with specific information gathering and moves toward more open conversation.

The tunnel sequence. The interview proceeds through a series of the same kind of questions throughout.

Environment

Physical surroundings profoundly affect the nature and outcome of an interview. The environment can range from reassuring to intimidating. (For an extreme example of the latter, think of the prisoner being questioned under a naked light bulb.) The employee selection interview (6.5.1) can be conducted in a pleasant room with both participants seated in comfortable chairs with no barriers between them. Or the applicant may face a panel of interviewers seated behind a large table.

The interviewer generally has some control over the environment and can usually arrange the furniture to reduce the physical barriers between participants. Even in a busy public library, the reference librarian can walk with the user into the stacks to gain more privacy. And the supervisor can choose a neutral room (neither the employee's office nor the employer's office) for a counseling interview.

6.3.3. All-Purpose Interviewing Skills

Certain basic skills are useful in every type of interview, including those conducted in settings as varied as social work, medicine, health services, management, vocational counseling, and journalism. To these settings, we can add information services. Allen E. Ivey has organized these basic skills as the microskills hierarchy (see 5.4). In libraries and information centers, the most useful skills for any kind of interview are those in the basic listening sequence—introduced in Chapter 2 of this book and elaborated in the sections on acknowledgment (3.2), encouragers (3.3), open questions (3.4), avoiding premature diagnosis (3.5), sense-making questions (3.6), follow-up questions (3.7), paraphrasing and summarization (3.8), reflecting feeling (3.9), and closure (3.11). In addition, the basic attending skills of culturally appropriate eye contact (1.2) and body language (1.3–1.5) enhance most kinds of interviews. The influencing skills—giving information, direction, explanation, feedback, and opinions (3.12–3.16)—are particularly useful for all types of interviews, including reference interviews, employment interviews, performance evaluation interviews, and counseling interviews.

Individual skills are learned one at a time. But once the individual skills have been mastered, the next step in the hierarchy is learning how to sequence and structure the interview. Finally comes the skill of integrating all these behaviors. In our discussion of this synthesizing process, where the focus is on the total interview, we will focus on interview situations unique to the information worker. The following section uses examples derived from what we are calling the *generic reference interview* or information interview.

6.4. Reference Interviews

Some say there's really no such thing as the reference interview—after all, library users are generally pretty clear about what they

---

Did You Know? ?

In some cultures, such as some North American Indian nations, people deliberately leave a silence between a statement or a question and the response as a sign that they are considering the answer very carefully. Many Anglo-Americans feel uneasy with this silence and tend to react by repeating or talking louder.

Did You Know? ?

Librarians aren't alone in making assumptions about what their users want. Other professionals do it too. Researchers who observed more than 400 counseling sessions found that in over half of these sessions, neither the client nor the counselor was aware, after the sessions, of what the other most wanted to discuss (Wertz, Sorenson, and Heeren, 1988).

want. They need only to be asked a question or two to clarify. And, anyway, how can you call a 90-second transaction an interview? On the other hand, that transaction is clearly a "conversation with a purpose." And learning more efficient and useful techniques for asking those one or two questions can help librarians provide more effective service.

The term *reference interview* suggests to most librarians a short interview conducted for the purpose of finding out what the user really wants to know. However, variations on this basic form often occur. For example, the interview tends to be longer when the user has already done a simple search on a search engine but has not found the needed information, quite possibly because the topic has complicated subject parameters. In other cases, where users prefer to do their own searching, the interview may include instruction in choosing an appropriate online database and constructing a search strategy. Then there is what we are calling the *secondhand reference interview* or imposed query—the interview in which you cannot communicate directly with the person who originated the question but must work through an intermediary. The *research reference interview*, conducted with researchers who often want very specialized information, offers further complications.

So far we have been mentioning interviews that use face-to-face communication that can take advantage of the rich information provided by voice and body language. In other forms, the information is reduced: the *telephone interview*, where the medium is the voice only; and *the virtual reference interview*, where the medium is text, transmitted through e-mail or instant messaging or chat. And finally there is the *readers' advisory interview*, where the librarian needs to find out what a user wants to read before making recommendations.

All of these interviews in their various guises can be defined simply as a conversation between the librarian and the user in which the librarian asks one or more questions in order to (1) get a clearer and more complete picture of what the user wants to know and (2) link the user to the system. In addition to these purposes of query negotiation, the reference interview may include related functions—giving instructions or directions (3.12); getting feedback (3.15); offering suggestions (3.16); and following up (3.7). See Ross, Nilsen, and Radford (2009: 1–4) for a discussion of how reference interviews differ from other interviews and why a well-conducted interview is not just a friendly conversation.

Did You Know? ?

In Maryland, a three-day workshop given to 200 staff in 14 public libraries raised the percentage of complete and accurate answers from 55 percent to 77 percent. The Maryland consultants identified the three most important reference behaviors in order of importance: paraphrasing or repeating the question (acknowledgment); asking a follow-up question; and using open questions (Isenstein, 1992).

6.4.1. The Generic Reference Interview

Although all reference interviews are unique, they have common structural features and go through similar stages: establishing contact with the user, finding out the user's need, and confirming. The interview can go wrong in predictable ways, and there are standard ways of recovering from "communication accidents." Your behavior during the interview is the major predictor of success. Users almost always attribute the success or failure of a reference transaction to relational factors (Radford, 1999: 76–77; Ross, Nilsen, and Radford, 2009: 10–15).

The Reference and User Services Association's (2004) "Guidelines for Behavioral Performance of Reference and Information Service Providers" provide benchmarking standards for both face-to-face and virtual reference interviews that you can use both to improve your own interview success and to train others. The guidelines list five component behaviors (approachability, interest, listening, inquiring, searching, and follow-up) that are essential for success. We discussed approachability as essential in the first 60 seconds of any one-to-one interaction (see 6.1.1). The remaining interpersonal communication behaviors (showing interest, listening, inquiring, and follow-up) are incorporated into the following discussion.

Establishing Contact

Reference interviews often start out in one of two ways: the user asks a very general question ("What have you got on transportation?") or the user asks a very specific question ("Could I see the *Encyclopedia of Addictions*?"). When these questions are answered literally ("Thousands of books, articles, and clippings on transportation" or "Here's the call number for that encyclopedia"), the answers may not help the user. Suppose, for example, the users in these examples wanted the name of the company that built a local incline railway or the times and places of nearby Narcotics Anonymous meetings. The literal answer may not help.

But why would a person wanting a company name ask for information on transportation? Why don't people say what they want in the first place? Brenda Dervin has coined the term *Bad Guy User* to describe the person who won't use the system on our terms—the one who refuses to read signs and follow instructions or the one who asks for "books on transportation" when it's clear there are thousands of such books. All of us, from time to time, are Bad Guy Users in other people's systems, particularly when that system is unfamiliar. (Have you ever called up a government department and asked for "information on bylaws" or asked a bus driver "Is this the bus to Albuquerque?" when the sign clearly says "Albuquerque"?)

Linguists have an explanation for what seems to be the perverse way in which people phrase their initial requests for help. This explanation is based on the fact that language can have several functions, including exchanging information and establishing contact. At the outset of the reference interview, the librarian expects from the user an exchange of information in the form of a clear statement of the information need. But the user's first concern is to establish contact. The user has tacit questions in mind that need answering before he can go on to clarify his need for information: Am I in the right place? Are you available and listening to me? Are you the person who's going to help me? Can you help me with a problem that falls into this general area?

You need to respond in a way that answers these unspoken questions. **PACT** is an acronym for remembering what the user wants to know first:

> **P**lace is right
> **A**vailable and listening
> **C**ontact made
> **T**opic (in general) understood

Communicate these responses through nonverbal skills such as eye contact, smiling, and standing up (see 1.1–1.5) and through verbal skills such as acknowledgment (3.2) and encouragers (3.3). When the user asks for books on transportation, look up, perhaps stand up, smile, and acknowledge the user immediately; for example, "'Transportation, uh-huh." By using PACT, you establish the contact that will encourage the user to tell you more.

Finding Out What Is Wanted

After you establish contact, you still have to find out what the person wants to know. This next stage in the reference interview involves the integration of skills introduced in Chapter 3 (see 3.4 for open and closed questions, 3.5 for avoiding premature diagnosis, 3.6 for sense-making questions, 3.10 for inclusion, and 3.12 for giving instructions).

Exercise

A Costly Misunderstanding
The user of a rural branch library has asked for "a book on bats." "Bats as in an animal? Not baseball bats?" asked the librarian, using acknowledgment to avoid premature diagnosis. "Bats that fly, yes," confirmed the user. So the librarian checked the system catalog, identified a new book on bats, ordered it from the central library, and within a week proudly presented the user with a beautiful natural history book that had a hundred color plates and everything you could possibly want to know about bats. But not quite everything. The user was very disappointed. "I wanted to know how to get rid of them," he said.

1. What could the librarian have asked the user to avoid this misunderstanding?
2. What could be the economic consequences of this misunderstanding?
3. Might there be other consequences?
4. How serious are the consequences from the viewpoint of the user, from the viewpoint of the branch librarian, and from the viewpoint of headquarters?
5. What training or procedures would help to avoid this problem in the future?

What's the Real Question?

This is a group exercise.

In your group, think back to a conversation that you had with a library user in which it was not initially clear what that person really wanted to find out. What did the user first ask? What did you think might be wanted? What did the problem turn out to be? How did you find this out? Collect examples and write keywords for each on the blackboard or flip chart under headings Initial Question and Negotiated Question, for example, Books on entomology and How to get rid of ants.

Leader's notes: This exercise is more useful for practitioners with some experience. Give each participant a few moments to recall a situation. Then ask for volunteers to describe, briefly, the user's first question and the question as it finally turned out. When you have five or six examples, open general discussion. What patterns, if any, can be seen in these examples? Why do you think someone would come into a library and say, "Where are your books on Canada?" when he really wants a picture of an attacking grizzly bear for a book he is illustrating?

A good reference librarian uses the skills intentionally and combines them to advance the purpose of the interview.

The **What People Really Want to Know** chart gives some examples of initial questions, as presented by actual library users, and the negotiated or "real" questions. Reference staff shared these examples with us in our various reference workshops when we asked participants, "Can you think of a time when the real question turned out to be something quite different from what the user initially asked for?"

What People Really Want to Know

Initial question	Negotiated question
Where are your books on entomology?	How do I get rid of ants?
Do you have a rare book collection?	Will you buy my grandmother's books?
I need a book on office organization.	How can I get along better with a co-worker?
Have you got *Down on Broad Street*?	I was told to ask for Dun and Bradstreet.
I need a book on fashion.	Where can I get advice on what to wear to a funeral?

Moving from the initial question to the negotiated question is much easier if you use microskills. If you take the question at face value, without encouraging the user to clarify and expand the question for you, you can both end up in real trouble, or at least waste a lot of time. Consider, for example, what might happen if you jump to conclusions about the following request, without asking any questions: "Do you have material on China?"

Six Common Causes of Communication Accidents

Inexperienced interviewers, including librarians conducting reference interviews, tend to have predictable communication accidents that can be avoided or at least remedied through the use of basic microskills. The following list provides you with six common causes of communication accidents:

1. **Not acknowledging the user.** Establish immediate contact with the user by acknowledging her presence

through eye contact (1.2) and gestures and by restating the initial question (3.2).

2. **Not listening.** The inexperienced interviewer talks more than the experienced interviewer, who listens more. Librarians who are talking or thinking ahead about search strategy aren't listening (2.3). Practice active listening. Pause (1.4) or use an encourager (3.3) instead of responding at length to everything the user says. To show that you are listening, use appropriate body language, reflect content and feeling (3.8 and 3.9), and summarize (3.8).

3. **Playing 20 questions.** An open (3.4) or sense-making (3.6) question such as "What would you like to know about X?" will get you further in less time than playing 20 questions and asking, "Is it this? Is it that?"

4. **Interrupting at inappropriate times.** If you're talking or cutting the user off when the user is telling you something that's relevant to the query, you're not listening (2.3). Use closure (3.11) to direct the conversation and pauses or encouragers to signal the user that it's her turn to talk.

5. **Making assumptions.** Some assumptions (e.g., that the user would like some kind of help) are necessary. Assumptions based on the user's appearance or on your own perception of the problem are usually inaccurate and may offend if you make them explicit. Avoid premature diagnosis (3.5). Instead, ask sense-making questions (3.6), such as, "Could you tell me a little bit about how you plan to use this information?"

6. **Not following up.** Recover from other communication accidents by following up (3.7). Ask a closed or open follow-up question: "Did that help you? What other help would you like?" Even when you're busy, invite the user to ask for further help or give instructions ("If you don't find it, ask the person at the Information Desk").

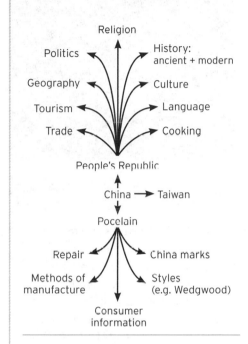

A Quick Tip ⏱

Are You Interested?

The Reference and User Services Association's (2004) guidelines say that users indicate higher levels of satisfaction when librarians demonstrate a high degree of interest in helping them. In face-to-face interviews, you do this by maintaining eye contact and signaling your understanding through verbal and nonverbal behavior. In virtual reference interviews, maintaining "word contact" lets the user know that you are still there and still interested.

Exercise 🔧

The 55 Percent Problem

Many research studies indicate that only about 55 percent of the answers provided by reference librarians are accurate. For a group discussion, ask group members to read the Hernon and McClure (1986) article that first articulated the 55 percent rule. Discuss to what extent the accuracy rate could be increased by a more effective reference interview.

Exercise

Discover the Real Question

This role-playing exercise can be done as a group exercise with two volunteers playing the part of the user and the librarian, with the rest of the group as observers. If desired, a new set of volunteers can be recruited for each role-played scenario. Materials needed are cards, prepared in advance, for the users' roles and a stop watch. Each user card includes a single initial question that the user asks, plus a scenario that gives some background information about the question. Some examples are given here. Think up initial questions and scenarios of your own for additional cards.

Scenarios

- **Initial question:** "I need to get some statistics." The user is a student who wants statistics on production of canola oil in various countries for a project assigned in a geography course.
- **Initial question:** "Where should I look for information on snow conditions?" The user is planning a trip to Colorado in early March and wants to know if there will still be any snow?
- **Initial question:** "Where should I look for information on allergies?" The user has a family member with allergies and wants recipes that do not contain gluten. The user would also be interested in contact information for a local support group for people with gluten allergies.
- **Initial question:** "Where is your music section?" The user wants to know why Nova Scotia fiddlers play Celtic music.
- **Initial question:** Where is your literature section? The user wants a list of local authors who write adult fiction to take to her next book club meeting. The user is interested in both literary fiction and popular fiction in any genre.

Roles

- **User role:** The user presents the initial question and thereafter answers only closed questions, responding "yes," "no," "this," or "that." The user must be careful not to volunteer any information and not to answer it by mistake if the librarian asks an open question before the three-minute time limit is up.
- **Librarian role:** The librarian is instructed to find out as quickly as possible what the user wants to know, using only closed questions.
- **Observer role:** Observers watch to make sure that all questions are closed, to count the number of closed questions asked, and to call time if the librarian does not discover the true query in three minutes. If the query is not fully negotiated in three minutes, the librarian may at this point ask open questions and the user improvises answers according to the scenario on the card.

Discussion

After each role-play, the group leader may ask the observers to analyze what happened in the interview. Which questions worked, which didn't, and what was the difference between asking open questions and closed questions?

6.4.2. The Secondhand Reference Interview and the Imposed Query

In some situations you cannot communicate directly or immediately with the user who has the question. You receive the reference query secondhand, mediated through a written message or through a second party, who might not know the context for the question. For example, you might be expected to do a search from a written request or search form that the user has filled in and left at the information desk. You could receive an interlibrary loan (ILL) request by telephone through an intermediary or be forwarded a question through a consortial reference agreement with another library. You might have just a secondhand account of the information needed. (A colleague might say to you, "Jen, I'm leaving now. Would you get some stuff on rock paintings for Mr. Martin? He'll pick it up at six" or "Jen, I'm leaving for the day. Dr. Habib is having her graduate class come over tonight. Could you pull some materials on U.S. economics for her?")

If you feel you don't have a complete picture of what the user wants, try to contact the person who spoke to the user. ("Hold it, Antonio, tell me more about what Mr. Martin said he needed. What kind of rock paintings? What does he want to know about rock painting?" or "Antonio, before you leave, do you have a phone extension for Dr. Habib, so I can call her to find out more about what her students need?") If the intermediary didn't do an adequate reference interview, you should contact the user directly before you put in much searching time, request an ILL, or e-mail or fax a lot of materials. When there's no way of contacting the user, the best you can do is to find one or two examples of what you think may be wanted (as a gesture of good intentions) and invite feedback through a note asking the user to e-mail or call back if this material doesn't help (a written version of the follow-up question).

A better way to solve this problem is to prevent it. Make sure that everyone who is in a position to receive requests knows the importance of the reference interview and knows how to ask at least one or two basic questions, such as, "What would you like to find out about X?" Then ask everyone who might receive a request to write down everything the user says while the conversation is happening—this reduces the chance of premature diagnosis (3.5) or incorrect interpretation. You can also avoid some communication accidents and save a lot of time by routinely asking the user, "If we have any trouble finding this, do you mind if we call you to get more information?" and take a number. These should be routine procedures for accepting requests, no matter how clear the requests may seem to be.

Imposed Queries

A variation of the secondhand reference interview is the "imposed query," a situation in which the question the user asks at the reference desk was actually generated by someone else. Imposed queries are asked at someone else's request: for example, a wife asks a question on behalf of her husband; a student asks a question that is generated by a school assignment; an employee asks a question to get information for a boss. When questions are imposed and not self-generated, problems often arise because the person asking the question may not fully understand it, may not know much about the context in which the question arose, and may not be aware of the use to which the desired information is to be put.

Melissa Gross (1995), whose pioneering work on the imposed query has established the terminology generally used, calls the person who generates the question "the imposer" and the person who asks the question "the agent." She has pointed out that when the person asking the question is not the person who generated the question, "many [of the recommended] question-negotiation techniques lose their effectiveness" (Gross, 1999: 54). That's because recommended interview skills succeed by tracking the question back to its origins in the life of the user, a limited strategy when the person you are dealing with doesn't know. Here are some tips for handling the imposed query:

- Identify at the outset the kind of question you are dealing with. Is it self-generated, or is it an imposed query? But avoid asking a closed question (3.4), such as, "Do you need this information for a school assignment?" Instead, ask something like, "Can you tell me a bit about how this information will be used?"
- Ask open questions that get the user to talk about what he *does* know, not what he doesn't. The agent doesn't know as much as the imposer, but he will know *something* about the context. A student with a school assignment may not know much about the topic but does know what course the assignment is for, what the grade level is, when the essay is due, and how long the essay is supposed to be. Ask:

What did your teacher tell you about this assignment?

If you have the assignment sheet handy that your
teacher gave you, it might help if I took a look
at it.

What requirements does your teacher have for this
assignment?

- In the case of an agent asking a question on behalf of a
  neighbor, friend, or family member, ask sense-making
  questions (3.6) that tap the situation, gaps, or uses,
  such as:

Can you give me some idea of how your friend/
husband/daughter/father will be using this
information?

Can you tell me a little bit about the situation
your friend is in, where he will be using this
information?

- In the case of an employee asking a question for a boss, give
  the agent something to take back to the boss—your best
  guess based on what is wanted. Then use a follow-up (3.7)
  with a special twist. Essentially you are teaching the agent
  how to ask the right question of the supervisor in order to
  be a better go-between. Say to the agent:

When you give this material to your supervisor, ask
if it completely answers her question. If not, tell
her that we can find other materials if she can tell
you what specifically is missing in the materials
provided.

If this isn't the information that your supervisor
wanted, it would help if you asked her what
specifically she wants to know about X and how
she hopes the information will help.

6.4.3. The Research Reference Interview

Reference interviews with users who are researchers (e.g., graduate
students, scholars or scientists affiliated with an institution, or adult

Did You Know? ?

Data curation seeks to manage research data for the long term so that it is available for reuse and preservation. Libraries are increasingly involved in curating these data, and reference librarians are often expected to take on this role. Jake Carlson (2012: 7) explains that conducting a data interview "can be a daunting task given the complexity of data curation and the lack of shared definitions . . . [and] reference librarians will need to be trained in conducting data interviews with researchers to better understand their data and associated needs."

independent learners) require the same skills that work for the generic reference interview, but there are also some important differences. Some librarians work in research libraries where they routinely work with researchers in the early stages of their projects. The librarian may be involved in planning search strategies, finding the needed literature, and, in some special libraries, preparing summaries of the literature. In other cases, before approaching the librarian, the researcher may have done some preliminary searching and not found the needed information. As with the generic reference interview, the librarian needs to find out specifically what a researcher wants to know. However, the interviewer needs to consider some special characteristics of the research interview:

- Because the research interview is often scheduled by appointment, there is more time and privacy. These conditions allow the interviewer to plan the structure of the interview, to probe more, and to encourage the user to talk more.
- The user's expectations will vary. Some researchers may think that the librarian really can't add anything to what they already know about finding information in their own field. Others may be more open to learning about various reference tools and the appropriate search strategies.
- Rapport and common ground needs to be established with the researcher. While the librarian tries to find out what the researcher needs to know, the researcher is evaluating the librarian's awareness of the research literature and the methodologies of the discipline. The questions the librarian asks will be used to judge the librarian's competence and/ or can be seen as a challenge to the researcher's own competence.
- The librarian's anxieties about understanding specialized technical terms, developing a good search strategy, recommending appropriate databases, and formulating search terms may interfere with her ability to listen.
- The librarian may need to do more initial information giving—why keyword searching may be insufficient, how a particular database differs from another, why a particular database provides more information than another, how multiple databases can be searched simultaneously, and so forth.

- System constraints make certain closed questions necessary: "Do you want abstracts or not? Just English or other languages?" Ask these after the interview but before you search.

Some Useful Questions for the Research Interview

Defining the problem:
Please tell me about the problem you're working on.
What would you like to find out about X?
What are some other things that X might be called?
If you could find the perfect journal article, what would its title be?

Helps and uses:
What do you hope to find out as a result of this search?
What will the search results help you do?
How are you going to use this information?

Identifying barriers:
What have you done so far?
What happened when you did that?
What has helped you the most so far?
What is still missing from the materials you've found so far?

Interviewing the End User

The end user is someone who is going to do his own online searching on the web or using the library's online collections. The end user interview is a conversation between the librarian and the end user that will mostly focus on what the user knows or doesn't know about the system, what help is needed, and how the user can get the best results. But it should also include some element of query negotiation, because the librarian needs to know enough about the query to give useful instructions or advice. The end user interview therefore has two levels and purposes:

> **A Quick Tip** 🕐
>
> **Adaptable Skills**
> Although ideas in this section are geared to complex subject searches, they can also be adapted for simpler tasks, such as helping users to search the library's catalog for a specific title.

- The query level, where the librarian's purpose is to find out about the problem that initiated the search
- The system level, where the librarian's purpose is to help the user with the searching procedures

At the query level, one of the most useful things the librarian can do is teach the end user how to interview himself. First, explain that a clearly formulated information need produces more effective search results. Ask the user to think about what he'd like to find out, how that would help him, and how he plans to use the information. Or make up a handout or poster listing such questions (see **Before Starting Your Search**). Explain that answering these questions will improve search results.

Before Starting Your Search Ask Yourself These Questions

- What do I know already about this topic?
- What do I want to know?
- How do I plan to use this information?
- How will the search results help me? What will they help me do?
- What aspect of this topic concerns me most?
- What results are not likely to help me? What do I *not* want to know?
- If I could have any help at all, what would it be? What format would it be in (e.g., maps, statistics, a bibliography)?

Thinking about the answers to these questions will help you improve your search results.

At the system level of the interview, the librarian needs to find out how much the user already knows about the system, what's missing in the user's understanding of the system, what might stop the user, and what kind of help the user needs. Avoid assumptions (3.5) about the user's experience and abilities. Leave the user in control by asking sense-making questions (3.6) such as:

> Tell me what you know about searching on this system.
> What happened the last time you did a search?
> What parts of this procedure concern you?
> What would help you most right now to get started with your search?

Other skills for helping the end user include giving instructions (3.12), inclusion (3.10), and giving suggestions (3.16). Remember to be specific, follow up, and ask for feedback. Don't overload the user with too much information at once.

6.4.4. The Telephone Reference Interview

In addition to the skills needed for effective telephone communication in general (see 6.2), there are additional skills needed to conduct the telephone reference interview. Special features of telephone reference are by-products of the technology used. You and the user can't see each other or rely on visual cues. You can't use the physical setting as a prop for the interaction or work through a problem by showing the user a book or resource and getting her feedback. And you can't very easily provide bibliographic instruction. But you can provide convenient service to mobile users who want to talk to a real person and connect from any location.

Interview Skills for the Telephone

Good interviewing skills and attentive listening are especially important in the telephone reference interview, because you lose all visual cues. Users don't see your welcoming smile, and they can't know what you are doing unless you tell them. Unlike in the e-mail or chat interview, however, nonverbal cues can be expressed through the voice. Remember that for the caller your voice represents the whole library.

In addition to general suggestions for using the telephone (section 6.2.1) and for conducting the generic reference interview (6.4.1), here are some specific suggestions for conducting a telephone reference interview:

- Use PACT (6.4.1) to establish contact and to reassure the user that you are indeed the right person to be answering the question.
- Acknowledge (3.2) the user's initial question by restating or rephrasing it.
- Ask open questions (3.4) and sense-making questions (3.6) to find out what the caller really wants to know.
- Listen. Listening skills (2.4) are even more important in the telephone interview than in the face-to-face interview, because you lack the visual cues that might let you know that things are going off track.
- Write down the question while the caller is still on the phone. Check spellings, dates, and other particulars with the caller. As you are writing it down, you may realize that

---

Did You Know? ?

Users who called the reference desk by telephone were the original remote, interactive real-time users. A 1956 advertisement for a library telephone service reads remarkably like promotions for today's chat services. It advised users, "You don't have to come to the library in person" (Kern, 2004: 12).

Did You Know? ?

Libraries continue to provide telephone reference, even as other forms of remote reference grow in popularity. Responding to a 2001 survey, all 70 university library directors indicated that their libraries still offered telephone reference. A 1993 analysis of telephone inquiries at a university library found that about one-third of the calls were reference queries, similar to results of a public library study a decade earlier (Agosto and Anderton, 2007: 45-46).

you don't quite understand what the caller really wants to know about migration patterns in Wales (or was it whales?).

- Explain what you are doing (3.10)—remember that the caller can't see you.
- Don't leave the caller on hold. If finding an answer will take longer than a minute or so, offer to take the number and call back or e-mail/text/fax the answer.
- Refer, if you can't answer the question yourself. Say something like, "Let me transfer you to Martha Avery, our reference librarian who specializes in legal materials."
- Say, "If this source doesn't completely answer your question, make sure you call back and we can try something else."
- Keep a record of the question and the sources found, especially if the question is likely to require a follow-up by someone else later.

6.4.5. The Virtual Reference Interview

Joe Janes (2008) says, "Give users and libraries the tools by which to communicate, and those tools will get used for reference transactions." He points out that successive waves of new technologies have been used for reference service: reference by letters mailed back and forth in the nineteenth century; telephone reference by the mid-1920s; e-mail reference by the 1990s. And now there's what looks like a deluge of digital options, some quite well established and others more experimental, such as reference provided in virtual reality systems such as Second Life and reference incorporated into a social networking site such as Facebook. In this section, we focus on what Janes calls "the stand-by tools" and emphasize the bias of communication introduced by the technology used for virtual or digital reference.

The main benefit of virtual reference for users is that they can now reach the library around the clock. The Reference and User Services Association (2010) defines virtual reference as a "reference service initiated electronically, often in real-time," where users' communication with reference staff is mediated through computers or other Internet technology, including e-mail, chat, videoconferencing, VoIP (voice-over Internet protocol), instant messaging (IM), and text messaging, also known as short message service (SMS). Questions arrive from users who may be on the other side of the world, or they may be working right in your own information commons.

The virtual reference interview can be sorted into categories along two different dimensions, depending on (1) whether it takes place synchronously (in real time) or asynchronously (not in real time) and (2) whether the medium is voice (or voice plus video) or text. Successful use of these media depends on paying attention to the bias of the medium used, maximizing strengths while trying to minimize limitations. The purpose of virtual reference remains the same as any other kind of reference service: to help users find the information they need to fulfill purposes in their own lives and to do it in a way that saves users' time and respects them as persons.

Dimensions of Technologies Used for VR Interviews

	Synchronous in Real Time	Asynchronous
Text-based	Instant messaging Chat	E-mail Texting (mobile phone)
Voice or voice plus video	Telephone VoIP Video-conferencing Skype	Voice mail

The first and second rules for providing a successful virtual reference service (VRS) are that people need to know that you offer the service and the service needs to be easily accessible. Just as the reference service in the physical library should not be hidden away, so the VRS should not be buried four levels deep in the website. A study based on focus group interviews with graduate students who were nonusers of VRS found that the most frequent reason given for nonuse (73 percent) was that they didn't know the service existed (Connaway, Radford, and Dickey, 2008).

The digital counterpart to creating a welcoming physical environment is creating visible, easy-to-use web links and well-designed, easily navigated webpages. VRS must be immediately available through highly visible links on the library's main page. When advertising your VRS, make sure that people understand your policy on the kinds of help they can (and can't) expect. For e-mail and texting, give people an idea of how long it will take for them to receive an answer. Connaway, Radford, and Dickey (2008) recommend that the best way to convert nonusers into users of VRS is to market to mobile users the convenience of a service available 24/7 from anywhere with net access. They also recommend that you emphasize the privacy and confidentiality of VRS and integrate VRS into library use instruction and courseware.

E-mail Reference Interviews

With a history in libraries that goes back at least 20 years, e-mail reference is a firmly established basic service with wide appeal. Many users choose the convenience of e-mail reference because they can ask their questions whenever they think of them, at any time of the day or night, and from any location. Texting reference questions using mobile phones is a newer twist (see 9.3.3). For both the users and the librarians, the advantages and drawbacks of e-mail reference are two sides of the same coin: its asynchronous, text-based nature. Here are some key features of this stripped-down, asynchronous environment that affect the reference interview:

- The text-based environment of e-mail, like that of chat and instant messaging, eliminates both visual and auditory cues. Correctly interpreting the tone of a text-based exchange can be challenging, and misunderstandings are not uncommon.
- Providing a typed rather than a spoken answer takes more time and requires writing skills, including the use of correct spelling and grammar. A higher standard is expected for e-mail writing in comparison with the less formal on-the-fly writing of chat sessions.
- Deprived of nonverbal cues, you can't tell whether the user is a child or a senior citizen, male or female. You will be less likely to jump to conclusions based on assumptions derived from physical appearances (see Avoiding Premature Diagnosis, 3.5). However, you still need to avoid making assumptions based on grammar, writing style, or spelling mistakes. For many topics, you will need to take extra steps to find out about the user's level of literacy and ability to make sense of specialized or technical information.
- In face-to-face, live chat, or phone reference interviews, turn-taking does not increase the total length of the transaction. Turns are often short—remember those minimal encouragers (3.3) such as "umm-hmm"—and

Did You Know? **?**

E-mail reference can be a useful option for people who are not native English speakers. They may not speak English well enough to feel comfortable asking questions face-to-face or by telephone, but often they can read and write English well enough to communicate.

the user's responses are immediate. But with the e-mail interview, turn-taking introduces delays, sometimes up to several days or more. The literature on e-reference refers to this phenomenon as "high dialogue penalties."

The secret to reducing turn-taking and its accompanying high dialogue penalties is to design a great webform. The form acts as a substitute for the reference interview and prompts the user to take many turns at once. Questions in a face-to-face reference interview are extended in time. The questions on the e-mail form are extended in space. The standard functions of welcoming the user, asking open and sense-making questions, using encouragers, avoiding premature diagnosis, and using inclusion all need to be incorporated into the form itself. If you use inclusion (3.10) to explain why you are asking for certain kinds of information, users are more likely to provide it.

Having set the stage by designing a good form, the next step is responding to the user's initial question that you get. In your first individualized reply, acknowledge the question by restating (3.2) what you understand the user has asked for. If your form has been well designed, you should be able to send some kind of answer immediately. But even with the best of forms, often a crucial piece of information is missing. Suppose the user has said, "I am working on a history paper on the Highland Clearances and immigration patterns, and I need materials and references. Any suggestions?"

Your response might acknowledge by saying, "I understand that you want information on immigration patterns of Highland Scots after 1745 and have assumed you are interested in emigration to North America. Here are the URLs for two sites that provide information on this (be sure to name the sites and indicate how to find the information). If this information isn't helpful or you want emigration to Australia or elsewhere or during a specific time period, please let me know what specifically is missing that you still need to know about." You will note that this response includes the follow-up, "If this information isn't helpful" (3.7). You may also want to encourage the user to give some kind of context for the search (e.g., "It often helps if you tell me a little bit about how you plan to use this information so that I can find the most helpful materials").

The key, as always, is to find out what the real question is. A well-designed form should eliminate many of the too-general initial questions ("everything on climate change"). But if the user's initial question is still unclear or too broad, there is no point in taking a

A Quick Tip ⏱

Copy a Good Model

When designing your form, look for good models. A good place to start is the Internet Public Library (IPL) reference question form (http://www.ipl.org/div/askus), which we think is one of the best—uncluttered and well laid out, with well-designed questions and explanations of why each question has been asked. For example, the excellent sense-making question, "How will you use this information?" is accompanied by this explanation: "Understanding the context and scope of your information needs helps us to deliver an answer that you will find useful."

scattergun approach to providing an answer, barraging the user with information in the hope that somehow some of it will be relevant. This approach doesn't work in face-to-face reference, and it won't work in the digital environment. It is better to respond with a small amount of information plus a request for clarification. Make sure that you ask in the same e-mail *all* the questions that you need to get answered.

Chat and Instant Messaging Reference Interviews

Virtual reference started with e-mail, but many libraries have augmented their e-mail reference service with a real-time live chat and instant messaging because they want to meet users where the users are. The 2004 Pew Internet and American Life surveys (Shiu and Lenhart, 2004) discovered that more than four in ten Americans who are online use instant messaging programs—some 53 million American adults. More recent data suggest that use of instant messaging could triple by 2016 because of the launch of new free services and the growing number of smartphone users (Ashdown, 2011).

Some libraries offer a stand-alone service, while others have joined consortia. National and international collaborative networks of linked libraries now enable an insomniac user in Pittsburgh to ask a question in the middle of the night and have it negotiated in real time by a librarian who is on duty at the virtual reference desk in England, India, or Australia. OCLC's QuestionPoint is the largest virtual reference collaborative, with more than 2,200 participating libraries in 100 countries and in 26 languages. Users of chat reference say that they appreciate the immediate response, the convenience of point-of-need help provided remotely, and the personalized service.

The key difference between e-mail reference on the one hand and chat and instant messaging reference service on the other is that the latter is offered in real time. The time lag between turns is a matter of seconds and minutes, not hours or days. As with face-to-face and telephone reference, you can ask for clarification or supplementary information and get it right away.

Chat and instant messaging reference shares with e-mail reference the lack of nonverbal cues. Connaway and Radford (2011: 45) stress that the chat librarian needs to take conscious steps to make up for the positive emotional and social cues that are missing in the text-based environment. A response intended to be simply concise may be interpreted as brusque or rude. They strongly recommend taking the time to add encouraging remarks, asking for patience,

A Quick Tip ⏱

Writing Text-Based Messages
Digital messaging presents special challenges. See section 9.3 for suggestions for writing messages in various platforms.

Did You Know? ?

A collaborative approach may involve as few as two libraries. But unless the participating libraries have different hours or are in different time zones, a 24/7 response is difficult to achieve. A large consortium can facilitate access to collection resources and specialized staff expertise. However, the participating library does need to adopt the policies and procedures of the consortium, even when these are not consistent with local preferences (Boss, 2010).

using a pleasant greeting and personal closing, and explaining what's going on—all ways to appear friendly in type when you can't do so in person.

One enhancement available with chat virtual reference technology is that it allows you to push webpages and co-browse databases with the user. You are able to demonstrate to the user how to find something on the web or how to enter search terms in databases. These features allow you to walk your user through the source to find the answers and to provide library use instruction. Complete transcripts of each chat session can be e-mailed to the user and archived so that a full record of the reference transaction is available, complete with URLs and instructions provided.

COMMUNICATION SKILLS FOR CHAT AND INSTANT MESSAGING

With real-time chat reference and instant messaging, everything has changed; nothing has changed. Well, actually both are true. The principles for the reference interview remain the same (see the generic reference interview in 6.4.1). People ask the same kinds of questions ("I want to find out if Johnny Depp has a band and if so how can I get their CD" [Radford, 2006: 1052]). Virtual reference users are just as likely as face-to-face users to ask an initial question that is too broad ("everything on autoimmune diseases") or too specific.

On the other hand, there are special challenges both in producing typed text quickly and in interpreting it in a context of overlapping transmissions, typographical shortcuts and errors, a lack of nonverbal cues, and a perceived need for speed. Marie Radford, who has done pioneering work on the relational aspects of face-to-face reference, has turned her attention to the dynamics of the chat reference interview. And what did she find? *Plus ça change, plus c'est la meme chose.*

Using an analytic framework that looks at conversational turns and sorts them into two categories—those that affect task functions and those that affect the relationship of the parties involved—Radford (2006) examined 44 chat reference transcripts submitted for a Samuel Swett Green Award for Exemplary Virtual Reference and compared them with 245 chat transcripts randomly selected from transactions of a statewide, chat reference service, Maryland AskUsNow! In particular, she focused on relational facilitators that enhanced communication and on relational barriers that hampered communication, illustrated with examples drawn from the transcripts.

Did You Know?   **?**

Transcripts of the chat reference transaction help users to capture the links to sites visited in the search. But transcripts are also useful as a training tool for chat reference librarians. Tammy Bobrowsky and colleagues from the University of Minnesota-Twin Cities point out, "A good chat transcript can teach a chat reference librarian how to conduct a chat reference interview or provide a good process to follow to find an answer. Transcripts are also great tools . . . to teach what not to do in a chat transaction" (Bobrowsky, Beck, and Grant, 2005: 179).

Did You Know?   **?**

The Seeking Synchronicity project (Connaway and Radford, 2011: 53) found that query clarification is almost always needed: "Our analysis revealed that only 4% (24) of interactions did not need some type of additional dialogue to further define the question." In virtual reference transactions, 74 percent (438) of librarians asked questions to find out what the user really wanted to know. This rate, said Connaway and Radford (2011: 53), is "higher than those reported in FTF [face-to-face] reference studies, which find that query clarification is done in between 45-60% of interactions" (Gers and Seward, 1985; Dewdney and Ross, 1994; Ross and Nilsen, 2000).

Relational facilitators included:

- rapport building ("conversation encouraging give and take, establishment of mutual understanding, and development of relationships");
- compensation for lack of nonverbal cues (e.g., use of informal shortcuts and text characteristics such as punctuation, emoticons, font, or abbreviations to convey meaning);
- deference (showing courtesy and respect for the other's experience, knowledge, or point of view); and
- the appropriate use of ritual greetings (e.g., "Hello" or "Hi") and ritual closings.

Relational barriers included:

- relational disconnect/failure to build rapport (failure to engage in the give and take that establishes mutual understanding and builds a trusting relationship); and
- closing problems (ending without a ritual goodbye or else using "negative closure," i.e., a strategy to end the transaction without providing a helpful answer).

It turns out that in computer-mediated communication, no less than in face-to-face communication, paying attention to relational aspects is not a frill but a critical element in being successful at the task.

Some Tips for Conducting the Chat Reference Interview

- Start with a personal greeting—it can be a quick "Hi!"—and use the person's first name in your exchanges.
- When reading the user's responses, look carefully for any self-disclosure that provides clues about the kind of help the user wants (something for a grade six student) or indicates something about the user's frame of mind (needs reassurance, is worried, etc.).
- Use reflection of feeling (3.9) when users self-disclose frustration or some difficulty (e.g., "Yes, it is frustrating when our technology doesn't work" or "I'm sorry you're not feeling well and can't travel to your library").
- Don't take the initial statement at face value and start firing off URLs right away. Ask open (3.4) or sense-making (3.6)

questions, such as, "What do you need to know about zebras?" or "What information on zebras would help you most?"

- If the information need is complex, let the user know how much time your search is likely to take (e.g., "I'm going to search sources X and Y, which may take about five minutes"). Ask if the user has the time to wait while you search.

- Maintain "word contact" with your user by providing short reassurances (e.g., "still searching . . .") so that users know that you are still working on their problem and haven't disconnected.

- Involve the user in the search process as a joint participant (e.g., "Let's try this" or "We'll look here first").

- Mirror the level of formality/informality of the users. If they use informal language, shortcuts, acronym, abbreviations, and emoticons, "chat speak," feel free to do so also (as appropriate and if you are comfortable doing so).

- Be deferential and respectful, using polite expressions such as *please*, *thanks*, *you're welcome* and apologizing as appropriate (e.g., *sorry*, *unfortunately*, *oops*).

- Always give a personal closing (can be a quick "Bye!") and end with an invitation to return if more help is needed (see discussion of follow-up in 3.7). (Adapted from © Marie L. Radford and OCLC Online Computer Library Center, Inc., 2008; see Ross, Nilsen, and Radford, 2009: 202, 204–205.)

Texting the Reference Interview

Integrating the use of mobile phones for texting using SMS into libraries' reference services has been underway since about 2005 in North America and earlier in Europe. SMS is a communications protocol that lets mobile phone users send text messages of 160 characters or fewer to one another, to an e-mail address, or to an instant message software application. Twitter supports an even briefer text message of up to 140 characters. Telephone reference (see 6.4.4) has a long history in libraries, and so it may seem odd to hear mobile phones being described as offering a new thing in reference service. Apart from the difference between voice-based and text-based communication, the new element here relates to mobility and the integration of mobile devices—and texting, tweeting, searching, reading, listening—into

---

Did You Know? ?

We might think of texting as a synchronous process—"you text me, I text you back"—but it is perfectly adaptable to asynchronous communication. Incoming texts can wait until you are able to answer. As with e-mail, auto-responses can be sent to the user letting them know their questions have been received and when they can expect a response.

Exercise

Anyone for Goldfish?

This exercise provides a chance to examine the dynamics of the text-based interview that takes place in real time. Here is an unedited transcript of a chat reference encounter in which a grade six student has asked for information on goldfish from the statewide, chat reference service Maryland AskUsNow! Published in Marie Radford's 2006 article, this transcript illustrates what can go wrong, even when the library staff member is doing a lot of things right. As background for your analysis of this transcript, take another look at the earlier material on relational facilitators and relational barriers. Note that the comments in square brackets in the transcript are prescripted messages.

1 Librarian: [A librarian will be with you in about 2 minutes.]

2 [Librarian XXX—A librarian has joined the session.]

3 Librarian: [Welcome to Maryland AskUsNow! I'm looking at your question right now; it will be just a moment.]

4 Librarian: What kind of information do you need about goldfish?

5 User: okay

6 User: I want to do alittle research for a school science fair project

7 Librarian: So you want to do a project with goldfish?

8 User: please don't send me things for science project ideas

9 User: thank you

10 Librarian: So what research do you need? There's lots of information about goldfish

11 User: i want to know everythingaboutfish and thier breathing rates with temperature

12 Librarian: OK, let me take a look

13 User: i want things for someone on a sixth grade level too

14 Librarian: I'll try. I'm looking

15 User: okay please hury it up thanks

<text omitted>

16 Librarian: I do have one page that may help. I'm sending it

17 [Item sent]

18 Librarian: The site is http://wise.berkeley.edu/WISE/evidence/220.html

19 Librarian: Take a look and I'm going to look a little further

20 Librarian: Here's another possibility. It's not goldfish specifically, but it's about fish

21 User: this is not what i'm looking for I want info on . . . . . . FISH!

[Item sent] http://wow.nrri.umn.edu/wow/under/parameters/oxygen.html

22 Librarian: You don't need to capitalize. Did you read the last paragraph?

23 User: I ONLY WANT GOLDFISH INFO GET THAT THROUGH YOUR THICK HEAD!

24 User: what is in the last paragraph?

25 Librarian: [If you need further assistance and can be more patient, please feel free to contact us again. Thank you for using Maryland AskUsNow! Goodbye!]

26 User: geta real job loser I bet your spose is cheatingon you! hahaha!

<end>

(Radford, 2006: 1054)

For discussion

1. Identify as many instances as you can of the librarian's effective use of communication skills. (For example, at line 4 the librarian asks a good open question, "What kind of information do you need about goldfish?") How many effective behaviors are related to the task of finding out what the user needs to know and providing an answer? How many are related to keeping the relationship on track—what Radford calls relational facilitators?

2. The user starts off using terms of politeness ("please" on line 8 and "thank you" on line 9) but becomes angry. Where do you think the transaction began to go off track and what makes you think so? What, if anything, could the librarian have done differently to produce a happier outcome?

3. Radford has identified behaviors by librarians that contribute to "relational disconnect" or failure to build rapport. These include: providing a robotic answer, reprimanding the user, limiting time, ignoring the user's question, condescending, ignoring self-disclosure, misunderstanding the user's question, mirroring the user's rude behavior. What role do any of these play in the dynamics of the transaction?

4. How do you think the computer-mediated communication may have affected the outcome of this transaction?

Exercise

Character Limit in SMS

Here are four of examples of questions received and questions answered by the Southeastern Louisiana University's text-a-librarian service, as provided by Hill, Hill, and Sherman (2007: 26). Note the range of reference questions asked and the ingenuity of the answers in compressing much in little. SMS and tweets are to texts what haiku is to poetry: a very condensed genre with its own specialized conventions.

Q1. *(question after Hurricane Katrina)* When does school start back, i dont have electricity so i can watch the news so i dont know if they said.

A. Classes resume Thurs, Sept. 8. Students have been advised 2 use their own judgment on returning 2 campus. Absences will B forgiven 4 the foreseeable future. (156 characters)

Q2. What year did Texas become a state?

A. Hi. The official annexation day for Texas was 12/29/1845. 4 More C the Texas Handbook: http://www. tsha.utexas.edu/Handbook /online/articles/AA/mga2.html (153 characters)

Q3. I need info on ethical issues of human cloning and stem cell research?

A. Under Databases, 1st look @ CQResearcher 4 a good overview, then try Academic Search Premier 4 journal articles. If U login 2 Chat we can show U more. (150 characters)

Q4. How do I find empirical articles online?

A. We've databases that will help U locate empirical research articles; e.g. PsycInfo 4 psychology. Many of the DBs have specific limits. What's your topic? (153 characters)

(From Hill, Hill, and Sherman, 2007: 26)

For discussion

1. How many *different* communication functions can you identify in the librarian's answers (e.g., greeting, information providing, providing instructions, evaluating, asking questions, following up, citing sources, etc.). Label each separate unit within the answer according to what function it performs. Are there any words or phrases that perform no function?
2. In which of these exchanges did a reference interview happen (i.e., the librarian asked one or more questions for the purpose of finding out what the user wanted)?
3. What communication skills does a reference librarian need to cultivate if she wants to be able to match these model SMS answers?

the warp and woof of phone users' daily lives on the move. A Pew Internet survey of mobile phone users (Rainie and Fox, 2012) reports the emergence of "a new culture of real-time information seekers and problem solvers." One finding was that 70 percent of all cell phone users and 86 percent of all smartphone users had used their phones in the past 30 days to get "just-in-time" information in the course of their everyday life—to coordinate a meeting, solve an unexpected problem, make a decision about a destination, settle an argument, or look up a sports score.

Some libraries have responded by setting up a text-a-librarian service that is incorporated into their suite of face-to-face, telephone, e-mail, and chat reference services. Many of the questions received are short and asked repeatedly (e.g., opening times, holiday schedules, location of library branches), and these can be answered using an answer template. Users can request renewals or holds, and library staff can text users regarding due dates, fines, and the like. But users are also asking reference questions, the majority being questions with expected short answers such as "Who wrote *The Sun Also Rises*?"

Libraries have so far reported low use of SMS reference, but use may grow. Hill, Hill, and Sherman (2007: 26) speculate that in college and university settings users are deterred by the character limit per message that makes for terse SMS communication. They suggest that e-mail and chat are "better suited for research questions that cannot be adequately answered by short answers."

Users, however, often don't know in advance how hard a question is or what kind of answer to expect. Staff of a new text-a-librarian service at Oregon State University anticipated questions that could be answered with quick simple responses, but one of their first questions was, "What is the function of interneurons?" (Miller, 2010). The expansion of texting as a communication medium and the unexpectedly complex nature of some questions suggest that reference staff need to use ingenuity when responding to short texted reference questions and find ways to create an integrated, flexible reference service where a question might start off as an SMS text or a tweet and then cross over into voice or face-to-face as appropriate. As Joe Janes of the University of Washington has said, "It's all reference."

6.4.6. The Readers' Advisory Interview

The readers' advisory interview is focused on helping readers find materials they want to read, listen to, or view for pleasure. In this section, we focus on the face-to-face readers' advisory interview, with the proviso that the principles be adapted to telephone and virtual reference as well.

In the revival of readers' advisory work that has happened since the early 1980s, the emphasis was initially on fiction books. More recently, however, the literature on readers' advisory has recognized that people also read nonfiction for pleasure and that a variety of formats are relevant, not just printed books but also e-books, audiobooks, and films. We use the term *book* in this section as a shorthand, but all kinds of materials that a user might want for pleasure should be understood. Whatever the genre and format desired, essentially the readers' advisory transaction is a matchmaking service. It's what happens when someone asks, "Can you recommend a good book?" (See also 8.5.2 on booktalking.)

The readers' advisory interview resembles the reference interview in requiring similar communication skills. First set the stage by being approachable, and then use appropriate skills of questioning and listening. However, the readers' advisory interview differs from the reference interview in one important way, which is the requirement to engage readers in a conversation about books. Readers must be encouraged to talk about the kinds of books they enjoy and conversely the kinds they do not enjoy. A good open question (3.4) that works well for readers' advisors is, "Can you tell me about a book you've read recently and really enjoyed?" followed up by a further probe, "What particularly did you like about it?"

The ability to listen with a tuned ear (2.4) and distill the essence of what users say is a crucial skill for all reference interviews but especially important in the readers' advisory context. The readers' advisor must pay close attention to what the reader says about a complex set of book appeal characteristics such as plot, characters, setting, pacing, preferred type of ending, literary quality, reading difficulty, and length ("quick reads" vs. "fat books")—in short, the "feel" of the desired reading experience.

The problem for readers' advisors is that the term *good book* is a relative term. Readers mean a good book for me; a book that suits my level of reading ability; a book that matches my mood right now; a book that satisfies my particular needs and interests. Therefore, it doesn't work to have on hand a list of "Good Books" (masterpieces of Western Civilization perhaps?) and recommend these same books to everyone. Nor should readers' advisors recommend their own personal favorites unless they have reason to believe that the user has the same reading tastes (e.g., "I've just read Kate Atkinson's *Started Early, Took My Dog* and absolutely loved it—you'll love it too").

You can't tell whether a reader will enjoy a particular book by considering the text alone, because the book is only half the equation. The other half is what the reader brings to the reading transaction. The reader's mood, skill as a reader, previous experiences with books, and current interests matter. That's why it's important to have a conversation with the reader about the kinds of reading experience she is looking for at present. You have to find out what each individual reader considers to be a "good book" at this particular time—hence the need for the readers' advisory interview.

> **A Quick Tip**
>
> **How Did You Like It?**
> If you are in a library small enough for you to get to know readers, talk to them about their reading. Ask them what they liked or didn't like about the books they are returning. Show an active interest.

Continued on p. 153

The readers' advisory interview has the characteristics of the generic reference interview (6.4.1), to which are added some further characteristics related to the activity of reading. Research has uncovered factors that are important to readers as they search for "a good book."

Factors That Affect Readers' Choices

The following list of factors that affect reading choices is adapted from Pejtersen and Austin (1983, 1984) and augmented with insights from Joyce Saricks (2005) about a book's appeal and from Catherine Ross (2001) on how readers choose books. When encouraged to talk about a book they have read and enjoyed, readers will single out certain features important to them ("I loved the strong female character," "The plot was fast-paced and suspenseful," "I loved learning so much about an archaeological dig/bell-ringing/knitting," "I laughed all the way through at the snappy dialogue"). Listen carefully to how the reader describes a book and identify which of these factors matter most to this particular reader:

Subject—what is the book about?

- What kind of *action* occurs in this book? Does the plot involve a conflict between two matched opponents, the uncovering of a mystery, the education of the central character, a quest or a journey, the gradual development of a love relationship? Is the action interior and psychological, or is it external, involving a lot of activity such as fights and chase scenes?
- What kinds of *characters* are featured in this book—a mother and daughter, a fellowship of elves, a strong woman who overcomes setbacks, a runaway, a private eye, a pirate king, vampires, members of a religious community, terrorists, a family of wolves or werewolves? What sorts of relationships take place among characters?
- What is the *theme*—love, war, survival, revenge, the conflict between good and evil, coping with adversity, coming of age, the discovery of identity?

Setting

- *When* does the story happen—past, present, or future? Time periods often offer clues to genre preferences, with the past associated with historical fiction or fantasy and the future associated with science fiction or speculative fiction.

- *Where* does the story happen—on another planet, an inner-city high school, a village in Kashmir, an advertising agency in Manhattan, the American frontier, a nursing home? Preferences for certain geographic settings provide clues to genre preferences, with glamorous, wealthy settings such as the perfume industry associated with bestselling melodrama and the frontier associated with the Western, the romance, or the family saga.

Kind of reading experience offered by the book

- Does the reader *learn something* from this book? For example, "I learned so much about Islamic family life in postwar Cairo" (or bee taxonomists, or the fashion industry in Paris, or how to break a horse, or the pioneer experience in Australia, or the partition of India).
- Does the reader *feel something* as a result of reading this book? For example, "It made me feel happy/sad/hopeful about human goodness" (or scared me, or made me laugh, or reassured me and confirmed my values, or challenged me to reassess my beliefs). Does the book have a happy ending? What is the mood engendered by reading this book?

Accessibility

- What *reading skills* are demanded by this book? Does this book use literary conventions that may be unfamiliar: stream of consciousness narrative method, an unreliable first-person narrator, flashbacks, literary parody?
- How *predictable* is it? The more conventional it is and the more it follows a formula, the more the reader already knows what to expect and the easier it will be for a novice to read.
- How *accessible is it physically* in terms of size and heaviness? In terms of the point size of the type?

Not all of these factors will be salient for all readers. A younger reader with strong arms and good eyesight may find the physical character-

Continued from p. 152

advisory mailing list, as well as its "Web Sites for Book Lovers" page with links to booklists, reading-related websites, genre fiction websites, and websites for e-books.
- For interactive access to the real experts—readers themselves—there are discussion lists and blogs and reviews, where readers chat about the latest, the best, and the worst. There are networking sites for every genre (see, e.g., The Romance Reader at http://www.theromancereader.com/). Post your difficult readers' advisory questions to the experts. And tell library users about these sites.
- Book-focused social networking sites such as GoodReads (http://www.goodreads.com/) and LibraryThing (http://www.librarything.com/) allow readers to catalog and tag their own books and find new books that other readers think have similar features. See Stover (2009: 246) for a list of other sites.

istics of the book irrelevant. A reader may not care where the book is set as long as it depicts strong, independent-minded female characters. On the other hand, a reader may refuse to read anything with too much sex and violence in it, or anything with confusing Russian names in it, or anything set in historical times. To find out which factors matter to an individual reader, ask open questions (3.4). The list **Some Questions for Readers' Advisors** provides some questions from which to choose the next time someone says, "Can you recommend a good book?"

Example: Readers' Advisory Interview

> **User:** Can you recommend a good book?
>
> **Librarian:** A good book to read, uh-huh (acknowledgment, 3.2). What kind of book are you in the mood for today (open question, 3.4)?
>
> **User:** I'd like a book I can get my teeth into. Preferably something with lots of different characters with complex relationships among them. Something I can take with me on my one-week holiday that will last me.
>
> **Librarian:** Can you give me an example of a book like that, which you have recently enjoyed (closed question that functions in the same way as the open question, "What would be an example of that?")?
>
> **User:** Well, I really liked Guy Gavriel Kay's *Sailing to Sarantium*.
>
> **Librarian:** *Sailing to Sarantium*, okay. What did you especially like about it?
>
> **User:** I liked the historical elements for sure. I liked the fact that a journey was involved. Oh, and I loved the talking birds! And I also like the fact that there is another book in the series, which I have also read.
>
> **Librarian:** Okay. And is there something that you would *not* like?
>
> **User:** Nothing depressing. No serial murderers. There's enough of that in real life without having to read about it. I want something with a bit of magic to it, not some sordid story that I could read in a newspaper.

Exercise 🔧

Role-Play Scenarios

Here are two role-play scenarios to help you practice the readers' advisory interview. In pairs, one person takes the role of the librarian, who must find out what sort of book the user would enjoy. The other person, who acts the part of the user, is given one of these scripts. If you are the user, don't spill the beans all at once, but answer the specific question you are asked. Switch roles for the second script. After each role-play, the actors should discuss how they felt about the interview, and then invite comments or suggestions from observers. After doing scenario 2, you could look again at 6.4.2 on the secondhand reference interview.

Scenario 1

You are going to the lake for a few weeks and want to bring along some mystery novels to read. You are tired of cozy mysteries that take place in small English

Continued on p. 155

Some Questions for Readers' Advisors

To initiate a readers' advisory interview:
Is there a special book you are looking for?
Are you finding what you're looking for?

To get a picture of previous reading patterns:
So that I can get a picture of your reading interests, can you tell me about a book/author that you've read and enjoyed?
What did you especially enjoy about that book (author/type of book)?
What do you *not* like and wouldn't want to read?
What elements do you usually look for in a novel (nonfiction book/biography/travel book/audiobook)?

To determine current reading preferences:
What are you in the mood for today?
What have you looked at so far? [to a person who has been looking unsuccessfully]
What did you *not* like about these books that you looked at?
If we could find the perfect book for you today, what would it be like? (What would it be about? What would you like best about it? What elements would it include?)

To understand the function of the book:
What kind of reading experience do you want to have?
What do you want to get from this book? What do you find satisfying?
What would you like this book to do for you?

To follow up on a recommendation:
If you find that these books weren't to your taste, get back to us and we can suggest something else.
What else can I help you with?

Continued from p. 154

villages, but you wouldn't object to Scandinavia, Italy, or even North America. However you don't want too many postmortem scenes of electric saws cutting into corpses or stories featuring body parts sent through the mail or stories told from the perspective of a warped serial murderer. You want a few good solid mysteries that feature a likeable protagonist, a good page-turning story, and an interesting setting. You approach the readers' advisor with this question: "Can you recommend some good books to read?"

Scenario 2
You are in the library to get some books for your aunt, who just broke her ankle skiing and is housebound. You know that your aunt reads a lot, she reads quickly, and she likes long books. You don't know exactly what she has been reading lately but rather think that she enjoys fantasy and books featuring strong female characters. You approach the readers' advisor with this question: "Where are your books for shut-ins?"

6.4.7. Integrating Reference Interview Skills

When librarians first attempt to apply new interviewing skills in an intentional, integrated way, they often wonder about the appropriateness of some skills and the effect the skill will have on the user. They are especially concerned about whether they will ever be able to use the skill without awkwardness. Here are some questions that trainees commonly ask about reference interview skills:

1. When someone asks for something specific, do I still need to conduct a reference interview? A common type of request is for a particular title or reference tool

such as Charles Dickens's *A Christmas Carol* or a directory. A reference interview might seem redundant because the user obviously knows what's wanted. But are you sure? It often turns out that the user, who is not familiar with the whole range of sources available, asks by name for the one source he happens to know about, not necessarily for the one that will actually answer the question.

A recommended approach is to acknowledge the request and fulfill it whenever it is possible to do so quickly. But follow up by checking to see if the requested item is really going to help. When the requested item is unavailable and you are about to suggest an interlibrary loan or reserve or refer the user to another library, try this instead: "Perhaps there's something else that would help you. What sort of information are you looking for?" In the case of *A Christmas Carol*, for example, it turned out that all copies were out. But the librarian was able to determine that the user wanted to put on a play with her grade seven class and was thinking of making a play out of Dickens's Christmas story. The librarian was then able to provide a book of Christmas plays that included a dramatic version of *A Christmas Carol*.

2. Doesn't it seem like prying to ask how someone plans to use the help they have asked for? Most people are quite willing to tell you if you ask the question appropriately. There are four guidelines for asking this sense-making question:

- **Never ask "why" directly.** "Why" often sounds judgmental. Moreover, "why" questions aren't necessarily efficient at eliciting answers about situations or uses. Users may answer by saying, "Because this library is closest," "Because the teacher told me to ask," or "Because I can't find what I want."
- **Clarify your intention.** Make it clear that you are asking this question because you can be more helpful if you know intended uses, not simply because you are curious. Say, for example, "We have a lot of material on Alzheimer's, and some might serve your purpose

better than others. Could you please tell me a bit more about what you are trying to find out?"

- **Avoid assumptions.** Let users tell you themselves what they are trying to do. Don't guess. Guessing is often inefficient and sometimes, when you guess wrong, can be offensive. It is much safer to ask questions that encourage users to describe the need in their own words.

- **Leave the other person in control.** When you ask a sense-making question like, "How do you plan to use this information?" users can say as much or as little as they want. They may tell you everything, which will help you suggest the most appropriate material. But if they choose to, they can say, "Oh, I'm just interested," a response that lets you know they don't want to say anything further.

3. Won't it take too long to ask open questions and use all these other skills? Well, extra time spent at the beginning to clarify what the user really wants often saves far more time later—time that would otherwise be wasted searching for the wrong thing. You can conduct short interviews by simply answering the user's initial question at face value ("Sorry, all our copies are out"), but is that real service? Besides, playing 20 questions isn't faster.

4. Won't I sound awkward to the user? When librarians first start practicing their new skills, they sometimes do sound awkward, but usually more awkward to themselves than to the user. The message that most users will get is that you're trying hard to help. Use the general practicing tips in section 5.7 and the **Five Easy Questions for the Reference Interview**.

Five Easy Questions for the Reference Interview

Ask	Instead of asking
What can I help you do today?	Do you need any help?
What have you done so far?	Have you looked in the catalog?
What would you like to know about X?	Do you want to know A or B?
What kind of help would you like?	Do you want me to do C?
What else can you tell me about X?	Is it this? Is it that?

6.5. The Employment Interview

Most people have been interviewed for a job. They have thought in advance about the interview and have likely consulted some of the many guidebooks on answering interview questions about their greatest weaknesses and where they want to be in five years. However, as a library professional, you will likely also be on the other side of the table, posing the questions. There has been comparatively little written on how to conduct employment interviews as opposed to being interviewed. We begin this section with the communication skills needed as an interviewer who wants to hire the best person for the job. Then we examine the communication skills needed by the applicant who wants the job. Although we consider the employment interview in this chapter on one-to-one communication along with other kinds of interviews, it needs to be stressed that many, if not most, job interviews in libraries are done as a group interview. Therefore Chapter 7 should also be consulted (see especially 7.4).

6.5.1. Conducting the Interview

As an interviewer, your first duty is to know about the job to be filled. Review the job description. Talk if possible with the person who has held the job before, and talk with the person who will supervise the new hire, if it's not you. If appropriate, discuss the job with people who will be working with the new hire. If you are interviewing as part of a group, you should do this work collaboratively, coordinated by the chair. This background work of thinking about the job will help you identify the aptitudes, experience, and knowledge needed by the successful candidate—topics that will guide your questioning. Your second duty is to review the interviewees' résumés before you meet them. This review will help you formulate questions intended to clarify or probe the candidates' particular qualifications. Before the interview begins, review the dimensions of the interview (6.3.2) and the interviewing skills you will need (6.3.3).

Before the Interview: Developing the Questions

Your selection process will be fairer and more effective if you develop in advance a list of questions, based on job-related criteria, that you will ask systematically of every candidate. If the interview is to be conducted by a group of people, the chair typically coordinates in advance the order of questioning and assigns particular questions to particular members of the interviewing group. This coordination heads off the danger of the interview's turning into a free-for-all, with important questions left unasked and unanswered.

What kind of questions should you formulate? Open questions (3.4) that contain no assumptions and that encourage the applicant to talk. As we have already seen, closed questions can sometimes be useful for confirming a fact but are poor tools to elicit information. Fear and Chiron (2002: 60) point out that if you ask the closed question, "Did you like the people there [in a former job]?" the obvious answer is, "Yes." Instead, you should ask, "How did you feel about the people there?" Moreover, as Ellis (2009: 37) points out, asking "too many closed questions can turn an interview into an interrogation" and not the trust-based, guided conversation that you want. After all, good employment interviewing is also an exercise in recruitment, leaving the best candidates with the desire to work in your library.

Because past performance very often predicts future performance, Richard Ellis (2009) recommends that interviewers use behavioral questions. These questions invite interviewees to talk about specific behaviors that they have actually used in the past (or claim to have used). He notes that hypothetical questions such as, "What would you do if X happened?" elicit answers that the interviewee thinks are wanted. Instead, consider the particular competencies required in the advertised position and ask questions designed to tap actual behaviors that demonstrate those competencies. Even if candidates have prepared potted answers, the follow-up questions and probes will provide the real test (Ellis, 2009: 37–38). Here are some examples, including follow-up probes:

> Please give us an example of a time on the job when you had to make a difficult decision. What process did you use? What happened?
> Have you ever had to handle conflict in a team? Tell us what you did and what you learned.
> How did you manage change in your last job? What would you do differently next time?

Then there are the questions that you should *not* ask. Be aware of Equity and Human Rights legislation in your jurisdiction. Know what questions are illegal or inappropriate (e.g., related to age, gender,

---

Did You Know?   ?

An effective and equitable process:
focuses on objective, job-related
  criteria;
gives people the chance to show off
  their full job qualifications; and
evaluates people on the basis of
  their ability to meet objective job
  requirements.

(From *The Employment Equity Guide*
at The University of Western Ontario,
available at http://www.uwo.ca/equity/
docs/fac_employ_equity_guide.pdf)

marital status, family, lifestyle, physical disabilities, race, ethnicity, national origin, religion, and political beliefs). If you are the chair, you might refresh the memories of the committee members by circulating a copy, if any exists, of your organization's guidelines on Employment Equity. Don't ask questions of women or minority members that you would not ask of men or nonminorities. Questions to avoid include Are you married? How will you be able to manage this job if you have young children? How old are you? Where were you born?

During the Interview

From the perspective of the employer, the interview serves two purposes. It allows you to gather critical evidence about the applicant's suitability for the job. But the interview is also a crucial element in the recruitment process in which you court excellent candidates. You haven't succeeded if you select a top-notch applicant but the chosen individual rejects the job, having been turned off by the insensitivity of the interview process. You want the best candidate to be impressed by the opportunities of the position and by the collegiality and friendliness of the other people who work there, including members of the selection committee. Therefore, a crucial first step is setting the applicant at ease at the outset and establishing rapport and trust (see the discussion of trust in Dimensions of the Interview, 6.3.2).

Some Tips for Conducting Employment Interviews

- Start the interview by putting the interviewee at ease. If this is a group interview, introduce other members of the hiring committee.
- Let the applicant know at the outset the format of the interview. For example, "In this interview, which will take about an hour, we will be asking you some questions relating to the three main areas of the job, namely, X, Y, and Z. At the end, however, there will be time for you to ask us any questions you may have about the job, our library system, or our city."
- Begin with a question or two that will be easy for the applicant to talk about—perhaps something from the résumé relating to an award or a distinction. For example, "I see that, when you were in the children's library, you got a

---

A Quick Tip 🕐

Softeners

To soften questions you plan to ask in tricky or sensitive areas, Fear and Chiron (2002: 69-70) suggest that you use qualifying introductory phrases such as "to what extent," "perhaps," "a little bit," or "might." Instead of asking, "Why did you have problems with the system implementation?" you could ask, "How did it happen that" or "To what do you attribute the problems in system implementation?"

Some Useful Questions for the Employment Interview

Follow up these questions, as appropriate, with probes and encouragers, such as "Can you provide an example?" "What happened in that situation?" and "Anything else?"

To find out about work history and the fit between the candidate and the job:
Suppose you start by telling us about your educational background/work experience/previous positions.
What does a job need to have for it to give you job satisfaction?
What attracts you to this position?

To find out about a candidate's strengths and possible weaknesses:
In your previous job(s), what did you learn about yourself in terms of your own special strengths?
For this new position, what skills or knowledge sets do you think you will need to acquire or bone up on?
How would your co-workers in your previous job describe you? Suppose you tell us three things your supervisor or co-workers might say.

To probe job-related competencies by asking about past behaviors:
Think of a recent situation in which you were required to demonstrate leadership (or teamwork/supervisory skill/creative problem-solving/ flexibility/the ability to deal with angry complaints, etc.). Please tell us a bit about the situation and what you did about it. What might you do differently next time?
Can you provide some examples of times when co-workers have asked you for help or advice or expertise? Can you provide examples of when you asked others for help?
This job sometimes requires attention to detail (or taking risks/making tough decisions, etc.). Suppose you talk about an instance in the past when you were required to demonstrate this quality. Tell us what happened.

To follow up:
What questions do you have for us?

leadership award for your work on literacy. Suppose you tell us what you did to earn this award?"

- Use appropriate eye contact and other nonverbal behaviors (Chapter 1) to show that you are interested, listening, and friendly. If this is a group interview, everyone on the committee should show active interest, not just the person who has asked the question.
- Listen actively. In the information-gathering part of the interview (i.e., all but the end where the interviewee is

invited to ask questions), the interviewee should be doing at least 90 percent of the talking.

- Use deliberate pauses (1.4) and minimal encouragers (3.3) to get the applicant to elaborate and provide a fuller answer.
- Be positive and encouraging in your response to all the candidate's answers. Do not signal with either your body language or your comments that a particular answer was deficient, even if you think it was.
- Deviate from your prepared questions to probe something that emerges in the course of the interview itself.
- Take notes during the interview so that you can compare the responses of the various candidates. But make sure that your note-taking doesn't interfere with using eye contact and encouraging body language.
- Allow time for the interviewee to ask questions.
- Wrap up the interview with a thank-you to the candidate and an explanation of what comes next. Explain the timelines for the selection process and when the candidate can expect to hear from you. (Adapted from Dodd, 2007: 236–251; Ellis, 2009: 35–41; Fear and Chiron, 2002: 71)

6.5.2. Being Interviewed

When you are the interviewee, your role is the flip side of the process discussed in 6.5.1 from the perspective of the employer. Like the interviewer, you also have to prepare carefully in advance of the interview and use your communication skills during the interview itself. Whereas the interviewer prepares by thinking carefully about job requirements, you prepare by identifying your own particular skills, competencies, and areas of strength in relation to the advertised position.

You initiate the interview process by supplying an up-to-date résumé or curriculum vitae and a supporting cover letter. Don't use the same résumé for every job you apply for, but revise your basic document to highlight how your strengths are a good fit for the advertised position and for the institution. Your cover letter should explain concisely why you should be considered for the position (see 9.5 on good news and neutral letters). Think of your cover letter and résumé as an audition—you have the employer's attention very briefly, and you want to make it as easy as possible for your good points to shine.

Once you have been selected to be interviewed, learn as much as you can in advance about the institution, the library, and the individuals who will be interviewing you. Explore the library's website thoroughly, and read the mission statement and latest annual report. Ferret out any information about current activities and future plans, and look at publications or presentations of staff members. Find out the venue of the interview, and figure out how to get there (where to park, transportation from airport, etc.). Arrive on time!

Just as the interviewer will prepare a set of questions in advance, you should anticipate questions in advance and think how you might answer them. Take a look at **Some Useful Questions for the Employment Interview** (6.5.1) as a starting point. Do some brainstorming about specific situations where you have used one of your signature strengths (e.g., calmness in a crisis, good analytic skills, team-building skills, ability to find creative solutions, ability to see the big picture). What did you do in the situation, and how did it help? Thinking in advance about specific strengths and specific instances when you used them will help you answer those behavioral questions that we recommend interviewers use (see 6.5.1).

Some Communication Tips for the Interviewee

- Do your part in making the interview into a *conversation* where a genuine exchange of information can take place. Maintain eye contact with the interviewers, and use positive body language (Chapter 1). Sound, as well as be, interested and enthusiastic about the job—vocal qualities go a long way toward conveying enthusiasm.
- Listen carefully to the questions asked. If you are not sure that you understood the whole question, use restatement (3.2), repeating what you did hear and providing an opportunity for the interviewer to fill in the gaps. For example, "You are interested in hearing about X and Y and you also wanted . . . what was that again?"
- Avoid falling into the yes/no routine. Not all interviewers are good at asking open questions (3.4). If they do ask a closed question, don't just say yes or no. Treat it as an open question and volunteer information.
- Watch the body language of the interviewees and shorten your responses if they give signals that they are becoming impatient or bored. (Of course, really good interviewers won't give anything away, no matter how far off the track your answers are going.)

> **Exercise**
>
> **Go for a Dry Run**
> Before you face the real interview, rehearse. Recruit someone who will role-play the interview with you, asking you questions in a mock interview. In advance, give your interviewer a copy of the job posting, a copy of your résumé, and a copy of the list **Some Useful Questions for the Employment Interview** found in 6.5.1. For the interview, choose a quiet setting where you will not be interrupted. Record the interview so that you can replay it and hear which questions you aced and which areas need more work.

- Be aware of timing and pacing of the interview. The interviewer(s) have scheduled a specific amount of time for the interview, which you should be told about. If not, assume it's not more than an hour. Aim for answers that are detailed, interesting, and pithy. The more you have thought in advance about possible questions and answers, the more likely that your answers will hit the Goldilocks standard of being not too long and boring, not too short and uninformative, but just right.
- If the interviewer is unskilled and takes up too much of the interview time in providing information rather than in gathering information, don't interrupt or try to wrest away the control of the interview. Listen and nod and smile and pay attention.
- If the interviewer has not given you a chance to talk about some key strength or achievement, at the end you could volunteer it. For example, "You might be interested to hear about the X project where I implemented a new system quite similar to the one you are considering."
- When invited to ask questions about the job, make sure you ask some. (Adapted in part from Ellis, 2009: 46–53)

Being Interviewed by Telephone

Many libraries now are using telephone interviews as a screening tool to learn more about potential candidates' suitability before short-listing those to be invited for an on-site interview. Typically you will be interviewed by several people on a conference call. For the interviewee, there is the added challenge that you can't readily tell who is speaking and you can't rely on body language to see how interested your interviewees are in what you are saying. Everything depends on voice. One thing you do know is that you yourself want to sound interested, enthusiastic, and confident. This is not the time to use that cell phone that loses signal strength, drops calls, and makes you sound as if you are speaking from inside a drain pipe.

To prepare for a telephone interview, review 6.2.1. Tiffany Eatman Allen (2007) recommends that you practice for the interview. She says you can (1) give a friend a list of questions that she can use to conduct a practice interview over the phone; (2) audiorecord a practice interview session and replay it to check for "clarity, enunciation, volume, and enthusiasm"; or (3) answer interview questions "while sitting back to back with a friend," a condition that mimics the reality of telephone interviews of talking without being able to see body language.

During the telephone interview itself, follow as appropriate the communication tips given earlier on being an interviewee. Here are two considerations of particular relevance to the telephone interview: (1) use restatement (3.2) if you are not sure that you understood the question fully, because you won't be able to see nonverbal cues that you are on the wrong track; and (2) don't worry about pauses. Because you can't see each other, pauses may be used to make sure each party is finished speaking. The interviewer may be taking notes.

6.6. Coping with Special Situations

In public service, special communication problems are often due to a barrier between you and the user. Such barriers may involve a physical disability, where the user has limitations in seeing, speaking, hearing, or moving. Or barriers may involve differences in language, speech, or culture. Special communication problems also arise when there is a conflict between the user's expectations and your own, as in situations where the user has a complaint that seems reasonable to him but unreasonable to you. And then, in an entirely different category, there is behavior that not only seems unreasonable but may also be disruptive or even dangerous

These various situations should be distinguished and correctly identified, because each type of situation requires different skills and attitudes. It is inappropriate, ineffective, and sometimes offensive to try to solve all special communication problems the same way. And, not least, it is most important to learn to judge when a situation is developing into more than a communication problem.

6.6.1. Helping People with Disabilities

A person with a disability is anyone who has any condition that limits movements, senses, or activities. People with disabilities may be apprehensive about how well they will be able do something or how they will be perceived in public places, including the library. Other people may fear or avoid situations where they need to communicate with a person with a disability. We can reduce this apprehension by learning more about specific disabilities and by learning skills for getting around any communication barriers that the disability may pose.

Libraries have worked hard to eliminate physical barriers that used to hamper access to libraries and to library materials by people with disabilities. The Americans with Disabilities Act (ADA), passed into law in 1990 and amended in 2008, applies in most U.S. libraries in both public and private settings. It has prompted the reassessment of library facilities, collections, and services. Libraries in Canada and other countries are also paying greater attention to removing physical barriers to library access, often in order to comply with legislation. American Library Association policies emphasize facilities, collections, and adaptive devices but do not explicitly address communication skills needed by staff members who respond to the information needs of persons with disabilities. Nevertheless, helping library staff acquire appropriate communication skills is a crucial element in providing equal access.

The key is to respect the user and take every question seriously—possibly even more seriously than usual. It can take more determination for a person with a disability to come to the library and approach a stranger to ask for help. A number of physical and mental conditions can make communication difficult. There are speech disorders, including problems of articulation, voice production, and rhythm, which can be caused by a variety of factors, including hearing impairment, head injuries, stroke, and cerebral palsy. Users with a mental illness may speak in a manner that appears inappropriate, possibly incoherent or too loud. Although the library literature sometimes refers to these users as "problem patrons" (see 6.7), the Americans with Disabilities Act recognizes that mental impairment is a disability. The ADA defines mental impairments as "any mental or psychological disorder, such as mental retardation, organic brain syndrome, emotional or mental illness, and specific learning disabilities."

Your library will provide services to users with a wide range of disabilities. The skills needed for assisting these users can be learned through self-education and practice. Workshops offered through agencies and community groups as well as web-based programs are available as well.

Twelve Tips for Communicating with People with Disabilities

1. **Know the facts** about specific disabilities. Needs and abilities vary with the kind and degree of disability.

2. **Leave the user in control.** Ask if he would like help or what kind of help is wanted.

3. **Don't make assumptions** about the user's abilities or needs. One physical disability doesn't necessarily mean other disabilities. For example, a speech disability may or may not affect a user's ability to hear or understand you.

4. **Treat the user as an individual.** Speak directly to her as you would to any other user. Don't ever talk about her in the third person ("Would she like help getting up-stairs?")

5. **Maintain appropriate nonverbal behavior.** Even if the user cannot see you, your physical bearing is conveyed in your voice (see 1.2 on eye contact and 1.3 on smiling and nodding).

6. **Don't underestimate people with disabilities.** Like all users, those with disabilities have a broad range of interests and mental abilities. Don't stereotype a user as unable to cope with challenging materials, but find out what level of material is wanted—just as you would with any user.

7. **Don't assume** (3.5) that the user wants special materials. You may have a fine collection of audiobooks, but these may not be what the user wants. Nor should you assume that the user wants information about disabilities.

8. **Know the limitations** of your library. The high shelves, narrow aisles, or stairs may be barriers. Be watchful—as you would with any library user—and be ready to give help as required or requested.

9. **Don't pretend** the disability doesn't exist. But don't be supersensitive or try to change your normal behavior. For example, users with visual disabilities understand the words *see* and *viewpoint* and are not offended by these terms.

10. **Support the user's independence.** Be patient, and don't interfere with the user who wants to do something him-

self, even though you could do it for him faster. Offering an orientation tour of the library often provides greater freedom and encourages future independence.

11. **Use follow-up questions.** Find out whether the user has received the kind of help wanted, or if there is anything else needed (see 3.7).

12. **Encourage feedback.** Users with disabilities can often make excellent suggestions for improving your facilities and services. Comments about barriers they have encountered are important—pass them on to the library decisionmakers. Let users know that you are concerned about the negative aspects of the library's environment and appreciate their comments (see 3.15 on receiving feedback). (Adapted from Rubin, 2001, and other sources.)

Communicating with People with Hearing Impairments

Know the facts about the kinds and degrees of hearing disabilities. People with hearing difficulties have different ways of communicating, depending on when the problem began. People who have been profoundly deaf from very early childhood have never heard spoken language and will often communicate using a sign language such as ASL (American Sign Language). For libraries serving such users, equitable access can be provided by hiring a staff member who can use sign language or by recruiting signing volunteers.

Some who have been hearing impaired from birth but have residual hearing might wish to communicate by speaking. Because their pronunciation may be nonstandard, you need to listen carefully, use acknowledgment (3.2), ask for repetition when necessary, and sometimes ask the user to write down the question. Those with hearing loss in later life can speak without difficulty but may have a problem understanding when you speak.

- Approach hearing-impaired people so that you can be seen. Get their attention before you start speaking.
- Don't assume a knowledge of sign language. Ask the individual how he prefers to communicate, and adopt the preferred form. If someone makes a request in writing, don't ask if he can read your lips.

- Face the person when you speak, and speak directly to her (not to an interpreter). Use eye contact and any gestures that you feel will help. Use all the nonverbal language available through your face, eyes, and hands.
- Don't exaggerate your speech. Speak at your normal pace, enunciating carefully. Make sure the light is on your face and not behind you. Keep your lips flexible, not rigid. Keep your hands away from your face.
- Write on paper if you do not understand the person or if she does not seem to understand you. Do this matter-of-factly, not apologetically.

Communicating with People with Motor Impairments

- Know the facts. People using wheelchairs, scooters, or walkers may have one or another condition, such as paraplegia, amputation, stroke paralysis, multiple sclerosis, or cardiovascular disease. The disability may be temporary, chronic, or progressive. Some users may be just learning to use their assistive device. Others have remarkable mobility and dexterity through long experience. People relying on assistive devices usually can use any kind of library material or service as long as it is physically accessible.
- Be aware of your library's physical barriers, and know how to help the person with a motor impairment overcome them. Using drinking fountains, reaching items on high shelves, or getting materials from narrow aisles may require your help. Do not touch or push the assistive device without permission.
- Put yourself at the person's eye level by sitting down. It is tiring for a wheelchair user to look up for any length of time.
- Don't think of people as confined by their mobility equipment—they are not "wheelchair bound." Think of the technology as enabling, in the same way that a car lets people go where they would otherwise not be able to go.

Communicating with People Who Are Visually Impaired or Blind

- Know the facts. The ability to see and read varies greatly. People who use guide dogs or white canes are legally blind

FIGURE 6.2. Wheelchair Accessibility Icon

Did You Know? ?

The 2010 National Health Interview Survey (NHIS) Preliminary Report found that some 21.5 million adult Americans reported that they either "have trouble" seeing, even when wearing glasses or contact lenses, or that they are blind or unable to see at all (see American Foundation for the Blind at http://www.afb.org/section .aspx?FolderID=2&SectionID=15).

(with less than 20/200 visual acuity) but may still be able to see contrasts of light and dark. A person with low vision has some useful sight but experiences limitations in various daily activities, such as driving and reading. Some people are born with visual impairments, while others, such as those with age-related macular degeneration, have lost visual acuity as they have grown older.

- Listen carefully. The visually impaired or blind person depends even more on speech than does the fully sighted person.
- Identify yourself and others with you. In a group discussion, identify the person you are addressing.
- Give precedence to the voice as a way of showing your welcome and helpfulness, but continue to use visual cues as well. Some of your nonverbal behavior is communicated through your voice, so don't stop smiling and nodding. However, because the person cannot read many of the messages conveyed through body language, be careful to acknowledge the person verbally with restatement (3.2) and verbal encouragers (3.3).
- Use the skill of inclusion (see 3.10) to describe what you are doing or where you are going. Don't simply walk away to check something, leaving the blind person talking to empty air.
- Make sure that library materials are available in a variety of formats, including large-print books, audiobooks, digital text, and Braille. Ask the user which formats are preferred.
- When giving directions, use the clock face as a method of orientation. For example, "The reference desk is at three o'clock from where you're standing."
- When guiding a person, allow her to take your arm. Don't grab her arm or hand.
- Don't treat guide dogs as pets. They are trained working animals. Don't allow other library users to distract them. "Please don't pet him; he's busy working!" will usually get the message across.

6.6.2. Language and Speech Barriers

Because the basis of communication is a common language, communication accidents can occur when you and the user do not share the same first language or dialect or when the user has a speech disorder.

For people for whom English is not the first language, talk clearly and a bit more slowly than usual. Avoid slang and idioms (or at least restate the meaning). And don't ask negative questions such as, "Don't you want this book?" or double-barreled questions like, "Do you want to search yourself, or do you want me to show you how?" For people with speech disorders, be patient—they may need extra time to communicate clearly—and don't finish their sentences for them.

If you cannot understand what the user is saying, try these four steps:

1. Restate what you do understand (see 3.2). If you catch the word *book* or *information*, respond with some acknowledgment, such as, "You're looking for a book on . . . ?" or "You need some information?" This establishes your willingness to help, encourages the user to repeat or fill in the part you missed, and gives you a second chance to listen.

2. Take ownership of the problem. Say, "I'm sorry, I seem to be having trouble understanding people today. Could you tell me again?"

3. If you still do not understand what the user wants, explain your difficulty and ask how you can communicate more easily. Offer writing as an alternative. Again, take ownership: "It would help me if you could just write the name (or topic) down on this paper." However, keep in mind that some people may not be able to write English and that some speech difficulties also make writing hard.

4. If all else fails, ask someone else to help. Sometimes another librarian will be able to hear immediately what the person is saying. Do this gracefully: "Maybe Mrs. Jones will be able to help. Let's just go over there and ask her." Often just moving with the user to another, less public, area will lessen tension or frustration for both of you and encourage the user to express the request in another way.

Always show the user respect. Remember, it may be more difficult for him to ask the question than for you to understand it. Never speak about the user in the third person ("Marge, I can't understand a word this person is saying"). Pay attention to cultural differences

---

A Quick Tip

Oranges and Peaches

Check out and confirm that you heard it right. Misunderstandings occur routinely between people even when they share the same language and dialect. A study of language accidents at the reference desk included these examples: "The book, *Oranges and Peaches*" (the user really wanted *On the Origin of Species*); "gynecology" (genealogy); and "house plants" (house plans). Then there was the user who asked to see ERIC, only to be told that no one called Eric worked at the library (Dewdney and Michell, 1996). And of course there was the sad case in Gilbert and Sullivan's *Pirates of Penzance*, where the hero Frederick was apprenticed by mistake to a pirate instead of to a pilot—all through the mishearing of a consonant.

as well as to language differences. In your effort to understand what the user is saying, you may be sending other, negative messages (such as asking too many questions or infringing on personal space) that hamper communication. Don't raise your voice—the user's difficulty in speaking doesn't necessarily have anything to do with her ability to hear you. A person who isn't fluent in English (or in your dialect of English) is not deaf.

Above all, stay calm and be patient. Don't tell yourself, "I didn't understand a word of what he said—and I never will." Work through the strategies of acknowledgment, taking ownership, asking the user to write the question down, and, finally, referral. One of these will work.

6.6.3. Cross-Cultural Communication

Throughout this book, we try to show how culture affects all types of communication. In this section, we point out a few of the communication accidents that can occur directly as a result of cultural differences. In our increasingly multicultural societies, "intercultural accidents" are more likely to happen both in person and on the web. We are encountering more people different from ourselves than ever before. We need to be aware of intercultural differences. But we also need a way of thinking about these differences that will help us develop intentional strategies for communicating effectively. A good place to start is the books by Samovar and Porter (2001, 2000). In these books and others like them, you will read about the main factors that affect intercultural communication.

The main differences between cultures are differing values and attitudes toward human relationships. McGuigan (2002) explains that if you are unaware of these differences, you may offend someone whose deeply held cultural values you have unknowingly violated. These cultural differences usually manifest themselves as differences in the following:

- Body language
- Sense of time
- Sense of personal space
- General rules for etiquette, for "being polite," and for showing respect

Did You Know? ?

Culture is not the same as ethnicity and national background, although they may be related. Consider, for example, a person who has lived most of his adult life in Detroit but was born and raised in Jamaica by parents who grew up in China. Because cultural behaviors are learned, not innate, people's "culture" tends to reflect the environment in which they have spent the most time, especially in childhood, rather than their national background or their ethnicity. Culture is learned. National background and ethnicity are not.

Some differences can seem quite arbitrary—for example, the thumbs up gesture means okay in North America, but to some people from southern Europe, Iran, and South America it is the equivalent of the American obscene gesture of the middle finger.

Most cultural differences are internally logical. Many are based on concepts of time, space, and one's social position in any given situation. For example, in some cultures, being late is a mark of your importance—it shows you are busy. Personal space (see 1.7) is also often culture specific: a distance of two feet between two people may be perceived as too close (read "pushy") by the British participant and too distant (read "unfriendly") by the Cuban. Touching is fraught with subtle cultural, social, and gender differences. A "friendly" tap on the shoulder of a South Asian female student by a male Anglo-American librarian will likely be considered as totally inappropriate.

In some cultures, space is perceived as communal, permitting people to jump queues. Conflict then occurs when an individual from a communal-space culture enters a culture that rigidly observes the "first come, first served" rule. Directness or "getting to the point" is valued by North Americans as an indication of efficiency and honesty, but, in some Asian and Middle Eastern cultures, it is perceived as impolite, if not offensive. The tolerance for conflict varies among cultures—saying "no" directly may be seen as a sign of disrespect by people whose culture values harmony. Someone from Japan might say "It's difficult" rather than flatly say no.

But here's where a caveat is needed: a little knowledge is a dangerous thing. It is tempting to overgeneralize behavior within a particular culture. Vast individual differences exist within any one culture—consider, for example, your own way of communicating compared with that of someone else from your own culture. Communication accidents arising between two people of different cultures may not, in fact, have their roots in culture at all, but may have resulted from other individual or situational factors. So there are no general "rules" for cross-cultural communication, except perhaps to assess the situation on its merits and show respect for the individual. However, here are a few tips for using nonverbal and speaking skills with people of another culture:

- Use body language that suggests approachability, respect, and willingness to help—smiling, standing up, and giving the user your full attention.

Did You Know? ?

The concept of time varies with culture. For example, "As soon as possible" may mean "immediately" to an Anglo-American, whose culture places a premium on time, but it may mean "whenever convenient" to Hispanic Americans. To avoid conflicting expectations, be explicit: "By Thursday at 5 p.m."

Exercise ⚒

Observe Eye Contact
Eye contact carries different meanings in different cultures. Berlanga-Cortéz (2000) explains that in the African American, Hispanic, and Asian cultures, *speakers* are expected to look at listeners directly in the eye, while *listeners* are expected to avert eyes to indicate respect and attention. On the other hand, in the Anglo-American culture listeners are expected to look at a speaker directly to indicate respect and attention, and speakers are expected to avert eye contact (especially in informal speaking). Make your own informal survey as you speak with colleagues and library users. Do your findings agree with Berlanga-Cortéz? What are the implications of this finding on cultural differences for reference interview success?

- Restate or paraphrase the user's words to allow the other person to correct you.
- Do not assume that the user's smile means agreement—check it out.
- Recognize that the user's silence or lack of eye contact may be a demonstration of respect rather than a lack of understanding.
- Make your questions clear, and wait for an answer. Avoid constructions with double negatives, such as "not doing nothing" or "not unexpected."
- If you do have a misunderstanding, apologize and say, "Let's start again."

6.6.4. Handling Complaints

Every organization receives complaints. Everyone in an organization—from the custodian to the chief executive officer—needs to know how to handle complaints efficiently, effectively, and tactfully. In libraries, the most common complaints from users involve circulation procedures: overdue fines, charges for lost books, and loan periods. Users may also complain about selection decisions such as holdings that they consider unsuitable for the library or material that the library doesn't have. Other types of complaints may involve parking availability, hours of opening, noise, or staff behavior.

Helpful hints for handling complaints are provided in many publications about what used to be called "problem patrons" or "awkward customers." However, it's important to remember that the largest proportion of unpleasant encounters originate not from unreasonable demands or deviant behavior but from legitimate concerns or misunderstandings. Treating the user as the bad guy, even if the complaint initially seems unreasonable, is an invitation to confrontation.

To prevent a complaint from escalating into a full-blown display of anger, make sure your responses follow these three stages: understand the problem, decide what you are going to do about the complaint, and take action toward resolving the complaint.

Understand the Problem

1. **Listen** to the complaint (2.2). Show that you are giving your full attention. Use eye contact, appropriate pos-

Did You Know? ?

For every complaint you receive, at least ten more library users have the same problem but haven't let you know. However, you can be sure that people who don't make a formal complaint are telling other people about their dissatisfaction. Give them a way to let *you* know so that you have a chance to solve the problem.

ture, and all those nonverbal skills that say, "I'm paying attention."

2. **Acknowledge the user's concern** and the user's right to question or criticize library regulations. Use restatement (3.2) to assure the user that you are listening ("You have just received this notice, hmm") and reflection of feeling (3.9) to communicate empathy ("I can see that this has really upset you").

3. **Allow the user to describe** the complaint fully without interrupting. Use encouragers (3.3) such as "Hmm," "I see," and "Tell me more about this." Ask the user to be specific ("Can you give me an example?") and to describe what has happened to cause this complaint. For example, the user may say that he is very angry about the way this library is run and especially about the way books are chosen. Rather than responding at this stage with an explanation of the book selection policy, find out what initiated the complaint. Ask an open or sense-making question (3.4 and 3.6), such as "What is it about our policy that upsets you?" "What aspect of this concerns you?" or "What has happened?"

4. **Let the user do the talking** at first. Don't be too quick to explain or defend. Often the user just wants to blow off steam and let someone know what has happened. In any case, the user isn't going to listen to you until he gets a chance to vent.

5. **Ask** (3.4), if it's not clear what the user expects. Try one of these: "What would help you?" "What would you like us to do about this?" "What can I do that would help resolve this situation?"

6. **Restate** (3.8) to confirm that you really understand what the user expects you to do. You could say, "You'd like us to remove this book from the collection" or "If I understand you correctly, you received a bill for a book that you already returned, and you want us to cancel the bill."

> **A Quick Tip** 🕐
>
> **Stand and Deliver**
> In cases when users are so furious that they can't hear what you're saying, Anne Turner (2004: 40) recommends the "stand and deliver technique." You listen, nod, stay calm, and make sympathetic noises until they run out of steam. She claims that labeling the technique helps staff handle the psychological burden of abuse.

These six steps are necessary before you make a decision or take action. Often, by the time you've worked through these steps in the first stage of handling the complaint, the user will no longer be angry or will at least be ready to listen to you.

Handling Complaints

In pairs, role-play these situations. Take turns being the user and the librarian. Practice one skill at a time: acknowledgment or restatement, encouragers, open questions, reflection of feeling, and broken record.

1. The user has not been able to find a parking space and had to circle the library lot for 15 minutes. He is now double-parked. He says to the circulation clerk: "You'd better do something about that parking lot."

2. A woman, whose 14-year-old daughter is an enthusiastic user of the public library's free Wi-Fi, wants to speak to "the head librarian" about pornography.

3. A professor has just discovered that the library has cancelled its subscription to his favorite (rather esoteric) journal. He demands its reinstatement.

A Quick Tip

Yes We Can

Rhea Rubin (2010) recommends that you stress what you and the library *can* do for the patron rather than what you cannot do. Instead of saying I can't do X," say, "What I can do is Y."

Decide What You Are Going to Do about the Complaint

To decide what you are going to do about the complaint, consider:

- Is this a situation over which you have control?
- Is it a common situation for which you have a standard procedure?
- Is it an unusual situation where no procedure exists but which you may be able to solve?
- Is it a situation that you must or should refer to someone else?

Take Action toward Resolving the Complaint

1. **Indicate what action** you are prepared to take—any action. Examples:

   - I'm going to report this immediately.
   - I'll check our files. Usually our records are accurate, but occasionally they are not.
   - What we do in these cases is to file a report and then check the shelves over the next two weeks until we find the book.
   - This is a serious problem, and the director would certainly want to know about it. I'll call her.

2. **Tell the user** what you are doing if you need to **refer**: "I'm not sure what to do about this, but Mrs. Harris, who is head of circulation, will know. If you will wait for a moment, I'll call her." Be prepared to make quick and accurate referrals.

3. **Explain what the user should expect** as a result of your action. For example, "You will not receive another notice unless we definitely cannot locate the book. If you don't hear from us within two weeks, you'll know we found it."

4. **Suggest what the user can do** to help resolve the situation. Make specific suggestions without implying that the problem is the user's fault. You could say, "While we're checking here, you might have another look at

home and ask your family when they last saw this book."

5. **Thank the user** for reporting the problem. You could say, "I'm glad that you brought this to our attention. It's only when people tell us that we can check into these records." Again, acknowledge the concern: "I'm very sorry that this happened to you. It was upsetting, I know" or "It never hurts to ask about the rules. I'm sorry that I couldn't let you take this magazine home."

These five steps resolve most complaints. However, sometimes the user becomes emotional or abusive, even when you have listened carefully and acted appropriately. In such cases, do not argue, bargain, or be drawn into unnecessary justification of library policy. Use the broken record technique (3.13) to emphasize your point.

BROKEN RECORD RESPONSE

User: That's ridiculous. What's the point of having magazines that don't circulate?

Librarian: We don't allow the latest issue to circulate, because we need to be sure it's here when someone wants to consult it in the library.

User: Nobody ever reads this magazine but me.

Librarian: Still, we need to have it here in case someone does.

User: How about letting me have it overnight?

Librarian: I'm sorry. We don't circulate the latest issue.

User: That's a stupid rule.

Librarian: That is our rule.

If the user is still not satisfied, refer to a supervisor who is immediately available. This referral provides an opportunity to remove the discussion from a public area and to allow someone else to try to solve the problem. Sometimes people feel their complaint has been taken more seriously if they are referred to a supervisor. If the supervisor is not immediately available, however, the user may feel that she is being given the runaround. A simple way of making this decision is to ask the user: "There are many people waiting to charge out their books, so I am wondering if you would like to talk to my supervisor about this? I can show you to her office."

Quick Tips for Handling Complaints

- **Remain calm.** Never argue or negotiate. Speak quietly. Be pleasant, no matter what the user says.
- **Listen.** Let the user blow off steam.
- **Don't take complaints personally.** Complaints are directed at the system. Taking them personally leads to burnout.
- **Avoid self-disclosure.** Don't give your own opinion or tell a story about something similar that happened to you. Self-disclosure is a skill that is often inappropriate for handling complaints: the user will either become impatient or feel encouraged to describe more complaints.
- **Refer** quickly and accurately when a complaint is beyond your control.
- **Communicate with staff.** When you receive repeated complaints about something outside of your control and for which there seems to be no appropriate policy, procedure, or referral, it's time to discuss the problem at a staff meeting.

6.7. Problematic Behavior

Before you can respond appropriately to problematic behavior, you need to identify the type of behavior at issue. Is the person's behavior dangerous? Disruptive? Merely annoying or eccentric? Annoying to you, but not to other staff or users? Much written about the so-called "problem patron" fails to distinguish between the kinds of behavior that pose the problems. If a person's behavior is dangerous or unlawful, it is probably also disruptive and inappropriate. But often a person's behavior is not dangerous—only inappropriate or mildly disruptive. Some library users become frustrated and angry and may be rude in their interactions with staff. Some, such as cell phone users, noisy teens, or argumentative seniors, are disruptive to other users (Sarkodie-Mensah, 2002).

Then there is the possibility that the "problem patron" has been labeled such because he doesn't fit library norms of the Good User— he asks too many questions, complains that he doesn't like the library's restrictive Wi-Fi policy, is thought to waste librarian's time, and so forth. So an important first step is to ask yourself what really is at issue here. What kind of problematic behavior are you dealing with? You also need to consider whether or not elements in the library system, including your own behaviors, are contributing to the problem.

Distinguishing between dangerous behavior and inappropriate behavior is important, because these two problems require very different responses at both the personal level (the staff member who experiences or observes the problem) and the institutional level (through policy statements and written procedures). Section 6.7.1 discusses the difference between routine problems that any public service worker can adequately handle with good communication skills (provided there is the support of written policies if required) and more difficult situations involving deviant or socially unacceptable behavior. Some situations require only an understanding of the behavior and do not require intervention until the behavior becomes disruptive or generally offensive in some way. Section 6.7.2 describes appropriate responses to behavior that may be unlawful or dangerous or both.

6.7.1. Disruptive and Inappropriate Behavior

This section considers behavior that includes the following: the eccentric; the disruptive; and the both eccentric and disruptive. The man who sleeps away the afternoon in the library may be eccentric, but he is harmless and not disruptive. This sort of behavior can usually be ignored. The behavior of the irate user may seem disruptive to the library staff but perfectly reasonable and completely justifiable to the user. This is usually a one-shot situation—behavior that is not habitual but arises from a user's reaction to a specific situation. As long as the irate user doesn't start throwing books or punching out the circulation clerk, library staff can usually resolve the problem with the communication skills described in the section on handling complaints (6.6.4).

The most common source of disruptive and inappropriate behavior is the rowdy student. But there are others: the regular user with strong and offensive body odor; the woman who wants to use two reading tables to spread out her Christmas cards on a busy day; the cell phone user who gets into a loud argument with the other party; and the sleeper when he begins to snore loudly. These people are all behaving in a way that impairs other people's ability to use the library. To this category we might add behavior that is both disruptive and eccentric but not dangerous: the man who talks to himself constantly or the woman who approaches other users or staff with peculiar stories or requests. This is deviant behavior but usually not a sign of dangerous

---

A Quick Tip 🕐

User Behavior Rules
Too many rules for user behavior are counterproductive. Anne Turner's (2004: 20) nine-point checklist for evaluating library behavior rules includes the following: Is the problem behavior already covered by law? Does the rule address a situation created by problem behavior, or is it really aimed at a specific individual or group? Can the majority of people understand what will happen if they don't follow the rule? And, finally, "a year later, do we still need this rule?"

Did You Know? ?

Many of the inappropriate or rude behaviors that happen in face-to-face encounters also happen in telephone, e-mail, or chat contacts, but ratcheted up a notch. Ann Curry (1996: 184) explains that the telephone or chat encounter provides the protection of "visual anonymity." The result may be that some people are more aggressive than they would be in person. You can use many of the same skills in telephone and virtual encounters that you would use in dealing with rude/impatient people in face-to-face encounters.

Exercise

Problems and Solutions

This exercise may be done individually or in small groups. Ask participants to suggest three ways in which a library staff member might respond to each of the following situations. Choose the best solution and justify your choice.

1. A group of five or six boys (around 11 years old) have been sitting at a table, getting increasingly louder–laughing, calling out to other students, using offensive language. One has now knocked over a chair. Other library users ask you to do something about the noise.
2. An elderly man in poor clothes has come in out of the rain. He seats himself in the corner of the reading lounge and produces a brown paper bag from which he takes a drink. (Your library allows eating and drinking.)

behavior. It helps to understand the reasons why people act this way and to develop communication skills that can modify the unsuitable behavior.

The communication skills that are most useful in problem situations are listening skills (2.4); nonverbal skills including tone of voice and gestures (Chapter 1); confrontation (3.13); and giving directions—to both users and staff (3.12). First, listen carefully and assess the situation before you act. Active listening (2.2) will help you pick up on cues to the user's behavior and intentions. Use a calm tone of voice; do not speak loudly or too quickly. Use gestures that communicate calmness and control. Never use sudden gestures.

Using Confrontation Skills: DESC and the Broken Record

Confrontation (3.13) is a skill that works well for changing behavior that is unacceptable or disruptive, but not dangerous. The DESC sequence is useful as a means of dealing with the rowdy student:

> **D**escribe: You are making a lot of noise.
> **E**xplain: This is preventing other people from working.
> **S**pecify: I would like you to stop talking.
> **C**onsequences: If you are quiet, you can stay. If you continue talking loudly, I will ask you to leave.

This approach will work better than: "You'll have to stop that noise right away, or else." If the DESC sequence doesn't work the first time, repeat the cycle:

> **D**escribe: A few minutes ago I asked you to stop talking loudly but you didn't stop.
> **E**xplain: Your talking is still bothering other people.
> **S**pecify: Pick up your books and walk out that door. Please don't come back tonight.
> **C**onsequences: If you don't do as I ask, I will call the security guard (or inform your school, mother, etc.).

Use the broken record technique to keep the conversation on track and to focus on the way you want the problem resolved:

> **User:** But I have to photocopy my hands.
> **Librarian:** I'm asking you to leave now.

User: I put my quarter in. I can do what I want.
Librarian: Please leave now.
User: I won't go.
Librarian: I'm asking you to leave now.
User: You're an old bag. [But she leaves.]

Finally, you may need to give instructions (3.12) either to the person who is creating the problem or to another staff member whom you ask to go for help. Instructions should be clear, concrete, and specific. Use a firm voice. For example:

> Take your hand out of the photocopier. Pick up your books, and leave the library. Please don't come back today.
>
> Robert, please use the phone in the back room. Ask Mrs. Newton to come to the front desk immediately.

6.7.2. Unlawful and Dangerous Behavior

Unlawful behavior includes contravention of library regulations and possibly criminal law. In this section, we are talking about the person who cuts up library books, defaces library signage, steals, threatens, or assaults. Unlawful behavior may or may not be overtly disruptive or dangerous, and the person who engages in it may or may not be mentally ill. In some cases it is not clear that the behavior is in fact "unlawful," and for repeated problems you will need to consult a lawyer. The best advice we can give is to use caution; such behavior may escalate and is unpredictable. These are not situations in which to practice your new communication skills. Do not attempt to do the work of the police or mental health professionals.

However, the fact remains that it is the frontline staff who first encounter these situations, often in the absence of a supervisor. There should be specific procedures to follow, and these procedures must be supported by institutional policies. Some libraries have written their own manuals for dealing with these problems, and if your library doesn't have such a manual, it should. For help in writing the manual and introducing it to staff, see Anne M. Turner's (2004: 104–111) excellent book *It Comes with the Territory: Handling Problem Situations in Libraries*. See also the American Library Association's Intellectual Freedom Committee guidelines on developing policies regarding patron behavior (American Library Association, 1993).

Exercise

Problematic Behavior

For each of the following scenarios, have one volunteer role-play the library user's part and another volunteer role-play the librarian's part. Experiment with different outcomes for the same scenario by having several people play the librarian's role, in turn.

1. A man has left a large pile of overdue books on the circulation desk and is walking away. Some books appear to be damaged. The man refuses to pay any fine. He gives the circulation clerk a hard time and is making a scene. You are the circulation supervisor and have been summoned to handle the situation.

2. A well-dressed professor is leaving the library, apparently empty-handed, when the security alarm goes off. When asked if she has forgotten to check out a book, she refuses to let you look in her briefcase and becomes abusive. She says she is a tenured full professor and threatens to call the board of regents.

3. A library user asks you to make copies of an article for him because he is in a hurry. You explain that staff members do not provide this service but that he can print the article himself in the library's copy area. He orders you to make the copies and begins to shout at you about poor service.

Exercise

Dangerous Customers

Discuss the appropriate procedures for dealing with these situations:

1. One of your student helpers is very upset because a man has exposed himself to her while she was shelving books. She thinks he is still in the building.
2. You have repeatedly asked two teenaged boys to leave the library. One of them says, "Make me!" and pulls out a knife.

The time to think about what to do in a potentially dangerous situation is *not* during the incident itself. The library system needs to have considered in advance possible scenarios and have put into place agreed upon procedures for what to do and not do in specific situations. Handling potentially dangerous situations is a good topic for a staff development session in which a panel of community experts is invited to speak, including a police officer and mental health professionals.

Quick Tips for Potentially Dangerous Situations

- Be alert. Initial signs of a problem situation include users moving away from another user; users staring at someone; and users looking at staff as a form of complaint.
- Stay calm. You may be able to defuse the situation or at least prevent it from escalating.
- Do *not* do any of the following: speak loudly, use patronizing phrases, make sudden gestures, confront the person, or approach too closely.
- Act immediately.
- Know the appropriate agency to call in the situation. Develop an unobtrusive signal system or code word that will alert another staff member to call library security or the police right away.
- Ask other users and staff to move away from the disturbed person for their safety.
- Do not attempt to prevent the person from leaving the library.
- File an incident report (see 9.6.1).

6.8. Annotated Bibliography

General Works, Initial Contacts, Telephone, and Voice Mail

Adler, Ronald B., and Jeanne Marquardt Elmhorst. 2008. *Communicating at Work: Principles and Practices for Business and the Professions*. 9th ed. New York: McGraw-Hill. This book offers good tips for using voice mail and other electronic media. It includes two chapters on interviewing.

Blicq, Ron S. 2005. *Communicating at Work: Creating Messages That Get Results*. 4th ed. Toronto: Prentice Hall Canada. This comprehensive guide to communicating in the electronic office includes suggestions for use of phone and voice mail.

La Guardia, Cheryl, et al. 1996. *Teaching the New Library: A How-To-Do-It Manual for Planning and Designing Instructional Programs*. New York: Neal-Schuman. See pages 109–134 for hints on helping users in the "electronic arcade."

Phone Pro—Leaders in Telephone Skills Training. 2010. http://www.phonepro.org/. This site offers telephone customer service training online. A number of free articles on customer service, culture and morale, and training and management are included.

Walters, Suzanne. 1994. *Customer Service: A How-To-Do-It Manual for Librarians*. New York: Neal-Schuman. See pages 45–47 for helpful hints on training staff to answer the telephone properly.

Principles and Skills of Interviewing

Ivey, Allen E., Mary Bradford Ivey, and Carlos P. Zalaquett. 2010. *Intentional Interviewing and Counseling: Facilitating Client Development in a Multicultural Society*. 7th ed. Pacific Grove, CA: Brooks/Cole. Chapter 13, "Skill Integration: Putting It All Together," provides an overview of the counseling interview, with a sample transcript illustrating individual microskills.

Shipley, Kenneth G., and Julie McNulty Wood. 1996. *The Elements of Interviewing*. San Diego: Singular Publishing Group. This is a useful introduction to basic interviewing skills in various contexts.

Spradley, James P. 1979. *The Ethnographic Interview*. New York: Holt, Rinehart and Winston. Written for the student of ethnography, this influential book clarifies the difference between a conversation and an interview and distinguishes between an interviewer style in which the interviewer learns the language of the interviewee versus the style in which the interviewee must learn the interviewer language.

Statze, Sarah R. 2003. *Public Speaking Handbook for Librarians and Information Professionals*. Jefferson, NC: McFarland. The second section of this handbook covers the interpersonal communication skills needed by library professionals to conduct interviews.

Stewart, Charles J., and William B. Cash. 2011. *Interviewing: Principles and Practices*. 13th ed. Boston: McGraw-Hill. This is a classic guide to various kinds of interviewing. Based on extensive research, it is both practical and easy to read. Each chapter includes training exercises.

Wertz, Dorothy C., James R. Sorenson, and Timothy C. Heeren. 1988. "Communication in Health Professional–Lay Encounters: How Often Does Each Party Know What the Other Wants to Discuss?" In *Information and Behavior*, Vol. 2, edited by Brent D. Ruben, 329–342. New Brunswick, NJ: Transaction Books. This is a much cited work.

The Reference Interview

Agosto, Denise, and Holly Anderton. 2007. "Whatever Happened to 'Always Cite the Source'? A Study of Source Citing and Other Issues Related to Telephone Reference." *Reference and User Services Quarterly* 47, no. 1: 44–54. This article includes a pertinent discussion of telephone reference issues, particularly the opportunity it offers for teaching users about information, and suggestions for improving service.

Carlson, Jake. 2012. "Demystifying the Data Interview: Developing a Foundation for Reference Librarians to Talk with Researchers about Their Data." *Reference Services Review* 40, no. 1: 7–23. This article provides practical information for public service librarians to help them conceptualize and conduct data interviews with researchers.

De Souza, Yvonne. 1996. "Reference Work with International Students: Making the Most Use of the Neutral Question." *Reference Services Review* 24, no. 4 (Winter): 41–48. This article provides suggestions on how to use sense-making questions with international students without intimidating them.

Dewdney, Patricia, and Gillian Michell. 1996. "Oranges and Peaches: Understanding Communication Accidents in the Reference Interview." *RQ* 35, no. 4 (Summer): 520–536. The authors recommend specific interview techniques to avert communication accidents.

———. 1997. "Asking 'Why' Questions in the Reference Interview: A Theoretical Justification." *Library Quarterly* 67, no. 1: 50–71. The authors explain the linguistic reasons that "why" questions are often misinterpreted and suggest other strategies for finding out "why."

Dewdney, Patricia, and Catherine Sheldrick Ross. 1994. "Flying a Light Aircraft: Reference Service Evaluation from a User's Viewpoint." *RQ* 34, no. 2 (Winter): 217–230. This article summarizes the experiences, both good and bad, of library users in the Library Visit Study who visited the library to ask a question that mattered to them personally.

Dyson, Lillie Seward. 1992. "Improving Reference Services: A Maryland Training Program Brings Positive Results." *Public Libraries* 31, no. 5 (September/October): 284–289. Persuasively makes the case that follow-up is one of the most important skills for the reference interview.

Gers, Ralph, and Lillie J. Seward. 1985. "Improving Reference Performance: Results of a Statewide Study." *Library Journal* 110, no. 8 (November 1): 32–35. This study revealed the importance of follow-up questions.

Gross, Melissa. 1995. "The Imposed Query." *RQ* 35, no. 2: 236–243. This article introduces the theoretical and practical aspects of the imposed query.

———. 1999. "Imposed versus Self-Generated Questions." *Reference and User Services Quarterly* 39, no. 1 (Fall): 53–61. The author argues that librarians need to identify questions as either imposed or self-generated and provides special treatment for imposed queries.

Gross, Melissa, and Matthew L. Saxton. 2001. "Who Wants to Know? Imposed Queries in the Public Library." *Public Libraries* 40: 170–176. This article reports on the first study of imposed queries at the adult reference desk.

Hernon, Peter, and Charles R. McClure. 1986. "Unobtrusive Reference Testing: The 55 Percent Rule." *Library Journal* 111, no. 7 (April 15): 37–41. This frequently cited article revealed that library users get the right answer slightly more than half the time.

Isenstein, Laura. 1992. "Get Your Reference Staff on the STAR Track." *Library Journal* 117, no. 7 (April 15): 34–37. This is a good example of a skills-based training program.

Jennerich, Elaine Z., and Edward J. Jennerich. 1997. *The Reference Interview as a Creative Art.* 2nd ed. Littleton, CO: Libraries Unlimited. This book includes an excellent discussion of verbal and nonverbal skills for the reference interview.

Kern, Kathleen. 2004. "Have(n't) We Been Here Before? Lessons from Telephone Reference." *The Reference Librarian* 85: 1–17. Kern compares the development and implementation of chat reference to telephone reference, noting that the similarities are greater than the differences.

Lynch, Mary Jo. 1978. "Reference Interviews in Public Libraries." *Library Quarterly* 48, no. 2 (April): 119–142. This is the report of a pioneering and still pertinent study of 751 reference transactions that occurred in four New Jersey public libraries.

McCain, Cheryl. 2007. "Telephone Calls Received at an Academic Library's Reference Desk: A New Analysis." *The Reference Librarian* 47, no. 2 (98): 5–16. The author presents an analysis of reference transactions at the University of Oklahoma.

Naylor, Sharon, Bruce Stoffel, and Sharon Van Der Laan. 2008. "Why Isn't Our Chat Reference Used More?" *Reference and User Services Quarterly* 47, no. 4 (Summer): 342–354. Students interviewed in focus groups supported a range of reference services rather than any one service and indicated a strong preference for personalized services.

Nebraska Library Commission. 1989. *The Nebraska STAR Reference Manual (Statewide Training for Accurate Reference).* http://nlc.state .ne.us/Ref/star/star.html. This excellent training manual is regularly updated online.

Radford, Marie L. 1998. "Approach or Avoidance? The Role of Nonverbal Communication in the Academic Library User's Decision to Initiate a Reference Encounter." *Library Trends* 46, no. 4: 699–717. The author reports on research on how library users make a decision as to which librarian to approach with a reference question.

———. 1999. *The Reference Encounter: Interpersonal Communication in the Academic Library.* Chicago: Association of College and Research Libraries. Chapter 1, "Literature on the Reference Interaction," reviews evaluative studies that report on reference success.

Reference and User Services Association. 2004. "Guidelines for Behavioral Performance of Reference and Information Service Providers." Reference and User Services Association. http://www.ala .org/rusa/resources/guidelines/guidelinesbehavioral. This resource includes techniques for showing approachability and interest, listening/inquiring, searching, and providing follow-up.

Ross, Catherine Sheldrick, and Kirsti Nilsen. 2000. "Has the Internet Changed Anything in Reference? The Library Visit Study, Phase 2." *Reference and User Services Quarterly* 40, no. 2: 147–155. User reports of reference transactions indicated that librarians bypassed the reference interview, made unmonitored referrals, and failed to ask follow-up questions.

Ross, Catherine Sheldrick, Kirsti Nilsen, and Marie Radford. 2009. *Conducting the Reference Interview.* 2nd ed. New York: Neal-Schuman. Based on research and practical experience, this book covers all aspects of the reference interview and includes tips and practical exercises for reference library staff and those who train them.

White, Marilyn Domas. 1981. "The Dimensions of the Reference Interview." *RQ* 20, no. 4 (Summer): 373–381. This article describes how librarians can increase the coherence of an interview by explaining to the user why they are asking the questions they ask.

The Virtual Reference Interview

Ashdown, Daniel. 2011. "Mobile Messaging Markets Report: SMS, IMS, IM and E-mail Strategies, 2011–2016." Juniper Research. http://www.juniperresearch.com/viewpressrelease.php?pr=337. This research report forecasts extensive growth in the use of instant messaging. A summary of findings is available in a Juniper Research press release dated September 12, 2012.

Bobrowsky, Tammy, Lynne Beck, and Malaika Grant. 2005. "The Chat Reference Interview: Practicalities and Advice." *The Reference Librarian* 43, no. 89/90: 179–191. This article provides practical suggestions for good communication in chat reference as well as pertinent examples.

Boss, Richard W. 2010. "Virtual Reference." *PLA TechNotes*. Public Library Association. http://www.ala.org/pla/tools/technotes/virtualreference. This is a succinct description of virtual reference.

Connaway, Lynn Silipigni, and Marie L. Radford. 2011. *Seeking Synchronicity: Revelations and Recommendations for Virtual Reference*. Dublin, OH: OCLC Research. http://www.oclc.org/reports/synchronicity/full.pdf. This is the report of a multiyear study of virtual reference.

Connaway, Lynn Silipigni, Marie L. Radford, and Timothy J. Dickey. 2008. "On the Trail of the Elusive Non-User: What Research in Virtual Reference Environments Reveals." *ASIST Bulletin* 34, no. 2 (December/January). http://www.asis.org/Bulletin/Dec-07/DecJan08_Connaway_etc.pdf. This article reports the findings of a focus group with graduate students who use Internet tools freely as well as face-to-face reference but do not use virtual reference service.

Fagan, Jody Condit, and Christina Desai. 2003. "Communication Strategies for Instant Messaging and Chat Reference Services." *The Reference Librarian* 79/80: 121–155. The authors argue that librarians can use deliberate strategies to compensate for the absence of nonverbal cues. A strength is the variety of examples drawn from real transactions in the Morris Library, Southern Illinois University at Carbondale.

Hill, J. B., Cherie Madarash Hill, and Dayne Sherman. 2007. "Text Messaging in an Academic Library: Integrating SMS into Digital Reference." *The Reference Librarian* 47, no. 1 (July): 17–29. The authors describe the text messaging reference experience at Southeastern Louisiana University's Sims Memorial Library.

Janes, Joe. 2008. "An Informal History (and Possible Future) of Digital Reference." *ASIST Bulletin* 34, no. 2. http://www.asis.org/Bulletin/Dec-07/janes.html. A spritely and informed article, it covers exactly what the title promises. The author argues that the future depends on making digital reference scalable and central to people's everyday lives.

Kwon, Nahyun, and Vicki L. Gregory. 2007. "The Effects of Librarians' Behavioral Performance on User Satisfaction in Chat Reference Services." *Reference and User Services Quarterly* 47, no. 2: 137–148. This article confirms the importance of communication behavior in virtual reference.

Miller, Mary Helen. 2010. "Librarians Answer Reference Questions with Text Messages." *The Chronicle of Higher Education*, March 25. http://chronicle.com/blogs/wiredcampus/librarians-answer-reference-questions-with-text-messages/22067. See also the responses to this brief article.

OCLC. 2013. *QuestionPoint: Cooperative Around-the-Clock Reference Services and Integrated Online Management Tools* [brochure]. OCLC Online Computer Library Center. http://www.oclc.org/services/brochures/211401usb_questionpoint.pdf.

Radford, Marie L. 2006. "Encountering Virtual Users: A Qualitative Investigation of Interpersonal Communication in Chat Reference." *Journal of the American Society for Information Science and Technology* 57, no. 8: 1046–1059. A thorough review of the literature on relational factors in chat reference, this article includes findings of research and provides illustrative examples of chat transactions.

Radford, Marie L., and Lynn Silipigni Connaway. 2009. "Seeking Synchronicity: Evaluating Virtual Reference Services from User, Non-User, and Librarian Perspectives." Funded by the Institute for Museum and Library Services; Rutgers, the State University of New Jersey; and OCLC, Online Computer Library Center. Last modified August 11. http://www.oclc.org/research/activities/synchronicity. This text provides an in-depth analysis of chat reference based on focus group interviews; online surveys of VRS users, nonusers, and librarians; and the analysis of 850 QuestionPoint transcripts.

Radford, Marie L., et al. 2011. "Are We Getting Warmer? Query Clarification in Live Chat Virtual Reference." *Reference and User Services Quarterly* 60, no. 3: 259–279. This article reports on an analysis of 592 chat transcripts that compares librarian and user query clarification.

Rainie, Lee, and Susannah Fox. 2012. "Just-in-Time Information through Mobile Connections." Pew Internet and American Life Project. http://pewinternet.org/~/media//Files/Reports/2012/PIP_Just_In_Time_Info.pdf. The authors provide the results of a 2012 survey of 2,254 adults concerning their use of cell phones for time-sensitive information.

Reference and User Services Association. 2010. "Guidelines for Implementing and Maintaining Virtual Reference Services." http://www.ala.org/rusa/sites/ala.org.rusa/files/content/resources/guidelines/virtual-reference-se.pdf. These guidelines provide recommendations for establishing effective virtual reference services. Section 4.4 covers service behaviors.

Shiu, Eulynn, and Amanda Lenhart. 2004. "How Americans Use Instant Messaging." Pew Internet and American Life Project. http://www.pewinternet.org/~/media//Files/Reports/2004/PIP_Instantmessage_Report.pdf. This report provides results of a daily tracking survey of 2,204 adults on their use of the Internet.

van Duinkerken, Wyoma, Karen I. MacDonald, and Jane Stephens. 2009. "The Chat Reference Interview: Seeking Evidence Based on RUSA's Guidelines: A Case Study at Texas A&M University Libraries." *New Library World* 110, no. 3/4: 107–121. The authors discover that chat reference librarians sometimes ditch the recommended practices of the Reference and User Services Association (RUSA) in the interest of speed. The authors end by questioning the applicability of RUSA guidelines in computer-mediated reference.

The Readers' Advisory Interview

Chelton, Mary K. 1993. "Read Any Good Books Lately? Helping Patrons Find What They Want." *Library Journal* 118, no. 8 (May 1): 33–37. This is an excellent short introduction to readers' advisory skills.

Jones, Patrick. 1997. *Connecting Young Adults and Libraries*. 2nd ed. New York: Neal-Schuman. This book includes a still-relevant section of dos and don'ts for talking with young adults.

Moyer, Jessica E., ed. 2008. *Research-Based Readers' Advisory*. Chicago: ALA Editions. A good summary of research as well as a source of additional references on readers' advisory service generally, this book includes some material on the readers' advisory interview.

Pejtersen, Annelise, and Jutta Austin. 1983, 1984. "Fiction Retrieval: Experimental Design and Evaluation of a Search System Based on Users' Value Criteria." Parts 1 and 2. *Journal of Documentation* 39, no. 4 (December): 230–246; 40, no. 1 (March): 25–35. The authors analyzed 300 user/librarian conversations as the basis for identifying the dimensions of fiction books that are important to readers.

Ross, Catherine Sheldrick. 2001. "Making Choices: What Readers Say about Choosing Books to Read for Pleasure." *The Acquisitions Librarian* 25: 5–21. The author analyzes 194 open-ended interviews with avid readers in order to understand how readers choose as well as reject books.

———. 2006. "The Readers' Advisory Interview." In *Genreflecting: A Guide to Popular Reading Interests*, 6th ed., edited by Diana Tixier Herald, 25–29. Westport, CT: Libraries Unlimited. *Genreflecting* is a classic work that emphasizes popular genres of fiction.

Ross, Catherine Sheldrick, Lynne (E. F.) McKechnie, and Paulette M. Rothbauer. 2006. *Reading Matters: What the Research Reveals about Reading, Libraries, and Community*. Westport, CT: Libraries Unlimited. By providing a road map to research findings on reading, audiences, genres, and the role of libraries in promoting literacy and reading, this guide offers a rationale for making pleasure reading a priority in the library and in schools.

Saricks, Joyce G. 2005. *Readers' Advisory Service in the Public Library*. 3rd ed. Chicago: American Library Association. This indispensible book introduces the concept of appeal factors and includes a chapter on the readers' advisory interview.

Stover, Kaite Mediatore. 2009. "Stalking the Wild Appeal Factor: Readers' Advisory and Social Networking Sites." *Reference and User Services Quarterly* 48, no. 3: 243–246. The article discusses how book-focused social media sites can be incorporated into readers' advisory practice.

The Employment Interview

Allen, Tiffany Eatman. 2007. "It's Your Call: Telephone Interview Strategies." LIScareer.com, Career Strategies for Librarians. http://www.liscareer.com/allen_phone.htm. This article provides good advice for interviewees.

Dodd, Carley H. 2007. *Managing Professional and Business Communication*. 2nd ed. Boston: Allyn and Bacon. See also the third edition, published in 2012. This useful resource book on all aspects of communication in the workplace includes excellent material

on a wide range of interviews. It covers interviews concerned
with complaints, grievances, discipline, and employment (both
interviewees and interviewers) and offers suggestions for telephone
interviews, group interviews, and videoconference interviews.

Ellis, Richard. 2009. *Communication Skills: Stepladders to Success for the Professional.* Bristol, UK: Intellect. This book includes chapters on interviewing and being interviewed. It is a concise guide with many good examples.

Fear, Richard A., and Robert J. Chiron. 2002. *The Valuation Interview: How to Probe Deeply, Get Candid Answers, and Predict the Performance of Job Candidates.* 5th ed. New York: McGraw-Hill. This is a valuable source of practical advice on all aspects of the employment interview from the interviewer's perspective.

Grasz, Jennifer. 2009. "45% Employers Use Facebook–Twitter to Screen Job Candidates." *Oregon Business Report*, August 24. http://oregonbusinessreport.com/2009/08/45-employers-use-facebook-twitter-to-screen-job-candidates/. This blog posting provides data from a Career Builder survey of 2,600 hiring managers on how social media postings are used to screen out job applicants.

People with Disabilities

Many social service agencies, health organizations, and self-help
groups publish pamphlets that increase understanding of specific
disabilities and include tips for communicating. Ask your local organizations to provide you with multiple copies for your staff and your
public. They also may provide speakers for staff training.

American Library Association. 2001. "Library Services for People with Disabilities Policy." Chicago: Association of Specialized and Cooperative Library Agencies. http://www.ala.org/ascla/asclaissues/libraryservices. This policy was developed to help libraries conform with the requirements of the Americans with Disabilities Act.

———. 2009. "Services to Persons with Disabilities: An Interpretation of the Library Bill of Rights." Chicago: American Library Association. http://www.ala.org/advocacy/intfreedom/librarybill/interpretations/servicespeopledisabilities. This interpretation clarifies the role of libraries in ensuring that people with disabilities are able to participate fully in society.

Americans with Disabilities Act. 1990. *U.S. Code.* Vol. 42, secs. 12101–12213. Amended in 2008. For a copy of the act complete with amendments, see http://www.ada.gov/pubs/ada.htm.

Dalton, Phyllis I. 1985. "Two-Way Communication." In *Library Service to the Deaf and Hearing Impaired*, 24–33. Phoenix, AZ: Oryx Press. The author discusses skills for working with groups and individuals, including American Sign Language and other systems.

Deines-Jones, Courtney, and Connie Van Fleet. 1995. *Preparing Staff to Serve Patrons with Disabilities: A How-To-Do-It Manual.* New York: Neal-Schuman. This book provides tips, resources, and frontline procedures for library staff to use with users with special needs. It also includes sections on the special needs of children and young adults.

International Federation of Library Associations. 2000. *Guidelines for Library Services to Deaf People*, 2nd ed., edited by John Michael Day. The Hague: IFLA. http://archive.ifla.org/VII/s9/nd1/iflapr-62e.pdf. The American Library Association's *Guidelines for Libraries and Information Services for the American Deaf Community*, edited by Martha L. Goddard (Chicago: Association of Specialized and Cooperative Library, 1996), is based on the first edition (1991) of the IFLA guidelines.

Mabry, Celia Hales. 2003. "Serving Seniors: Dos and Don'ts at the Desk." *American Libraries* 34, no. 1: 64–65. This article provides several practical recommendations for helping older adults, as well as statistics on disabilities for this population.

Rubin, Rhea Joyce. 2001. *Planning for Library Services for People with Disabilities.* Chicago: Association of Specialized and Cooperative Library Agencies. This planning manual includes a glossary of terms, guidelines for descriptive language use, and tip sheets for communicating with people with disabilities.

Tinerella, Vincent P., and Marcia A. Dick. 2005. "Academic Reference Service for the Visually Impaired: A Guide for the Non-specialist." *College and Research Libraries News* 66, no. 1 (January): 29–32 . This article includes recommendations on communication.

Walling, Linda Lucas, and Marilyn M. Irwin, eds. 1995. *Information Services for People with Developmental Disabilities: The Library Manager's Handbook.* Westport, CT: Greenwood Press. This text is still useful in helping librarians recognize the range of developmental disabilities, including difficulties with language and communication, perception, learning and cognition, and emotional and social development.

Wright, Keith C., and Judith F. Davie. 1991. *Serving the Disabled: A How-To-Do-It Manual for Librarians*. New York: Neal-Schuman. This book focuses on attitudes rather than technologies, but includes a chapter on what "going electronic" means for people with disabilities. It provides exercises, tests, and staff development simulations.

Language Barriers and Cross-Cultural Communication

Adler, Ronald B., and Jeanne Marquardt Elmhorst. 2010. *Communicating at Work: Principles and Practices for Business and the Professions*. 10th ed. New York: McGraw-Hill. This business communication text has a strong multicultural focus.

Berlanga-Cortéz, Graciela. 2000. "Cross-Cultural Communication: Identifying Barriers to Information Retrieval with Culturally and Linguistically Different Library Patrons." In *Library Services to Latinos: An Anthology*, edited by Salvador Güereña, 51–60. Jefferson, NC: McFarland. This chapter provides a good discussion of the impact of nonverbal communication on cross-cultural communication.

Garner, Sarah Devotion. 2003. "Bridging an Intercultural Communication Gap at the Reference Desk: How to Have an Effective Reference Interaction with Asian LL.M Students." *Legal Reference Services Quarterly* 22, no. 2/3: 7–39. Garner provides a thorough discussion of intercultural communication. Recommended strategies and tips apply to many situations, in addition to the specific user group described.

Hall, Edward T. 1959, 1973. *The Silent Language*. Garden City, NY: Doubleday. The classic work on cross-cultural differences in communication. See also his 1976 book *Beyond Culture* (New York: Doubleday).

McGuigan, Glenn S. 2002. "When in Rome: A Rationale and Selection of Resources in International Business Etiquette and Intercultural Communication." *Reference and User Services Quarterly* 41, no. 3 (Spring): 220–227. This article describes the problems for business of intercultural miscommunication and provides an annotated list of books that could be helpful for library staff.

Nebraska Library Commission. 1989. *The Nebraska STAR Reference Manual (Statewide Training for Accurate Reference)*. http://www.nlc .state.ne.us/Ref/star/star.html. This manual includes tips for working with people from a different culture and with non-native English speakers. It provides information on Hispanic first and last names and Asian naming systems.

Rentz, Kathryn, Marie Flatley, and Paula Lentz. 2010. *Lesikar's Business Communication: Connecting in a Digital World*. 12th ed. New York: McGraw-Hill. This book has a good chapter on cross-cultural communication (face-to-face, on the telephone, and in writing).

Samovar, Larry A., and Richard E. Porter. 2001. *Communication between Cultures*. 4th ed. Belmont, CA: Wadsworth/Thomson Learning. This textbook includes chapters on cultural identification and the use of language. See also from the same authors and publisher *Intercultural Communication: A Reader* (9th ed., 2000), a research-based anthology of 42 articles that help the reader attain intercultural communication competence. Both books are useful for staff discussion.

Handling Problematic Situations and Behavior

American Library Association. 1993. "Guidelines for the Development of Policies Regarding Patron Behavior and Library Usage." Chicago: American Library Association, Intellectual Freedom Committee. http://www.ala.org/Template.cfm?Section=otherpolicies&Template=/ContentManagement/ContentDisplay.cfm&ContentID=78183. Revised in 2000 and 2005. These guidelines provide advice on creating patron behavior policies.

Curry, Ann. 1996. "Managing the Problem Patron." *Public Libraries* 35, no. 3: 181–188. The author analyzes problems arising from differing expectations of staff and users, including seniors and teens. The article includes a case study of sexual harassment and recommends appropriate policy and procedures.

Ferrell, Shelley. 2010. "Who Says There's a Problem? A New Way to Approach the Issue of 'Problem Patrons.'" *Reference and User Services Quarterly* 50, no. 2: 141–151. The author compares the concept of "problem patron" in the LIS and nursing literature, proposes a multilevel approach—is it a community problem, a library level problem, or an interpersonal problem?—and suggests responses to each type of problem.

Hecker, Thomas E. 1996. "Patrons with Disabilities or Problem Patrons: Which Model Should Librarians Apply to People with Mental Illness?" *The Reference Librarian* 53: 5–12. The author argues that those with mental illness should be treated as persons with a disability and not as "problem patrons."

Maness, Jack M., Sarah Naper, and Jayati Chaudhuri. 2009. "The Good, the Bad, but Mostly the Ugly: Adherence to RUSA Guidelines during Encounters with Inappropriate Behavior Online." *Reference and User*

Services Quarterly 49, no. 2: 151–162. The authors compare librarian behavior when faced with appropriate and inappropriate patron behavior in chat reference encounters.

McNeil, Beth, and Denise J. Johnson. 1996. *Patron Behavior in Libraries: A Handbook of Positive Approaches to Negative Situations.* Chicago: American Library Association. Sixteen experts provide authoritative recommendations for dealing with negative situations in public and academic libraries, including how to handle the homeless, the mentally ill, and specific populations such as young adults.

Radford, Marie L. 2006. "Investigating Interpersonal Communication in Chat Reference: Dealing with Impatient Users and Rude Encounters." In *The Virtual Reference Desk: Creating a Reference Future*, edited by R. David Lankes et al., 23–45. New York: Neal-Schuman. This chapter describes the experiences of librarians dealing with impatient users and the communication skills needed for chat interactions.

Rubin, Rhea Joyce. 2010. *Defusing the Angry Patron: A How-To-Do-It-Manual for Librarians.* 2nd ed. New York: Neal-Schuman. This book includes 25 coping strategies that help you deal with angry patrons as well as preventative measures. It also includes examples, scenarios, exercises, and self-tests that can be used in training.

Sarkodie-Mensah, Kwasi, ed. 2002. *Helping the Difficult Library Patron: New Approaches to Examining and Resolving a Long-Standing and Ongoing Problem.* Binghamton, NY: Haworth Press. Also published as *The Reference Librarian* 75/76. This work includes 25 articles on problematic patrons of various types, with much good advice on many aspects of the topic.

Turner, Anne M. 2004. *It Comes with the Territory: Handling Problem Situations in Libraries.* 2nd ed. Jefferson, NC: McFarland. Highly recommended. The author discusses some common "problems that plague us" and provides practical advice as well as guidelines and procedures that can be put in place.

Walters, Suzanne. 1994. *Customer Service: A How-To-Do-It Manual for Librarians.* New York: Neal-Schuman. This book provides excellent tips on problem solving and complaint management.

Videos

The following videos are available from Library Video Network, http://www.lvn.org/.

Library Video Network. 1994. *Be Prepared.* DVD or VHS. 10835B (DVD) or 10177B (VHS). 35 min. Security experts and library staff discuss the best ways to develop a security policy, approach disruptive users including those carrying weapons, and deal with emergency situations.

———. 1995. *Differences Make Us Stronger.* VHS. 10266D. 40 min. This video looks at diversity in the context of serving the internal and external customers and helps you set up your own diversity policies and procedures. It covers customer service, among other topics.

———. 2000. *Diversity in the Library.* DVD or VHS. 41055D (VHS). 20 min. Based on scenarios drawn from library staff members' experiences, this video was designed to help staff examine stereotyped assumptions that can create barriers to public service.

———. 2003. *Solving Difficult Situations.* DVD or VHS. 10886S (DVD) or 10622S (VHS). 28 min. This video shows recommended ways of handling difficult situations, including potentially violent patrons, bomb threats, sexual harassment, and inappropriate Internet browsing.

———. 2004. *Conducting the Reference Interview.* DVD or VHS. 10843C (DVD) or 1072XC (VHS). 29 min. This video covers the stages of a reference interview and the behaviors necessary to conduct a successful reference interview in both face-to-face and virtual interviews.

———. 2006a. *I Need a Book! A Guide to Readers Advisory.* DVD or VHS. 11017I (DVD) or 11009I (VHS). 25 min. This video shows how to identify appeal characteristics of books to help patrons find reading materials and demonstrates how to use the "Quick Dip" in order to learn about a book without reading it.

———. 2006b. *Putting Customers First.* DVD or VHS. 11041P (DVD) or 11033P (VHS). 40 min. Using examples of two libraries that transformed their service, this video emphasizes excellent customer service in person, on the phone, and online. It includes strategies for handling chat, phone, and e-mail transactions.

———. 2010. *Customer Service Basics.* DVD or VHS. 11203C (DVD) or 11211C (VHS). 15 min. This video covers approachability, how to complete a transaction, coping with unhappy users, and good listening skills.

Working in Groups

7.1. Why Work in Groups?

The best idea produced by a group is almost always better than any one of the best ideas from individuals working alone. Group judgments are generally superior to those of one individual because the judgments are evaluated and refined by several people with varying skills and perspectives. Studies suggest that groups of individuals tend to accomplish more creative thinking than individuals who are isolated. The probability of productive discussion, however, is related to the quality of interaction within the group and to the purpose for establishing the group.

When to work in a group:

- To generate ideas or alternatives
- To use the resources of more than two people
- To explore a complex issue or solve a complex problem
- To gather information or opinions from people who have varying perspectives
- To share responsibility for a decision
- To get the group's commitment to implementing the decision
- To develop motivation and leadership ability
- To allow people to share ideas or opinions about a film, book, or presentation that has been made
- To obtain feedback on decisions, instructions, or directions

Exercise 🔧

Purposes of Groups

Look at the following examples of groups commonly found in libraries. Which of these groups hold meetings in your organization?

Branch or departmental staff

A union or staff association

A board of trustees and its committees

Management committees

Task forces, ad hoc committees, special work groups

Citizen participation groups for library planning

Fundraising groups

Discussion groups for staff

Discussion groups for the public—book or issue oriented

Social committees

Seminars, classes, instruction groups

Choose three of these groups for discussion. What is the primary purpose of each of these groups? What are the secondary purposes? Could the primary purpose be accomplished in some other way? Why or why not?

But group work is not always necessary, desirable, or even possible. Moreover, when an emergency decision has to be made, valuable time can be lost in getting a group together. When the group cannot do the job better than a single individual could, don't work in groups.

7.2. Characteristics of Groups

In this book, we use the word *group* to mean more than just a collection of individuals. A group is a collection of individuals who have come together to achieve an explicit, shared goal (even if the goal is simply to exchange viewpoints) and who perceive themselves as members of the group. Group behavior is determined, or at least evaluated, by mutually accepted standards. Group members communicate primarily by talking to each other face-to-face, except in the case of virtual groups, which is discussed in 7.6. Groups may be further described in terms of their purpose, duration, size, personality, and communication structure.

Purpose. Although most groups regularly perform several functions at any one session, a group is usually established to achieve one primary purpose (which purpose may or may not be shared by every individual member). Some reasons that people establish or join groups include these:

- To get to know each other better
- To solve joint problems
- To explore issues of common interest
- To give or receive information
- To make decisions

Think, for example, of the stated purposes of a staff meeting or a meeting of the board of trustees. The purpose of the group determines many of the other characteristics of the group. Individual members may also have hidden agendas that affect the nature of the group. For some individuals, the social purposes of the group may be more important than the task-oriented purposes.

Duration. Groups may be short-lived (such as an emergency meeting of people who normally do not meet) or long lived (such as regular staff meetings where there isn't much staff turnover or a book discussion group of old friends who have been meeting for years). Voluntary groups survive when the members continue to share a common purpose and when the dynamics of the group are healthy.

Size. The optimal group size varies, depending on the purpose of the group. For productive group discussion, a suitable number is 10 to 15 people. In groups of more than 15 people, the communication pattern changes in the direction of a more formal meeting structure in which communication is channeled through the designated leader and the group can no longer be called a small group. Having fewer than ten members limits the range of differing perspectives, abilities, and expertise available for the work of the group. Very small groups—such as buzz groups—of three to four people can still operate productively as a group for certain purposes.

Group personality. Over time, groups take on a life of their own as they develop their own standards and cohesiveness. Groups are greater than the sum of their parts. The personality of a group may be completely different from the personalities of individual members. Have you ever noticed how two groups of similar people working on the same issue can be very different?

Structure. The communication structure of a group refers to the way in which members interact with each other, the relationships among members, and the position of each member in relation to the leader. Communication structures are usually imposed externally, at least initially, and should be appropriate to the size and purpose of the group. For example, a budget committee is established with a specific number of members, a chairperson, and procedures for determining how members communicate with each other and with the parent organization. In very formal structures, the designated (or elected) head makes decisions about who can speak, to whom, when, and about what. A panel discussion is a group that operates for the benefit of a larger group—the audience, with whom the panelists may interact in a controlled and limited way, such as through questions and answers. A discussion group (for the purpose of personal growth or problem solving) is designed for the benefit of the participants rather than the audience and works best with a small number of people who participate equally. Such groups may have a designated leader who facilitates discussion, but the group usually monitors itself. This latter type of group is usually what we think of when we use the term *small group*.

A Quick Tip 🕐

A Perfect Storm
Tuckman (1965) examined the question of why some groups work well and others never manage to complete their tasks. He discovered that successful groups pass through four stages, which Ellis (2009: 86-87) describes as follows:

1. Forming (a group comes together and starts to find its feet)
2. Storming (ground rules get established: agendas are sorted out, roles clarified, purpose and terms of reference settled)
3. Norming (group develops norms of behavior)
4. Performing (group is working and focused on the task)

The second stage is crucial. It is about "getting conflict on the table where it can be talked through and resolved." Ellis (2009: 86-87) states that it's up to "each and every member of the group to see that storming is carried through."

Did You Know? ?

The right size for a group meeting depends on the purpose of the meeting. Groups of three solve easy problems more efficiently than larger groups, but groups of six are more successful in solving complex problems. Groups with more than six members tend to have more behavioral problems and find it harder to find a time when all can attend a meeting. The most common sizes of committees are five, seven, and nine members. For a group to identify a problem, ten or fewer members work best.

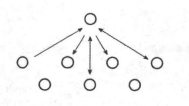

FIGURE 7.1.
Formal or Hierarchical Communication

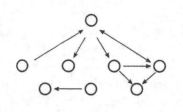

FIGURE 7.2. Semiformal Group

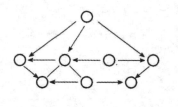

FIGURE 7.3.
All-Channel Communication

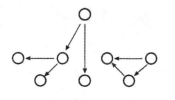

FIGURE 7.4. Splinter Group

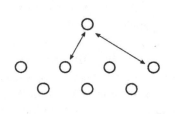

FIGURE 7.5. Monopolization

7.3. Patterns of Communication

Sometimes the leader controls communication within a group so that all discussion is channeled through the leader. Other group members talk, when recognized by the leader, but not directly with each other (Figure 7.1). This pattern is appropriate for a formal meeting, but it doesn't work so well for a small group discussion or joint problem solving. When a number of speakers raise a hand to speak, the chair calls on each of them in sequence, with the result that the discussion may have moved on to a new topic by the time a speaker gets a chance to contribute.

In Figure 7.2, more communication occurs between the group members, but the leader is still a strong focus. This pattern is not appropriate for a very formal meeting when the chairperson needs to control who speaks when and about what. Nor is it the best pattern of communication for a small group. It works best for informal classes or large groups in which some controlled interaction is desirable.

In a true small group, communication flows freely among group members with the leader appearing to take little or no part in directing the group's activities (Figure 7.3). Still, discussion is democratic and productive.

Each of these three basic patterns can be effective, depending on the size and the purpose of the group. But some communication patterns never produce effective group discussion. Splinter discussions (Figure 7.4) occur when a few people in a group split off to talk with each other. They become their own small groups, excluding others and preventing the larger group from functioning. Monopolization (Figure 7.5) is another common problem in which a few people do all the talking and most people in the group do not contribute.

7.4. Group Dynamics

For any group to achieve its goals, it must balance two functions: the *task* function (getting things done: making the decision, discussing the options, or accomplishing whatever the group got together for) and the *maintenance* function (building a good communication climate in which people feel both free and able to participate). In addition, a third set of *self-oriented* functions can often be identified; these are discussed in a later section on problem behavior (7.7).

7.4.1. Task Functions

The following are the roles that people can take in order to facilitate the task functions of the group. A good group member often performs a number of roles at any one meeting, choosing the role according to what is needed at any particular time to further the discussion:

- **Initiating.** Getting the group started, defining goals and problems, and making group objectives explicit. "We're here today to talk about X. Let's start by going around the table and stating our individual interests in X."
- **Asking for information.** Seeking facts. "Who was previously involved in this?" "What are other small libraries doing about this issue?"
- **Giving information.** Providing facts or information, defining. "SL in this report stands for Second Life, not Student Loan."
- **Asking for clarification.** "I'm not sure what we actually decided upon here." "I missed what you said—could you say it again please?"
- **Clarifying.** Restating or paraphrasing. "What I mean by X is . . ." "What you said suggests to me that . . ."
- **Seeking consensus.** "Is there a basic condition that we all agree is necessary?"
- **Asking for opinions.** Requesting others to state beliefs or make judgments. "What do you think we should do?" "How do you feel about the suggestion that we add a school librarian to the committee?"
- **Giving opinions.** Stating beliefs or making evaluative statements. "I think this is too important to ignore. We ought to hire a fundraiser."
- **Linking.** Explaining relationships between ideas or information previously contributed. "Joe has been talking about problems in the circulation department, and earlier we heard from Rosa about a new program in systems. Could a similar program be applied in the circ department?"
- **Summarizing.** Briefly restating group actions or concerns. "We've decided that we ought to do X, but we seem to disagree on exactly how to do this."

> **Did You Know?** ?
>
> In general, the larger the group, the less involved each member is in the meeting. Therefore, meetings with large groups should be shorter than meetings with small groups.

> **Did You Know?** ?
>
> A pioneer in the study of small group behavior and what he called "interaction process analysis," Bales (1950) concluded that almost all group behaviors can be categorized as task oriented or maintenance oriented. This categorization of task functions and group roles continues to be a useful tool for the analysis of group behavior. In a case study of a library management team, for example, Bradigan and Powell (2004: 146) described one team member as a "challenger," while another was considered a "collaborator." They argued that bringing different viewpoints to team decisions allows the team "to look at diverse aspects of an issue before making a decision or a recommendation." (See 7.5.5 and 7.6.1 for more on teams.)

- **Testing.** Trying an idea out in order to explore it more deeply. "Would that work in this situation?" "What would happen if . . . ?"
- **Expediting.** Performing routine activities such as rearranging chairs, handing out paper, and writing down group members' suggestions on a blackboard so that they can be discussed later.
- **Recording.** Writing down major points or decisions made by the group.

7.4.2. Maintenance Functions

People rarely question the need for task functions in a group. But some are unaware of the importance of maintenance functions and may be inclined to label as a waste of time activities that are in fact crucial to the group's continued survival. Here are some roles that help in maintaining the group:

- **Supporting.** Agreeing, praising. "That's a good idea, Barbara."
- **Harmonizing.** Reconciling differences, mediating. "I can see why Jake is concerned, because it is a big risk. On the other hand, we should maybe look carefully at what Liwen is proposing and see if that can be done in a way that won't hurt Jake's department."
- **Gatekeeping.** Facilitating equal participation in the group, preventing monopolization, structuring discussion. "George hasn't said what he thinks yet."
- **Reflecting group feelings.** "Maybe we've gone as far as we can with this point." "I think some of us are feeling a little lost."
- **Relieving tension.** Telling a joke, story, or personal experience to defuse negative feelings.

Do some of these task and maintenance functions sound familiar? The microskills described in Chapters 1–3 are skills for group work as well as for one-to-one communication.

In any group, attending skills such as acknowledgment (3.2) and eye contact (1.2) can function as maintenance skills by helping the group feel comfortable or as task skills by helping to focus on the task at hand. Questioning skills (3.4 and 3.6) contribute to the task functions of information gathering, checking out facts, comparing opinions, and probing. As in the interview, open questions (e.g., "What are your expectations for this group?") work very well at the beginning of a group session. Sense-making questions (3.6) can be used to find out what has brought this group together, what the members' concerns are and what they need or want to find out, and what would help the group achieve its purpose.

Confronting as an assertiveness skill (3.13) contributes to the maintenance of the group when it is used effectively to handle problem behavior. Summarization and reflection of feeling (3.8 and 3.9) are particularly important skills for group leaders, because they convey to the group the leader's understanding of what has been accomplished so far and how the group feels. Research among politicians has shown that the most successful political leaders are those who can explicitly state the common feelings and opinions of the population.

Role-Playing Exercise

This exercise provides an opportunity for group members to examine the effects of task and maintenance functions in a discussion group. The exercise works best when participants already have some understanding of group dynamics and have been introduced to the concept of task and maintenance functions and to the various roles that people may play in groups. Participants with an awareness of group dynamics are less likely to feel overwhelmed by being assigned a role that happens to be "out of character."

Each group member is given a card on which is described the role that member is to play. The group member reads the card silently but does not let anyone else know what is on the card. Each person plays the assigned role in a group discussion, without explicitly revealing the role. (The person who gets the supporter role supports other people's contributions but never says anything like, "Because I'm supposed to be the supporter . . .") The topic of discussion should be a question on which there is likely to be diversity of opinion: for example, what should the public library's position be on Internet content filtering? (Other possible topics: Is unionization a good move for professional librarians? Should academic librarians push for faculty status?)

When participants have read and understood their roles, discussion begins and continues for 10 to 15 minutes. At the end of the role-played discussion, talk about these questions:

- What role do you think other people were assigned, and what made you think so? (If a correct matching of person to role is made, the role-player should declare it.)
- When in the discussion did the roles emerge most clearly?
- What effect did each role have on the way the discussion developed?
- How did each participant feel about his or her role?

ROLES

(*Note:* The roles of opinion-giver and information-giver should each be assigned to at least two people. In a smaller group, assign the roles in the order below, leaving out the roles of supporter, tension-reliever, or observer as needed. In a larger group, the role of observer may be assigned to more than one member.)

- **Group leader.** Your role is to be the group leader. Get the discussion started by posing the question or topic. Keep it going by asking questions as needed. Encourage everyone to provide opinions and information. Don't give opinions or information yourself. At the end of the discussion, summarize points on which the group has agreed (or disagreed) as a wrap-up to the work achieved by the group. End the discussion in approximately ten minutes.
- **Information- or opinion-seeker.** Your role is to ask for facts, relevant information, ideas, suggestions, or opinions about the topic. Don't contribute facts or opinions yourself.
- **Information-giver.** Your role is to provide information—facts, statistics, relevant experiences, and so forth. Volunteer facts (make them up, if you like), and give information on what you have read or heard about this issue.
- **Opinion-giver.** Your role is to say what you think about the issue, providing opinions. You can be a devil's advocate, if you wish, for the sake of generating discussion.
- **Clarifier or elaborator.** Your role is to clarify or elaborate on what has been said to make sure that everyone in the group is talking about the same thing and understands it the same way. For example, "Do you mean . . . ?" or "Could you give an example?" or "If that is true, then what we could expect to happen would be . . ."
- **Evaluator.** Your role is to get the group to weigh the quality of ideas and solutions. When a suggestion is made,

encourage the group to test it out. For example, "Would this work if . . . ?" "What would prevent this from working?"

- **Harmonizer.** Your role is to build consensus and find common ground. Try to reconcile different viewpoints. Suggest compromises. Smooth over the rough spots. Don't say much about your own opinions.
- **Supporter.** Your role is to support other people's contributions to the discussion. Agree with one or another position or opinion expressed by others. Show support by encouraging others. Do not give any new information or opinions of your own.
- **Tension-reliever.** Your role in this group is to be a tension-reliever. Make humorous comments, encourage informality, and help people to be at ease. Don't offer many opinions. Just do your best to see that people are getting along and enjoying themselves.
- **Observer.** Your role in this group is to be an observer. Contribute to the discussion occasionally, but focus on what others are doing and saying.

7.4.3. Group Leadership

Every group has at least one leader. The leader may be the formal, designated leader (the chairperson or the group trainer) or an informal leader who holds no specified title but is able to influence group behavior and help the group work toward its goal. The leader's responsibilities are to:

- get the group started;
- guide the group through the stages of information-sharing, exploration of ideas, and evaluation or decision making;
- keep the group on track;
- encourage equal participation from group members;
- summarize group activity; and
- look after resources and physical arrangements.

A good leader is above all a good listener (Chapter 2). The leader should not express personal opinions but help others to achieve the group's purpose.

> **Did You Know?** ?
>
> Walt Crawford (2003: 116-117) provides these tips for discussion leaders:
>
> 1. Introduce the topic at the outset, and gently bring the discussion back when it strays.
> 2. Encourage all participants to take part without putting anyone on the spot.
> 3. Discourage dominant personalities from taking over the show.
> 4. Listen a lot more than you talk.
> 5. Head off personal attacks and incendiary remarks.
> 6. Ask someone else to serve as note-taker.

Learning How to Lead

Studies of leadership show that leadership ability is not innate but involves skills that are learned. Many styles of leadership can be identified, but here we are concerned with facilitative leadership or the ability to help a group identify, analyze, and reach its goals. Individuals who have been formally designated as group leaders may or may not be effective leaders.

However, the responsibility for effective group performance belongs to everyone in the group. If an important task or maintenance function is not being attended to, someone in the group should step in to perform the needed role. One way to provide leadership practice is to establish procedures for shared leadership. The designated leadership for an ongoing group may be rotated among all group members. An easy way to introduce this concept is to have co-leaders: an experienced and an apprentice leader work together for one or two sessions or for parts of a session. The apprentice leader then takes on the co-leadership with a new apprentice leader until everyone has become more experienced as a leader.

Quick Tips for Co-leaders

- Meet with your co-leader well in advance of the group session to plan who will do what and when.
- Share responsibilities for booking the room, sending out notices of meetings, preparing materials to be distributed in advance or at the meeting, and organizing refreshments.
- Designate sections of the discussion to be led primarily by one person. The other person then acts in a supporting role only during that section.
- When you are in the supporting role, listen carefully so that you know where your co-leader is taking the discussion.
- When you are in a supporting leadership role, be alert to the general tone of the group—observe body language, and note what's happening. Help your co-leader to recognize members who want to contribute.

Quick Tips for Getting Discussion Started

- Suggest that each person begin with a self-introduction and say something about his or her reasons for joining the

---

Exercise

Sharing Leadership

Practice shared leadership by working with a co-leader to plan and lead a short discussion in a group of five or six people. Decide who will take the primary leadership role first, and plan when you will switch roles. After the discussion is over, give feedback to your co-leader. What helped you? What other help did you need? How flexible were you? What could you do to improve the way you work together?

group. Ensure that this self-introduction doesn't turn into a status-definition procedure.

- Ask each participant to contribute something from personal experience. For example, "Let's go round the table and each describe a recent problem you have had with the reserve system. Try to be brief and specific."
- Help the group make an inventory of the problems or issues they would like to have discussed in the group. Write all suggestions on a flip chart or blackboard.
- Begin with a provocative statement or radical proposition. Ask individuals to react. For example, "An extreme solution is simply to reduce library hours right across the system. How do you react to that?"
- Brainstorm for ideas. Generate as many ideas as possible, without evaluation or criticism.

7.4.4. Being a Good Group Participant

All group members, not just the group leader, have a responsibility for making the group work productively. Even if you have no official leadership role, you still need to be aware of group dynamics and play an active part in helping the group achieve its goals:

1. Pay attention to your own behavior. What are you doing to help the group? Are you doing anything to hinder it?
2. Help the group by reinforcing positive group behavior ("That's an excellent suggestion, Ahmed."). Step in as needed to discourage negative behavior ("That's interesting about your fishing trip, but we do have a limited amount of time and maybe we ought to get back to the main issue" or "I know feelings are running high on this issue, but we still need to listen to each other respectfully").
3. Call attention to a problem in group functioning, even if you can't think of a solution ("Look, I feel that we're going around in circles. What can we do to get back on track?"). You're not doing yourself or the group a service by bottling up your feelings of dissatisfaction with how things are going.

A Quick Tip 🕐

Brainstorming

Brainstorming is a good way to stimulate original ideas in a group or simply to warm up a group so that members are more open to new ideas. To lead a brainstorming session, ask the group members to call out as many ideas as they can in response to the topic at hand (e.g., How can we draw attention to Library Awareness Week?). Explain that you will accept any idea, no matter how far-fetched or off-the-wall, and that the group should not stop to evaluate or discuss ideas. The purpose is solely to generate ideas. Keep the ideas coming as quickly as you can write them on a flip chart. Don't allow any embellishment or evaluation of ideas. When the brainstorming is working well, some ideas will be predictable, and others will be amusing or even ridiculous (e.g., put an ad in the paper, give away free books, invite the Pope, burn books in the library garden). Stop only when no one can think of another idea. To proceed to the next stage, get the group to identify the most interesting ideas for further discussion.

7.5. Group Work in Libraries: Five Types of Face-to-Face Communication

So far we have talked about group dynamics and leadership in general terms. The section that follows examines five representative types of group discussions that commonly occur in libraries. We start with the *book discussion group* as an example of an informal group in which the leadership function is distributed. The *problem-solving group*, while still informal in its communication patterns, is usually more structured. The *focus group* has a highly structured form and purpose, although the discussion can be free-ranging. The *formal meeting* usually involves the greatest numbers of people and is the most structured group of all. Our final example is *self-managed teams*, which can include various kinds of group interactions, informal and formal meetings, and problem-solving discussions, usually with a specific goal in mind. In a later section (7.6), we discuss virtual groups, which may have similar purposes to these five kinds of face-to-face groups but have different constraints.

7.5.1. The Book Discussion

Contrary to what you might think, the desirable outcome of a book discussion is *not* that group members end up with a comprehensive set of facts or a so-called correct interpretation of the book. A book discussion is successful when it allows all members to share their responses to the book, compare their differing interpretations, and ask each other questions. Something has gone wrong if the discussion turns into a lecture in which one person presents an expert interpretation and everyone else listens respectfully. Remember that a book discussion is *not* a booktalk—you will find information on booktalks in 8.5.2. However, it does involve talking about books.

Aidan Chambers in *Booktalk* speaks of the need to discover a repertoire of questions about the reading experience that helps rather than hinders the discussion of books. He developed what he calls the "Tell me" approach for use with children, but these open questions are fruitful for discussing books with readers of all ages:

Did You Know? ?

To facilitate meetings for large groups of people, Deschamps (2010) explains that libraries can use Large Group Methods (LGM). The meetings themselves are called "unconferences" or "camps." Open-space technology (OST) is the most popular method of hosting an unconference. Social media such as Facebook and Twitter are used to promote the event. The Open Space website explains that OST was developed in the 1980s when Harrison Owen found that conference participants identified the coffee break as the most interesting part of a conference he organized. "He perfected a meeting method where the 'coffeebreak' became the key element." For an explanation of how OST works, see Harrison Owen's "Brief User's Guide to Open Space Technology" at http://www.openspaceworld.com/users_quide.htm.

Tell me . . . when you first saw the book, even before you read it,
   what kind of book did you think it was going to be? (probe:
   Can you tell me what made you think this?)

What struck you particularly about the book?

Was there anything that surprised you? Puzzled you? Bored you?

Have you read other books (stories/plays/poems) like this? How
   does this one differ?

Which character (or, in a nonfiction book, which section)
   interested you the most?

Did you notice anything about the novel that made a pattern?

If the author asked you what could be improved about this book,
   what would you say?

We've heard each other's ideas on this book. Are you surprised by
   anything that anyone else has said?

When you think about this book now, after all we've said, what is
   the most important thing about it for you? (Chambers, 1985:
   168–173)

The book discussion is one of the best ways to learn group leadership skills and to teach them to others, including library users. A volunteer leadership training program should include an introduction to group dynamics, basic listening and questioning skills, and a great deal of practice within the training group. The following tips for book discussion leaders can easily be adapted for discussions of films.

Some Tips for Book Discussion Leaders

- Be prepared. Make an outline in advance of some possible questions and issues, but don't cling to it too closely. Let the group's interest determine what gets discussed. Let the discussion go on as long as it is relevant to the text.

- Maintain an open communication climate. Get everyone into the discussion early. Encourage everyone to question each other.

- Don't try to cover the whole book in every aspect. Focus on about four issues, but encourage the group to spend some time considering the book as a whole.

- Keep your questions short. Don't preface your question with a preamble that turns into a minilecture.

- Don't stop with agreement. Go on to find out why: Why did you all find it hard to get into the book? What made

---

Exercise ⚒

Leading a Discussion
Practice leading a discussion by using as your text a short document such as the American Library Association's "The Freedom to Read" document (http://www .ifmanual.org/ftrstatement) or something similar. Each participant takes turns being the leader for about three minutes. The task of the first leader is to get the discussion started by asking open questions (3.4) to clarify meanings and get opinions about intellectual freedom. The second leader continues this line of questioning but probes more deeply, and so on.

A Quick Tip ⏱

Book Discussion Novice?
If you are a book discussion novice or just want to brush up on your skills, expert readers' advisor Joyce Saricks (2009) recommends that you subscribe to *Booklist*'s book discussion blog *Book Group Buzz* (http://bookgroupbuzz. booklistonline.com/).

the setting the most interesting part of the book for most of you?

- Use provocative or "devil's advocate" questions to encourage opposing points of view.
- Stay on track. Don't let the discussion wander too far from the book itself, but don't rule out contributions about how a situation in the book resonated with a reader's own life experience.
- Redirect the discussion from the monopolizer and nonreader.

7.5.2. The Problem-Solving Discussion

Basic attending and questioning skills are useful in all groups, including book discussion groups and problem-solving groups. In addition to these basic skills, problem-solving groups also need to use analytic and evaluative skills in a systematic, structured way. The following is an outline that a leader might use to prepare for leading a problem-solving group. These suggestions apply to committee meetings as well as to ad hoc groups that get together informally to address a problem:

1. Describe the problem: What is its nature and extent?

    a. What background information is needed?
    b. What is the specific question to be decided?
    c. How serious is the problem?
    d. What factors should be considered in deciding on a solution?

2. What solutions are proposed?

    a. List solutions without evaluating.
    b. What are the advantages of each solution?
    c. What are the disadvantages of each solution?
    d. Which solutions can be discarded because no one considers them workable?

3. What is the group's initial reaction?

    a. On what points does the group substantially agree?
    b. What are the chief differences on matters of fact?
    c. What are the chief differences on matters of opinion?
    d. How fundamental are these differences?

4. Which solution, or combination of solutions, seems
   best?

   a. Can a compromise be reached that will find general
      approval?
   b. If not, which solution, after debate, is favored by the
      majority?

5. How will the chosen solution be implemented and
   made effective?

   a. What can this group do?
   b. What can each member do?
   c. How will the implementation be evaluated?

In this description, it is assumed that the problem solution will be
approved by a majority vote. However, there are other ways to come
to a decision: consensus (where everyone agrees); deferring to expert
opinion; and authority rule (where the final decision is made at a
higher administrative level, often after advice from the group). Adler
and Elmhorst (2010) explain that the choice of a decision-making
method depends on the type of decision to be made, the importance
of the decision, the available time, and the personal relationships
among members.

7.5.3. The Focus Group

First developed by market researchers, the focus group is a popular
format for gathering information and opinions. A focus group brings
together a small number of people (usually six to ten, but no more
than twelve) who represent a particular interest or characteristic for
a group interview on a particular topic. For example, people with
several different kinds of disabilities might be invited to share their
views on what the library could do to become more user friendly. Or
a randomly selected group of regular library users might be asked
what features they would like to see included in the design of a new
library building. Focus groups differ from individual interviews or
questionnaires (and other types of discussion groups) in several ways:

- Focus group participants are encouraged to discuss the
  topic in their own language and talk about the aspect of the
  topic that interests them.

> **Did You Know?** ?
>
> Focus groups provide a simple and
> flexible method to elicit opinions
> from library users (and nonusers)
> at relatively low cost. You can use
> in-house staff, and the results are
> easily understood. However, the
> results are only as good as the skills
> of the moderator, who must be able
> to encourage all participants to talk
> but must also keep the discussion
> on topic in an unobtrusive manner
> (Glitz, 1998).

- The group leader or moderator often starts the discussion with some ground rules and an introduction of the topic and then steps back and lets the discussion unfold naturally, intervening only when the talk veers off topic. The moderator's role is important but unobtrusive.
- Discussion reveals attitudes and the language that participants themselves use when talking about the topic.
- Group interaction produces a range of responses as well as reasons for these responses.
- Information can be gathered from otherwise hard-to-reach populations.
- Results help the library to understand complex issues from a variety of perspectives.

Running a focus group involves most of the skills necessary for any other group activity—keeping the group on track, ensuring that all participants express themselves, keeping a record, and so forth. It differs from most other types of groups in these ways:

- The selection process is crucial. If you want to get a wide range of opinions and ideas, use purposive sampling to select people who are very different from each other. If you are more interested in the "average" viewpoint of a particular group, take a random sample from your population (e.g., senior library users). To be sure of having enough participants, recruit a larger number of participants than is your target number. Some people will be unable to attend.
- Because it's often a one-shot meeting, more emphasis must be placed on building group trust within a short space of time (usually the meeting lasts one to two hours).
- To accomplish the task, leaders often use a semistructured interview guide with questions prepared in advance.
- Often the meeting is recorded so that all ideas can be analyzed later. The leader must ensure that people are aware of the audiorecording but comfortable enough to express their true opinions.

7.5.4. The Formal Meeting

Meetings can range from informal discussion groups to very formal meetings governed by specified rules of order. Some examples of formal meetings are the annual meetings of the national library associations or the regular meetings of a board of governors or trustees. Formal procedures are useful when the following conditions are present:

- The decisions made by a group are important and must be formally recorded.
- The topic is contentious.
- The group is large.
- A mass of routine business must be dealt with expeditiously.

If you become the president of the American Library Association or another large association, you will need to know how to conduct a formal meeting according to the rules of parliamentary procedure. These rules, which have been developed over the centuries as a way of maintaining order in democratic assemblies, are recorded in such standard works as *Robert's Rules of Order* (Robert et al., 2011) and the *Standard Code of Parliamentary Procedure* (American Institute of Parliamentarians, 2011). But even if you are never called on to preside, you still need to know the basics of how formal and semiformal meetings work in order to be an effective group member. This section is a basic introduction.

Establishing the Rules

Your group need not adopt procedures exactly as set out in *Robert's*. Some adaptations may well be desirable to streamline procedures and suit the rules to the particular needs of the group. In general, the larger the group, the more formally the rules are followed. But keep in mind that rules are not ends in themselves. They should be used to help in the transaction of business and not be used as technicalities to frustrate and obstruct the will of the majority. The basic principles lying behind the rules should always be honored:

- There should be justice and courtesy for all.
- The will of the majority should rule.
- The rights of the minority should be protected.
- Every proposition is entitled to a full hearing.
- Only one thing should be dealt with at a time.

> **A Quick Tip** 🕐
>
> **Rules for Small Groups**
> Check out some of the procedures manuals for small groups, such as *Democratic Rules of Order* (Francis and Francis, 2010) and *Roberta's Rules of Order* (Cochran, 2004). You may think that it's possible to function in a small group without procedural rules, but that way lies meeting chaos. John Gastil (1993: 60) suggests that procedures can be adapted to changing memberships, issues, and situations. For example, in some cases of decision making you might want to seek consensus, while in others you might rely on majority rule.

Planning the Meeting

The constitution and bylaws of your association or organization usually specify how often regular and general meetings must be held and who must be invited. When the date of the meeting is set, distribute a notice of the meeting and a brief agenda to members at least one week in advance (or more, if the constitution requires more advanced notice). The notice should contain the place, date, and time of the meeting and the name of a contact person to notify regarding attendance. The agenda, or order of business to be brought before the meeting, usually consists of certain standard items:

- Approval of minutes of the last meeting
- Reports of officers and standing committees
- Reports of special committees
- Unfinished business
- New business

It may also include appendixes containing materials for group members to read before the meeting.

Conducting the Business of the Meeting

The *motion* is the main tool used to conduct the business of the meeting, although groups vary in the way they use motions. In some informal meetings, motions are not used: members make proposals and carry on discussion and debate until some consensus is reached. In formal meetings, members must formally move and second a motion before a proposal is open to discussion. In semiformal meetings, members can discuss a problem and consider a number of solutions before someone formally proposes the adoption of one of these solutions in a motion.

What, then, is a motion? A motion is a proposal for the group to take a certain action. Most people, hearing the term *motion*, bring to mind proposals such as:

- I move that we adopt the committee's report.
- I move that the library be closed on Mondays.
- I move a vote of thanks to Shania for her excellent work on the Community Walks project.

A Quick Tip 🕐

Managing Meeting Time
Wait no more than five minutes for latecomers. People will learn after the first time. Meeting leaders (including teleconference moderators) who manage to end meetings slightly ahead of time are perceived as more efficient.

These are *main motions*. Main motions, which constitute the majority of motions brought forward, are the only ones that introduce business for consideration and action. However, there are three other categories of motions, any of which can be made while the main motion is pending: privileged, incidental, and subsidiary motions. Any motion in these three categories takes precedence over the main motion and must be dealt with before the group can return to the main motion.

Privileged motions have no connection with the main motion but are considered so important that they get immediate attention. Examples include motions to adjourn, to recess, or to raise a question of privilege (e.g., to point out that the room is stuffy and ask that the windows be opened). *Incidental motions* deal with questions of procedure that arise from the business at hand, usually another pending motion (to raise a point of order, to object to consideration, to withdraw a motion, to appeal the ruling of the chair). *Subsidiary motions* are for the purpose of dealing with or disposing of the main motion. Examples include motions to lay on the table, to call for the previous question (close debate and vote immediately), to limit debate, to refer to a committee, and to amend.

If you are going to chair a large formal meeting, make sure that you know the standard characteristics pertaining to different kinds of motions:

- What is the order of precedence for motions? (All other kinds of motion take precedence over the main motion.)
- Which motions require a second?
- Which motions cannot be amended?
- Which motions can be debated? Which ones can't be debated but must be voted on immediately?
- Which motions are carried by a simple majority? Which ones require a two-thirds majority? Which ones are settled by a ruling of the chair?

Standard manuals like *Robert's Rules of Order* usually provide charts, tables, and lists intended to clarify these points.

As a member of a group, you can probably get through most meetings without ever encountering many of these privileged, incidental, and subsidiary motions. However, you do need to understand some basic procedures and use some ordinary common sense and courtesy. The outline for a meeting presented later includes only the common elements that are likely to arise in every meeting.

Responsibilities of the Chair

The success or failure of the formal meeting largely depends on the chair. The formal responsibilities of the chair are easy to enumerate (although not so easy to carry off successfully):

- Checking to see if there is a quorum (the minimum number of members required to hold a legal meeting, as specified in the bylaws)
- Calling the meeting to order at the appointed time
- Following the order of business as outlined on the agenda
- Deciding all points of order
- Recognizing members who are entitled to the floor
- Guiding the discussion so that it does not digress
- Stating and putting to a vote all legitimate motions
- Ruling out of order motions that are deliberately frivolous or obstructive
- Making sure that all points of view get a hearing
- Adjourning the meeting

In performing these responsibilities, the chair should avoid expressing personal opinions on the merits of the proposals before the group. The presiding officer's job is to help the group discover the will of the majority by doing such things as sampling opinion, summarizing arguments, summarizing the feelings of the group, and suggesting procedural solutions. These activities can be carried out successfully only when the group perceives the chair as impartial.

There are four additional things that you should do when presiding over a meeting:

- Be alert to physical problems with the environment and fix them. Is there something wrong with the arrangement of the chairs? Is the room too hot or too cold? Is sunlight pouring in through the window and blinding some members? It shouldn't require a member's rising to a point of privilege to attract the chair's attention to such problems.
- While you listen to the speaker who has the floor, surreptitiously scan the whole room on a regular basis, watching for signs of difficulty such as puzzled expressions, raised hands, whispering, and inattention. Respond to these signs of difficulty. For example, if Bob Black looks puzzled

at a speaker's proposal, wait until the speaker is finished and then call upon Bob to explain his difficulty with the proposal. If participants seem weary and inattentive, you can suggest a brief recess.

- Facilitate discussion. The proper parliamentary practice for debate is that each speaker must first be recognized by the chair. Because this practice can be cumbersome and slow, it is common in semiformal meetings for the chair sometimes to allow two speakers to engage in rapid-fire, back-and-forth debate when this sort of exchange seems efficient. As chair, you can allow this mode—what William Carnes (1987) has called the "self-disciplined Ping-Pong mode"—but be vigilant for signs that order is breaking down or that the debate has lost the interest of the group as a whole. Never allow speakers, unrecognized by the chair, to speak at the same time or to speak randomly on unconnected issues.
- Listen for the sense of what is meant. If you can't understand what a speaker means by a proposal, probably no one else can either. As chair, either you should ask the speaker to clarify or you should summarize (see 3.8) succinctly what you thought was meant and ask the speaker if you got it right.

Common Faults of Committee Leaders

- Calling a meeting that is not necessary. Don't call a meeting just because it's the time for a regular meeting. If you can't write a one-sentence objective about what the meeting is supposed to accomplish, then don't call the meeting.
- Not circulating in advance a meeting agenda that is specific enough that group members know what topics will be discussed and can therefore prepare in advance for the discussion.
- Coming to the meeting unprepared. ("Let's see. What are we discussing today?")
- Losing control of the meeting so that the discussion goes off topic, splinter discussions develop, or monopolizers take over. Good leaders know when to practice closure (3.11).
- Refusing to handle dysfunctional behavior. Do not permit unproductive or irrelevant discussion. Don't allow strong emotion to inhibit progress. Make sure everyone

Some Quick Tips

Good Behavior for Meetings

Ellis (2009: 96) suggests what attendees can do to make meetings more effective:

Arrive on time.
Read the background papers and minutes in advance.
Help maintain peace and harmony. Say, "Can we take a ten-minute cooling off period?"
Ensure that everyone is clear. Ask, "Can we have an explanation of . . . ?"
Advance the discussion by offering a specific action. Say, "May I propose that we circulate this to . . . ?"

participates in an appropriate role and that decisions are made without bullying.

- Not controlling the time: not starting the meeting on time; not ending on time; or letting discussion drag on unprofitably on some minor issue so that no time is left for the major topic. Start on time, even if not everyone is present. Latecomers will soon learn. Finish on time, even if you have to refer an item to the next meeting. Allot a certain amount of time for each item on the agenda, and then move on.

Keeping a Record

The purpose of minutes is threefold: (1) to refresh the memory of those present about what was done at the meeting; (2) to inform those who were absent; and (3) to provide a historical record of resolutions, decisions, and acts. Effective minutes save time by providing continuity from meeting to meeting and by preventing the wasteful duplication of action. They also remind members what they agreed to do by including action items.

The minutes, which are written up by the secretary and circulated to members, should contain the following information:

1. Details of who, where, when:

- the kind of meeting (e.g., regular, special);
- the name of the group;
- the date and time and the place (unless the place is always the same); and
- the names of those present, including whether or not the regular chair and secretary were present or who substituted for them (the names of those who sent regrets are sometimes included).

2. Approval of the minutes:

- whether the minutes of the last meeting were approved as read or circulated (or corrected and approved as corrected).

A Quick Tip

Electronic Agendas and Minutes

Distributing agendas and minutes electronically is essential for virtual meetings, but for face-to-face meetings you may still want to make some paper copies available as well because participants need copies at the meeting and may not print them off beforehand. If the group is always electronically connected, using laptops or tablets may provide sufficient access to agendas and minutes at the meeting. Minutes can be archived in a shared meeting folder with read-only access.

3. What was done at the meeting:

- a summary of what was done at the meeting in the order in which it happened; and
- for each main motion, it is necessary to record the exact wording of the motion, the name of the mover and the seconder, and what happened to the motion. (It is not desirable to record everything that was said. But it is often useful to record the reasons for a decision in sufficient detail that people consulting the minutes for guidance some time in the future can understand the rationale for decisions.)

4. The time of adjournment.

Some Quick Tips for Writing Minutes

- Be tactful and avoid making personal references. Instead of saying, "Bill went on his usual rampage about user fees," the minutes might say, "One member expressed strong opposition to user fees."
- Be selective, clear, and succinct. Minutes should provide a record of what was done without being encumbered with a mass of unnecessary detail. Highlight those things that furthered the objectives of the meeting, particular decisions made, and action items.
- Include a summary of strong minority points of view so as to acknowledge that these opinions were heard and taken into account although in the end rejected by the majority.
- Write up the first draft of your meeting notes within a few hours, while events are fresh in your mind.
- See 9.11 on committee communications.

A Quick Tip

Know Your Readership
Ellis (2009: 101) suggests that minute-takers be aware beforehand who is likely to read the minutes. If only those attending the meeting will read them, you can summarize the proceedings more tersely. If the readership includes those who do not normally attend, you might need to expand some of the discussion (explain jargon or abbreviations, for example, or provide more background).

A Model Outline for a Typical Meeting

Chair: The meeting will now come to order. The first item of business is the minutes of the last meeting of October 17, which were distributed. Are there any errors or omissions? [An opportunity is provided for group members to point out corrections.] If there are no (further) corrections, the minutes are approved as read (or corrected).

[Some organizations prefer having a formal motion to approve the minutes, in which case the chair says, "Can we have a motion to approve the minutes? Seconder? All in favor?"]

Chair: The second item is a matter arising from the minutes. At our last meeting, we asked an ad hoc committee consisting of Bob Black, Shania Robinson, and Kwame Kundi to look into the question of X and make recommendations. Bob, can I call on you to tell us what your committee discovered?

Bob Black: Thank you, Mme. Chair. Our committee . . . [summary of the committee's deliberations]. Therefore, I am prepared to move that [wording of the motion].

Chair: Is there a seconder? [A main motion must have a seconder before it can be considered. The chair acknowledges the seconder.] It has been moved and seconded that [restatement of the motion]. Is there any discussion? Yes, Barbara Green. [Only the person recognized by the chair can speak. The chair recognizes in turn everyone who wants to speak on the question but disallows discussion that is not related to the present motion.]

Barbara Green: I move to amend the motion by deleting [such and such word, phrase, or sentence]. [Motions can also be amended by inserting or adding words or by striking words and substituting others. If the motion to amend is hostile or irrelevant to the main motion, it should be ruled out of order. Discussion, if any, follows as in the handling of the original motion.]

Martin Grey: I second the motion to amend.

Chair: We have a motion before us to amend the main motion so that it reads [statement of the amended motion]. Any discussion? [pause followed by a discussion, if any] If you're ready, I'll call the question. The motion before us is to amend the main motion by deleting [such and such] so that it would read [restatement]. All in favor of the motion to amend? [Those in favor raise a hand.] Opposed? [Those opposed raise a hand.] Carried [or defeated]. The motion, as amended, now reads [restatement]. [If the motion to amend was defeated, the chair would say, "The original motion is . . ."] Is there any further discussion of the motion? [pause] If not, I'll call the question. All in favor of the motion [restatement of the motion]? Opposed? The motion is carried [or defeated].

> **Chair:** The next piece of business is Item 3, the report from the Standing Committee on [such and such]. [Calls on the chair of the committee for a report.]
> [And so on through the order of business.]
> **Chair:** Is there any further business that you'd like to address? [pause] If not, can we have a motion to adjourn?

7.5.5. Self-Directed Work Teams

Teams are self-managed groups from within an organization, the members of which are focused on a joint goal or project. They do not have a supervisor but direct their own work under the coordination of a team leader whom they select. Katzenbach and Smith (2003: 21) define teams as "a small group of people (typically under twenty) with complementary skills committed to a common purpose and set of performance goals." This definition provides the keywords that distinguish teams from other work groups: small, complementary skills, common purpose, and performance goals. Simply labeling a group a team does not make it a team. A team is not just any group working together—committees, councils, and task forces are not usually teams.

Katzenbach and Smith (2003: 279) note that team performance requires both individual and mutual accountability. Team members "hold themselves accountable for their individual contribution, for their mutual collective contributions, and for whether the team achieves its purpose and goals." Teams may be short term (project teams established to deal with a particular project, for example) or long term (management teams established permanently to manage a function).

Project teams are usually organized by a project manager, who must take responsibility for the results. The project manager selects the team leader who, in turn, selects and assigns tasks to the team members, directs the work, and encourages the team members to complete the tasks. Depending on the nature of the project, team members can be pulled together from across departments or job functions. Many of the task and maintenance functions (see 7.4.1 and 7.4.2) of participants and leaders of project teams are the same as for other work-related groups. Success of project teams depends on training, motivation, and recognition.

Management teams are self-directed groups with responsibility for a substantial, but defined and manageable, part of the work that an organization does. Team members usually come from within the

Did You Know?

Robert Kling and Christina Courtright (2003: 224) note that a convenient way to categorize the different forms of social organization, both face-to-face and online, is to sort them in terms of their relationship to paid employment. Members of work-oriented groups such as work teams recognize that their participation is "either compulsory or highly-beneficial for work-oriented advancement." They therefore participate differently than people do in nonwork groups such as clubs and nonprofessional associations, self-help groups, and the like.

Did You Know?

Bradigan and Powell (2004: 146-147) found that while a team needs to have regularly scheduled face-to-face meetings, the number of these meetings can be reduced by using an electronic team discussion list. Team members can communicate easily, hold informal meetings, provide informal feedback to each other, and exchange documents. (See 7.6.3 on virtual discussion sites.)

same department or work area (e.g., all from information services). The team manages itself and the work it does. Individuals within the team may have specific day-to-day responsibilities, but the team has oversight over overall policy and any changes in practice within the area for which it has responsibility.

Both kinds of teams require participants who are "good team players," able to work cooperatively with others. Interpersonal communication skills are just as important assets for team members as are problem-solving and decision-making skills. Team members should be able to listen actively, state their opinions clearly, and provide helpful suggestions and feedback to others. Technology allows for "virtual teams" (7.6.1) assembled with participants from anywhere in the world. The interpersonal skills needed for working on virtual teams are, if anything, even more important than for face-to-face teams.

7.6. Virtual Groups

Communications technology mediates the relationship between space and time, breaking the tyranny that used to require group members to be in the same place and work at the same time. In 7.1–7.5 on face-to-face groups, we have had in mind for the most part a small group with certain characteristics: a closed set of a fairly small number of members who know each other, who interact with each other in the same physical space, who have a sense of their own identity as a group member, and who are aware of who else belongs in the group.

With communications technology, we now have entities that are called "groups" that have a porous membership of up to thousands of people who may be anonymous. Individuals may be brought together by a common practice or interest or goal, without necessarily having much idea of who else is in the group or how big the group may be. On the other hand, some virtual groups, especially work-related ones, resemble many face-to-face groups in being formally constituted with a fixed membership list of individuals who already know something about each other.

In a nutshell, a virtual group can be a lot of different things and can vary from a smallish group of people who work with each other (e.g., a virtual team, see 7.6.1) to an unbounded group of thousands, many of whom may drop in, lurk, or drop out (e.g., an e-forum or discussion site). When they are formally constituted, virtual groups

Did You Know?

The library staff at the University of Northern Iowa used e-mail brainstorming to develop their strategic plan (Neuhaus, 1997). The software they used allowed the facilitator to broadcast messages in groups of eight to avoid information overload while encouraging spontaneity. Online brainstorming can be done using e-mail, chat, Twitter, or a brainstorming software app (just search "brainstorming apps" on Google). Research on online brainstorming indicates that the online medium generates more novel ideas than does face-to-face brainstorming. Why? It seems that people in anonymous online groups feel less normative pressure, produce more ideas, and engage more equally in discussion (Luppicini, 2007).

may be created for a variety of purposes—formal meetings, basic problem solving, certain kinds of decision making, discussion including book discussion, information giving, information gathering, and brainstorming.

In this section, we discuss three kinds of virtual group situations commonly used in libraries—virtual teams, virtual conferencing, and virtual discussion sites—presented in order of diminishing structure and increasingly porous membership. We focus on the basic features and communication practices of each form, whatever the particular technology involved.

Most of the basic principles of group dynamics discussed in 7.4 apply to virtual groups too. Why? Because when people interact using communications technology, they bring into the interaction a set of social rules that have been developed in the face-to-face world of interpersonal relationships. Just as in face-to-face groups, both maintenance and task functions need attention. And, of course, whatever the group's task may be, whether making a decision or exchanging ideas, a requirement for success is good communication. Linda Harasim, a professor at Simon Fraser University who is a pioneer in developing distance education networks, knows a lot about collaborative learning and the building of online communities. The suggestions she provides for building a sense of community in an online group are good advice for face-to-face groups as well. She recommends the following: respond promptly; use first names or nicknames; use reinforcing phrases, such as "Good idea, Barbara"; show good humor; promote cooperation by offering help and sharing ideas; and don't beat anybody up (Harasim et al., 1995).

A growing body of research has focused, with mixed success, on teasing out the differences between interaction in face-to-face groups and in virtual groups. The field of education has a special interest in computer-mediated communication (CMC) as a tool for learners in distance education. Rocci Luppicini (2007) reviewed 170 recent research articles in 78 journals that addressed CMC in education. Some consensus seems to have emerged. When participants in online groups don't know each other's identities or status, they are less inhibited by the fear of being evaluated. They are therefore less likely to withhold ideas and contributions. An online decision-making group is less likely than a group that meets face-to-face to be taken over by a few dominating personalities.

The same lack of inhibition that encourages more equal participation among anonymous online group members also leads to more expression of personal viewpoints, more novel ideas, but also more argumentation. However, as Hollingshead and Contractor (2006: 126) point out, everything changes when the members' identities and statuses are known in advance or available visually—in this condition, there was "no evidence of the participation equalization effect" in the computer-mediated setting.

Earlier empirical work done on face-to-face versus CMC used concepts such as "media richness" and "reduced cues" and "cues-filtered-out" to investigate differences. The thinking was that the lack of nonverbal cues in text-based communication necessarily made the text-based medium impersonal and lacking in socioemotional content. Walther (1996) argued in a much-cited paper that this simply is not the case. When group members "have time to exchange information, to build impressions, and to compare values," CMC becomes interpersonal. It just takes longer than it does in face-to-face groups for members to get to know one another.

When we consider the role of technology to mediate communication in virtual groups, it can be helpful to keep these points in mind:

- Users adopt new communications technologies and integrate them into their repertoire, alongside the older tools (Quan-Haase and Young, 2010).
- New tools don't usually kill off older ones. But when the new technology is introduced, it often changes the order that existed before. For example, television didn't kill radio, but now people use radio differently than they did when people gathered around the radio to hear Roosevelt's fireside chats. The telegraph is one of the exceptions, killed off by e-mail after 155 years.
- The older medium has a continued existence because it finds a special niche, performing a particular function very, very well or very conveniently. Sometimes, as in the case of the smartphone, new functions and affordances transform use.
- Communications media can be usefully sorted according to the type of communication they support: one way or two way; one-to-one, one-to-many, or many-to-many; synchronous or asynchronous; text based, voice based, or voice and video. For group communication, the dominant channels must be two way and many-to-many. But one-way channels are used in supplementary ways, for example, to distribute agendas, minutes, and documentation.

Did You Know? ?

Early studies generally agreed that CMC of groups is impersonal. But it seems that the impersonality finding was an artifact of the way the experimental studies were designed. The studies used one-shot designs that put together groups of people who didn't know each other and never expected to meet again and then got them to work together on a timed task. However, when group members are given time to know each other in a real-life situation, their communication becomes interpersonal (Walther, 1996). Hollingshead and Contractor (2006: 127) report that longitudinal research with real groups indicates that CMC is a stumbling block to interaction initially but that over time the virtual group catches up.

- "Every tool shapes the task," as Ursula Franklin (1996) has pointed out. Tools are not neutral. Communication software that is adopted to manage communication among groups of people has a shaping power over what happens in the group, whether it's a classroom of learners or a group making a decision.
- Notwithstanding the importance of the constraints and affordances of technologies, that is not the whole story. Equally important are usage practices and what people themselves decide to do with the tools (Kling and Courtright, 2003).

7.6.1. Virtual Teams

A virtual team is one in which the team members work on projects from different locations and rarely, if ever, meet face-to-face. But they do communicate on a regular basis by phone, e-mail, instant messaging, videoconference, or web conferencing software. CMC supports teamwork in various ways enumerated by Michelle Boule (2008b: 7). Because team members can come from anywhere with an Internet connection, the criteria for choosing membership can be quality and diversity of expertise, not simply geographic propinquity. Because all documents and work are in a shared virtual space, team resources can be accessed from wherever the team members happen to be. And because people communicate through a variety of technological tools, both synchronous and asynchronous, discussions and decisions need not be postponed until a meeting can be scheduled.

Virtual teams seem to work best if members can be brought together at the outset for a face-to-face meeting to get to know each other. As Walther (1996: 10) points out, "the accrual of interpersonal effects is slower in CMC and develop in proportion to accumulation of message exchanges." It takes longer to write than to talk. However, you can jumpstart the process. Caroline Haythornthwaite et al. (2000) describe how the University of Illinois at Urbana–Champaign has set up a compulsory two-week face-to-face boot camp for each new cohort of students in the distance option (LEEP) of its graduate LIS program; she says, "Boot camp unites members of each year's cohort and builds a community for them." Similarly for virtual teams, Hinds and Weisband (2003: 33–34) recommend that members meet face-to-face early in the process "so that rapport and common ground can be established before misconceptions arise." To sustain the bonds, it

---

Did You Know? ❓

Ursula Franklin, Canadian metallurgist, feminist, and champion of human rights, warns, "Be mindful of how the tool shapes the task. And that you only find this out when you really learn about the tool" (Franklin, 1996: 11-12). She points out that when you get a food processor, suddenly everything you cook needs slicing and dicing and you stop using your old recipes.

Did You Know? ❓

When groups have access to a variety of tools, communication can occur almost simultaneously through multiple media rather than sequentially. In a study of the use of multiple media in a firm, Quan-Haase, Cothrel, and Wellman (2005) found that employees did not switch between media and people to communicate but used various media simultaneously to interact with different people. "People use the media that their communication partners prefer. Besides having a good understanding of individual preferences in media use, people also know the best way to reach particular people."

can be helpful for members to meet face-to-face at least once a year, changing up the location so that members get to visit each other's sites.

Some Tips for Virtual Teams

If you are the team leader:

- Consciously foster the team's sense of a shared group identity.
- Establish shared ground rules for respectful group interaction.
- Be the facilitator of the team's work, making sure that members stay engaged and deadlines are met.
- Provide constructive feedback (3.14).
- Provide multiple means of communication for sustaining group interaction: synchronous and asynchronous; one-to-one, one-to-many, and many-to-many; public and private; formal and informal.
- Recognize which team members respond best to a phone call, e-mail, or instant messaging, and use the preferred channel. (Adapted from Boule, 2008a: 29; RW³ Culture Wizard, 2010: 34)

If you are a team member:

- Take responsibility yourself for fostering the team's cohesiveness and sense of identity as a group.
- Use your communication skills of using encouragers (3.3), asking questions (3.4), reflecting content and feeling (3.8 and 3.9), offering instructions (3.12), offering opinions and suggestions (3.16), and providing feedback (3.14) to keep the project on track.
- Be willing to volunteer information to advance collaborative work.
- Be a good team citizen. Be accountable to the group's goals, meet deadlines, and follow the work rules that the group establishes.
- Check in frequently with the team, following agreed upon routines (such as checking into the team site five times a week).

- Be aware of cultural differences among team members and the way that those differences may lead to misunderstandings and communication accidents. (Adapted from Boule, 2008a: 30; RW³ Culture Wizard, 2010: 16)

7.6.2. Virtual Conferencing

Virtual conferences allow people physically located in different places to meet, using electronic communications equipment to hear, and often see, one another as they interact. Virtual conferencing is a cost-effective way of bringing people together. It can work well, especially if the people involved have already met each other in person. But there are situations when virtual conferencing is *not* suitable:

- Making major or very complex decisions with far-reaching consequences (e.g., you might hire an entry-level librarian in a teleconference, but you would probably want to be face-to-face with a prospective new CEO)
- Giving bad news to employees, especially if it affects them in different ways

There are various methods of virtual conferencing—in this section we consider teleconferencing, videoconferencing, and web conferencing as three types with different affordances. The behaviors of participants in virtual conferencing depend on how much the technology allows them to share. Voice-only as in teleconferencing? Both voice and video as in videoconferencing? Or voice and possibly video plus the ability to see and exchange documents during the conference as in web conferencing? The basic task and maintenance functions of group members (described in 7.4) must also be considered in terms of how they can be achieved in virtual conferences.

Teleconferencing

As a member of a work team or an association committee, you may have participated in a voice-only teleconference, which is still used to facilitate meetings when participants are geographically scattered. Originally, teleconferencing meant telephone landlines and a maximum of three geographic areas included in the conference. Now the addition of mobile phones and the ability to connect more than three

Did You Know? ?

Chilcoat and DeWine (1985) examined the interpersonal perceptions that people had of each other when they communicated synchronously using three different media: audioconferencing with voice only, videoconferencing with voice and image, and face-to-face. Consistent with a "cues-filtered-out" theory, the researchers expected that the fewer the cues available, the less favorable the perceptions would be. However, the opposite was the case. Audioconferencing partners produced higher ratings of their partner's similarity of attitude and higher ratings of physical and social attractiveness than did those using video or face-to-face. Raters thought their partners more attractive in the only condition in which they could *not* actually see each other.

Did You Know? ?

In addition to the usual problems that plague group meetings (e.g., people not showing up, participants not reading the background material in advance, poor leadership by the chair), there are some extra causes for poor-quality conference calls:

- Lack of experience with how group dynamics work in a conference of many voices
- Lack of familiarity with the technology
- Background noise and disturbances that are multiplied when there are so many participants located in different settings

parties have opened things up and made teleconferencing more useful for group interaction.

As with any other meeting, teleconferences are productive when participants are well-prepared and have an effective leader. Usually it's the moderator's job to ensure that people are prepared—by sending out the background material and agenda, as well as by explaining the procedure, including time limits. It is also the moderator's job to make participants feel welcome, encourage their contributions, thank them for participating, and prevent disparaging remarks about group contributions.

When the teleconference begins, the moderator should do a roll-call (so that everyone can hear everyone else's voice), restate the purpose of the meeting, and set out the guidelines for discussion. For example, the moderator should specify the time allotted for each section of the agenda and remind the participants to identify themselves each time they speak ("This is Martha again"). Because some participants are reluctant to speak, the moderator should ensure that everyone participates by calling on each person occasionally or by using a gatekeeping strategy ("Let's hear from someone who hasn't had a chance to speak. Robert, what are your concerns about this proposal?").

Because nonverbal cues are unavailable in a voice-only environment, you should use even more intensively some of the verbal skills described in Chapter 3. Appropriate skills include encouragers ("That's interesting"), restatement ("So, Jake, you think we should get some outside help"), reflection of feeling ("Donna, you don't sound happy with that decision"), and check-out questions ("Is that what you're saying, Peter?"). It's often hard to tell who's saying what on a teleconference. Identify yourself before speaking, and use names of others ("This is Lee again. I agree with Mario because . . .").

At the end of the conference, the leader should summarize key points and restate what decisions have been made and what actions will follow. The recorder should ensure that a call summary or the minutes of the teleconference are sent to everyone within a few days of the meeting, both to participants and to those who were invited but could not attend. Like traditional meeting minutes (see 7.5.4), this record should contain the names of participants, the highlights of the discussion, and a description of major decisions made.

Videoconferencing

Videoconferencing and Skype combine voice and picture. To the cues available in teleconferencing (words, tone of voice, pitch), video-based technologies add nonverbal cues such as gestures, gaze, facial expressions, posture, and movement (see Chapter 1).

Sue Potton (1996) advises that, when you are on camera, your appearance, interactions with others, and mannerisms can convey unintended messages. Behaviors that might not be noticed so much in a face-to-face meeting (wrinkling your nose, smiling inappropriately, yawning, doodling, tuning out, working on something else, rolling your eyes, wearing unprofessional attire)—all these behaviors are magnified on video. Moreover, they may be preserved, to be seen again in a repeat viewing and possibly transmitted to a wider audience.

So practice before you go live. For a major presentation, practice before a video camera and ask others for feedback. And consider the background. Take a cue from those experts on television who are interviewed remotely through a satellite connection—they almost always appear in front of a suitable, orderly, and nondistracting background.

Organizing a videoconference demands advance work. If participants are in different time zones, the coordinator needs to make sure that everybody knows the time of the conference in their own specific time zone. A copy of the agenda should be sent out before the event, along with a list of the names of all attendees. If people are participating from distant places, a local moderator should be appointed who can ensure participation is managed effectively at each location. The moderator will need to ensure that all the necessary equipment is in place and fully functional. Be prepared for possible technical failure. Prepare a contingency plan for alternative communication, and let participants know what the plan is (see "The Art of Videoconferencing" at http://www.worketiquette.co.uk/the-art-of-video-conferencing .html).

Web Conferencing

Web conferencing provides the opportunity for group meetings over the Internet. A web conference is similar to a conference call but with an added Internet component that allows for richer engagement. Participants sit at their own computer and connect to the web conference

---

Did You Know? ?

At its simplest, videoconferencing provides transmission of static images and text between two locations. At its most sophisticated, it provides transmission of full-motion video images and high-quality audio between multiple locations

A Quick Tip 🕐

Webinars
Check out free library webinars (web + seminar) as a way of learning new skills and finding out about new developments in the library world on everything from Defending the Right to Read to Disaster Recovery in the Cloud. A webinar is a live online educational presentation, typically an hour in length. Attendees, who usually register in advance, can participate by submitting questions and comments during the live presentation. If you can't make the live viewing, you may be able to see the archived presentation later in an on-demand viewing. You can find good tips at TechSoup (http://www .techsoupforlibraries.org/events/ archive).

through the Internet plus a phone connection or alternatively VoIP. When logged onto a website, participants can view slides, a whiteboard, or documents and co-browse. Depending on the specialized software used, there may also be support for online chat, video, and online polling of attendees. Recording of conference proceedings is automatic and can be kept on your hard drive or, in some cases, archived. Designed initially for corporate use, web conferencing systems are available at various levels of functionality, bells-and-whistles, and cost.

Web conferencing is being adopted by libraries and used not only for online meetings but also for training programs, lectures, presentations, book discussions, and web seminars (webinars). In *Library Programs Online: Possibilities and Practicalities of Web Conferencing*, Thomas A. Peters (2009) has provided a guide written with such library programs in mind. Peters was involved with Online Programming for All Libraries (OPAL), a collaborative effort by libraries to provide web-based programs and training for library users and library staff. Because of archiving, a web conference event may be synchronous for the real-time participants and asynchronous for people who catch it later as a podcast or webcast. In some cases, the original live online event may have had 15 participants, but later hundreds may see the recorded version, which is archived and indexed in search engines.

Peters (2010) provided some tips for presenters. People who participate from home on their computers may be multitasking, with lots of competition for the scarce resource of their attention. Therefore, programs should be kept short, say an hour maximum. Elements for audience engagement should be built in—for example, opportunities to ask questions through online chat or to answer yes or no to a polling question. Because of the potential for software incompatibilities with different versions of web browsers and different operating systems, you should anticipate a possible problem loading your presentation slides into the web conference software. Slides can shift, resize, and experience other unexpected quirks. Therefore, keep the slides simple and, if you use any embedded image files, keep them small (8.3.6).

7.6.3. Virtual Discussion Sites

You have probably participated in or "lurked" on an online library discussion group or electronic discussion list at some time or participated in an Internet forum or message board on a topic of personal interest. An Internet discussion provides a structured space where people can have conversations in the form of posted messages that many people will read and some will answer. The communication is interactive, but the interaction is asynchronous—time delays occur between responses. Unlike chat, the text messages are archived and available indefinitely. See 9.3.5 for tips on writing the messages.

Unlike in a face-to-face group, you don't get many social context clues about the other participants, whom you may know only by some alias such as Roadscout or Bookgrrl. Instead, you build images of what people are like based on the meager information of what they write. This means that whatever minimal cues do appear take on "particularly great value" (Walther, 1996), because there are no other cues provided that could be used to temper an impression. For example, on a discussion forum on the website Engadget concerning the promised date for the release of an operating system update, one contributor said, "It'll be nice if the update is released on Tuesday Feb. 21st, but I don't believe it, I don't believe the post because of the spelling error on the word 'unteathered.' No way this could've been put out by top executives in a company." In the absence of other cues, a disproportionate weight was given to a spelling mistake. Readers are always filling in the gaps in trying to make sense of a text. When the gaps are large and information sparse, readers may form an impression of the message writer that is either idealized or sharply negative—what Walther (1996) calls "hyperpersonal" computer-mediated communication. In this situation, CMC is far from impersonal—it becomes *more* personal and more intense than would a corresponding face-to-face interaction.

It is common to talk of interactive electronic media as creating a level playing field, democratizing communication, and creating a space where anyone can freely communicate with anyone else. However, Kling and Courtright (2003) recommend that we take a sociotechnical view. We should pay attention to how sites are structured by the affordances of the technologies involved, the social and institutional factors, and the various rules about who can participate and who can't, what modes of communication are acceptable, and what actions the participants are able to do (post/read/buy/sell/role-play, etc.). Kling and Courtright (2003: 222) note, "Some of these sites rely upon passwords for protection; others use IP addresses. In short, rather than the level and undifferentiated view of the Internet . . . , this sociotechnical view emphasizes carefully structured electronic

Did You Know? ?

People who participate in an electronic forum (e-forum) or a professional electronic discussion list do not automatically become a "community." Kling and Courtright argue that the casual use of the term *community* to refer to people who may occasionally post in the same forum is "seriously misguided" and short-changes the real work needed to create community. They say, "developing a group into a community is a major accomplishment that requires special processes and practices" (Kling and Courtright, 2003: 221).

forums where people experience walls, hallways, and doors with electronic locks."

Though rules and norms vary in different sites, some standards for communicating in an online discussion group are commonly accepted and are found on many sites. Briefly, here's how to behave in an e-forum or learning group:

- Stick to the topic. If you want to talk about something different, start a new thread.
- Avoid flaming, profanity, and racist or sexist remarks.
- Be concise. And don't clutter up your response with the complete text of the message to which you are replying.
- If someone has requested personal assistance, send your message only to that person, not to the whole list.
- Know the difference between sending a command (e.g., to unsubscribe) to the moderator/owner/server and sending it to all participants. You might not want 3,000 people to know that you're going out of town.

7.7. When Your Group Has Problems

In both virtual and face-to-face groups, problem behavior may occur because individuals have not yet learned how groups work, or they are unaware of the need for people to participate equally and constructively. People who are not used to working in groups often erroneously think that the person who has the most subject expertise or experience should do the most talking and, conversely, that people who have no expertise or experience have nothing to contribute. At other times, problem behavior occurs because participants do not yet have the skills for group work. They are not sure how to ask the right questions or how to express their feelings appropriately. A third reason for problem behavior is that some members of the group may have a hidden agenda that involves self-aggrandizement or even perpetuating the problem that the group is trying to solve.

7.7.1. Self-Oriented Functions

In addition to the task and maintenance functions listed earlier (7.4.1 and 7.4.2), there is another category of group functions called "self-oriented." These functions are destructive unless they are immediately addressed. Some common self-oriented functions are:

- **Blocking.** Disagreeing without a rationale or alternative; preventing the group from moving on; repeatedly taking a negative approach.
- **Attacking.** Criticizing individuals rather than their opinions and behavior; criticizing the group and its purpose without reason.
- **Attention-seeking.** Bragging; recounting personal experiences in a self-important way; constantly seeking recognition.
- **Withdrawing.** Refusing to talk or listen; doodling; behaving excessively formally; conducting splinter discussions.
- **Monopolizing.** Exerting authority or superiority; manipulating group behavior; interrupting; talking excessively.
- **Horsing around.** Excessive joking; not taking other people's contributions seriously.

One way for a leader (or any participant) to prevent problem behavior in a group is to describe the purpose of group work and to make the expectations explicit: "We are here today to discuss X. Some of us have had previous experience with this, and some have not. Because we want to generate as many ideas as possible, it is important for everyone to participate in this discussion. We need to see the issue from everyone's perspective."

If a group is really committed to its task, the members themselves will eventually deal with problem behavior—sometimes very skill-fully. Still, it is safer and more efficient for the leader to handle the problem promptly before it begins to affect the group's ability to function.

Exercise: Negative Roles in Groups

To illustrate the effects of self-oriented behavior, use the role-playing exercise in 7.4.2, but add one or two of the following dysfunctional roles. (Don't add more than two of the monopolizer/blocker/digressor roles at any one time or the group becomes hopelessly dysfunctional. With the addition of even two of these negative roles, it takes a strong group leader to prevent the discussion from going off track.) This exercise should be used only with groups that have already developed some understanding of how groups work and when there is some assurance that the designated leader will not feel overwhelmed.

- **Monopolizer.** Your role is to steal the show. Say as much as you possibly can. Make all your opinions known. Interrupt others.
- **Nonparticipant.** Your role is to try to be invisible. Never volunteer anything. If you are spoken to, say you have no opinion or don't know. Behave as if you are very shy.
- **Blocker.** Your role is to be a stumbling block to the group's achieving its goals. Object to everything. Bring up points for further consideration that the group has already rejected. Try to prevent any agreement. Say things like, "We've tried this before and it never works" or "There's no point in trying to do that because no one will cooperate." Object to the group's procedures, and say they are very flawed.
- **Digressor.** Your role is to try to get the group off topic. Say that the topic under consideration reminds you of another (dissimilar) experience that you had once and begin to describe your experience. Introduce red herrings into the discussion.

7.7.2. How to Handle Problem Behavior

Here are some quick tips for handling the talker, the know-it-all, two kinds of clams, and the joker.

Quick Tips for Handling the Talker

Some individuals talk excessively in a group for various reasons—self-importance, enthusiasm, special knowledge or expertise on a topic, even nervousness. The talker may in fact be interesting, entertaining, and have wonderful ideas and suggestions. But he's monopolizing discussion time to the exclusion of other people who may have equally wonderful ideas and who, in any case, are there to work through the group's task together, not to hear a lecture. Individuals talk excessively only because someone else lets them. The power to redistribute the discussion lies not only with the designated leader but also with the group. In any long-term group, the members will eventually deal with the talker, but it's more efficient if the leader handles the problem promptly. The following tips for face-to-face interaction can also be adapted to virtual groups:

- Use the skill of closure (3.11). Wait for the talker to finish a sentence or take a breath; then acknowledge her contribution or expertise, and shift the focus of discussion through a question directed to others: "That's useful information, Mary. We may get back to it. In the meantime, what do the rest of you think?"
- If the talker doesn't get the hint after you redirect the discussion, make your request more explicit. Interrupt if necessary: "Hold it, Mary. What you've said is useful, but one of the purposes of this meeting is to get everybody's ideas. So I'm going to limit the next part of the discussion to those people who haven't said anything yet."
- Mary may be dying to start talking again, with your permission. Don't make eye contact with her, and don't acknowledge her gestures—if you do, that's an invitation for her to start all over again. Even if she's the only one waving her hand, look elsewhere or change the topic. In a virtual group, you can't depend on body language, so use microskills that discourage Mary—avoid acknowledgment, and don't ask Mary a question.
- In large groups where there are a few people who do all the talking, try this: "One of the purposes of this meeting is to get everyone's ideas, but some people haven't had a chance to get a word in edgewise. For the next 20 minutes (or for today's session), I'm going to ask the people who usually say a lot not to say anything, and I'm going to ask the people who usually don't say anything to say a lot. You all know who you are, so let's start the discussion." This approach doesn't hurt anyone's feelings (never mention names) and reflects group feeling—everyone knows that a balanced discussion is better. You may not think that this will work, but it almost always does!

A Quick Tip for Handling the Know-It-All

The know-it-all wants everyone to know that he's an expert. He tried that plan before and it didn't work; he has read all the important literature; he alone knows what decision should be made. Handle the know-it-all as a special case of the talker, and use the strategies listed above.

Quick Tips for Handling Two Kinds of Clams

At the other end of the scale are the clams, people who never contribute to the discussion. The first type of clam is the person who never speaks but would like to. The shy person needs an atmosphere in which it is safe to speak without fear of saying the wrong thing or of being ignored.

- Get the shy person into the discussion early—the longer a person goes without speaking, the harder it is for her to join in. In a virtual group, call on the lurkers—people who read the postings but never contribute.
- If necessary, call on that person by name and ask a question in a way that leaves the person in control and does not demand too much. For example, "Jean, what do you think about that?" or "What experience do you have in that area?" If Jean answers, "I'm not sure" or "I haven't had any experience," follow up with a positive statement: "I think we're all a little uncertain about which way to go" or "This is a new experience for several of us—that's why we're here to talk about it." Pause to give Jean time to add more, and if she doesn't, move on.
- Periodically, give Jean another chance to participate. When Jean does make a contribution, don't interrupt. Instead, be patient and use encouragers and restatement (3.3 and 3.8). Remember that shy people are often good listeners and will make more contributions in smaller groups.

But there is another kind of clam in many face-to-face groups—someone who doesn't speak, not from shyness but for some other reason. He or she is usually not a good listener either and may deliberately withdraw either by not showing up or by using body language that says, "I don't want to be here."

- Use the same questioning techniques as with the shy person, but when you get an "I don't know," probe further: "Do you mostly agree? Disagree? Give us an example."

- In a long-term group and only when initial trust has been built up, use reflection of feeling (3.9) to deal with the problem: "Joe, I get the feeling you wish you didn't have to come to these meetings. Am I right?" Then follow up: "What could we do that would make you feel more involved in this issue?"
- You might want to speak to Joe privately, using a confrontation skill, DESC (3.13). Describe the facts: "Joe, we've had three meetings now and you haven't said anything." Express, or explain, the problem: "When some people don't say anything, we can never be sure that we've explored everyone's concerns." Specify what you'd like to see happen: "It would be helpful to the group if you could express your opinion occasionally, even if it's only a brief statement." State the consequences: "If you don't give an opinion, we could end up with a decision with which you don't agree."

Quick Tips for Handling the Joker

This person is a grown-up version of the class clown, always ready with a smart remark, a joke, a funny face. His behavior can function positively by reducing tension and by helping people relax. But the behavior becomes negative when it happens so often that the group cannot concentrate on the task or members feel they are not being taken seriously.

- At first, ignore the behavior. Don't encourage the joker by acknowledging his behavior, even by saying, "That's very funny, but . . ." If you reinforce the behavior by commenting on it ("The class clown, I see") you may be typecasting the joker permanently and he may not be able to break out of it, even when he wants to get serious.
- If necessary, use the DESC sequence (3.13): "You made a joke but, instead of helping us get this job done, it makes me feel as if our job isn't serious. I'd like us to get serious for a while and leave the jokes till after the meeting so that we can focus on the issue."
- In face-to-face groups, you can also confront with nonverbal skills—a long, deliberately awkward pause, direct eye contact, all the disapproving gestures that your teachers

used to use. This usually works in the short term, but it may create an authoritarian image that inhibits shared leadership in a long-term group.

7.8. Annotated Bibliography

Group Theory and Practice

Adler, Ronald B., and Jeanne Marquardt Elmhorst. 2010. *Communicating at Work: Principles and Practices for Business and the Professions*. 10th ed. New York: McGraw-Hill. See Chapter 8, "Working in Teams" (pp. 223–259), for decision-making groups, and Chapter 9, "Effective Meetings" (pp. 261–328).

Bales, Robert F. 1950. *Interaction Process Analysis: A Method for the Study of Small Groups*. Cambridge, MA: Addison-Wesley. This is a classic study of small group interaction.

Ellis, Richard. 2009. *Communication Skills: Stepladders to Success for the Professional*. 2nd ed. Chicago: University of Chicago Press. Chapter 10 (pp. 85–92) covers group communication in general, and Chapter 11 (pp. 93–107) covers communicating in meetings.

Fujishin, Randy. 2007. *Creating Effective Groups: The Art of Small Group Communication*. 2nd ed. Lanham, MD: Rowman and Littlefield. This text covers the communication skills necessary for small group communication. Each chapter includes individual and group exercises.

Galanes, Gloria J., and Katherine Adams. 2010. *Effective Group Discussion: Theory and Practice*. 13th ed. Boston: McGraw-Hill. This frequently revised classic text covers all kinds of smaller groups, such as committees, work groups, and task forces, and others that aim to find solutions to problems, create policies, and so forth. It includes many useful definitions, examples, and exercises (which can easily be adapted for in-service training).

Hargie, Owen, and David Dickson. 2010. *Social Skills in Interpersonal Communication*. 4th ed. London: Routledge. Chapter 14, "Groups and Group Interaction" (pp. 401–437), introduces the theory of group dynamics and leadership. The book includes a brief review of research on groups and discusses task and maintenance skills. It is useful for trainers.

Janis, Irving L. 1982. *Groupthink: A Psychological Study of Foreign-Policy Decisions and Fiascoes.* 2nd ed. Boston: Houghton Mifflin. The first edition (1973) was titled *Victims of Groupthink.* Janis's book introduced the term *groupthink.*

Johnson, David W., and Frank P. Johnson. 2009. *Joining Together: Group Theory and Group Skills.* 10th ed. Boston: Merrill. This work takes an experiential approach to small group dynamics. It includes good exercises for problem-solving and decision-making groups and provides useful strategies for problem solving. It is frequently revised.

Rentz, Kathryn, Marie Flatley, and Paula Lentz. 2010. *Lesikar's Business Communication: Connecting in a Digital World.* 12th ed. New York: McGraw-Hill. This edition of a classic text includes discussion of current challengers for business communication.

Tuckman, Bruce W. 1965. "Developmental Sequences in Small Groups." *Psychological Bulletin* 63, no. 6: 384–399. This is an influential article on group stages.

Wenger, Etienne. 1998. *Communities of Practice: Learning, Meaning, and Identity.* Cambridge, England: Cambridge University Press. This book popularized the concept of the community of practice, which is a group that shares a profession or craft and learns from each other by exchanging information in the domain of interest.

General Works on Technology as a Tool

Franklin, Ursula. 1996. *Every Tool Shapes the Task: Communities and the Information Highway.* Vancouver, BC: Lazara Press. This text is a warning about the mutual shaping of people and technology.

Lievrouw, Leah A., and Sonia Livingstone, eds. 2006. *Handbook of New Media: Social Shaping and Social Consequences of ICTs.* Updated Student Edition. Thousand Oaks, CA: Sage. With 22 chapters by authoritative authors, this handbook offers a helpful guide to many aspects of new media but also includes chapters focused on communication, interpersonal life online, and interactivity.

Book Discussions

Balcom, Ted, ed. 1997. *Serving Readers.* Atkinson, WI: Highsmith. This book includes a chapter on establishing book discussion groups. See also his highly recommended *Book Discussions for Adults: A Leader's Guide* (Chicago: ALA, 1992).

Chambers, Aidan. 1985. *Booktalk: Occasional Writing on Literature and Children*. London: Bodley Head. This collection of articles, lectures, and essays is an excellent book for anyone interested in children's literature, reading response, and book discussions.

Larrabee, Nancy. 2006. "Creating Connections in Your Community: Starting and Leading a Book Discussion Group." LISCareer.com. Career Strategies for Librarians. http://www.liscareer.com/larrabee_book.htm. This article contains some good hints for leading book discussions.

Saricks, Joyce. 2009. "At Leisure with Joyce Saricks: Leading Book Discussions." *Booklist* 36, no. 1 (September 1): 37. http://www.booklistonline.com/ProductInfo.aspx?pid=3713804&AspxAutoDetectCookieSupport=1. Saricks explains why librarians enjoy leading book discussions, with suggestions for enhancing your skills.

Focus Groups

Glitz, Beryl. 1998. *Focus Groups for Libraries and Librarians*. New York: Forbes Custom Publications. Glitz highlights the strengths and weaknesses of focus groups in library settings. Selection criteria for choosing a professional or layperson moderator are nicely detailed, as are necessary qualifications, skills, and characteristics. It also provides concrete tips for moderators on setting room ambiance, building rapport, encouraging discussion, focusing the discussion, and closing the group.

Johnson, Debra Wilcox. 1996. "Focus Groups." In *The Tell It! Manual: The Complete Program for Evaluating Library Performance*, edited by Douglas Zweizig, Debra Wilcox Johnson, and Jane Robbins with Michele Besant, 176–187. Chicago: American Library Association. This chapter includes a basic introduction to using focus groups for evaluation, with a sample interview guide and a training checklist.

King, Jean A., Richard A. Krueger, and David L. Morgan. 1998. *Focus Group Kit*. Thousand Oaks, CA: Sage. This text provides complete information on the focus group process, including a chapter specifically on moderating groups.

Krueger, Richard A., and Mary Anne Casey. 2009. *Focus Groups: A Practical Guide for Applied Research*. 4th ed. Newbury Park, CA: Sage. This book provides practical advice on setting up and running focus groups both externally and within organizations. It covers skills needed for moderating focus groups and includes chapters on

interviewing cross-cultural groups and young people and on group
interviewing using telephone and the Internet.

Mellinger, Margaret, and May Chau. 2010. "Conducting Focus Groups
with Library Staff: Best Practices and Participant Perceptions." *Library
Management* 31, no 4/5: 267–278. This is one of the few articles on
using focus groups with library staff.

Meetings, Formal and Informal

American Institute of Parliamentarians. 2011. *Standard Code of
Parliamentary Procedure.* 5th ed. New York: McGraw-Hill.
Formerly titled *Sturgis Standard Code.* This is a simplified and more
streamlined guide to parliamentary procedure than *Robert's Rules of
Order.*

Carnes, William T. 1987. *Effective Meetings for Busy People: Let's Decide
It and Go Home.* New York: IEEE Press. An experienced meeting
leader discusses, with helpful practical advice, his adaptation of
parliamentary procedures for more effective decision making in
deliberative assemblies.

Cochran, Alice Collier. 2004. *Roberta's Rules of Order: Sail through
Meetings for Stellar Results without the Gavel: A Guide for Nonprofits
and Other Teams.* San Francisco: Jossey-Bass. This text provides
practical principles for effective meetings and governance.

Crawford, Walt. 2003. *First Have Something to Say: Writing for the Library
Profession.* Chicago: American Library Association. In addition to lots
of tips on writing, Crawford covers how to lead discussions.

Deschamps, Ryan. 2010. "Building Communities with Large Group
Methods and Social Media." *Feliciter* 56, no. 5: 198–200. This article
discusses how libraries can organize "unconferences."

Dewey, Barbara I., and Sheila D. Creth. 1993. *Team Power: Making
Library Meetings Work.* Chicago: American Library Association. This
book includes suggestions for planning for effective communication
in library meetings.

Francis, Fred, and Peg Francis. 2010. *Democratic Rules of Order: Easy to
Use Rules for Meetings of Any Size.* 9th ed. Vancouver, BC: Cool Heads
Publishing. A compact pocket guide of 80 pages, written in plain
language, this text includes an example of a meeting governed by
these rules of order.

Gastil, John. 1993. *Democracy in Small Groups: Participation, Decision
Making, and Communication.* Philadelphia: New Society Publishers.
An interesting discussion of the various ways that small groups can

operate, this work is available as a free download at http://www.la1
.psu.edu/cas/jgastil/pdfs/Democracy%20in%20Small%20Groups%20
-%20Complete.pdf.

Maier, Norman R. F. 1963. *Problem Solving Discussions and Conferences:
Leadership Methods and Skills*. New York: McGraw-Hill. Though
published years ago, this is still considered an excellent resource.
See the summary of guidelines by Scott Armstrong at http://www
.calstatela.edu/academic/aa/cetl/resources/guidelines-for-problem-
solving-meetings.pdf.

Race, Phil, and Brenda Smith. 1996. *500 Tips for Trainers*. Houston, TX:
Gulf Professional Publishing. Practical suggestions for working with
small groups. For brainstorming procedures, see pages 41–42.

Robert, Henry M. III, Daniel H. Honemann, Thomas J. Balch, Daniel
E. Seabold, and Shmuel Gerber. 2011. *Robert's Rules of Order:
Newly Revised*. 11th ed. Cambridge, MA: Da Capo Press. This is the
standard guide. Earlier editions are still useful.

Soete, George J. 2000. *The Library Meeting Survival Manual*. San Diego:
Tulane Street Publications. This is a practical guide to meeting
management.

Stanford, Geoffrey H., ed. 1994. *Bourinot's Rules of Order*. 4th ed. Toronto:
McClelland and Stewart. This is a popular Canadian guide.

Streibel, Barbara J. 2007. *Plan and Conduct Effective Meetings: 24 Steps
to Generate Meaningful Results*. New York: McGraw-Hill. This
book covers many techniques for making meetings more effective,
including how to deal with problems and how to neutralize
interpersonal conflicts. It also discusses video- and teleconferencing.

Wilson, Gerald L. 2005. *Groups in Context: Leadership and Participation
in Small Groups*. 7th ed. Boston: McGraw-Hill. This text includes
chapters on preparing for and participating in group meetings.
It covers leading meetings, improving group climates, and
promoting cohesiveness and satisfaction, as well as managing
conflict. Appendixes cover small group presentations and designing
presentation graphics.

Teams (Face-to-Face and Virtual)

Bradigan, Pamela S., and Carol A. Powell. 2004. "The Reference and
Information Services Team: An Alternative Model for Managing
Reference Services." *Reference and User Services Quarterly* 44, no.
2 (Winter): 143–148. This article describes the operation of a self-
directed management team in an academic health sciences library.

DeRosa, Darleen, and Richard Lepsinger. 2010. *Virtual Team Success: A Practical Guide for Working and Leading from a Distance.* San Francisco: Jossey-Bass. A useful resource for team leaders and team members, this book is based on both extensive research and practical experience.

Duarte, Deborah L., and Nancy Tennant Snyder. 2006. *Mastering Virtual Teams: Strategies, Tools, and Techniques.* 3rd ed. San Francisco: Jossey-Bass. This toolkit for leaders and members of virtual teams includes guidelines, strategies, and best practices for working cross-culturally and cross-functionally, across time and distance.

Hinds, Pamela J., and Suzanne P. Weisband. 2003. "Knowledge Sharing and Shared Understanding in Virtual Teams." In *Virtual Teams That Work: Creating Conditions for Virtual Team Effectiveness*, edited by Cristina B. Gibson and Susan G. Cohen, 21–36. San Francisco: Jossey-Bass. This chapter focuses on real problems that virtual teams experience and on solutions.

Katzenbach, Jon R., and Douglas K. Smith. 2003. *The Wisdom of Teams: Creating the High Performance Organization.* Boston: Harvard Business Press. This is a widely used classic. See also their *The Discipline of Teams* (Boston: Harvard Business Press, 2009), which includes two chapters on the unique challenges confronting virtual teams.

Lipnack, Jessica, and Jeffrey Stamps. 2000. *Virtual Teams: People Working across Boundaries with Technology.* 2nd ed. New York: John Wiley and Sons. This text claims that a virtual team's success is based 90 percent on the people involved and 10 percent on the technology.

RW[3] Culture Wizard. 2010. *The Challenge of Working on Virtual Teams: The Virtual Teams Survey Report.* RW[3] LLC. http://rw-3.com/VTSReportv7.pdf. This text presents the findings of a survey of employees of multinational firms.

Computer-Mediated Communication for Group Work

Barnhart, Anne C., and Andrea G. Stanfield. 2011. "When Coming to Campus Is Not an Option: Using Web Conferencing to Deliver Library Instruction." *Reference Services Review* 39, no. 1: 58–65. This article describes an experiment using collaborative software for instruction.

Boule, Michelle. 2008a. "Best Practices for Working in a Virtual Environment." *Library Technology Reports* 44, no. 1: 29–31. This article provides guidelines covering organizational practices, team leadership, and team practices that apply as much to face-to-face teams as to virtual teams.

————. 2008b. "Changing the Way We Work." *Library Technology Reports* 44, no. 1: 6–9. This article is on how to integrate new technology into group work.

Chilcoat, Yvonne, and Sue DeWine. 1985. "Teleconferencing and Interpersonal Communication Perception." *Journal of Applied Communication Research* 13, no. 1: 14–32. One conclusion of the research is that audio-only conferencing can be more satisfactory than videoconferencing when the purpose is information sharing (rather than problem solving) and/or when the speaker displays negative nonverbal cues.

Griffith, Terri L., Elizabeth A. Mannix, and Margaret L. Neale. 2003. "Conflict and Virtual Teams." In *Virtual Teams That Work: Creating Conditions for Virtual Team Effectiveness*, edited by Cristina B. Gibson and Susan G. Cohen, 335–352. San Francisco: Jossey-Bass. The authors argue that "[s]kill in face-to-face communication and conflict management does not necessarily map on to virtual communication and (virtual) management of conflict" (p. 335).

Griffiths, Kami, and Chris Peters. 2009. "Ten Steps for Planning a Successful Webinar." TechSoup. http://www.techsoup.org/ learningcenter/training/page11252.cfm?cg=tsblog&sg=webconf. This detailed site provides good advice for organizing and producing online seminars for nonprofit organizations.

Hara, Noriko, Pnina Shachaf, and Sharon Stoerger. 2009. "Online Communities of Practice." *Journal of Information Science* 35, no. 6: 740–759. This article examines three electronic discussion lists, including one devoted to digital reference, as examples of online communities of practice.

Harasim, Linda. 2012. *Learning Theory and Online Technologies*. New York: Routledge. An overview of the current state of e-learning, this book addresses learning theory, pedagogy, and evaluation as well as online collaborative learning and online communities of practice.

Harasim, Linda, et al. 1995. *Learning Networks: A Field Guide to Teaching and Learning Online*. Cambridge, MA: The MIT Press. This much-cited pioneering work considers the dynamics of distance learning groups.

Haythornthwaite, Carolyn, et al. 2000. "Community Development among Distance Learners: Temporal and Technological Dimensions." *Journal of Computer-Mediated Communication* 6, no. 1. http://onlinelibrary .wiley.com/doi/10.1111/j.1083-6101.2000.tb00114.x/full. This article examines the concept of community through the case of the online master's program at the Graduate School of Library and Information Science at the University of Illinois at Urbana–Champaign.

Hogan, Bernie, and Anabel Quan-Haase. 2010. "Persistence and Change in Social Media." *Bulletin of Science, Technology and Society* 30, no. 5: 309–315. An introduction to a special issue with the same title, this paper looks for broad patterns and generalizable statements about social media.

Hollingshead, Andrea B., and Noshir S. Contractor. 2006. "New Media and Small Group Organizing." In *Handbook of New Media: Social Shaping and Social Consequences of ICTs*, Updated Student Edition, edited by Leah A. Lievrouw and Sonia Livingstone, 114–133. Thousand Oaks, CA: Sage. This is an informed overview of theoretical frameworks and empirical findings in the area of new media and groups at work.

Kling, Rob, and Christina Courtright. 2003. "Group Behavior and Learning in Electronic Forums: A Sociotechnical Approach." *The Information Society* 19, no. 3: 221–235. The authors present a research-based evaluation of the effectiveness of IT-led forums versus IT-supported forums.

Luppicini, Rocci. 2007. "Review of Computer Mediated Communication Research for Education." *Instructional Science* 35: 141–180. This review article summarizes 170 recent research articles in 78 journals that addressed CMC in education—specifically the relation of CMC to learning and learning processes, group problem solving, group decision making, group dynamics, gender differences, anonymity, and writing.

Neuhaus, Chris. 1997. "Creating an E-mail Brainstorm." *Library Administration and Management* 11, no. 4 (Fall): 217–221. This article explains how libraries can use e-mail to conduct successful large-group brainstorming sessions.

Peters, Thomas A. 2009. *Library Programs Online: Possibilities and Practicalities of Web Conferencing*. Santa Barbara, CA: Libraries Unlimited. Written with a public library emphasis by the Director of OPAL (Online Programming for All Libraries), this book explains how libraries can deliver programs such as lectures, book discussions, storytimes, workshops, and conferences online.

———. 2010. "Using OPAL for Easy Online Meetings, CE, and Public Programs." Previously archived at http://www.opal-online.org/archiveopal.htm. This online program demonstrated features of web conferencing, including VoIP, text chatting, presentation slides, and co-browsing.

Potton, Sue. 1996. "A Very Candid Camera." *Successful Meetings* 45, no 1: 84–85. The author discusses how to present a confident on-screen image in videoconference groups.

Quan-Haase, Anabel, Joseph Cothrel, and Barry Wellman. 2005. "Instant Messaging for Collaboration: A Case Study of a High-Tech Firm." *Journal of Computer Mediated Communication* 10, no. 4: article 13. http://jcmc.indiana.edu/vol10/issue4/quan-haase.html. This article examines perceptions of users of various media for work-related communication.

Quan-Haase, Anabel, and Alyson Young. 2010. "Uses and Gratifications of Social Media: A Comparison of Facebook and Instant Messaging." *Bulletin of Science, Technology and Society* (October) 30, no. 5: 350–361. Researchers found that undergraduates used Facebook for entertainment, for being connected with a social network, and to find out social information about peers. The near-synchronous instant messaging was preferred for intimate personal exchanges.

Walther, Joseph B. 1996. "Computer-Mediated Communication: Impersonal, Interpersonal, and Hyperpersonal Interaction." *Communication Research*, 23, 1: 3–43. This frequently cited article argues that it is *not* true that CMC is intrinsically impersonal: "as goes f2f, so goes CMC, given the opportunity for message-exchange and accompanying relational development" (p. 11).

———. 2008. "Problems and Interventions in Computer Mediated Virtual Groups." In *Mediated Interpersonal Communication*, edited by Elly A. Konijn et al., 271–289. New York: Routledge. This chapter reviews research on the interpersonal dynamics of virtual groups in a professional context.

Whitehill, Gary. 2010. "Communicating as a Leader: Conference Call Mistakes and How to Avoid Them." *Entrepreneur Week*, March 11. http://www.entrepreneurweek.net/articles/communicating-as-a -leader-conference-call-mistakes-and-how-to-avoid-them. This work includes some good tips.

Videos

Library Video Network. 2000. *Team Work Basics*. VHS. 15 min. http:// www.lvn.org/store/index.html. This video reviews basic teamwork components and how they can be applied in libraries, rotating team memberships, and role of team facilitator.

———. 2006. *Holding an Effective Meeting.* DVD and VHS. 19 min. http://www.lvn.org/store/index.html. Among the topics covered in this video are the role of the moderator, setting a workable agenda, keeping the discussion on topic, and dealing with difficult meeting participants.

Video Arts. 1993. *Meetings Bloody Meetings.* DVD. 30 min. John Cleese dramatizes typical faults that make meetings unproductive. See also *More Bloody Meetings*, 1994.

Making Presentations

8

8.1. General Considerations

Who needs to be able to speak effectively in public? Anyone whose job involves any of the following:

- Introducing or thanking a speaker
- Doing a booktalk
- Giving a library tour
- Providing library instruction to groups
- Speaking about the library to outside groups
- Providing staff training

Your choice is probably not between speaking in public or not speaking. It is between doing the job well or doing it badly. Think of the last time you heard an ineffective public speech. What made it poor? Probably something that, with some effort, could have been corrected. In this chapter, we are talking mostly about a face-to-face presentation. But the majority of elements that make for a successful face-to-face talk are also needed for a virtual presentation, including knowing your purpose, analyzing the intended audience, finding and developing a topic, arranging materials, using audiovisual aids, and so forth. If your talk is mediated by virtual conferencing (see 7.6.2), you still need to be concerned about delivery.

Many speakers go wrong because they forget that a speech is intended primarily for the ear. They fail to consider the differences between an oral medium intended for groups and a visual medium intended for individual readers. Readers have more control than listeners do over how they receive a message and adapt it to their own needs. Readers can choose to skim a text, skip boring paragraphs, and read the end before the beginning. They can carefully reread passages that puzzled them the first time. They can speed up their reading for familiar content or slow it down for difficult, unfamiliar content. They can examine the physical features of the text to determine, in advance of reading it, how long it is, how many sections it has, and what each of the sections is titled.

All audience members, in contrast, listen at the same speed to the same words in the same order. They can't go back to clarify something that they missed. And they never know in advance, unless you tell them, how long the speech is or where it is going. As a speaker, you must make allowances for these limitations of the spoken presentation. Keep your pace brisk enough that you don't bore your listeners but not so brisk that you leave them behind. Help your listeners get a handle on your talk by giving them, at the beginning, an agenda or brief outline of what you intend to speak about. If you are using presentation software for a talk of 30 minutes or more, your first slide (after the one showing your name, affiliation, and title of your talk) should be the agenda. As you go along, you can help your audience remember important points from your talk by writing keywords on a blackboard or flip chart or by using a summary slide in your presentation software.

Remember, however, your advantage over writers: you have a direct relationship with your audience. Because you know who your audience is, you can tailor what you say to the needs of this specific audience. You can see how the group is reacting to your talk and can correct problems as you go along, abbreviating a part that seems to be boring everyone, explaining a concept when you see puzzled looks, and so forth. You can make the session interactive by frequently providing an opportunity for your audience to ask you questions. And you can use gestures and qualities of voice to dramatize your message and give it impact. When you are giving a speech, take advantage of these strengths of an oral presentation.

8.2. Arranging for Other People to Speak

The only time your audience thinks about the arranger's job is when something goes wrong. Then people ask: who chose this dull speaker? Why doesn't the speaker start on time? Why doesn't someone do something about the uncomfortable chairs/unsuitable size of the room/unbearably hot and stuffy atmosphere/inadequate sound system? Why is the speaker allowed to go on so long? Why doesn't someone control how much time each panelist got so that each person got an equal chance to speak? Why isn't the session ending on time? To make sure your background role as arranger stays in the background, here are some suggestions for anticipating and avoiding glitches.

Quick Tips for Arranging Guest Presentations

- Start your planning early. For some large, formal speaking occasions, starting six months in advance is not too soon. Assess your audience's needs and decide what kind of presentation will suit these needs.
- Don't select a speaker on the basis of her written work. Interesting writers can sometimes be very dull speakers. Get some feedback from someone who has recently heard the person speak. Make sure that the proposed speaker's abilities match your specific needs.
- Be forthright upfront on the issues of costs, fees, and honoraria. You and the speaker should both clearly understand in advance what travel costs are covered, whether or not a fee is being paid, and how much it will be.
- When negotiating with the speaker, don't just say, "Will you speak to our group?" Tell the speaker exactly what kind of presentation you expect (an amusing, 15-minute after-dinner speech; or a formal, 30-minute keynote address to open a research-oriented conference; or a one-hour workshop on how to run children's storytimes). Be very clear about the amount of time that is allotted for the speech itself and how much time, if any, should be saved for questions from the audience. If your speaker is to be on a panel with others, explain all that too. Describe the

<hr>

Exercise

Checklist for Arrangements
Create a checklist. If you will soon be performing an arranger role, make your checklist with this future event in mind. (Otherwise think about an event that you might be expected to be involved with.) Pick from "Quick Tips for Arranging Guest Presentations" only those action items that apply to the event you have in mind. Use a spreadsheet to make your checklist. Create at least four columns: Action Item; Date to Be Done By; Who Does It?; Item Completed. Fill in the Action Item column with the activities that apply to your event.

intended audience in terms of its size, its average age, its interests, and its level of knowledge about the topic. Explain any relevant details about the context of the presentation (the talk is last in a sequence of speeches on the same topic). Leave no room for misunderstanding.

- Suggest a slant on the topic that you think would interest the audience.
- Suit the room to the audience. Put 40 people in a room with seats for 50 and the atmosphere seems cozy. Put them in a room with seats for 100 and it looks as if half the audience stayed home.
- Arrange to have refreshments if possible. Refreshments do wonders to improve the audience's frame of mind. And remember that not everyone drinks coffee.
- In good time before the presentation, ask the speaker if he will need any special equipment or facilities. Well-prepared speakers, taking nothing for granted, always specify their needs for computers, compatible presentation software, data projectors, lecterns, flip charts, special seating arrangements, and so forth. But don't wait for your speaker to volunteer this information. Ask.
- Several days before the actual presentation, find some excuse to call up your speaker. Your real purpose is to remind him of the time and date of the speaking engagement and confirm that he is actually coming and hasn't gotten the month wrong. When you call, say something like this: "Can I help you with anything before your talk this Wednesday?" With a speaker from out of town, you might say you are calling to confirm plans for meeting the plane and driving him to his hotel.
- Make sure that the speaker's time with you is enjoyable, especially if he is from out of town. You could arrange for a social event, depending on time available—take him to lunch or dinner. Speakers go to a lot of trouble preparing a talk and often travel a considerable distance. As Janet Swan Hill reminds us, speakers are not "hired hands" but your colleagues and your guests (Hall and Hill, 2002: 66–67).
- On the day of the presentation, look after your speaker. Meet her and take her to the room at least half an hour before the audience is due to arrive. Suggest that she will probably want to check out in advance the room and the

equipment. Remind her once again about the length of time allotted to her talk.

- After the presentation is over, don't abandon her. Make arrangements to get her home (or to the hotel or airport).
- Thank the speaker in person after the talk. Thank her again in a personal letter or card, mentioning favorable comments from the audience and any initiatives that may have been sparked by the talk.

8.2.1. Introducing a Speaker

The speech of introduction has an important function. It focuses the audience's attention, settles people down, and prepares them to listen with interest to the speaker. All this can, and should, be done briefly. In four to six sentences, you can:

1. State the title of the talk: "Today's topic for our Noon Hour Speakers' Series is: 'Franchising: Is It for You?'"
2. Say briefly but specifically why this topic will interest this particular audience: Not "I'm sure all of us here are interested in this topic," but rather, "In our fall survey of the interests of this group, franchising came out on top, which is why . . ."
3. Explain briefly the speaker's qualifications to talk about the topic and end with the speaker's name: "Our speaker opened her first Yum-Yums store three years ago to sell chocolate specialties. Since then she has franchised and now has over 40 stores selling her treats. She has agreed to tell us today some of the things she learned the hard way about franchising. I'm pleased to introduce to you [one-second pause]—Mary Maddox."

Quick Tips for Introducing a Speaker

- Check the equipment. Before the audience begins to arrive, make sure that everything works. The first words of your speech of introduction should not be excuses for why a glitch has delayed the talk.
- Create a positive atmosphere for the talk to come. But don't overdo your praise: overpraise can embarrass the speaker

---

Exercise 🔧

Clichés
Make a list of clichés to avoid when introducing a speaker. Here are some obvious ones:

Without further ado . . .
Here is a speaker who needs no introduction.
You didn't come here to listen to me.

How many more can you think of?

A Quick Tip ⏱

Cross-Cultural Introductions
When you are introducing someone from another culture, remember that some people prefer to be introduced formally, using a formal title. Check with the speaker on how she would like to be introduced (Walters, 1993: 412).

and lead to disappointed expectations on the part of the audience.

- Don't talk about yourself or take over the role of the invited speaker by expressing your own views on the speaker's topic.
- Never apologize or dwell on the negative aspects of the event. It only depresses the audience to hear things like: "It's too bad we have such a poor turnout tonight" or "Thank you for coming out on this stormy night when you'd probably rather be home watching hockey."
- Be selective. The audience doesn't want to hear a detailed list of the speaker's every university degree, administrative role, honor, affiliation, and publication. Mention only those accomplishments, especially recent ones, of particular relevance to the audience, the occasion, or the topic of the speech. The better known the speaker, the less you need to say. But avoid clichés such as "Our speaker tonight needs no introduction."
- Write down the title of the talk and the speaker's name on a card and keep the card handy but unobtrusive. This way you avoid the embarrassment of saying: "I'm pleased to introduce—um, um, er."
- Say it as if you mean it, and know what you are talking about. Don't turn your statements into a question by ending on a rising inflection (1.8): "Last year our speaker received the Young Innovators Award?"
- End decisively with the speaker's name. Don't say: "I'd like to introduce Mary Maddox [the beginning of applause]. But before I do, let me remind all those who haven't signed up for the next session to do so before they leave. There is coffee available following the talk, and we hope as many of you as possible . . ."
- Give the speaker your full attention once the speech has started. Do not distract the audience by fiddling with your notes or writing out your thank-you speech.

8.2.2. Thanking a Speaker

The speech of thanks can be even briefer than the introduction. It should include these elements:

- a sincere thank-you,
- a specific reference to something significant and interesting in the speech,
- a statement about why this particular item was valuable to the audience, and
- another sincere thank-you.

Following this, lead the audience in applause.

Write a thank-you note to the speaker—handwritten will be appreciated more than an e-mail, but an e-mail is better than nothing.

8.2.3. Chairing a Panel

The chairperson plays an important role in the success of the panel. But remember that your role as chair is to choreograph the speaking of others, not to give a speech yourself. Limit yourself to the following facilitating activities: double-check the arrangements; briefly introduce the topic and the speakers at the beginning; call upon each speaker in turn; control the time they speak; be a gatekeeper in coordinating questions from the audience; and provide a definite ending point to the event by briefly thanking contributors and leading the audience in applause. Your biggest problem will be controlling the time. Every speaker thinks his or her speech deserves at least ten minutes longer than the allotted time.

Quick Tips for Chairing a Panel

- Be specific about what each panelist is expected to talk about and for how long. Put the agenda and format in writing, and give it to your panelists in advance.
- Timing is crucial. To help panelists stick to their time allotment, you might say to them ahead of time, "It's often hard for a speaker to keep track of how much time is left. So when I give you this sign [demonstrate it], you will know that you have three minutes left." If this doesn't work (and often it won't), you can always stand up. Begin moving relentlessly toward the microphone, if there is one. This body language conveys a powerful hint that you mean what you say about timing.
- Check to make sure that chairs, tables, lecterns, and screens are positioned properly; that the microphones work; and

> **A Quick Tip** 🕐
>
> **Who Else Is Speaking?**
> Let speakers and panelists and reactors know in advance who else is on the program roster. Janet Swan Hill recommends that you provide program participants with their co-presenters' names, addresses, phone numbers, and e-mail addresses. Do so far enough in advance to allow them to consult each other, if desired. For out-of-town speakers, provide local information—details about the hotel arrangements and phone numbers of people whom the speaker may need to contact (Hall and Hill, 2002: 66-67).

that water is available for the speakers. Do this *before* the audience arrives.

- Write down on a card the names of the speakers and key information about them. If you go blank on a name during your introduction, you can glance at your card. Check pronunciations, and practice pronouncing difficult names in advance so that you don't stumble over them during the introduction.

- Be brief. Your introduction of each panelist should be even shorter than an introduction of a single speaker. In most cases, all that needs to be said about each panelist is the name and why this person is qualified to speak on the topic.

- Help panelists as needed with lights, presentation software, and so forth, during the panel discussion itself.

- Control the question period by soliciting questions, calling on the questioners in turn, and then repeating the questions so that everyone can hear them. Limit the number of questions so that the program ends promptly at the advertised time. You could say, "We have time now for one more question." Then move on firmly to thanking the panelists briefly and leading the audience in applause. Don't let the question period drag on so long that audience members trickle away, one by one.

8.3. Making a Presentation Yourself

Before you do anything else, you should ask yourself whether or not to agree to give the presentation in the first place. Richard Ellis (2009:109) notes that, when an inexperienced speaker is invited to give a presentation, he is likely to think, "Can I do this talk?" "What should I say?" But experienced speakers ask themselves some other questions before agreeing to speak:

- Is there a better way to achieve the intended purpose than by a presentation?
- Is the effort involved likely to pay off from a personal point of view? From the perspective of achieving the intended purpose?

A Quick Tip 🕐

Establish a Speakers Bureau

To spread the word about your library and its services, Lisa Wolfe (2005: 191-193) recommends developing a list of library staff who are available and willing to make presentations to outside organizations and to groups within the library. The listing should include the topics that each speaker is willing to talk about. For example, the local history librarian could list "Tools for Genealogists," which would appeal to genealogical groups, but she might also list "Architecture and Heritage Preservation," a topic of potential interest to other groups. A staff member who is a mystery or fantasy buff might be an outstanding booktalker whether or not his job is related to collection development or readers' advisory. Wolfe recommends developing a list of possible presentation topics and distributing it to local service organizations. She also recommends publicizing the speakers bureau regularly in the library newsletter.

- If yes, am I the right person to give this particular talk? (If not, refer.)
- Is the title/topic of the talk fixed, or can it be negotiated? (Adapted from Ellis, 2009: 109)

8.3.1. Knowing Your Purpose

Be clear about what your purpose is in giving this speech. To make Loretta feel appreciated by her colleagues on the occasion of her retirement dinner? To entertain the audience and make them laugh? To explain a process? To present new information? To change or confirm attitudes? To persuade the audience to some course of action? To whip up enthusiasm for a cause, an idea, or a proposal? If you can't explain to yourself in one sentence what you would like to see happen as a result of your speech, your efforts will lack focus. It helps to write down, in specific behavioral terms, your objectives. Here are examples of specific objectives:

- **For informative talks:** Staff members will learn enough about the new software to start using it immediately for chat reference.
- **For persuasive talks:** Library board members will approve a change in policy with respect to handling young adult materials.
- **For inspirational talks:** The reference staff will be filled with new energy and enthusiasm for answering people's questions.
- **For ceremonial talks:** Listeners will feel that the new branch library was opened with style and dignity.

8.3.2. Analyzing the Audience

Ask yourself these questions about the audience:

1. What do you want to happen as a result of your talk? What do you want/expect your audience to do/learn?
2. Who will make up the audience?
3. How many people do you expect?
4. What are your audience members' main reasons for being at your talk? What do they want/expect to get from the talk?

> ### Exercise
>
> **On Oral Presentations**
> Consider the difference between an oral presentation and a written presentation. Suppose that you have written a 25-page report for your library system assessing the need for a new branch in a subdivision. You have been asked to present your report at a meeting of senior administrators. (You realize, of course, that you can't simply read the report from page one onward until some desperate audience member stops you.) What steps will you have to take to turn a 25-page written report into an effective oral presentation? How does the difference between a written presentation and a spoken presentation affect your approach to the problem?

5. What is your audience's most pertinent problem? How can you help audience members to solve it?

6. How much do they already know about your topic? Are they specialists? Do they have a good, general background? Do they know just a little bit? Are they new to the topic? Will the audience be mixed in terms of its familiarity with your topic? If you don't know their level of knowledge, find out.

7. How receptive are they to your message? Are they very receptive? Somewhat receptive? Indifferent? Somewhat hostile? Very hostile?

8. What do you know about their age, gender, culture, ethnic origin, educational background, cultural interests, political and religious affiliation, or other factors that will affect their reception of your talk?

9. What kinds of material are most likely to succeed with this audience? (Inversely, what probably *won't* succeed?) Here are some possibilities: stories and anecdotes, facts, statistics, testimony, analogies, hands-on demonstrations. What else?

8.3.3. Finding a Topic

Often your topic will be decided for you by the context in which you give the speech or presentation. You may have been invited to speak because you have experience or expertise with some particular topic. For example, a high school teacher asks you to tell her history class about the documents in your regional history collection; a local reading group invites you to give a booktalk; the local Special Libraries Association chapter asks you to discuss the implications of proposed changes to copyright legislation; your job requires you to provide library tours and instruction. In these cases, the main challenge is to find the right slant on the topic to suit the interests and level of understanding of the particular audience.

Sometimes, however, you will have considerable freedom of choice in selecting your topic. Suppose a service group has asked you to speak after dinner at the annual meeting. The topic is to be "anything you like." You could talk about your bird-watching hobby, but after all you have been invited because you are a library professional. This is your chance to increase community awareness about the library and what it does. On the other hand, an after-dinner speech should be lively and entertaining. After the double chocolate layer cake, few want to hear a factual speech on international standards for serials.

Consider how you might adapt your chosen topic to accommodate the audience's known interests. For example, suppose your topic is information service. If the group you are talking to is dedicated to helping young people become entrepreneurs, you could focus on the variety of unusual resources in the library helpful to anyone starting a small business: government statistics; census data; statutes and regulations; and the like. Illustrate this talk with interesting and little-known examples and anecdotes of success. For a more general audience, you could talk about how the library answers questions and use as illustrations three diverse cases where the questions were challenging and unusual and the answers were interesting, surprising, or funny.

8.3.4. Developing the Topic

A speech includes two elements: (1) a governing idea, message, or thesis; and (2) supporting materials that develop or reinforce the governing idea. Let us suppose that you have a topic: technostress among librarians. That's the subject, but you don't have a message or governing idea until you know what you want to say about technostress. For example, "Technostress is a permanent, everyday part of librarianship today, not a temporary challenge" or "You can handle technostress by following these three strategies."

The first step, then, is deciding upon your governing idea, message, or thesis. With your main thesis clearly in mind, you can proceed efficiently to the next step of gathering the supporting materials. Supporting materials that are not directly related to your governing idea should be ruthlessly rejected as irrelevant, however interesting you may otherwise find them.

These are sources for material:

- Yourself—your professional expertise and your memory of examples and anecdotes (this is the most important source)
- Your own research
- Talking with other people
- Reading other people's material and research (in most cases, you should use this one only as a supplement)

To develop your governing idea, use one or more of the following kinds of supporting materials.

Impromptu

This exercise on developing a topic can be done on your own, but it's more fun in a small group.

Write a number of everyday topics chosen at random on small pieces of paper and put the pieces of paper inside a hat or bowl. Good topics are ones that can be talked about from a number of different perspectives, for example, apples, dust, paper, chairs, skiing, holidays, retirement savings funds, molasses, tweets, life jackets, red shoes.

Each person in turn draws a topic from the hat. The speaker is given three minutes to organize a two-minute talk on the topic, after which he gives the talk. Appoint a timer, who makes sure the time limits are followed. Other people in the group can provide feedback (3.14).

Suppose the topic apples is drawn. The first step is to decide on the governing idea, such as "The apple has been a source of mischief to humanity ever since Eve," or "The apple that we find in stores today is a designer product," or "Here's an inexpensive but exotic dessert you can make with apples."

The next step is to develop this governing idea through one or more kinds of supporting materials: anecdotes of disasters, such as the Trojan War, that were caused by apples; an explanation of how genetic selection has much reduced genetic variation in apples since the days of Johnny Appleseed; or instructions on making the tempting apple dessert. The choice of suitable supporting materials follows from the governing idea.

Illustrative Examples: Stories, Anecdotes, Case Studies

One of the most interesting and effective ways of developing an idea is to tell a story. For retirement tributes, anniversary lunches, ceremonial occasions, and after-dinner speeches, especially, the best material is often a series of well-chosen and appropriate anecdotes that have some bearing on the occasion.

Facts and Statistics

Use statistics sparingly. Long lists of numbers are hard for the ear to take in. Space out your facts. If a number is important, repeat it. Translate the fact into terms that make sense to the listeners—the needed library budget increase would cost each taxpayer the price of one cup of coffee a week.

Testimony

Quote respected authorities on the topic. Of course the quotations must be accurate and must not be distorted by being taken out of context.

Analogies

Compare a lesser known subject with a more familiar subject in order to make a point. In explaining the classification system to students, you could say that methods of ordering books on the shelf are like methods of organizing food in supermarkets. Although each store is different, all supermarkets put meats together in one place, cereals together in another, condiments in another. Likewise libraries, and so on.

Demonstrations and Modeling

When you want an audience to understand an object or a process, you can show it to them or model it for them. For example, you could demonstrate how to use NoveList Plus to find an entertaining book to read for pleasure by demonstrating a search. The audience members will be able to follow the steps as they watch the output displayed on a large screen.

8.3.5. Choosing an Appropriate Arrangement

The supporting materials discussed in 8.3.4 are the basic building blocks of the speech. But they are still just raw materials until you organize them into an effective pattern. Experienced speakers have found that certain standard formulas work well as frameworks within which to organize materials. Here are some suggestions:

1. Tell 'em

A popular design for presenting information is the old "Tell 'em" formula, where the message is hammered home through repetition:

> Tell 'em what you're going to tell 'em.
> Tell 'em.
> Tell 'em what you told 'em.

This is a good design to use when you want the audience to learn something. It takes into account the situation of listeners. Unlike readers, they cannot skim over the text in advance to orient themselves, and they can't go back to review points they missed. The preview works as an advance organizer, telling listeners what to expect. It helps them comprehend, assimilate, and remember the details. The summary at the end reinforces and confirms the main message. Use this direct strategy with audiences who (1) are receptive to your message or (2) are busy and want a straightforward approach. The structure of a talk using this formula looks like this:

- **Introduction:** Catch the audience's attention with a brief illustrative story, a startling fact, or a vivid quotation from an authority (e.g., "One out of every seven North Americans lack basic literacy skills. They can't read instructions on a bottle of medicine, find information on the Internet, or use the index in a newspaper."). The introduction prepares the audience for the substance of the talk at the same time that it emphasizes the importance of the main message. State the message, and provide a preview of key points ("So how do these findings about literacy affect us in public libraries? I'm going to tell you today about three implications: [one], [two], and [three].").

> **A Quick Tip**
>
> **Friendly Persuasion**
> Clarify your ideas before you decide on the best arrangement. Here is a useful framework for clarifying in your own mind your ideas about a persuasive talk:
>
> I want the audience to . . .
> They will do this because it will benefit them by . . .
> So I must . . .

- **Body:**

  First point—Examples, testimony, statistics, facts, or
       other supporting data
  Second point—Examples, testimony, etc.
  Third point—Examples, testimony, etc.

  Three main points are usually enough for all but the longest
  of speeches, and the number three has a satisfying ring
  to it and the sanction of precedent. For suggestions about
  putting the points into an appropriate order, see the patterns
  of organization of written texts, 4.5.

- **Conclusion:**

  Summary of key points
  Repetition of main message

2. The HWFS Approach

A variation that works well for persuasive speeches is one first recommended a long time ago by Richard C. Borden (1935: 3). Use it when
you want to get the audience to act:

  Ho hum.
  Why bring that up?
  For instance.
  So what?

In other words, first you wake up the listener and grab his attention
(perhaps by a story, a startling statistic, analogy, or testimony). Then
you show why your message is relevant to the listener's interest. Then
you reinforce your point with specific cases (the illustrative examples).
Finally you ask for action ("You can help in the fight for literacy by
participating in our 'Let's Read' family literacy program").

3. Motivated Sequence

With an indifferent or hostile audience, the "Tell 'em-right-away"
approach runs the risk of provoking resistance to your message.
People tend to become defensive, reject what you have to say, and stop
listening. (See barriers to listening in 2.3.) Therefore, you should delay
your real message. First you highlight a problem that the audience

faces. Then you reveal your message, which you present as the solution to the audience's problem. An effective method is *the motivated sequence*, which ties the speaker's message to the audience's needs:

Attention. You catch your audience's attention.
Need. You focus that attention on a problem or concern.
Satisfaction. You present your solution to the problem.
Visualization. You explain the benefit of your solution to your listeners (the what's-in-it-for-you theme).
Action. You ask for approval of your solution.

These ways of organizing speeches are traditional forms of European rhetoric, but it is worth remembering that the act of public speaking carries culture-specific values and norms. For example, if you are bolstering your point with "evidence," remember that what constitutes good evidence varies from culture to culture, and this in turn will affect the structure and content of the speech. Statistics may not be as well received as stories from the elders, for example. And the "tell 'em" strategy may not work when your audience prefers a less direct approach or can tolerate more ambiguity. As Clella Jaffe points out, both the topic of public discussion and the way in which it is discussed can send different signals to different audiences. For further help, see Jaffe's discussion of ways to organize a speech, including not only the topical, chronological, or pro–con pattern, but also the wave pattern (remember Dr. Martin Luther King's most famous speech?), the star pattern, and the spiral pattern (Jaffe, 2006: 155–172).

8.3.6. Using Audiovisual Aids and Presentation Software

Well-presented audiovisual aids can hold your audience's attention and help people remember the important ideas in your talk. But your aids should supplement your talk, not upstage you. You don't want to reduce your role to that of technical support for the equipment. However, well used, audiovisual aids can enhance understanding. Many people learn better when they can use both eyes and ears, both the visual and auditory channels (Mayer, 2001: 7). A visual aid used in a talk can range from something low tech such as a map and a pointer to something quite elaborate such as a multimedia presentation

Quick Tip ⏱

Avoid Death by PowerPoint
The murder weapon in this case is the blunt instrument. The victim is bludgeoned to death by a surfeit of slides and too many bullet points and nested hierarchies.

Did You Know? ?

Less is more! Edward Tufte's advice on ready-made PowerPoint templates is to use restraint: "No matter how beautiful your PP ready-made template is, it would be better if there was less of it. Never use PP templates for arraying words or numbers. Avoid elaborate hierarchies of bullet lists" (Tufte, 2003: 22).

involving film clips. The aid most often used is presentation software for projecting overhead slides.

The size of the audience and the size of the room are factors to consider when deciding whether or not to use presentation software. For an audience of ten people in an intimate room, you may prefer to avoid the regimented lock-step of prepared slides and the soporific effect of the darkened room. For an audience of 100 or more and a large room, projected overhead visuals are a good way to focus the attention of the audience. If you are speaking to an international audience whose members speak English as a second language, seeing the words on the screen aids in comprehension.

For some in-between-sized audiences and rooms, you might decide that low tech is better. Your visual aid could be the old standby of chalk and a blackboard or a marker and a flip chart. As is often the case, it's a swings-and-roundabouts situation, and the best advice is that it all depends. There are several advantages to the low-tech option. There is no barrier between you and the audience. You can adapt your talk to the interest of the audience, for example, by silently omitting a section of lesser interest without being tied to the lock-step of sequenced slides. You don't have to worry about an equipment malfunction. All your efforts can go into great content.

However, presentation software can be very effective if used strategically. It is very useful if you want to show images—say, of book covers to illustrate a book talk on a number of titles. And if you want to present multimedia clips or be able to call up webpages easily, presentation software allows for a smoothly synchronized performance. A newer platform, Prezi (http://prezi.com/) is cloud-based presentation software that allows you to put text and graphics on a virtual canvas and then zoom in and out, navigating in a nonlinear way through information.

If you do plan to use presentation software, take the time to do a professional job. Audience members have already sat through too many tormented PowerPoint presentations with unreadable fonts, overcrowded text-heavy pages, cheesy cartoons, overvibrant colors, distracting backgrounds, dancing animations, and zooming page transitions to want to be subjected to another one. Edward Tufte (2003: 22), international authority on the visual presentation of information, has this to say about the pitfalls of PowerPoint, which he feels is too often used as a crutch for the presenter rather than as an aid for the audience:

Presentations largely stand or fall depending on the quality, relevance and integrity of the content. The way to make big improvements in presentation is to get better content. Designer formats will not salvage weak content. If your numbers are boring, then you've got the wrong numbers. If your words or images are not on point, making them dance in color won't make them relevant. Audience boredom is usually a content failure, not a decoration failure. At a minimum, a presentation should *do no harm* to content.

Getting the Aid Ready to Use

There are two kinds of aids that you can use to enhance your talk: those you prepare ahead of time and those you create during the presentation itself. Aids that you prepare in advance include:

- overheads such as PowerPoint slides to present keywords, diagrams, images, charts, and tables;
- audio or video clips to present material such as role-played interviews for staff training; and
- printed handouts to provide the audience with material to take home and consult later. When a great deal of supportive material is to be distributed to audience members, you may wish to distribute the material in the form of electronic files that attendees can read on-screen or print themselves.

These aids give you control over your presentation, but they cannot accommodate participation from the audience. To involve participants in a spontaneous way, you can ask for ideas, examples, and suggestions and record them as they are offered so that everyone can see them and think about them. Use one of the following:

- a chalkboard,
- a flip chart, or
- software that allows you to write on a pad and project your inscription onto a large screen.

The single most common fault with visual aids is that they are too small for the audience who is intended to see them. Charts often can't be read past the third row. Too many speakers try to cram long chunks of text onto their presentation slides. And some speakers even wave small objects in front of their audiences and say, "Unfortunately, you can't really see this. But if you could, you would notice . . ." This point cannot be stressed too much: your visual aids must be big enough for the audience to see; your audio aids must be loud enough for the audience to hear. Check out ahead of time, preferably in the room you will be using for the talk, the visibility or audibility of your prepared materials.

Preparing Overheads

If you do decide to use presentation software, here are some tips:

- Choose a font size that is large enough for the audience to read without strain—24 point would be good for the main body of the slide and larger for titles. Lowercase type is easier to read than all capitals. A sans serif typeface like Arial works well (see readability of fonts, 4.10). Avoid fantasy fonts—they are hard to read when projected on a screen.
- Use a clean, uncluttered design, and leave lots of white space. Don't distract from the content of the slide by choosing a fussy background or by adorning your slides with graphics that are unconnected to your point.
- Use keywords, not whole sentences. Your talk expands upon the keywords. (Never, under any circumstances, try to put the whole talk on the slides themselves.) Some authorities recommend the rule of six—no more than six words to a line and no more than six lines to a page. Some recommend even greater austerity.
- Don't numb your audience with too many slides. Use no more than 15 to 18 slides max in a half-hour presentation and preferably fewer.
- Seek variety. Avoid showing a whole series of slides that are all alike—all tables or all text or all graphs or all bullet points.
- Give each slide an interpretive title that tells the audience what the overhead is about.
- If you use images or text taken from the Internet, acknowledge your sources and pay attention to copyright restrictions.
- Keep charts uncluttered. Your audience cannot see or absorb a lot of detail. Label all charts clearly (see 4.9).

- Proofread. Do your own proofreading first, but also get someone else to check for errors you may have missed.
- Rehearse your presentation, paying attention to such details as where you will stand to avoid blocking the audience's line of vision, how you will operate the equipment, and how loudly you will speak. Practice until you feel so comfortable with the machinery that you can look at the audience and not at the buttons and controls.
- Have a contingency plan. Things can go wrong with technology. What would you do if your presentation software can't be made to work?
- Get to the room early on the day of the talk and check the equipment—for example, the projector and the microphone. Learn where the light switches are and how to dim the lights. The point to remember is that you do all the setup work *before* the audience arrives.

Using Visual Aids Effectively during the Presentation

A visual aid should increase the impact of what you are saying, not set up an interference pattern. Therefore, control *when* your audience sees your visual aid. Keep your visual aid hidden until the moment in the talk when you begin to talk about it. Your audience should be listening to you and not puzzling over the significance of a slide, map, model, chart, or box of baby kittens that you have not yet started to talk about. When using presentation slides, you should consciously control and synchronize what the audience reads when. Whenever a slide is on the screen, you should be talking about the topic of that slide. A slide about a different topic—one you have finished talking about or one you haven't gotten to yet—will compete with your talk and distract the audience. Darken the screen between slides if necessary.

Speakers can lose their audience by introducing materials too early that compete for attention. If you have produced a kit of handouts, don't hand it out until the end. If you want audience members to be able to consult handouts during the talk, hand out the kit at the beginning but ask people to put it away. Say that you will let them know when they will need to refer to something from the kit. Don't pass out materials like books or pictures while you are talking. When each person is examining some different item, no one is listening to you. Instead, set aside some time solely for the purpose of examining the materials.

Arial Typeface

6 point Arial

10 point Arial

12 point Arial

16 point Arial

20 pt Arial

24 pt Arial

36 pt Ari

48 pt A

FIGURE 8.1. A Sampler of Font Sizes

A Quick Tip 🕐

Presentation Software

A quick search on Google leads to many sites offering advice on how to make good use of presentation software. Here's one example: "Ten Tips for More Effective PowerPoint Presentations" by Dustin Wax (http://www.lifehack.org/articles/technology/10-tips-for-more-effective-powerpoint-presentations.html).

A Quick Tip 🕐

Stand Up and Stand Still
Chapple Langemack (2003: 69) laments that many speakers get a lot of things right and then blow it all by aimless, ritualized movement unrelated to the point they are trying to make. She says, "I've seen some do a little box step in place . . . and others, in an effort to work two sides of a room, pace in a little aimless half-moon. I worry about them. Where is it they want to go? Will they get there? Will they ever stop?"

Did You Know? ?

These are the most common vocal problems in speech delivery:

- The "uh" problem (You know what we–uh, er, um–mean!)
- Voice drop (If words trail off, the meaning gets lost.)
- Faulty pronunciation (Mispronunciation is distracting and undermines confidence.)
- Poor enunciation (Consonants and not vowels are the real keys to effective enunciation.)

(Adapted from Morrisey, Sechrest, and Warman, 1997: 126-129)

8.3.7. Delivery

Excellent delivery can sometimes rescue a weak speech, but a badly delivered speech almost always fails. Important elements of good delivery include good vocal quality (1.8), use of appropriate gestures (and absence of distracting gestures), pauses (1.4), and eye contact (1.2) with the audience.

Never read a speech if you can avoid it. Actors can read without sounding as though they are reading, but most people can't. Know your material well enough that you can speak from your notes as if you were having a conversation with your audience. Record one or two rehearsals of the speech so that you can listen for qualities of voice that need improvement (see 1.8). Your voice should be loud enough to be heard, clearly articulated enough to be understood, and expressive enough to keep the audience interested. Speak as if you are speaking to a friend.

Think of yourself as being onstage. Use the resources of a good actor: variety of pitch and emphasis, changes of pace, pauses for effect, gestures and movement. Look at your audience and not down at your page or at some spot on the ceiling. Vary your visual focus. Don't look mostly at people on one side of the room or the other. If your audience is large, divide it into quadrants and make sure that you look at each quadrant on a regular basis. Every member of an audience of hundreds will think that you have been looking directly at her.

8.3.8. Overcoming Stage Fright

Stage fright is a normal part of making presentations in public. All speakers experience it. But good speakers are able to use their nervousness to charge their talk with energy. They don't let it cripple their performance. A good strategy for dealing with anxiety is to ask yourself: what is the worst thing that could happen? Your secret phobia might be one of these:

- Tripping on your way up to the podium; falling over; falling off the stage
- Dropping your notes and having them get out of order
- Shaking uncontrollably
- Losing your voice; not being able to get out even the first sentence
- Stuttering or mispronouncing words

- Going blank and forgetting your whole speech
- Making some horrible mistake that the audience will all laugh at and remember with merriment for the rest of their lives
- Discovering in the middle of your speech that your fly is undone (or even that you have on no clothes at all)

Whatever your fear is, the strategy is the same: (1) plan what you will do to prevent this mistake from happening and (2) plan what you will do to recover if it does happen. Successful speakers are not people who make no errors. They are people who make fewer errors and have a recovery plan to deal with the ones they do make. For example, if you fear you may trip, wear comfortable, safe shoes that are easy to walk in. If you fear your notes may get out of order, print them on cards and use three rings to attach the cards together. If you do make a mistake, pull yourself together, maintain the appearance of calm, and don't draw attention to the gaffe by apologizing. If you can forget about the mistake and carry on, the audience will be able to do so as well.

A useful formula for overcoming stage fright is 70 percent preparation ahead of time, 15 percent good breathing technique, and 15 percent strategies for coping with problems. Here are some specific things you can do to lessen anxiety about speaking.

Prepare Thoroughly

After you have developed your speech, rehearse it. Record your rehearsal so that you can play it back and correct problems. You might also want to rehearse your talk in front of friends, who can offer suggestions for improvements (see discussion of receiving feedback in 3.15). If possible, rehearse aloud in the room in which you will actually deliver the talk. Time your speech. If it is too long, make cuts. Remember that it takes longer to deliver a speech to an audience than to an audiorecorder. If you plan to use audiovisual aids, always rehearse with them. Feeling prepared will give you confidence.

Use Notes

Don't try to memorize the speech word for word. With a memorized talk, the danger is that either you will go completely blank or you will rattle through your speech at top speed. Instead of memorizing, speak

> **Did You Know?** ?
>
> Koegel (2010) argues that poor planning is the number one reason virtual presentations fail, and advises that you don't leave presentations to chance: "practice." See his chapter on planning virtual presentations (pp. 27-35).

from notes on which you outline the key ideas of your talk. If you find regular 8.5" by 11" paper hard to hold and liable to rattle and signal nervousness, transfer your notes to cards (4" by 6" or 5" by 7"). Here are some pitfalls to avoid:

- Don't clutch your notes. Instead, place them on a lectern or desk.
- Don't try to conceal that you have notes.
- Don't plan to read notes from your computer screen.

Be Positive about Your Role as Speaker

Act confident even if you don't feel confident. Walk briskly to the platform. Stand straight. Look as if you are enjoying yourself. Look directly at your audience, smile, and take a deep breath. Pause for a moment before you begin speaking. Be enthusiastic about your topic. You will find that, after the first few minutes, the panic subsides and you become as confident as you look.

Relax

If you are offstage and out of sight, do some neck rolls. Let your head droop forward to your chest, allowing your muscles to relax and your cheeks to sag. Inhale. Turn your head to the right and hold while you count five. Exhale and let your head drop back to your chest. Inhale. Turn your head to the left and hold while you count five. Exhale and let your head drop back to your chest. Repeat. This exercise helps to get rid of the tension in your neck and shoulders.

You can do this next exercise right in the conference room and no one will notice. Take a deep breath, keeping your upper chest still and expanding the diaphragm and abdomen. Let out the breath slowly in a sigh. (But don't hyperventilate.)

Cope with Signs of Nervousness

For a dry mouth, keep a glass of water handy and take a small sip, not a gulp. If there is no water available, you can stimulate saliva by biting (not too hard) the side of your tongue. Avoid hard candies, which will interfere with your articulation and may choke you.

Shaking is caused by an excess of energy. You can't stop shaking by going rigid, clutching the lectern, and trying not to move. But you

---

A Quick Tip

Don't Apologize
Start your talk with a bang, not an apology. Don't say things like, "I'm sorry I haven't had much time to prepare, so this is off the top of my head," or "I don't really know much about this topic," or "Someone else would probably be better able to talk about this than me." You may think it sounds like becoming modesty, but the audience will lose confidence in you.

can use this energy in a positive way by directing it into motivated movement and gestures. These movements should not be fidgets and random pacing but movements that reinforce the meaning of what you are saying or that bring you into closer connection with your audience. It is reassuring, however, to realize that trembling that seems violent to the speaker is usually not noticeable to the audience. If you think the shakes may be a problem, put your notes on cards of heavy stock that won't rattle, and don't wear jangly bracelets.

If you suddenly go blank and can't remember the next sentence, pause. Take a deep breath. Exhale. Look down at your notes to find your place. Do not fill up the silence by babbling. A pause that seems excruciating to you will not seem long to your audience.

If you garble your words, don't draw attention to it by saying, "Oh dear, I've made a mess of this." Make the correction smoothly and confidently and go on. Television announcers sail right over errors: "The spokesperson for management—for labor, rather—said that he expected . . ." If you make total nonsense out of a whole thought, say, "I'll repeat that last point to make sure it's clear."

The good news for anxious speakers is that people in the audience can't tell how nervous you feel. Your heart may be pounding, your palms sweating, your mouth dry, and your stomach fluttering—but the audience can't tell. (Unless you tell them, which of course you should never do.)

8.3.9. Public Speaking: A Checklist

Before You Give the Talk

- ❑ Do you clearly understand what kind of speech you are being asked to give?
- ❑ Have you analyzed your audience? Have you geared your speech to your expected audience?
- ❑ Have you rehearsed your presentation, including your visual aids, ahead of time?
- ❑ Have you timed the talk to be slightly shorter than the allotted time?
- ❑ Is your clothing appropriate for your intended audience? Is it consistent with a professional image?
- ❑ Can you operate all the equipment that you plan to use?
- ❑ Do you plan to come to the room early enough to correct for problems with seating or equipment?

During the Presentation

❏ Will your talk entertain as well as inform your audience? It helps some speakers to think of the presentation as a performance.

❏ Are you looking at your audience and talking directly to audience members, not to your notes?

❏ Are you speaking loudly enough that you can be heard from anywhere in the room?

❏ Are you paying strict attention to timing? Starting on time? Ending on time?

❏ Are you providing variety and a change of pace?

❏ Are you observing your audience's reactions and adjusting your presentation accordingly? Cut short a section that seems to be boring the audience.

❏ Are your presentation slides, if any, easy to read, uncluttered, and pertinent?

What Not to Do

❏ Never apologize. Don't say at the outset that you fear that the talk may be a waste of time or that somebody else would probably do a much better job.

❏ Don't stand in front of the screen, blocking sightlines. Ask whether the audience can see, and make changes if anyone cannot.

❏ Don't pass out to audience members competing materials such as books or pictures, while you are talking.

❏ Don't use distracting mannerisms (rattling change in your pockets, twisting a strand of hair, rubbing your chin, or saying "um" or "you know" too often).

❏ Don't draw attention to the fact that you have had to cut something out. Don't say, "It's too bad that we didn't have time to talk about X because X is probably the most important aspect of the topic."

❏ Don't run overtime.

8.4. Making Longer Presentations at Workshops and Conference Sessions

You may be asked to give a longer presentation or a poster session (see 8.5.1) at either an in-house training session or at a conference or workshop. In addition to paying close attention to the topics discussed in section 8.3, you should be aware of some considerations peculiar to longer sessions.

8.4.1. Requirements of Longer Presentations

The most important thing to remember is that the longer the presentation is, the more energy you need to put into keeping your audience interested, comfortable, awake, and involved. A low-key delivery that succeeds for a brief talk may put an audience to sleep during a one-hour talk. Chairs that are acceptable for 30-minute talks may be intolerable for a three-hour workshop. Long presentations in lecture format without audience involvement are almost always deadly. The longer presentation is harder and takes more confidence and expertise. Get experience with the shorter ones first.

Accepting the Invitation

Are you capable of giving the kind of presentation that is expected? If not, don't be afraid to say "No" when you are first invited (see 8.3 for more on whether or not to accept the invitation). Later on, it will be too late to back out. Once you have decided to accept, confirm your acceptance in a letter or e-mail to the organizers. Your message should include:

- a confirmation of the terms agreed on,
- a list of the equipment and supplies you will need,
- specifications for the setup of the room, and
- a statement of any other special arrangements as applicable (e.g., that you will send them a file that includes formatted pages for ten handouts that they should print on colored paper and assemble into a kit for participants).

In addition, you should send information that the organizers can use for publicizing the program.

> **Did You Know?** ?
>
> "People do not fly across the world to attend conferences to sit in a dark room and look at the back of someone's head while they read incomplete sentences on a projector screen. People attend conferences to share their insights, take part in conversations, contribute to the solutions to problems, and take information back to the library" (Brier and Lebbin, 2009: 361).

Publicity and Promotion

Often longer presentations are advertised ahead of time in posters, flyers, and so forth. It's safest if you supply the organizers with your own copy that they can adapt for their advertising. Include the following:

- your name in the form in which you wish it to appear;
- the exact title of your talk;
- biographical details of relevance, including your qualifications for giving this talk (e.g., you have been responsible for the design and implementation of the system you plan to talk about);
- what your audience can expect as a result of hearing your talk (they will learn X or will be able to do Y or will experience Z); and
- the format (e.g., the workshop involves minilectures, role-plays, and group exercises or a presentation followed by group discussion).

8.4.2. Designing the Presentation

Prepare two agendas—one that you give your audience and one that you use yourself. Providing your audience with an agenda has two advantages. The process of preparing the agenda in advance (either on an overhead or as a handout) helps you by forcing you to think realistically about the timing and the structure of your presentation. Having an agenda helps the audience members listen better because they know what to expect. In drawing up the agenda that you give your audience, don't be either too general or too detailed. Leave some flex time.

In drawing up the agenda that you will follow yourself, be more detailed. Plan exactly what you are going to do, minute by minute of the presentation, whether it's one and a half hours, three hours, or six hours. Don't imagine that you can wing it. (You might be able to, but that's just lucky.) Work out in five-minute blocks exactly what you plan to do. In your design, pay special attention to pacing and to providing flexibility.

A Quick Tip

Name Tags

For workshops where participants don't know each other, make name badges for everybody. Use 18 or 24 point type so that names can be read without close inspection of the upper body (Race and Smith, 1996: 19-20)!

Pacing

All of us have relatively short attention spans, possibly as short as 15 minutes when we are listening to a lecture. This means that variety is important to recover the audience's flagging interest. So after you've done one kind of thing, such as lecture for 15 minutes, do something else. Change it up. Involve the audience by asking them questions. Let the audience ask you questions. Do a role-play. Tell a joke. Get your colleague to do something. If one voice has lulled the audience, the switch to another voice may wake it up.

If you are talking to a group who has just come back from a large lunch, you will have to use extra energy to combat post-lunch drowsiness. One way of keeping the audience awake is to encourage its active participation. Instead of lecturing, involve the audience in an exercise, a discussion, or a role-play.

Providing Flexibility

Draw up a very detailed plan in advance, but be prepared to be flexible if necessary in the event itself. Work out alternate strategies of what to do in case something goes wrong or in case you need to respond to the group's concern.

It often happens at a conference that things get behind schedule. You may have been billed to start your one and a half hour presentation at 10.30 a.m., but it is actually 11:15 before you can get going. There are three things that you should *not* do in this situation. Do not run over into the scheduled lunch hour; your audience will be hungry and blame you. Do not try to dash through your talk at double speed; it won't work, and you will ruin your delivery. Do not present the first half of your talk and then say at noon, "Too bad we ran out of time before we got to the most important part." Instead, make a silent cut so that you do cover the most important things in the time you have available. Be prepared for this contingency by planning ahead what, if necessary, you will cut. If you are using presentation software (see 8.3.6), it is unfortunately harder to drop out a whole section without signaling the cut to the audience. So plan ahead what you can do to abbreviate the presentation without drawing attention to the cut. Conversely, bring extra material to use if you get ahead of schedule—you probably won't need it, but having it available will make you feel more secure.

> **A Quick Tip** 🕐
>
> **Practice, Practice, Practice**
> Cultural and language concerns can create anxiety for those who are not native speakers of English. They may fear that public speaking will reveal their weaknesses, for example, in usage or of words. One of the best remedies for this is rehearsal and practice.

Adapt your presentation to the needs of your audience. Don't go on doggedly with uninteresting material just because it is in your notes. If you see that your audience is losing interest or has grasped something faster than you thought it would, cut short your presentation on this point and go on to something else. Cutting it short does not mean running through the same material at a faster clip; it means reducing your illustrative examples and providing summaries instead of a detailed development.

Rehearsing

Rehearse until you are thoroughly familiar with your material. It is a paradox that the more thoroughly you have rehearsed the freer you will feel to depart from your plan if necessary and the more flexible you can be. Then you can wing it.

8.4.3. Getting the Audience Involved

We know from our own experience that there are definite limits to how many facts we can absorb from a lecturer who stands at the front and talks at us. People learn best when they are actively involved. So try interspersing your lecture presentation with opportunities for your audience to participate. The following ways of involving the audience are popular techniques used by trainers.

Introduce participants. At workshops, participants welcome the opportunity to meet other people who share their concerns. So, if the participants don't already know each other, you can give them a chance to introduce themselves briefly at the beginning. With a small group, you can ask each person to say who he is and where he's from. With a group of more than 15, you won't have time to hear from everybody, but you can ask for volunteers. Suppose that you have come to speak to a group of librarians from different libraries on the topic of problems of doing legal reference work. Ask participants to tell the group what particular problems they are facing. Get a few different experiences by asking questions that invite sharing: "Has anybody here had a different problem?" "Anything else?" "Who else has a different problem?"

Ask your audience questions. Questions encourage active participation because all audience members, not just the ones who actually answer, get involved in thinking about their response. Be aware of the effects of the kinds of questions you use (see 3.4). Three kinds of questions usually don't work in generating discussion: (1) closed questions that can be answered with a yes or no answer; (2) questions with only one right answer, such as, "What was the name of the first Librarian of Congress?"; and (3) questions that are too broad, such as, "What do you think about censorship?" Instead ask open questions that:

- get participants to share relevant experiences,
- elicit opinions or feelings, and
- invite critical scrutiny of an issue.

You could ask, "How do you handle this problem in your library?" "What do you think would be the hardest part of this plan to implement?" "How do you feel about this way of handling grievances?" or "What reservations do you have about using this skill?"

When you ask a question, wait for the answer. It often takes participants a while to formulate their ideas. Don't confuse them by asking another question or by rephrasing the first one. And don't answer the question yourself. Treat with respect all answers that you do get.

Invite structured discussion. For example, instead of telling your audience of children's librarians what to look for in a good book for children, you can ask people what they look for themselves. Write down points, as they are suggested, on a flip chart or whiteboard. Adult learners learn best when they are encouraged to draw upon their own past experiences (10.2). However, many people with excellent ideas are reluctant to express them to a group of 40, although they may be happy to share them with a group of five. So another option is to break up the audience into small buzz groups of from three to seven people. This way you get more individuals actually involved. Buzz groups are given a task to work on, a specified time to work on it, and the responsibility of later reporting their findings to the group as a whole. Before they break up into their separate groups, tell people clearly what they are supposed to be discussing and how long the discussion is to last. Ask them to appoint a spokesperson to report the group's response to the task (its recommendations, its list of important questions, its best one or two ideas on the topic, etc.).

Use case studies. Case studies are useful in getting participants to deal with concrete specifics. Participants receive a printed description

> **A Quick Tip** 🕐
>
> **Humming Along**
> Buzz groups are easiest to manage if three to seven participants are sitting at round tables. Give them three to ten minutes to consider a question, such as "What's the most contentious thing you heard today?," or give them a case study to read and analyze.

of some particular problem situation. Their task is to bring problem-solving skills to bear on the case in order to come up with a solution, decision, recommendation, or plan of action. Fruitful cases are usually ones in which more than one good solution is possible. Case studies are popular tasks to give to buzz groups. After the buzz group discussion, the spokesperson from each group can share its solution with the whole group.

Do an exercise. In a training workshop, you can give the audience members an exercise in which they use the skills you have just presented. The exercise provides an immediate application in which the learner can test out what has been learned. You can get participants to do the exercises individually, in pairs, or in groups of three to five.

Involve the audience in simple role-plays. For example, in a workshop on answering reference questions, you could ask for volunteers who will play the part of the users. Make it easy by giving cards to the "users" from which they can read off their reference question. Ask audience members to take the part of the "librarian." The librarian responds to the "user" by using the skill that you have just taught. If the "librarian" succeeds only partially at demonstrating the skill, focus on the strength, not on the weakness, of the performance (see giving feedback, 3.14). When learners are learning a new skill, they rarely get all of it right on the first trial. But they get some of it right. Reinforce what they do well. People learn by successive approximations to the desired behavior. Two things are important with role-playing: (1) never put anyone on the spot, and (2) never set up a situation in which the volunteer can be made to feel foolish or incompetent.

Get your audience to ask you questions. You can either encourage your listeners to ask for clarification as you go along or specify when you will be allowing time for questions and ask them to hold their questions until then. Your handling of the first few questions determines whether or not the audience will ask anything more. If you imply that an audience member's question is silly, further questions will dry up. Input from the audience is valuable, but you should control how much and when. If someone asks you to discuss a point that you had planned to cover later, you may want to say something like, "That's an extremely important aspect. I'm going to discuss it in this afternoon's session, after lunch, so I'll ask you to bring up your question again then." But give a brief answer at the time so that you don't appear too smug.

8.4.4. Answering Questions from the Audience

Here are some suggestions for handling the question period at the end of a presentation:

- Do your homework. Prepare answers in advance for questions that you can anticipate being asked.
- Provide a positive climate by treating each questioner with respect and each question as valuable. You can say, "That's an interesting point to raise, because . . ." or "I'm glad you asked that because it's a question a lot of people may wonder about."
- Repeat the question to make sure everyone has heard it before you begin your answer. This repetition is especially important in a large room.
- If you don't know the answer, say so and promise to find out. Don't waffle.

These techniques can help you with troublesome questioners:

- **Incomprehensible questioners:** If, instead of an actual question, you get a long, rambling, incomprehensible statement of opinion or an anecdote, don't ask the questioner to repeat the question. The second attempt probably won't be any clearer. Instead, agree with the participant on some point that you were able to understand and comment on that: "I agree with you, sir. It is certainly true that libraries are very different places from what they were 50 years ago. A lot has certainly changed." Then turn away and look at another questioner.
- **Monopolizers:** Handle a monopolizer by taking one step toward her and looking at her as you answer her question. When you've finished your answer, don't provide another opening by saying, "Does that answer your question?" Instead, break eye contact, look away to another part of the room, and field a question from someone else.

- **Hostile questioners:** The important thing is to keep cool and not be baited into going on the attack yourself. It sometimes works to turn the question back on the questioner: "I see that you are doubtful about my solution. How would you handle the problem?" If this doesn't work, use the "monopolizer tip." Don't get drawn into an argument or an angry exchange.

Some Quick Tips: Dealing with Difficult Questions

Here are a few tips, adapted from Race and Smith (1996: 94–95), for handling difficult questions:

- Ask for suggestions from the audience. Say, "That situation comes up a lot, and when it does it can be bad news. Can we hear from someone who has faced this situation in your library? What did you do?"
- Welcome difficult questions. Say, "This is important. Thank you for raising this issue."
- Get a few possible responses from the audience, list them, and then get participants to rate them. Ask, "What's the best thing about this approach? What's the danger with this approach?"

8.4.5. Evaluating the Presentation

The test of your presentation is how well you satisfied the needs of your audience. Get feedback by asking audience members to fill out an evaluation form. The decision about when to collect the forms involves a trade-off. If the evaluation form is completed and collected at the end of the presentation, you may get a response from everyone. But you won't be able to ask questions about the usefulness of the presentation to participants once they return to the job.

On your evaluation form, use a combination of open and closed questions (3.4). The closed question "Would you recommend this workshop to a colleague?" or some variant thereof provides clear-cut evidence as to how many participants were satisfied. The open questions allow participants to make suggestions in their own words about what helped them and what didn't.

Keep the form short—usually a single page is enough. See the **Sample Workshop Evaluation Form** in 10.9.1 for an example.

8.5. Some Specialized Forms of Presentation

In this section, we consider three different specialized forms of presentation that are often given by library professionals. Each form has its own challenges. The *poster presentation* is a miniature form that combines documentary and oral elements and requires, above all, succinctness and clarity. *Booktalking* is a pitch designed to sell reading for pleasure. *Leading tours* is an ambulatory exercise that requires the presenter to take an audience through a physical (or sometimes virtual) space. In examining these three forms, we consider common elements such as the need to analyze the intended audience. But we also examine some issues peculiar to each form: the integration of text and graphical elements in a poster presentation; the matchmaking needed in a booktalk between the interests of the audience and the appeal factors of particular books; and the progress through a space as the organizing principle of the tour.

8.5.1. Poster Presentations

A poster presentation is a hybrid form—part document (the poster itself) and part oral presentation (what you say about the poster at the poster session). Poster sessions are like an audition, providing a brief opportunity to engage an audience, a few people at a time. The poster itself is a condensed version of your research story. You should be able to walk someone through your poster in a few minutes.

A good poster includes the following elements and does so in 800 words or fewer:

- A catchy short **title** that encapsulates what the poster is about, plus your name and affiliation at the top
- A brief section called **Research Questions**
- An overview of **methods** that you used to answer your questions
- A report of your **findings** in a section with a descriptive header that works like a newspaper headline (i.e., not "Findings" but something that summarizes the main finding, like, "Good readers also watch more TV")

- An interesting **discussion** of the findings and their implications (similarly given an informative label, not just "Discussion")
- **References** to articles important to your topic
- An **acknowledgment** of help, advice, and financial support you received

Don't waste words on an abstract. Your poster itself is the abstract. To get onto the program of a conference poster session, however, you must write and submit a poster abstract, which is either accepted or not. If your poster abstract is accepted, you next need to consider how best to present your topic both as a document and as a talk. At the conference itself, your poster will be set up, along with 20 to 200 others, in a designated area where it will remain for a day or two. (It may also be mounted on the conference website.) In his informative document "Designing Conference Posters," Colin Purrington (2013) says, "The best general advice I can give a first-time poster constructor is to describe the circumstances in which a poster will eventually be viewed: a hot, loud, congested room, with really bad lighting." Forewarned is forearmed.

During the poster session itself, your job is to stand beside your poster and explain your work to attendees who walk by, look at your poster, and sometimes ask questions. The advantage to presenting a poster rather than giving a talk is that a well-designed poster on an interesting topic can attract attendees who didn't realize they were interested in your topic until they saw your terrific poster. Also you can interact personally with people who are especially interested. But remember that the average person walking past your poster doesn't want to hear more than about two sentences on the methods used in the study or other technical details. Give more information only in response to expressed interest. You may wish to provide handouts to those who want more detail (see 9.13.3 on handouts). Have some business cards on hand to make it easier to contact you about your research.

Preparing the Poster

A good poster is like a spread in a comic book. It combines words and images in a unified whole. It grabs the reader's attention by subordinating detail to a strong, arresting pattern. The design should make it easy for the reader to navigate through sections in the right

---

A Quick Tip ⏱

See the Good (and the Bad)
To see examples of some really good posters, as well as some really terrible posters, see the Flickr site of pictures of posters and people at poster sessions (http://www.flickr .com/groups/368476@N21/pool/). For critiques of posters and lots of other useful stuff, see the blog *Better Posters* (http://betterposters. blogspot.ca/).

order. It's bad news when the reader has to wonder, Where next? On the one hand, the poster must be a stand-alone work that readers can understand without the supplement of oral explanation. On the other hand, it should intrigue readers and prompt them to ask you questions at the poster session.

Don't underestimate the amount of work that it takes to produce a good poster. It is a demanding creative process. The text must be sparse, clear, and economical; the graphics informative. Text and graphics must work together to explain and illustrate the project clearly. The biggest mistake made in poster design is trying to cram in too much—too many words, too many images. The design should attract viewers and intrigue them sufficiently that they want to find out more about the project (see 4.10 on graphic design). A good way to attract eyes is to use digital photographs, preferably ones that you have taken yourself, rather than stock, generic images.

With page layout applications, the entire poster—often four or more panels—can be designed and printed directly onto poster board, which is sized to the required dimensions. A poster often has an afterlife, becoming a semipermanent record of your work when the poster is mounted on the conference website.

SOME TIPS FOR CREATING POSTERS

- Follow carefully any instructions provided by the conference organizers. If your poster does not fit the size specification, it may be disqualified from the poster session.
- Get professional help for layout and design, even if only at the local print shop.
- Think carefully about what story you want your poster to tell. Then think about how to tell it. Which details do you need to explain in the text? Which details are best conveyed in images, charts, or graphs (see 4.9)? What title best encapsulates the story?
- Use a logical structure to present the content of your poster so that readers can immediately grasp the story without reading all the details.
- Be brief. Cut out all unnecessary words, and use white space as a design element (see 4.10 on formatting the page).
- Make the title legible to a person standing 12 feet away and the body text legible at eight feet away. For the title and headings, use a sans serif font. Do not use ALL CAPS,

> **Did You Know?** ?
>
> Your poster needs to be self-explanatory because it might be seen by people who cannot attend the scheduled poster session and by people who see it mounted on the conference website. Your poster should be self-contained—understandable without an accompanying handout or the supplement of oral comments—but richer when the handout or comments are added.

which are hard to read. For the body text, use a serif font. Don't use a dark background.

- Use headers that are informative about your specific content, not the generic "Introduction," "Findings," and "Discussion." Give your graphics an informative, legible label, not "Figure 1.1."
- Use graphical elements that are clear, simple, informative, and closely related to the text.
- Go for a clean look—informative and beautiful. Too much text, too many busy graphics, or too many colors stupefy the viewer and discourage engagement.
- Proofread and double-check all the information and data. Posters can't be altered after final printing. (Adapted from Purrington, 2013; De Castro, 2009: 115–120; "Better Posters: A Resource for Improving Poster Presentations," http://betterposters.blogspot.ca; plus good advice from Paulette Rothbauer)

At the Poster Session

Unlike a speech or conference presentation, where you hope that audience members stay for the entire talk, a poster session allows people to drift by, linger, ask questions if they are interested, or move on to the next poster if they are not. Your personal presence at the poster session and your response to questions can generate interest in your poster. The oral part of a poster presentation is less like a speech and more like a conversation, guided by the questions and interests of the audience. But you still need to be prepared, anticipate questions, formulate answers, and practice. Interacting with your audience demands that you think on your feet, apply nonverbal and verbal communication skills, and provide short, clear, and concise explanations.

SOME TIPS FOR INTERACTING WITH YOUR AUDIENCE AT A POSTER SESSION

- Make sure you can sum up the main story of your poster in two to three sentences.
- Practice 30-second, 2-minute, and 4-minute versions of your poster presentation.

- Think about which parts of your poster will be the most challenging to explain, and polish your explanations— a short two-sentence version and a longer version.
- Greet people with a smile, and show your enthusiasm for your work.
- Find out why they are interested in your poster before you begin speaking about it. That way you will be able to address their specific interests and tell them something they want to hear.
- Do not stand in front of your poster where you might block people's view. Stand to the side of your poster (but don't block the adjacent poster).
- Maintain eye contact with people as you present your poster. Do not look at the poster or read directly from it.
- If people approach your poster after you have begun to talk about it to others, pause to welcome them and let them know where you are in the story: "Hi, I'm just explaining the methods we used to do X."
- Thank people. You could say, "Thanks for stopping to talk with me" or "Thanks for your feedback on the XXX program." (Adapted from the Cain Project, 2003)

8.5.2. Booktalking

The purpose of booktalking is to turn people on to books they will enjoy reading. Two essential elements are (1) selecting books appropriate to the intended audience and (2) talking about the books in such an interesting way that people want to read the book. A booktalk is not the same as a book review or a piece of literary criticism. It does not evaluate or offer a balanced assessment. It sells the book. You start with a book that you like and that you think the audience will like. Then you entertain with a come-on for the book. You tell what was funny, interesting, exciting, scary, or moving about the book. You want your talk to result in people borrowing and reading the books you've discussed. Good booktalks boost circulation and generate excitement about reading. And of course booktalking is not restricted to physical books. You can booktalk e-books, audiobooks, and films.

Booktalks vary. They can be impromptu on-the-floor discussions with one person who has asked for a good book, or they can be presented more formally to a whole roomful of people. They can be aimed at children, young adults, or adults. They can be presented face-

Did You Know? ?

You should aim for not too much and not too little, but "just right." Langemack (2003: 29) says, "Booktalking is giving just enough information to convey the feeling of the book. You want your audience to be intrigued by the book and interested enough to investigate further."

to-face in the library, in schools, and community settings. Or they can be broadcast over local radio or TV or made available through podcasts and YouTube. A short booktalk on a single book may be less than a minute long, and a long one may last three to five minutes. Booktalks to groups usually present a number of different books that have something in common with each other, such as an author, a genre, an appeal factor (e.g., complex character development), or a topic (e.g., survival stories). They differ from library instruction (8.6) in being designed not to teach how to use a particular book but rather to sell the experience of pleasure reading and the role of the library in providing enjoyable books to read.

In preparing to do a booktalk presentation, you analyze the audience, just as you would before giving any presentation. Like a readers' advisor (see 6.4.6), you are providing a matchmaking service, connecting readers to books that they are likely to enjoy. Your purpose is to recommend books that have the potential to interest not just a single user but a group of users. Questions to ask about the audience include: What is the nature of the group—is it a grade nine English class? A book club? A group of retirees? A naturalists' club? What is the ratio of males to females? What is this group interested in? What is the reading level of group members? What are their reading tastes? What books have you presented to this group before? How long a presentation are they expecting to hear?

In making your presentation, keep in mind all those things that are crucial to the success of any talk: the use of eye contact, delivery (8.3.7), and controlling stage fright (see 8.3.8).

Usually a formal booktalk presentation consists of a series of shorter booktalks, varying in length from long to short and strung together with transitional sentences. As you begin to talk about each book, you pick it up and show it to the audience, stating clearly the author and title. If your audience is too large to be able to see a book held in your hand, show the cover art by using an overhead and presentation software (8.3.6). Your first sentence grabs the audience's attention by introducing the main character or by putting the audience into the midst of the action. By the second sentence, you are well into the main action, theme, or dilemma of the book, which you elaborate with a few (but not too many) concrete details. The last sentence is a cliffhanger that restates the author and title, while leaving unanswered questions in the listeners' minds. Then you move on to the next book.

Aim for variety in the books you select and in the way that you present them. Alternate a long booktalk with a short booktalk. If you start off with an action book, the next book you discuss may be a bit quieter and more reflective. Suggest some challenging books that stretch the best readers in the audience, but make sure that you also talk about some books within the reach of the less practiced readers. At the end of the presentation, you invite the audience to look at the books and ask questions.

Some Tips on Booktalking

- Don't generate a demand that you can't fill. Talk about enough titles that you can spread the demand over a number of books. But have multiple copies available of books you expect to be most popular.
- Don't try to memorize your whole talk. Speak directly to the audience, using notes (see 8.3.7 on delivery).
- Don't spill all the beans, or your listeners will feel they don't need to read the book. Never tell the ending.
- Read sparingly, if at all, from the text—four or five sentences at most. Listeners usually find it boring to hear long passages read, no matter how well you read. It's better to quote a number of short, especially apt phrases interspersed throughout the talk.
- Sketch out the essential action of the book in bold strokes. Don't get bogged down in complicated details and long descriptions.
- Your booktalk should convey the essential flavor of the book and the element in the book that is likely to appeal to a reader (see "Factors That Affect Readers' Choices" in 6.4.6). If a novel is a complex study in character, don't imply by your discussion that it's full of exciting action. Don't oversell a book, or your audience won't believe you the next time. If, however, the book has a slow beginning, warn your listeners that it is worth persevering to Chapter 2.
- Anticipate and avoid problems. For example, Mary K. Chelton (1976) points out that it can be dangerous to start off a booktalk with a reference to a noticeable physical trait. Ask, "What do you suppose it feels like to be the tallest girl in the whole school and have everybody call you beanpole?" and the entire audience may simultaneously turn and look at the tallest girl in the class.

> **A Quick Tip** 🕐
>
> **Handouts for Adults**
> When your booktalk audience is a group of adults, Baker (2010: 238) recommends that you provide each person with a list of all the booktalked books in the order in which you present them. The list helps listeners concentrate on what you are saying rather than on trying to write down the names of authors and book titles.

- Keep records of which books you've talked about with which audiences. When you talk to the same group again next year, you won't want to repeat yourself.

Digital Booktalking

Booktalkers can now use technological solutions to make booktalks available to readers any time anywhere. Wikis and podcasts allow you to create multimedia booktalks that are accessible from your library's website. These can incorporate voice, images, and video and can be as simple as a recording of a booktalk or as complex as something that incorporates a reenactment of a scene from a book. Video booktalks can be used effectively by librarians in school libraries, but they can also be assigned to students to produce as a class assignment, teaching them not only booktalking skills but also how to incorporate audio-visual materials. Keane and Cavanaugh (2009) explain how to create both audio (podcast and CD) and video booktalks.

8.5.3. Leading Tours

A tour provides participants with firsthand experience of a particular physical area, giving a sense of context or atmosphere that description alone cannot provide. A guided tour for an individual or a group is useful for:

- supplementing an orientation process,
- introducing staff members in their own environment, and
- encouraging people who wouldn't normally use your library or who aren't motivated to visit on their own.

But consider your purpose carefully (see 8.3.1). If you simply want to describe the functions of a department, give a history of the building, or demonstrate particular reference sources, don't organize a tour. Instead, use a lecture or display format—or just give people a map.

Consider your audience carefully, too (8.3.2). The kind of tour you organize for the board of governors or for new staff members will differ substantially from the kind of tour you organize for first-year students in an information literacy course or for people from a local service club. Assess the level of motivation, interests, and needs of the group. How is the tour going to help this group? What do you most want the group to understand about your library through this

---

A Quick Tip 🕐

Learn Booktalking Online
YALSA (Young Adult Library Services Association) offers an online course for YA librarians, "Booktalks Quick and Simple," that can be licensed for presentation in your library (http://www.ala.org/yalsa/onlinelearning/onlinecourses/booktalks_quick).

Did You Know? ?

A virtual tour is convenient for people who can't get to the scheduled face-to-face tours. Put a link to a "Library Tours" page on the homepage of your library's website, where you list the types of tours offered (e.g., general tours, school visits, information services tours to meet the needs of particular groups, or tours related to special exhibits) as well as schedules and contact information to arrange a tour. The webpage can also provide links to the library floor plan (see, e.g., Virginia Tech's Newman Library "tour options" page at http://www.lib.vt.edu/instruct/toursked.html).

tour? Keep your objectives simple. You may have achieved your purpose if your students see for themselves that there are five floors in the library and meet some pleasant, accessible librarians. It may be enough for your new board members to get an impression of the complexity and variety of library services and understand the growing role of digital resources, or for nonusers to find out that you have more than books, or for new staff members to be able to associate a few faces with locations.

Quick Tips for Giving Tours

- **Keep the group size manageable.** Arrange several separate tours for small groups rather than trying to conduct a large group tour, which may be disruptive to normal operations and may not be informative for participants. The maximum number is usually 12 to 15 people.
- **Speak clearly and slowly.** Don't shout. At the beginning, ask if everyone can hear you. If not, take a deep breath, pitch your voice to the person furthest from you, and ask again. Use short sentences.
- **Don't talk while you walk.** Stop periodically, face the group, pause, then make your point or ask your question. Don't get involved with private conversations with individuals in the group as you walk along. Very experienced leaders can talk while they walk backwards (but first they check for kick-stools in the aisles), but we don't recommend it for first-time tour guides.
- **Don't use the tour as a lecture platform.** Make only essential points, and leave the rest for another time. Inexperienced tour leaders provide too much or irrelevant information. Don't overload people. Less is more.
- **Involve participants.** Use questions as well as statements. For example, when demonstrating subject headings, ask someone to suggest a topic of interest. Or ask people to guess the age of a building. If you can, find out the interests of your group in advance. Address people by name if possible.
- **Introduce staff members** as you go along. At the very least introduce the group. For example, "Hi Aviva, these are visiting guidance counselors. [To the group] Aviva is one of the people who prepares book orders." Staff members like to

---

Exercise 🔧

Practice Being a Tour Guide
Take one or two friends on a ten-minute tour of a place that you know well (not necessarily a library). Pick a place where the tour is not likely to be disruptive, but if necessary explain to curious bystanders that you're practicing being a tour guide. For this exercise, pay special attention to personalizing the tour to meet the particular interests of your audience. After the tour, ask for feedback (3.15). What did they remember most clearly? What did they find most interesting? Least interesting? What did they learn that might be useful in the future? What would you do next time to make the tour more interesting or useful?

be acknowledged and respected for their work. Moreover, when you introduce employees, you give tour members the confidence to approach these people for help later. To vary the pace of the tour, you might ask the staff member to answer a simple question: "About how many books do you process each month?" Avoid leading questions ("You enjoy working here, don't you?") or questions to which the staff member may not immediately know the answer.

- **Keep the tour short.** People don't learn when they are tired or overloaded with information. A reasonable attention span in a tour is probably 20 minutes or less.
- **Combine formats.** Arrange a meeting or short lecture before the tour to present factual information and give an overview. Or bring people together after the tour so that they can ask questions about what they've seen. You might provide a short break between two parts of the tour. This helps to solve the problem of information overload. Consider combining classroom discussion with a self-guided audio tour or a self-guided tour brochure. If necessary, you can motivate participants to take a self-guided tour by providing an easy exercise or assignment (like a treasure hunt) that will take them through all the areas of interest.

8.6. Providing Library Use and Information Literacy Instruction

Librarians in all types of libraries are called on to provide user education, including library use instruction (bibliographic instruction or BI) and information literacy instruction. The terms are somewhat confusing and the definitions overlapping:

- **User education** refers to all the activities involved in teaching users how to make the best possible use of library resources, services, and facilities. It includes formal and informal instruction delivered either one-to-one or in a group. It also includes behind-the-scenes preparation of online tutorials, audiovisual materials, and printed guides and pathfinders.

- **Library use instruction** (synonymous with BI) teaches library users how to find information independently. The instruction may cover the library's system of organizing materials, the structure of the literature of a field, research methods appropriate to a selected discipline, and specific resources and finding tools.
- **Information literacy instruction** aims to teach both information skills (organization of libraries, library resources, etc.) and skills in critical evaluation and effective use of information content. (From *Online Dictionary for Library and Information Science*, ODLIS, http://www.abc-clio.com/ODLIS/odlis_i.aspx)

Library use instruction and information literacy instruction are now a larger part of staff duties in academic, school, and public libraries, and even in special libraries, largely because of ever-changing electronic resources. Instruction may take place in the classroom, in a lab, on a tour of the library, or on a one-to-one basis. Librarians are called on to consult with teachers and learners and to provide training in information literacy skills. Effective instruction requires the instructor to master, in addition to subject expertise, three types of teaching skills:

- organizing skills, including the ability to assess needs, set objectives, and design the curriculum or program;
- writing skills and skills of graphic presentation; and
- interpersonal skills for communicating effectively with individuals and groups.

The majority of the library literature on instruction concerns the first two categories of skills. Excellent articles and books cover instructional approaches such as the following: problem solving and critical thinking; curriculum content; and creative teaching methods specific to the library context. Most formalized instruction also involves writing for preparation of course outlines, exercises, pathfinders, handouts, lists of frequently asked questions (FAQs), and visual aids. These writing skills are described in Chapters 4 and 9 and are also included in the Annotated Bibliography on instruction at the end of this chapter. Unfortunately, the personal communication skills required of the instructor are not well covered in most of the literature on instruction. Because library instruction provides an excellent example of a specialized application for many of the nonverbal, listening, and speaking skills described in Chapters 1–3 of this book, this section focuses on a few ways in which selected skills may be used in instruction.

Quick Tips for Instruction in a Classroom

- Your primary tool for instruction is your voice. When speaking to a class, think about projection, pace, and modulation. Make sure that everyone can hear you—check with class members at the beginning, and adjust your volume if necessary. Don't go so fast that people can't keep up or so slow that people get bored and tune out (see 1.4 and 1.8 on projection, pace, and voice qualities). Use pauses strategically before an important point, but avoid long silences while you are opening a browser or waiting for a search to run. Use that time to explain what you are doing (see inclusion in 3.10).
- Avoid library-speak. Remember that your goal is to help students learn the concepts and skills of library research, not the specialized jargon of the library world.
- Make eye contact with your audience (1.2). Make sure that you look at audience members in all parts of the room, not just at the front row or at one section of the room. Some instructors break the room up into sections and make a point of regularly looking from section to section in order to connect with the entire class.
- Show your enthusiasm for your topic. If you sound bored, why would your students think the topic interesting or important?

See the University of Texas Libraries' "Tips and Techniques for Library Instruction" (http://www.lib.utexas.edu/services/instruction/tips/eval_index.html) for more information on evaluating both student learning and your own presentation.

8.6.1. Attending and Influencing Skills for Instruction

Experts in instruction recommend a variety of "teaching modes"—not just lectures but also labs, discussions, demonstrations, tours, indi-

Did You Know? **?**

The average student's attention span in a lecture is 15 minutes.

vidual assistance at the point of service, and online instruction with minimal intervention from the instructor. The particular interpersonal skills needed depend on the instructional format. One-to-one instruction requires all the nonverbal and speaking skills described in Chapters 1–3, but these skills are also essential when working with groups. Listening (Chapter 2), acknowledging (3.2), and encouraging (3.3) are basic attending skills that help to establish a productive communication climate in which potential library users feel that their problems, experiences, and ideas are respected. Inclusion (3.10), the skill of explaining what you are doing, is useful in demonstrations where you need to describe or explain a procedure as you carry it out. This is especially the case when instructing large groups, because not everyone can see exactly what you are doing. Instructions and directions (3.12) need to be clear and specific so that there is no doubt as to what is required. In a group situation, it's important to wait until the group is ready to hear the instructions (you may need to pause until you have everyone's attention) and to ask for confirmation of your instructions: "Now, before you begin, tell me what I've asked you to do."

8.6.2. Questioning Skills for Instruction

Asking questions is a skill useful not only for one-to-one instruction but also for working with groups. Questioning is a more versatile technique than many teachers suspect and need not be limited to the usual "test" question ("What are three points of access to a catalog?") that anticipates one correct response from the keenest student. Questions can be used to perform other functions. First, open questions (3.4) and the more structured sense-making questions (3.6) can encourage participation, motivate students, and establish a good communication climate. "Tell us a little about your first experience in using a library" is a good ice-breaker that also provides an opportunity for the instructor to assess the diversity of experience, expertise, and motivation in a group. Encourage a variety of responses. Listen carefully, and keep your comments brief and nonjudgmental. Questions may also be used to instruct. Draw on expertise within the group ("Who has used *Psychological Abstracts*? Tell us briefly what you used it for and how it helped you"); brainstorm ("If you were looking for information on X, where would you begin? Tell me all the possible places you can think of"); identify unexpected problems using an open question ("What problems did you have when you did this search?"); and find out what's missing in the student's understanding by asking sense-making questions ("How did this index *not* help you? What got you stuck? What else did you want to find out?").

Questions can also help you to evaluate both student progress and your own. Giving and receiving feedback (3.14 and 3.15) is an essential part of any instructional program and should occur periodically throughout a program, not just at the end. By requesting and receiving feedback, you learn what aspects of your teaching are helpful (or not helpful) to the students and what you could do to improve the program or your teaching techniques. For example, "Last session we talked about business databases. How did that discussion help (or not help) you? Give an example of something it helped you do or understand" or "What could be done to make this course more helpful to you?"

When you give feedback (written or spoken) to students, you are letting them know how well they are doing. Use the steps suggested in 3.14 on giving feedback. Start with something positive ("You found the two most important periodical indexes"). Describe rather than judge ("Your literature search included only popular articles and no other types of sources" rather than "Your literature search wasn't very good"). Be concrete ("You did not mention *Dissertation Abstracts*" rather than "Your literature search was incomplete"). Be realistic ("For the next assignment, try to find two more different types of reference tools" not "You must list all types of reference tools"). Limit suggestions for improvement to two or three. And suggest rather than prescribe ("You might want to look at X").

Questions That Instruct: Some Examples

> Suppose I've never used an index before in my life. Explain this to me so that I understand.
> If you had to find a biography of this artist, what would you do first? Next? Next?
> What does this citation *not* tell you?

8.6.3. Group Skills for Instruction

Understanding how groups work (Chapter 7) helps in teaching small or large groups of potential library users. Discussion, exercises, and demonstrations also provide necessary variation in the pace of the session. Handling problem behavior (7.7.2) sometimes becomes necessary in a group, especially when students are not equally motivated to attend the session. When the instruction program involves a lecture, presentation skills are important (8.3). First, examine the purpose of the lecture and the audience by using the checklist in 8.3.9. Consider the structure of the lecture (the "tell 'em" approach described in 8.3.5 works perfectly for instruction); use audiovisual aids skillfully (8.3.6); and work on your delivery skills (8.3.7), including overcoming stage fright if necessary (8.3.8). Use the presentation checklist (8.3.9) if this is your first attempt to teach library use in a large group. Don't forget your nonverbal communication (Chapter 1): eye contact, posture, and vocal qualities can help to make "using the library" a more interesting topic than your audience may have anticipated. These skills are also important in giving tours of the library (8.5.3), which are often part of education programs.

Evaluating Student Learning

You can evaluate student learning using brief and in-depth assignments. The latter require cooperation and advance planning with the faculty member. On the other hand, you can simply give students brief assignments to help you evaluate your presentation, such as:

1. **Three Things You Learned.** At the end of the session, ask students to write down on an index card three things that they learned. You can review these cards to find out if the instructional session has achieved your goals.

2. **The Muddiest Point.** At the end of the session ask students to write down on a piece of paper what they found most confusing. You can use this feedback to devise new ways to discuss those confusing points.

3. **Index Card Assignment.** When students arrive for the session, give them index cards and ask them to write down three questions they have about the library or about research. Collect these cards before you start the discussion. At the end of the session, read the questions and have students answer them. You will find out if they learned what you set out to teach them or if they had any questions you did not address during the session.

A Quick Tip

Hold the Stage

Carla List-Handley (2008) recommends that you approach classroom teaching as a performance, using movement, gesture, and voice to reinforce important points of your talk. Handle the student who is acting up by fixing him with a direct look—"the look" can stop disruptive behavior in its tracks. Smiling conveys enthusiasm and helps the voice by lifting the soft palate and improving the way sound is generated in the mouth.

4. **Pre- and post-quizzes.** Create a quiz that addresses the areas you will cover in the session. Copy it on both sides of a sheet of paper. At the beginning of the session, have students take the quiz. When they are through, tell them to set it aside. At the end of the session, ask students to turn the sheets over and take the same quiz again. They will immediately be able to see what they learned. So will you when they pass it in. Save enough time to go over the correct answers during class. If you do not have time, make sure that students are given a handout or a follow-up e-mail with the correct answers.

See the University of Texas Libraries' "Tips and Techniques for Library Instruction—Evaluation" (http://www.lib.utexas.edu/services/instruction/tips/eval_index.html) for more suggestions on evaluation.

8.7. The Media Interview

The media interview is a hybrid. It differs from the other kinds of public speaking discussed in this section, while at the same time it shares characteristics with PR, publicity, and promotion (9.13) and with interviews (6.3). In the media interview, your communication with the public is mediated through an interview, which is then edited into either a printed or online news article or a recorded radio or television clip. This mediating and editing process, in which you have a lot of input but little control, is what makes the media interview challenging. Many of the tips offered in this section are related to the problem of reducing distortion and ensuring that you are conveying the message that you want to convey.

Usually, media interviews with library representatives occur in response to your media advisory or news release (9.13.1) or because the reporter wants to obtain an informed opinion on a library-related issue. The interview may take the form of a short phone conversation (recorded for radio but dependent on the interviewer's notes for a magazine or newspaper) or a television interview taped at the library or at the studio. In some cases, you may participate in an online text-based interview in which the reporter either sends you a list of questions to answer at your convenience or else interviews you

---

Did You Know? **?**

Your library should have an overall philosophy and policy about how to handle inquiries from reporters. In large organizations, a communications officer often fields media questions and connects journalists to the people most knowledgeable about the topic at hand. In a smaller organization, a designated spokespeople should be identified. "A media relations policy prevents a reporter from putting your circulation clerk on the spot with a question about a recently challenged book—the staff person can simply tell the reporter that the interview must be cleared by the library director" (Wolfe, 2005: 92).

synchronously through the give-and-take of typed messages. Skype can be used for virtual face-to-face interviews. In any of these situations, the interviewer may sometimes go over questions with you in advance and may or may not ask exactly the same questions in the recorded interview.

For all media interviews, be prepared. Ask how long the interview will take (so that you can give shorter or longer answers) and what the main focus will be (so that you can address the major points). Have facts at your fingertips—don't guess. Never speak off the cuff or off the record. Assume that everything you say may be reported, even small talk before the official beginning of the interview. Treat the interviewer as neither an adversary nor a friend but as someone whose objective is to get information efficiently and effectively.

Tips for Getting Your Points Across

These tips apply to all forms of media interviews:

- Before the interview, become familiar with the style of the interviewer. Read articles written by the interviewer, listen to the talk show host, or watch the television interviewer in action.
- Define for yourself in advance the position statements that you would like to make about the issue or topic, whether or not you get asked about them. During the interview, fit them in, using a transition such as, "I'm glad you mentioned that because [position statement]" or "You may not be aware of this but [position statement]" or "Your viewers would probably be interested to learn that [position statement]."
- Communicate enthusiasm, concern, and authority through your tone of voice and what you say ("This is an important issue for the library and for the taxpayer" or "We've been studying this very carefully").
- Listen carefully to the question. If you don't understand, ask that it be repeated. If the question is difficult, pause first and think what you want to say before you begin to speak.
- Use the inverted pyramid structure for your responses (see 4.5). Give a general reply, then make it more specific, and finally give examples. If, as often happens, the whole

interview is cut to 20 seconds, the editor can use your first few sentences, which encapsulate the key points.

- Use short words, simple sentences, and analogies that the audience can understand (see 4.2 and 4.4—many of the hints for writing clear, understandable prose apply here too). Avoid jargon and buzzwords.
- Don't repeat an interviewer's words if they contain false premises (e.g., "Why are libraries needed any more now that everything is on the Internet?"). Instead, correct or rephrase the question. Explain why the premise is misleading, only partially true, or completely wrong.
- Set the record straight by saying, "A lot of people think that . . . but that's not true and here's why. . . ."
- Don't try to answer hypothetical questions. Instead, state your general position and offer your own example.
- Avoid off-the-cuff remarks, which can hurt your credibility and that of your organization.

Tips for Newspaper or Magazine Interviews

These tips apply in particular to print-based media:

- Make sure that what you say is what you want to see in print. Rephrase or repeat your answers if necessary.
- Don't expect to review the article before it appears. This is never permitted by large media organizations and rarely permitted by freelance writers.
- Provide background facts (including spelling of names, full titles or positions, and statistics) in writing to avoid errors. Encourage the reporter to call you for further information or clarification if necessary—then make sure you are available.

Tips for Television Interviews

These tips are directed particularly to making the most of the visual medium of television:

- For on-site television interviews, be prepared to suggest a couple of locations for the interview. Consider background noise, whether or not privacy is important, equipment

A Quick Tip 🕐

Nonverbal Behavior

The ALA Communications Handbook notes that a lot of communication problems in media interviews are nonverbal. Problems may include "adopting a wooden body posture; presenting material too technically; averting, darting, or poorly using eyes; ineffective use of hands; lack of facial expression or one that communicates fear, hostility, arrogance, or defensiveness; low energy; humorlessness; and use of boring language" (American Library Association, 2004: 30).

facilities, and the visual background. But follow the crew's advice. Don't try to tell media people how to do their job.

- Wear appropriate clothing—lightweight (because the lights are hot) in solid, midrange colors (blue, teal, rose, and burgundy work well). Avoid white and black or other strong contrasts. Avoid shiny or noisy jewelry. Wear business clothes. If you are wearing trousers, wear socks high enough to avoid gaps when you cross your legs. Stick with simple lines so that the viewer focuses on your message, not your outfit. Men should wear jackets. Women should avoid low-cut or sleeveless blouses and short skirts.

- Maintain eye contact with the interviewer. Look at the camera only when you are introduced or to make a special point.

- Gesture naturally. Don't fold your arms across your chest (it makes you look defensive), wring your hands, or fidget with jewelry or the microphone.

- Stay calm and don't lose your temper, no matter what the interviewer says.

Tips for Radio Interviews

These tips are directed particularly to making the most of the voice-based medium of radio:

- If the reporter doesn't tell you when the recording is to start, ask.

- If you use notes, put them on cards, not on paper that rustles.

- Avoid tinkling jewelry—it's even worse on radio than on television.

- Speak loudly and clearly, with the voice supported from the diaphragm, not from the throat. Vary your voice quality for emphasis (see 1.8).

- If you are on the air for a call-in talk show, organize some friends of your library to call in with some good questions—this will break the ice and show support.

- Mention your library's name at least twice (people tune in and out and may miss the introduction).

Exercise

Television Interviews
Watch two or three televised interviews on your local station. For each, pay attention to one aspect of the interviewee's behavior—body language, voice quality, appearance, or structure of responses. What behavior contributes to a good interview? What behavior distracts or is dysfunctional?

Did You Know?

Because radio and television producers often use a different "clip" for each broadcast, only a part of what you say in the interview may be heard at any one time. Try to ensure that each individual statement can stand on its own, out of the context of the whole interview.

8.8. Annotated Bibliography

General Works on Making Presentations

Adler, Ronald B., and Jeanne Marquardt Elmhorst. 2010. *Communicating at Work: Principles and Practices for Business and the Professions.* 10th ed. New York: McGraw-Hill. See Part V, "Making Effective Presentations," which comprises chapters on developing, organizing, and delivering business presentations. An appendix includes a sample presentation.

Blicq, Ron S. 2005. *Communicating at Work: Creating Messages That Get Results.* 4th ed. Toronto: Prentice Hall Canada. Presenting yourself well is covered in Part IV of this book, which includes Chapter 11, "Speaking Before a Business Audience" (pp. 259–286).

Borden, Richard C. 1935. *Public Speaking as Listeners Like It!* New York: Harper and Row. This has been described as the best short book ever published on public speaking.

Ellis, Richard. 2009. *Communication Skills: Stepladders to Success for the Professional.* 2nd ed. Chicago: University of Chicago Press. Chapter 12 (pp. 109–129) provides excellent advice on all aspects of presentations.

Jaffe, Clella Iles. 2006. *Public Speaking: Concepts and Skills for a Diverse Society.* 5th ed. Boston: Wadsworth/Cengage Learning. This thorough textbook covers basic public speaking skills, rhetorical foundations, and technology and is well worth studying. See the latest edition (7th, 2012) as well.

Koegel, Timothy J. 2010. *The Exceptional Presenter Goes Virtual.* Austin, TX: Greenleaf Book Group Press. This book covers all types of virtual, online, or distance presentations. It complements his earlier book *The Exceptional Presenter* (2002, 2007), which provides guidelines and tips that can help both new and experienced public speakers.

Morrisey, George L., Thomas L. Sechrest, and Wendy B. Warman. 1997. *Loud and Clear: How to Prepare Effective Business and Technical Presentations.* 4th ed. Reading, MA: Addison-Wesley. This is highly recommended as a concise and practical text for professionals. Appendix A provides worksheets and guidelines.

Motley, Michael T. 1997. *Overcoming Your Fear of Public Speaking: A Proven Method.* Boston: Houghton Mifflin. This brief 40-page handbook focuses on speeches as communication rather than as performance. It includes exercises.

Race, Phil, and Brenda Smith. 1996. *500 Tips for Trainers*. Houston, TX: Gulf Professional Publishing. This text provides useful tips on working with guest speakers, using work space and video playback units to your advantage, and ensuring that your body language is sending the right message to the audience.

Statze, Sarah R. 2003. *Public Speaking Handbook for Librarians and Information Professionals*. Jefferson, NC: McFarland. The first section of this well-written handbook provides basic principles of speech preparation and delivery, with suggestions and strategies for anyone making group presentations. The second section focuses on interpersonal communication and public speaking skills needed by library professionals to conduct interviews, run meetings, provide instruction, and make presentations to large and small groups of all kinds.

Walters, Lilly. 1993. *Secrets of Successful Speakers: How You Can Motivate, Captivate, and Persuade*. New York: McGraw-Hill. This book includes ways of building rapport with cross-cultural audiences.

Arranging for Others to Speak

Burkhardt, Joanna M., Mary C. MacDonald, and Andrée J. Rathemacher. 2001. "Blueprint for Planning a Successful Program." *American Libraries* 32, no. 10 (November): 48–50. This article succinctly outlines the steps to follow in planning a continuing education program. It is applicable for any kind of conference or workshop planning.

Follos, Alison M. G. 2006. *Reviving Reading: School Library Programming, Author Visits, and Books That Rock!* Westport, CT: Libraries Unlimited. This work includes several pages (pp. 89–101) on planning for author visits.

Hall, Danelle, and Janet Swan Hill. 2002. "Care and Feeding of Speakers and the Spoken-To." *American Libraries* 33, no. 5 (May): 64–67. This work includes two short articles, "A View from the Back Row" (pp. 64–65) and "A View from the Podium" (pp. 66–67).

Hart, Lois B., and Gordon Scheicher. 1993. *A Conference and Workshop Planner's Manual*. Amherst, MA: HRD Press. This manual systematically presents the steps for conference and workshop planning. It includes many sample checklists, letters, and schedule sheets that the reader can adapt.

Watkins, Jan. 1996. *Programming Author Visits*. ALSC Program Support Publications. Chicago: American Library Association. This is a step-by-step guide to planning and preparing for author and illustrator visits in children's and school libraries.

Visual Aids, Posters, and Presentation Software

Avery, Elizabeth Fussler, Terry Dahlin, and Deborah Carver, eds. 2001. *Staff Development: A Practical Guide*. 3rd ed. Chicago: American Library Association. See especially "How to Use Audiovisual Aids Effectively" by Maggie Weaver (pp. 139–142) and "How to Make Effective Presentations" by Melissa A. Wong (pp. 143–146). See also the 4th ed. (2012), edited by Carol Zsulya, Andrea Stewart, and Carlette Washington-Hoagland.

Brier, David J., and Vickery Kaye Lebbin. 2009. "Perception and Use of PowerPoint at Library Instruction Conferences." *Reference and User Services Quarterly* 48, no. 4: 352–361. The authors surveyed librarians attending LOEX conferences and conducted a content analysis of presentations at these conferences. They identify annoying elements of PowerPoint presentations and conclude that many librarians have produced and viewed too many unproductive PowerPoint presentations.

Cain Project. 2003. "A Guide to Presenting a Poster." Cain Project in Engineering and Professional Communication, Rice University. http://www.owlnet.rice.edu/~cainproj/presenting.html. This helpful site also includes "Presentation Resources" covering planning, effective data display, design of PowerPoint presentations. See also the presentation checklist.

De Castro, Paola. 2009. *Librarians of Babel: A Toolkit for Effective Communication*. London: Chandos. This book includes solid advice on visual aids, presentation software, and posters.

Hilyer, Lee Andrew. 2008. *Presentations for Librarians: A Complete Guide to Creating Effective Learner-Centred Presentations*. Oxford: Chandos. This practical book is based on Richard E. Mayer's cognitive theory of multimedia learning and covers how we learn from presentations and how to create them. Chapter 10 covers delivering successful presentations. An appendix provides hints on using presentation software (PowerPoint and Apple Keynote). See also Hilyer's blog, *Presentations for Librarians: Your Guide to Creating Effective Learner-Centered Publications*, at http://presentations4librarians.wordpress.com/.

Parker, Roger C. 2006. *Looking Good in Print: A Guide to Basic Design for Desktop Publishing*. 6th ed. Sebastopol, CA: Paraglyph Press/ O'Reilly Media. This book is full of tips on preparing graphics for presentations, with comparative examples.

Purrington, Colin B. 2013. "Designing Conference Posters." http:// colinpurrington.com/tips/academic/posterdesign. This is an excellent overview of what poster designers need to know, with examples of terrible and good posters, tips, recommendations for graphics packages and page layout programs, and a bibliography of further sources.

Tufte, Edward R. 2003. *The Cognitive Style of PowerPoint*. Cheshire, CT: Graphics Press. This is a much-cited critique of presentation software. Copies of this brief book can be found on the web, along with critiques of his critique.

Booktalking

Baker, Jennifer. 2010. "Booktalking for Adult Audiences." *Reference and User Services Quarterly* 49, no. 3: 234–238. Baker provides suggestions for working with adults and advice on choosing the right books for different audiences.

Baxter, Kathleen A. 1998. "Booktalking Basics." *School Library Journal* 44, no. 6 (June): 70. In addition to her *SLJ* column, "Nonfiction Booktalker," Baxter has published several books with co-author Marcia Agness Kochel on nonfiction booktalking for children. The most recent is *Gotcha Again for Guys! More Nonfiction Books to Get Boys Excited about Reading* (Santa Barbara, CA: ABC-CLIO, 2010).

Bodart, Joni Richards. 2010. *Radical Reads 2: Working with the Newest Edgy Titles for Teens*. 2nd ed. Lanham, MD: Scarecrow Press. This is the latest of the many books by Bodart on booktalking. For example, see *Booktalk! 5: More Selections from The Booktalker for All Ages and Audiences* (New York: H. W. Wilson, 1993), an excellent how-to-do-it guide on booktalking for librarians and teachers.

Chelton, Mary K. 1976. "Booktalking: You Can Do It." *School Library Journal* 22, no. 8 (April): 39–43. This article includes a one-page "Guide for Booktalkers" that contains 19 useful tips.

Keane, Nancy J., and Terence W. Cavanaugh. 2009. *The Tech-Savvy Booktalker: A Guide for 21st-Century Educators*. Westport, CT: Libraries Unlimited. This book includes ideas and instructions for integrating technology into presentations. Designed for teachers and school librarians, it is also useful for public librarians.

Langemack, Chapple. 2003. *The Booktalker's Bible: How to Talk about the Books You Love to Any Audience.* Westport, CT: Libraries Unlimited. This is a lively practical guide to all aspects of booktalking.

Wolfe, Lisa. 2005. *Library Public Relations, Promotions, and Communications.* 2nd ed. New York: Neal-Schuman. Chapter 12 discusses using library staff members as community volunteers and as booktalkers.

Providing Library Use and Information Literacy Instruction

Cox, Christopher N., and Elizabeth Blakesley Lindsay (eds.). 2008. *Information Literacy Instruction Handbook.* Chicago: ACRL. An update to ACRL's *Sourcebook for Bibliographic Instruction and Learning to Teach* (1993), this book includes discussion of the history, learning theory, program management, assessment, instructional technologies, collaboration, curriculum, and future of information literacy instruction.

Grassian, Esther, and Joan R. Kaplowitz. 2009. *Information Literacy Instruction: Theory and Practice.* 2nd ed. New York: Neal-Schuman. Part IV (pp. 221–266) covers delivery of information literacy instruction, with tips on taking a learner-centered approach, listening to and engaging learners, dealing with stage fright, and getting students' attention. Chapter 13 addresses teaching diverse populations and teaching in different types of libraries.

Kilcullen, Maureen. 1998. "Teaching Librarians to Teach: Recommendations on What We Need to Know." *Reference Services Review* 26, no. 2: 7–18. Kilcullen provides a summary of useful information to help librarians learn to deliver a lecture.

Lederer, Naomi. 2005. *Ideas for Librarians Who Teach: With Suggestions for Teachers and Business Presenters.* Lanham, MD: Scarecrow Press. This practical manual is packed with advice for anyone required to teach, lead workshops, or do presentations. It offers good advice on creating visual aids with and without technology.

List-Handley, Carla. 2008. "Teaching as Performance." In *Information Literacy Instruction Handbook*, edited by Christopher N. Cox and Elizabeth Blakesley Lindsay, 65–73. Chicago: Association of College and Research Libraries. An information literacy specialist emphasizes the importance of incorporating performance skills into presentations.

Mayer, Richard E. 2001. *Multimedia Learning*. Cambridge, England: Cambridge University Press. In this book, Mayer provides a cognitive theory of multimedia learning and seven principles for the design of multimedia messages. See also his many other books on human cognition and learning.

McCroskey, James C., Virginia P. Richmond, and Linda L. McCroskey. 2006. "Nonverbal Communication in Instruction Contexts." In *Sage Handbook of Nonverbal Communication*, edited by Valerie Manusov and Miles Patterson, 421–436. Thousand Oaks, CA: Sage. This chapter covers the research on nonverbal communication in teaching.

Vossler, Joshua, and Scott Sheidlower. 2011. *Humor and Information Literacy: Practical Techniques for Library Instruction*. Santa Barbara, CA: Libraries Unlimited. This book reviews the literature regarding the effective use of humor in teaching, especially in library science. It includes personal experiences of instruction librarians.

The Media Interview

American Library Association. 2004. *Communications Handbook for Libraries*. Chicago: American Library Association. http://www.ala.org/ala/issuesadvocacy/advleg/advocacyuniversity/advclearinghouse/commhandbook.pdf. This brief (39-page) handbook includes helpful advice on media communications, with many tips for doing media interviews.

Byrne, Judith. 2003. *Face the Media: The Complete Guide to Getting Publicity and Handling Media Opportunities*. 2nd ed. Oxford: How To Books. This book contains guidelines and tips for handling media interviews.

McLaughlinm, Paul. 1990. *How to Interview: The Art of the Media Interview*. Vancouver, BC: International Self-Counsel Press. This text explains in detail the process of the media interview and covers differences between print and broadcast. Although written for journalists, it is equally useful to those being interviewed.

Wolfe, Lisa. 2005. *Library Public Relations, Promotions, and Communications*. 2nd ed. New York: Neal-Schuman. Chapter 8 covers preparing for successful media relations.

Videos

Library Video Network (http://www.lvn.org/store/index.html) lists several videos featuring Arch Lustberg, including these:

Library Video Network. 1992. *Perfecting Presentations.* VHS. 37 min. Closed-captioned. In this amusing video Arch Lustberg presents proven techniques (e.g., "the power of the pause" and "the rhythm of eye contact") for high-impact presentations. An order includes his book *Podium Power.*

———. 1994. *Testifying with Impact.* VHS. 41 min. Closed-captioned. Includes book. Media coach Arch Lustberg shows how to present testimony and other kinds of information to friendly or hostile audiences.

———. 1995. *Using the Media to Your Advantage.* VHS. 50 min. Closed-captioned. Arch Lustberg gives tips for communicating on radio, on television, and in print.

Producing Texts

9.1. When to Write and When Not to Write

The first decision you must make is whether or not to write your message. You might do better to communicate in person—either over the telephone or face-to-face. If you choose to write, you have a further choice between print and electronic forms. Here are some guidelines.

When to Write

- To convey routine information that doesn't require a response
- To allow the reader time to consider your question or request before formulating an answer
- To communicate efficiently to a number of people who are separated geographically (It can take much longer to telephone each person separately than to send out a group or mass mailing of a letter or memo.)
- To create a permanent record of the communication (A memo can be filed and used later to resolve a dispute over what was actually written. A written thank-you note for a job well done can be included in a dossier and used at performance appraisal time to document a success.)
- To convey complex or detailed information (Written instructions decrease the chances of misunderstanding or error. You should write down dates, times, deadlines,

individual responsibilities, or numbers that you don't want the reader to forget or confuse.)

- To aid the memory (Handouts given out at staff training sessions and minutes of meetings are both examples of aids to the memory. These should also be made available on the library's intranet.)
- To increase confidentiality (But keep in mind, however, that electronic messages are not always secure. A sealed reference letter, marked "confidential," will be more secure than a fax or e-mail. Of course, letters that are not treated confidentially are even less secure than other message forms.)

When to Communicate in Person

- To avoid creating a record of the communication (A message committed to paper or electronically is easily copied and distributed. If you don't want the message to be reread later by unauthorized third parties, then it may be prudent not to write it down. Although there is no paper copy of cell phone calls, such calls are not entirely secure.)
- To make sure that the person actually does take note of the message (Often, people file or delete messages without reading them.)
- To convey information that is sensitive or painful (Face-to-face, you can see how the other person is reacting and can correct misunderstandings immediately.)
- To encourage dialogue and discussion (The person you are talking to can ask questions and can contribute ideas of her own.)
- To get an immediate answer or make a direct, personal contact

Sometimes it's best to combine both written and spoken communication—perhaps a telephone call followed by a written memo. Staff training is a good example of a situation that benefits from the use of both kinds of communication. The spoken presentation makes a direct contact with participants and fosters interaction; the handouts are permanent records that aid the memory. If you need to send a bad news e-mail, it is more compassionate to talk to the person by phone or face-to-face to provide advance warning (e.g., "I'm calling to let you know that we got the decision today on funding and I'm sorry to say your proposal wasn't funded. I'll be sending along the official decision by e-mail attachment. I hope we can talk about it after you have had a chance to read it").

9.2. Internal Communication versus External Communication

Before you start writing, consider this. Are you are writing for readers who are internal to the library (administrators, library technicians, librarians)? Or are your readers external to the library (members of the public, job applicants, newspaper reporters, government officials)? Writing for an internal audience differs from writing for an external audience in the following ways:

- You can make some assumptions about what an internal audience already knows. Because you share with your readers a common language of jargon, acronyms, and technical terms, you may be able to use terms like OCLC or LC in the expectation that your readers will understand them. The specialized language of jargon develops because it allows insiders to communicate concisely about matters specific to a field. When writing for an external audience, you should either avoid such terms or else explain them.
- You can use a more conversational and informal style if you are writing to your colleagues rather than to a member of the public or government official (see discussion of appropriate style in 4.2).

Common forms of internal communication are messages, memos, letters (good news, bad news, and neutral), reports of various kinds (committee reports, progress or periodic reports, incident reports, formal reports issuing from feasibility or planning studies), policy statements, manuals, procedures, instructions, agendas and minutes for meetings, performance appraisals, training materials, staff news-letters, and announcements.

External communication often uses some of the same forms, especially messages, letters, instructions, newsletters, and reports, but these are aimed at a different audience. For example, annual reports

---

A Quick Tip ⏰

Writing Interculturally

Be aware of intercultural differences when you write. In addition to translation difficulties, four of the most common writing problems between cultures are these:

- Choosing to write when you should speak face-to-face or vice versa
- Lacking awareness of the correspondence format of other cultures
- Adopting a casual tone when you should be more formal
- Neglecting the personal dimensions of the relationship (Although Americans consider it efficient and courteous to get to the point immediately, Middle Eastern and some Asian cultures demonstrate respect for the relationship by prefacing the "business" with personal greetings and "small talk.")

See also 4.6 on using inclusive and nondiscriminatory language.

are intended to reach a broader public. Some of the most common forms of communication designed primarily for people who do not work in the institution are signs, briefs to commissions or government bodies, publicity announcements, media releases, booklists, pathfinders, book reviews, library orientation materials, project proposals, requests for funds from external agencies, and newsletters for the public.

This chapter includes guidelines for selected types of both kinds of communication. We've concentrated on those forms that are most commonly generated by library staff or those that seem to pose frequent problems. Fortunately, a great many excellent manuals on effective writing are available as well as many reliable Internet resources for improving writing skills. For aspects that we do not cover in this chapter, see the Annotated Bibliography in section 9.17.

9.3. Messages

Whenever the technology is available, it appears that people will use it enthusiastically to send short messages—millions and millions of them. The first short message formats were the telegram and the postcard. According to John Freeman (2009: 46), the first postcard was mailed in England in 1871. Two years later, 72 million postcards were posted in England and 26 million in Germany—an impressively rapid adoption. The key characteristic of both the telegram and the postcard was brevity. A similarly rapid adoption has happened with a whole new set of ways to send short messages: e-mail, instant messaging (IM), online chat, social networking sites such as Facebook, and texting using Twitter and SMS (short message service) on mobile phones. In 6.4.5 we discussed the use for virtual reference of some of these technologies for exchanging short messages. In this section, we focus on more general kinds of message exchange when brevity is desired. Freeman (2009: 81) reports an exchange of telegrams between Oscar Wilde, who wanted to know how sales were going for his new novel, and his publisher. Wilde's message: "?" The publisher's reply: "!" Brevity is also desirable in these newer electronic formats (see discussion of writing digitally in 4.11).

9.3.1. E-mail

In 1971, the first e-mail message was sent, and by 2011 some 35 trillion e-mail messages flew back and forth among the world's 3 billion e-mail accounts. A Stanford survey found that 90 percent of all Internet users use e-mail (Freeman, 2009: 4). The average corporate office worker sends or receives some 100 e-mails a day. So you undoubtedly use e-mail daily in your professional work. You know the importance of an informative subject line and a brief, clear message. Possibly through sad experience, you have learned to reread and edit carefully each professional message before you hit the "Send" button, and you are very cautious about using "Reply All."

You find e-mail a very useful professional tool and think it saves you time and makes you more productive. But from time to time, you feel swamped. You worry that when you return from your holidays, it will take you days to catch up on your e-mail. And then there are those e-mail messages that left you puzzled about the sender's intention. Is the message some elaborate joke? Is the sender angry? You may also be able to recall an e-mail exchange that took a surprising and rapid downward spiral into a vituperative exchange that you think would not have happened face-to-face. So e-mail is a special type of written communication with its own rules and conventions for reading and writing and its own pitfalls.

E-mail is generally an informal medium but for professional messages aim for a middle style—businesslike but friendly and not stuffy. Ellis (2009: 183) recommends that when responding to an e-mail, "take your tone and style from the sender's own." However, in the case of a rude sender, politeness trumps style-matching.

Some Tips for E-mail

- Don't send e-mail unless the message is essential. E-mail begets more e-mail and requires more of your time to answer it.
- Don't send copies to everyone and her dog—cc only those who really need to know.
- Be aware of the high potential for misunderstandings in the "cues-filtered-out" medium of text-only. Take steps to avoid them when you read and write e-mail (see discussion of reduced cues in 7.6).

A Quick Tip 🕐

Write in Haste, Repent at Leisure

The immediacy of electronic communication can sometimes be a disadvantage. If you are feeling hot under the collar, save your message overnight and look at it again in the morning. You may decide to moderate your tone before clicking "Send."

A Quick Tip 🕐

Don't Send
In *The Tyranny of E-mail* John Freeman (2009: 206) reports that "one of the biggest generators of excess mail is a medium-sized message sent to a group of people, which then causes a pinball effect as people chime in and comment, having a virtual discussion."

A Quick Tip 🕐

Where Are You?
On your outgoing e-mail, always provide instructions for alternate forms of communication: your name, mailing address, fax, and phone. Not everyone who receives your e-mail message will use e-mail to reply. Your correspondent may want to fax or phone you or know where you are physically located.

- Attend to correct spelling, grammar, and punctuation in e-mail, just as you would in print. You're still leaving an impression.
- Get to the point before the reader has to scroll down the screen. (Readers sometimes fail to notice that scrolling is needed and think the message is complete on the first screen.) Remember he or she probably has 50 other messages to read. Make every word count.
- Break up a long message into sections with subheadings or lists with bullets. Even better, keep your e-mail message short and attach a file that can be read separately.
- Provide an "executive summary" on the first screen in a longer message—or at least say what kind of response you want, for example, "Please read this report and submit your suggestions for changes to me by Monday, October 13."
- Keep an exchange of e-mails as a record when a written trail is important. In such cases, don't change the subject line without warning, and don't delete the message you are replying to.
- Don't send back your correspondent's entire last message if a complete record isn't necessary. You can leave in key phrases for some context, to which you can reply.
- Always include a signature file. Include your name, title, and contact information. Don't clutter up your signature file with lengthy quotations, overly elaborate boxes, or fancy fonts or graphics.
- Use a descriptive subject line. "Your request" isn't as good as "Your vacation schedule."
- Don't write anything you wouldn't want posted on the staff bulletin board tomorrow morning. Your correspondent may innocently (or not so innocently) forward your message to others, possibly to the entire staff.

9.3.2. Instant Messaging and Online Chat

Instant messaging (IM) and online chat both allow people to communicate one-to-one or within groups in real time. Despite being text based rather than voice based, IM and online chat resemble a telephone conversation. You can conduct private text-based conversations with specified known users in real time. Like e-mail, both IM and chat messages can usually be saved for future reference. Unlike texting (see 9.3.3), there is no limit on message length.

Instant Messaging

IM is a practical and inexpensive means of communication among a known group of individuals. In 2010, there were 2.4 billion IM accounts worldwide. IM is popular with teens, who can privately converse with others on their contact (or buddy) list. Quan-Haase and Young (2010: 359) report that IM is often used among young people to provide and receive social and emotional support from friends: "In this way, exchanges over IM emulate in-person conversations, allowing for intimacy and a sense of connection." Because it works well for a known group of users, IM is particularly useful for collaborative work in organizations. It can be used both in one-to-one communication and in group communication, combining features of the telephone, e-mail, and chat into one (Thimm, 2010: 67). IM software increasingly includes audio and video components.

IM is useful for collaborative work in your library (see virtual teams, 7.6.1), but it can also be used to communicate with users. Some libraries are using IM for virtual reference (see 6.4.5). It is much less expensive than chat software, but it does have limitations—you can't push pages or co-browse. Otherwise, an IM reference transaction is very similar to a chat transaction.

Online Chat

Online chat can be used for a variety of purposes in both one-to-one conversations and group conversations. Online chat requires the installation of specific chat software that allows for communication between, for example, a library and multiple individual users, who can be anonymous. Unlike IM, some chat software permits messages to be sent to users who are not logged on at the time of sending. Libraries have found it useful for virtual reference because the software not only allows for a real-time reference interview but also allows you to push webpages and to co-browse databases. Records of the transaction can be sent to the user, eliminating the need for note-taking (see 6.4.5 on virtual reference).

SOME TIPS FOR INSTANT MESSAGING AND ONLINE CHAT

- Wait for a response to each of your comments before adding more. Otherwise, you won't be sure which comment the other person is addressing.

Did You Know? ?

In a study of the use of multiple media in a business organization, Quan-Haase, Cothrel, and Wellman (2005) reported, "IM supports one-to-one communication (user to user), one-to-many communication (user to multiple users), and many-to-many communication (where a user can initiate a session in which all invitees can interact with one another). Many-to-many communication can foster a sense of community among participants, since users become more aware of one another and their opinions, understandings, likes, and dislikes."

A Quick Tip ⏲

Providing Nonverbal Cues
Users of e-mail, IM, chat, and other text-based media have found creative substitutes for the missing nonverbal cues. Caja Thimm (2010: 65) identifies emoticons and chat-speak as examples of "secondary orality." Check out PC.net (http://pc.net/), which provides thorough lists of emoticons and chat acronyms such as HTH (hope this helps) and CYE (check your e-mail). For more on emoticons, see the **Take the Shortcut** tip in 4.2 in the section on formality.

- Keep your messages short, and limit the conversation to one subject at a time. If you will be away from the keyboard for a while, explain what you are doing: "I'm just checking in our catalog."
- Suggest moving the exchange to e-mail or phone if the topic starts to become complex.
- End the conversation with "I am signing off now" so that the other person knows that you believe the exchange is complete. But wait a few moments to see whether the other person acknowledges your sign-off or instead says, "Wait—there's more!"
- Remember that IM conversations are not necessarily private and can be shared with others. (Adapted from Gaertner-Johnson, 2010)

9.3.3. Text Messaging

Text messaging (commonly just "texting") allows people to send short messages of up to 160 alpha-numeric characters to and from a mobile phone (or fax machine and/or IP address) over a phone network. Sometimes known as short message service or SMS, text messages originally could not contain images or graphics. Now multimedia messaging service (MMS) allows for the inclusion of image, video, and sound. Because texting can be expensive, libraries find it prudent to reserve it for occasions when there is some urgency.

Texting, and the use of mobile devices generally, has profoundly affected interpersonal communication. Individuals making or receiving a text can be anywhere at any time. Text messaging is most often used between mobile phone users as a substitute for voice calls when voice communication is impossible or undesirable. Exchanges can be managed without the other person's being required to reply immediately. Of particular interest to this chapter, texting has resulted in new economical writing patterns.

Some Tips for Texting

- Identify yourself and your library.
- Reserve texting for messages that can be conveyed in 160 characters or fewer. If it can't be, use e-mail instead.
- Use abbreviations and shortcuts when you have reason to think the recipient will understand.

- Be complete. If the recipient needs to do something (pick up a requested book), provide full instructions (where to go, which desk to approach, your phone number if you want them to call).
- Edit your message before sending it.

9.3.4. Facebook

Facebook is one of the most popular of the many social networking services that allow for the exchange of user-generated content. Accessible from computers and from mobile devices, Facebook supports large volumes of short messages and pictures, posted on a public wall, which can be seen and commented on.

Launched in 2004, Facebook took off initially as a university students-only space for people with a .edu e-mail address. When Facebook expanded to include the general public, it became a way for individuals to connect with friends and family and to share photographs and personal news. It has since been adopted by businesses and organizations, which use Facebook to take advantage of its asynchronous, many-to-many communication to post messages to followers. Individuals who join Facebook create a personal profile, post messages or pictures on their wall, and add other Facebook users as Friends—that is, people who can look at their posts and comment on them. In 2007, it became possible for corporate entities, such as businesses, educational institutions, and libraries, to create an institutional Facebook page. Other Facebook users can access the content of institutional pages and can choose to become a "Fan" (the equivalent of being added as a "Friend" by a personal user). Settings of the Facebook page can be configured to allow fans to write on the wall and post photos, videos, and links. Fans also receive automatic updates when the page changes (e.g., a new posting for an upcoming library event).

By making it very easy for people to connect with others on their friends list, Facebook creates a sense of membership in a peer community. This many-to-many communication chiefly distinguishes social networking sites such as Facebook from IM or online chat (9.3.2), where the focus is on a conversation within a small group or between two participants. Less private than IM messages, Facebook interactions are visible to the entire community of friends, which in some cases may number thousands of people. Because of its public nature, Facebook postings to some extent resemble online discussions

> **Did You Know?** ?
>
> A text message is known by many names. It may be called simply a "text" in North America, Australia, the Philippines, and the United Kingdom. It is an "SMS" in most of mainland Europe, and it is a "TMS" or "SMS" in the Middle East and Asia ("Text Messaging," *Wikipedia*, http://en.wikipedia.org/wiki/Text_messaging).

A Quick Tip ⏱

Why Create an Institutional Facebook Page?

There are a lot of reasons to create an institutional page for your library; here are two you might not have thought of:

- Search engines index Facebook institutional pages (but not personal profiles of individuals).
- There are no limits on the number of fans an institutional page can have, while individual pages are limited to 5,000 friends. You can access data on who "liked" your library, how they interacted with it, and what content was most viewed. See Terra Jacobson (2011) for an example of research based on such data.

(9.3.5) or forums (Quan-Haase and Young, 2010: 359). Facebook's strict policy against the use of pseudonyms distinguishes it from sites such as Second Life, where people use avatars that may or may not bear any resemblance to their identities in the everyday world.

The institutional Facebook page for libraries is picking up momentum as a way to connect with users and post information about events and services. Because of its interactivity and huge number of signed-up members, Facebook has a lot of potential as a tool for publicity and promotion (see 9.13.4), but the jury is still out about its actual effectiveness to date. Two research studies that examined postings on Facebook walls of academic libraries reported very low incidence of fan posts or user discussion (Gerolimos, 2011; Jacobson, 2011). Gerolimos (2011) analyzed 3,513 posts on the walls of 20 randomly chosen academic libraries. Of these posts, 477 included comments, and the rest were clicks on "Like." The majority of posters were librarians, other staff members from the same institution, and alumni, but not the faculty and students who were the target audience. However, it appears that there is a huge gap between the institutional Facebook pages that have many fans—such as Yale University Library and the New York Public Library—and the lackluster ones that have just a handful of fans. Check out some of the best ones to see what strategies they use to stimulate user engagement and interactivity.

Noting the downside of interactivity (posting of false information, hate speech, etc.), Fernandez (2009: 10–11) has pointed out that the library has "an ethical obligation to be aware of potential abuses, and determine how it wants to regulate the interactions that occur on its site." Judicious use of the site's privacy settings can help. When Gerolimos (2011) performed a content analysis of wall posts, he reassuringly found no instances of hate speech and no instances of offensive language, possibly because posters could not be anonymous.

One caveat for libraries: the library needs to be prepared to invest ongoing attention and resources in maintaining its Facebook page. Private individuals may set up a Facebook account and then use it rarely to post an occasional picture of the baby or shots of the family at Aunt Mildred's ninetieth birthday party. Libraries, on the other hand, need to maintain an active presence with new content posted at least weekly—or else they shouldn't have a Facebook presence at all. In her research on actual use of Facebook in libraries, Jacobson (2011: 88) found that because its "top use is for announcements and marketing," Facebook is "a better tool for 'active libraries,' or libraries that host a lot of events, exhibits, workshops, and other activities."

Tips for Writing Facebook Posts

- Keep posts brief—see discussion of writing digitally (4.11) on how people scan rather than read.
- Seed content on your page that will promote discussion, responses, and user involvement.
- Provide essential details—the five Ws (who, what, where, when, why). If you're talking about an upcoming event at the library, give the name, date, time, and a link to more information.
- Write as though you are talking directly to a person, using personal pronouns and contractions and a relaxed, friendly tone.
- Ask questions to encourage interactivity, which is the lifeblood of social networking communication.
- Aim for variety and novelty in your messages, and update frequently to bring traffic back to your page.
- Provide a prompt—"Click 'Like' if you enjoyed X." People are a lot more likely to interact with your site if you tell them how they can participate.
- If the library's Facebook posts never get comments, reevaluate. Are the posts interesting, clear and concise, positive and engaging? Do they encourage interaction?

9.3.5. Virtual Discussion Sites

Virtual discussion sites have been a medium for posting public messages since at least the mid-1980s. In Chapter 7, we considered virtual discussion sites in terms of their role in facilitating group communication (see 7.6.3). In this section, we focus on issues related to writing and reading posts on these sites, often called "listservs," "electronic discussion lists," "bulletin boards," or "newsgroups." Usually focused on a specific topic of interest, they allow participants with a common interest (e.g., reading romance fiction or living with Tourette's syndrome or bee-keeping or library education) to post messages, ask questions, and provide information. They are still widely used, despite the increased use of blogs and social media sites. Unlike Facebook (9.3.4), discussion groups are usually centrally administered, meaning that posted items may be withdrawn after a specific time period. Many are also monitored so that postings are vetted before distribution.

Did You Know? ?

There is a good reason to understand and use Facebook privacy settings. Fernandez (2009: 11) points out that libraries using Facebook for outreach want "to keep their settings relatively open, or risk creating barriers" to interactivity and participation. But librarians also need to be aware of the danger that actions taken within the site that they intended to be private could be automatically pushed out to users. Understanding how privacy settings work helps librarians be "aware of what they can and cannot do to proactively control or promote certain types of communication."

A Quick Tip 🕐

Find Your Group
There are hundreds of library-related discussion lists for librarians. Try a Google search using "Electronic Discussion Lists for Librarians," and you'll find many possibilities. For example, New Mexico State Library publishes "Electronic Discussion Lists for Librarians" (http://www .nmstatelibrary.org/services-for -nm-libraries/programs-services/ librarians-toolkit/listservs-for -librarians) that covers local (New Mexico), nationwide, and worldwide lists.

When you join a discussion group, the first thing you should do is read the FAQs (frequently asked questions). You may choose to lurk (reading the messages but not posting any yourself) for a while until you get a sense for the interests, tone, and dynamics of the group. Lurking gives you a good idea of the most common communication accidents, errors, and social infractions on discussion groups, such as asking a question that is covered in the FAQs file; accidentally sending a private message to the group as a whole; meaningless subject lines (e.g., "More about That"); and sending the same message to multiple lists. Poorly constructed postings may be flamed, or attacked, but are more likely to be ignored. You can increase the likelihood of getting responses by writing briefly, correctly, and aptly. Combine the skills for good writing (Chapter 4) together with the skills for group interaction (Chapter 7), and add a dollop of good common sense. For example, if you want a lively discussion on a new topic, don't ask in the midst of a discussion of software for virtual reference, "Why doesn't anyone say anything about staff burnout?" Start a new thread yourself, introducing the discussion with an interesting observation followed by a question to elicit responses. In addition to the rules and norms for communicating in an online discussion group listed in 7.6.3, here are a few more suggestions related to writing.

Tips for Writing for Virtual Discussion Groups

- Be brief, concise, and on-topic.
- Remember that discussion groups have no geographical boundaries. Use culturally appropriate language, and provide complete addresses (e.g., "Hamilton" could be in Australia, Bermuda, Canada, Scotland, or elsewhere).
- Acknowledge the contributions of others ("As Lee pointed out . . .").
- Use neutral language when you disagree ("There is another way of solving the problem that Lee described" not "Lee is clearly not a professional librarian or he would know . . .").
- Practice reciprocity if you have canvassed the group asking for examples. Post a summary for others to use (e.g., a listing of titles suggested in response to a request for humorous novels featuring werewolves or zombies).
- Point out mistakes privately by e-mailing only the person who posted the message, not the whole group. If you make a mistake yourself, post a correction or apology immediately.

- To speed the termination of an issue that's become tiresome, try reflecting feeling ("I don't seem to be alone in thinking we've explored this issue as far as we can for now, so it may be time to move on to something else" instead of "If I see one more message about users reading pornography in the public library, I'm going to unsubscribe from this list").
- Finally, remember that anyone with an Internet search engine can read your posting, whether a group member or not.

9.3.6. Blogs

Most blogs (originally "weblogs") resemble a personal journal dealing with the blogger's personal experience and reflections, often on a specialized topic, but they do allow for interpersonal communication via comments from readers. The blogger and the readers can link to additional information on the web or in other blogs. Unlike on Facebook, discussion can be controlled by the originator, who can edit or delete contributions to it.

Librarians are avid bloggers, and libraries themselves sponsor blogs (to find some, do a Google search on "blogs written by librarians"). These library blogs might focus on specific library-related activities, such as cataloging, the use of e-books in libraries, social networking in libraries, children's literature, or—pertinent to this chapter—librarians writing for publication (e.g., http://academicwritinglibrarian. blogspot.ca/). Blogs by librarians might provide information about activities at specific branches (such as updates on a new construction project) or focus on good sources of information about various topics (e.g., new books, career help, health). Thimm (2010: 68) argues that blogs can have a significant influence on public opinion. Along with websites and Facebook pages, libraries can use blogs for publicity and promotion (9.13).

Some Tips for Writing Blog Posts

- Choose an appropriate tone for your blog's audience, conversational but professional.
- Provide clear and concise titles for your blog posts so that readers know what they are about.
- Avoid a text-heavy appearance. Use informative headings for each section so that your readers can scan easily. Write

short paragraphs—two or three sentences. Use lots of white space.

- Choose high-contrast graphics that have a strong relationship to the text and are not too small and too detailed.
- Provide some commentary and analysis for any links you include, explaining why you have chosen them (and don't provide too many).
- Know the copyright rules, and provide attribution to text and images you use in your blog.

9.4. Memos

With some exceptions, memoranda or memos are written to people within an organization, whereas letters are written to people outside. Hence, the format of the memo dispenses with some formalities of the letter in order to achieve speed, directness, and consistency. Memos may be sent in electronic or, more rarely, hard copy form. Organizations typically provide preformatted memo forms, with headings like these:

To:
From:
Date:
Subject:

Memos are generally not signed, although many writers like to initial their printed name on the "From" line.

Memos are a flexible form for communicating vertically or horizontally within an organization. A memo can serve the same purpose as an ordinary letter—providing information, asking for information, making a request, giving instructions, and so forth. Longer memos are closer in function and form to a report (see 9.6). Memos can be printed and distributed to recipients or sent as e-mail attachments or informally within the body of an e-mail.

The most common writing problem that can arise with memos is that they beat around the bush, waste the reader's time, and don't organize the information in the order that the reader needs to read it. Write your memo with the needs of your reader in mind. Unless there is some evident reason not to (see 9.5 for the indirect approach to use with bad news), start by explaining:

- why you are writing and
- what, if anything, you want the reader to do about it.

The following opening gambits are useful because they answer the reader's tacit question, "What's this got to do with me?"

- This memo is to let you know the details of the planned move to City Mall.
- Please read the attached plan for the move to City Mall and let me know if you approve of it.
- You will be pleased to learn that . . .
- If you are in category A (e.g., have people in your department who will be requesting maternity leave), then you will be interested in the following details. [This saves time by telling a reader who is not in category A not to bother reading the memo.]
- You asked me to let you know when Z was completed. . . .
- I read with great interest your report on X and am writing to respond to your recommendations.

If you are making a request for action, don't bury your request in the middle of paragraph three, where it may be missed. Instead, try something like this:

> To: Larry Stevens, Branch Supervisor
> From: Enrico Murray, Financial Officer
> Date: January 3, 2013
> Subject: Branch budget due February 3
> So that we can submit the budget to the Library Board on time, please do the following:
> 1. Discuss your staff's annual budget requirements with Mr. Crabgrass by January 15.
> 2. Send me the final branch budget request by February 3.

After you have made your request, provide any necessary background information, for example, explaining the necessary format for the budget submission or mentioning that the branch budget must be submitted by Friday in order to meet the deadline for distribution to City Hall staff.

Some Tips for Writing Memos

- Be personal and conversational. Try reading your memo out loud. If you would never say anything like this in a face-to-face encounter, the memo's style is probably too stuffy or too formal or too bureaucratic. Don't say, "Please be advised that your report was received today by our department." Simply say, "Thank you for your report."
- Use the word *you*. Emphasize the way the situation looks from the perspective of the reader, not the writer. A writer-oriented statement is: "I am pleased to report . . ." A reader-oriented statement is: "You will be happy to learn . . ."
- Be concise. If possible, get your memo all on one page. But remember that your motive for conciseness is to save the reader time. If your memo is so short that it leaves out essential information, your reader will have to waste time in writing you another memo asking for clarification.
- Make your message complete. Anticipate and include in your memo all the details that the reader will need to know.
- Be specific. On your "Subject" line, don't just say "Draft proposal" or "Recommendations." Better to say "Draft proposal of the Computer Users Committee" or "Recommendations on choosing a jobber."
- Use headings. Divide up the text of longer memos with headings such as "Need for a quick decision" or "Action requested, rationale, background." Headings make information easier to find and assimilate.
- Use checklists if you are making a number of requests. The reader can check off the requests as he or she complies with them.

For an example of a bad and a good memo report, see 9.6.1.

9.5. Letters

Letters come in two categories: (1) good news or neutral messages and (2) bad news messages. Letters in the former category are straightforward and easy to write because your reader will be receptive to your message. You may, for example, be writing to supply requested information, to grant someone a request, to congratulate someone, or to offer a job. Bad news letters require more care. You may have to turn down a request, complain to an outside supplier or vendor, or make a negative evaluation. The challenge is to say "No" or to phrase your complaint in a way that makes your position clear but respects the feelings of the reader. Letters to the editor are a different kettle of fish and fall into the category of publicity and promotion—see 9.13.

The sort of message you are writing determines the approach to take in organizing the letter. The governing question to ask is, how can you best accommodate the needs of your reader? To which approach will your reader respond best?

Your letter can be printed and mailed by post, sent as an e-mail attachment, or, less formally, simply written in the body of an e-mail. Which choice you make depends on the purpose of the letter and its intended audience. In general, letters should be considered formal documents and sent by post, faxed, or attached as PDFs to an e-mail.

Good News Letters and Neutral Letters

Take the direct approach. Get to the point immediately, without minor preliminaries. If you are writing good news, your reader will be anxious to hear it right away and not be left in suspense. If you are sending a complaint or making a claim, your reader will appreciate that your directness is saving time.

This formula is most commonly recommended for good news or neutral letters:

1. Start with the main point.
2. Provide explanations or supporting detail.
3. End with a statement of goodwill.

This means that if you are able to make a favorable reply to a question or request, your opening sentence should be the answer. Instead of writing, "Thank you for your letter of January 10," try "The answer to your question about X, raised in your January 10 letter, is . . ." Instead of writing, "Thank you for your inquiry asking about reserving rooms in the Central Library," try "We have booked Room 3 for your Reading Group on Thursday, October 15, from 8:00 to 10:00 p.m." (We offer more later on how to write the response when turning down the request to book a room.)

A Quick Tip 🕐

Good News, Bad News
If the news is partly good and partly bad, it is usually best to write the letter as a good news letter, playing up what you can do, not what you can't. However, you will have to use your common sense in deciding which approach to take.

EXAMPLE [TO GRANT A REQUEST]

[Main idea:]

Here is the book list that you requested containing suggestions for good books to share with your preschool children.

[Supporting detail:]

This reading list is a good starting point, and you can also access it and other reading lists on the library's website at [URL]. But if you want more information, you might want to come to the library and look at some of our books written for parents like yourself. In particular, I would recommend . . .

[Positive ending:]

I would be happy to show you these books and answer your questions about our collection of books for children.

This same direct approach works when you are making routine claims. The supplier or vendor should have a claims section on its website that you can use, but sometimes you may need to write a letter. You may think that, because complaints or claims are prompted by some failure of performance or service, you should follow the indirect approach of the bad news letter. But the direct approach has two advantages: it appeals to the idea that companies want satisfied customers and need to know when things go wrong; and it gives strength to the claim.

Start by specifying what action you want from the reader. Then provide, as supporting detail, an explanation of why the requested action is warranted. Use unemotional, measured language when describing the problem. Avoid gratuitous insults or threats as well as typographical signs of intemperateness such as exclamation points. By your calm tone, you indicate that you have confidence in the fairness and goodwill of the other party.

EXAMPLE [COMPLAINT OR CLAIMS LETTER]

Ineffective version

Until now, we have always found your reference tools very reliable and have a number of them in our library. Therefore, you can imagine my surprise when a user tried to look up chrysanthemum in *The Complete Gardener's Encyclopedia* and couldn't find it anywhere. It took us quite a while to discover that all the entries were missing for B and C. Somebody has been guilty of pretty shoddy workmanship somewhere. Please remedy this situation.

Note that this poor version makes several mistakes. It starts off with general statements and includes irrelevant details about how the problem was discovered. Remarks about poor workmanship are unnecessarily abrasive. The main point of the letter is buried in the last sentence. Moreover, the writer fails to specify exactly what remedy is wanted.

A better version

Please send another copy of *The Complete Gardener's Encyclopedia* to replace the imperfect copy that I am returning. I have enclosed the invoice that came with the book.

The returned copy apparently lacks an entire gathering. You will see that 32 pages are missing so that entries starting with B and C are missing.

If you could send the replacement copy soon, I would be grateful.

Bad News Letters

The indirect approach usually works best when the news that you have to give is unpleasant. Because your main point is unwelcome to the reader, don't announce it flatly in the first sentence. Delay it until you have explained the reasons for the bad news. By the time the reader gets to the actual refusal, he or she will be psychologically prepared for it.

As you write the bad news letter, you should put yourself in the place of the reader. Ask: How would I respond to this language, to this opening paragraph, or to this letter? Does the message seem too abrupt? Unnecessarily negative? You want the reader to finish reading the letter, with self-respect intact, thinking that your explanations, though disappointing, have been fair and reasonable.

This is the commonly recommended pattern for the bad news letter:

1. Start with a pleasant, neutral statement that is related to the topic. Begin, if you can, with an area of common agreement.
2. Explain in general terms the reasons for the refusal. If the reason is library policy, point out why this policy ultimately benefits everyone, including the reader.

Exercise

Effective Letters

Write a letter that would be suitable in the following situations:

1. Martha Lorenz, an alumna from your university, has written to your academic library to ask for a custom-made bibliography on the topic of reader-response criticism for a project that she is doing. You don't have the staff time to prepare an individualized bibliography. However, you can refer her to online sources, provide the link to some pertinent pages from the *Modern Language Association International Bibliography* for more recent work, and refer her to an annotated bibliography of early work in a book by Jane Tompkins titled *Reader-Response Criticism: From Formalism to Post-Structuralism* (Baltimore: Johns Hopkins University Press, 1986).

Continued on p. 327

3. State the bad news, as gently and as briefly as possible. Leave no room for misunderstanding, but don't belabor the point.

4. End with a statement of goodwill. When you can, offer an acceptable alternative or a helpful suggestion. Avoid referring again to the refusal.

This organization goes from general (the policy or the conditions for granting requests) to the specific (the refusal of the particular request). You explain, for example, that your library rooms are made available to nonprofit groups. Then when you refuse the use of the room to a small business, the refusal does not seem personal but the logical outcome of the general policy. Then as a goodwill close, you provide the names of facilities that do make their rooms available to small business groups.

EXAMPLE [TURNING DOWN A BOOK REMOVAL REQUEST]

Ineffective version

You will be disappointed to learn that we have decided to turn down your request to remove from the shelf Maurice Sendak's *Where the Wild Things Are*. Your son's response to the book, though unfortunate, is not typical. If we can be of further help, don't hesitate to let us know.

A better version

We appreciate the care you took in making us aware of your four-year-old son's response to Maurice Sendak's *Where the Wild Things Are*. We share your concern that a child may be frightened by a particular book, especially because it is very hard to predict individual responses.

As you know, the Children's Department is responsible for providing the public with picture books of high quality. As a book by an award-winning illustrator, *Where the Wild Things Are* is in great demand both by children themselves and by students of children's literature. That is why we must continue to make this book available. We encourage parents to make the judgment about suitable books for their own child. Because all children are different, parents are usually the most qualified persons to withhold a book that they think might be frightening to their own child.

Thank you for this opportunity to explain the policy of the Children's Department on our collection of picture books.

SOME TIPS FOR WRITING BAD NEWS LETTERS

Don't use a form letter if you can avoid it. People who have put a lot of time and energy into sending a proposal, coming for a job interview, and so forth, find a "Dear Sir/Madam" letter particularly heartless and uncaring.

- Avoid negative or accusatory language. Don't start off your letter with phrases like: "We regret," "we must refuse," "we have turned down," "we have rejected," "I'm afraid you may be disappointed," "unfortunately," "impossible," "cannot," "will not," "unable," and so on. If your reasons for the bad news have to do with the reader's behavior, don't use words like "negligent," "irresponsible," "careless," or say "you failed," "disregarded," "neglected," "refused," or "forgot" or "if you had read our policy statement, you would realize." Avoid referring to a statement made by the reader in terms suggesting distrust, such as "although you claim," "according to you," and "as you allege."

- Use the passive voice. This is one of the few cases in which the weakness of the passive voice is an advantage—see writing with impact (4.3). Instead of "You left the CDs in a hot place, which caused them to warp," try "The warping was caused because the CDs were left in a hot place." Instead of "The committee voted overwhelmingly against your proposal," try "Your proposal was not adopted."

- Explain your reasons. Don't just say that library policy prohibits granting the request. Explain why you have this policy and why the policy benefits all library users.

- Don't overdo your apologies, if you have to turn down a request. It won't sound sincere, given that your refusal has been based on a good reason. On the other hand, if you or the library is at fault, then you should convey your genuine regret and acknowledge the problem and fix it.

- Play up the positive. If you cannot satisfy the reader's request, you could explain the conditions under which you would be able to satisfy it. Instead of saying, "We can't do X," you might say, "As soon as [specify condition], we will be pleased to do X." Or you might be able to suggest an acceptable alternative: "The best we can do is Y."

- Avoid ending with a cliché. A perfunctory conclusion like "Don't hesitate to contact me if I can be of any further help"

Continued from p. 326

2. Jim Thompson, a longtime registered borrower at your public library, has e-mailed to complain of the treatment he received at the circulation desk when he tried to take out books. The circulation assistant had explained that he would be unable to charge out the books until he paid $25.00 in charges for fines and a lost book. Mr. Thompson says that he refused to pay this $25.00 charge because he doesn't remember even taking out the so-called lost book. However, he's upset at what happened. He wants an apology, and he also wants to be able to take out books in the future without paying the charge. You are going to have to turn down his request, but you want to keep his goodwill as a longtime patron of the library. (For some help with what you might say, see 6.6.4 on handling complaints).

is especially galling if you have been of absolutely no help so far. The more you can personalize your ending for the particular reader, the better.

9.6. Reports

Written reports vary in length, appearance, purpose, and formality. They may be a page long or 100 pages long. They may be in the form of a memo, a letter, or a multipage document in multiple sections. They may be a web document, a PDF, or a bound, professionally printed document. They may be written to answer a request, supply information, or help in decision making. They may be an internal or an external form of communication. What they have in common is that they are all organized presentations of material, written to convey the impression of objectivity. Reports present accurate factual information as the basis for informed evaluation. The kinds of reports typically written in libraries include progress reports, feasibility reports, investigative reports, committee reports, monthly and annual reports, planning reports, and research reports.

Reports may be either formal or informal. Informal reports, often written as a letter or a memo, include only the essentials—an introduction containing background information, a body that tells the reader about the investigation of the problem, and a conclusion containing whatever recommendations there may be. Formal reports often include, in addition to these essentials, the following: a cover, letter of transmittal, title page, abstract, table of contents, executive summary, bibliography, and appendix.

For examples of actual reports representing different formats and styles, see the texts recommended in the Annotated Bibliography at the end of this chapter (9.17).

General Characteristics of Reports

These defining characteristics of reports influence how they should be written:

1. Reports are usually written for busy readers who want to grasp the essentials quickly and not hunt for the main points. They should be able to get the gist of the

report without having to read the whole thing. There-fore, you should begin with a summary statement that puts the essence of the report in a nutshell.

2. Report writing is often an assigned job. The person or group who asked you to write the report usually knows what kind of report is wanted and should tell you. If not, you should ask.

3. A report is often written initially for a small number of identifiable readers who have authorized the report for a specific reason. (The report may later, of course, be read by secondary readers.) Identify your readers, and analyze their needs (see 4.1 on analyzing the audience).

4. A report may go up a hierarchy—to directors, boards, legislative bodies, and the like. Therefore, in analyzing your audience, you need to keep in mind the needs of readers at all levels in the hierarchy.

5. Because a report usually presents a lot of complex information, reports must be well organized. Organi-zation is a matter of putting like things together into groups and then ordering the groups into a helpful sequence. There is no single best way to organize (see 4.5 on organizing). Everything depends on the topic and on how you have investigated it. For a short infor-mal report, it may be enough to arrange three or four points in an itemized list. For a long formal report, a classification system may be desirable to show the reader the parts of a report and their relation to each other. Here is one popular option:

```
1.0
    1.1
    1.2
    1.3
2.0
    2.1
        2.1.1
        2.1.2
    2.2
    2.3 (etc.)
```

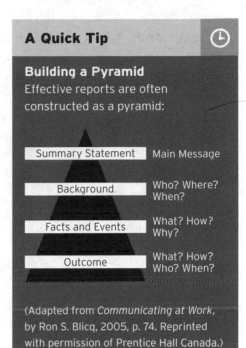

A Quick Tip

Building a Pyramid
Effective reports are often constructed as a pyramid:

Summary Statement	Main Message
Background	Who? Where? When?
Facts and Events	What? How? Why?
Outcome	What? How? Who? When?

(Adapted from *Communicating at Work*, by Ron S. Blicq, 2005, p. 74. Reprinted with permission of Prentice Hall Canada.)

> **Did You Know?** ❓
>
> To design information for maximum effect, match the choice of type font to the document's purpose. Serif font is easier to read than sans serif and therefore is best for long printed documents (the opposite is true of documents intended to be read on screens). Documents are easier to read if they are left justified with ragged right margins.

Layout, or the way the report looks on the page, is important, especially in a long report. Page after page of uninterrupted text discourages readers (see 4.10 on formatting). Help your readers deal with masses of evidence and complex arguments by using these techniques:

- Headings and subheadings in bold type
- Bulleted or numbered lists
- Graphic presentations such as tables, graphs, charts, and flowcharts (see 4.9 on tables and charts)
- Quotes in sidebars to highlight key points
- Lots of white space

There are some differences when writing for the web (see 4.11 and 9.13.4).

9.6.1. Informal Reports

Most of the reports written in libraries are informal reports, written for an internal readership. Because you are writing for colleagues, your tone is informal (see 4.2 on appropriate style). Your report may be in the form of a letter or a memo, but it should be divided into sections, and sometimes subsections, with headings. These are the usual parts of an informal report:

- **Introduction stating the purpose.** Sometimes a single sentence is enough, explaining why the report was written and what the major findings are. For example, "As requested, I have investigated the feasibility of Sunday opening and recommend that we open the Martindale branch on Sundays from 1:30 to 5:00 p.m. on a trial basis for six months." In an investigative report, this section might discuss the problem, outline its previous history, refer to earlier reports on the same problem, and define the scope of the analysis to follow (sometimes in the form of a list of questions to be answered).
- **Body.** This section presents the facts and explains where these facts came from. In an investigative report, you say what you were trying to do in your investigation, what you actually did do, and what you found out. In a progress report, you answer questions about the status of the project: Is it on schedule? Is it within budget? Are there any

unexpected problems or requirements for new resources? In a periodic report, you talk about work performed during the period, special accomplishments, problems encountered and remedies taken, and project plans. In a feasibility study, you point out alternatives and present evidence, as fairly and objectively as you can, both for and against each alternative. (Don't forget that one of the possible options is to do nothing: to buy none of the products considered or to make no changes to the policy, etc.)

- **Conclusions and recommendations or discussion.** The conclusion is your interpretation of the evidence presented in the body of the report. Recommendations advise what to do about a conclusion, what course of action to follow, which alternative to prefer. For example, if you are writing a report to evaluate different digital scanners, evidence might include facts such as these: Brand C is less expensive; Brand C is just as reliable and easy to use as Brand A and Brand B; surveyed users like Brand C and Brand A equally, and prefer both to Brand B. The conclusion would then follow: Brand C is the best buy. And the recommendation would be: Buy Brand C.

> ### A Quick Tip ⏱
>
> **The Five Ws (and an H)**
> You can assess how quickly your report gets to the point. Check how far into the report the reader has to read to get at least summary answers to the questions:
>
> - Who?
> - What?
> - Why?
> - Where?
> - When?
> - How?

Of the many different kinds of informal reports, the following are most often encountered in libraries.

Trip Report

Employees who go on work-related trips are often encouraged to write trip reports, usually in the form of a memo to a supervisor. The trip report provides a record of the trip and its achievements so that the information gained by one person can be shared by others. Your report should include a statement of purpose (why you made the trip), where you went, who you talked to, and what you achieved or found out. In providing details, be selective. Don't start at the beginning and tell everything that happened, hour by hour. Highlight the significant events or discoveries. The bottom line for a trip report is that it should answer the question: Why was this trip worthwhile? In your conclusion, you may also discuss the need for similar trips in the future or acknowledge people who have helped.

Accident Report, Incident Report, or Trouble Report

When an accident or breakdown occurs, the person in charge may be required to write up a report of the incident. Sometimes the report is written solely to provide information, as in this case of a building superintendent writing to a library director: "I thought you should know that there were two dead cats in the book chute again this morning." At other times, an accident report will include recommendations for action, such as "A handrail should be installed on all staircases."

It is particularly important to be factual, accurate, and prompt in writing up accident reports because they may be used as evidence in the case of lawsuits or insurance claims. Include the following kinds of information:

- The exact time, date, and place of the incident
- What happened, described in objective factual terms
- Who was present or involved
- The precise nature of the injuries or damage
- Treatment or remedies undertaken
- What has been done (or should be done) to address the cause of the incident
- Any other pertinent information

In your analysis of what you think caused the problem, omit speculations and interpretations unsupported by evidence. Avoid a heated, condemnatory tone.

Here is an outline for a typical trouble or accident report:

- **Summary** stating in a concise sentence or two the essence of what happened (e.g., "The Library Board Chair collapsed while at the circulation desk. An ambulance came promptly and took her to Memorial Hospital, where her condition has been reported as good").
- **Details** of the incident, in which you specify time, date, place of the incident; who was present; what happened.
- **Conclusion** in which you evaluate the implications of what happened. (Here's where you would make any recommendations, if appropriate, on how to prevent a recurrence of the problem or on how to draw up a disaster plan.)

Investigative Report

An investigative report is written in response to a demand for information and is used as the basis for making a decision. For example, you might be asked to find out what users think about the new chat reference service; to discover what other services are available in the city for young adults; to assess whether buying a new piece of equipment is warranted; to evaluate the success of a staff training program; or to investigate whether to expand use of text messages and Twitter to communicate with users. A memo format is common for this kind of report. Here is an outline for an investigative report:

- **Introduction** in which you get right to the point. Explain what you were supposed to find out and what you did find out: "As you requested, I have assessed our need for a digital scanner. My judgment is that we should buy our own equipment, and I am recommending X." In other words, start with what the reader wants to know.
- **Supporting details** under headings such as Background of the Problem. (Under this heading would go details such as: What happened that made a decision necessary? What is the extent of the problem? What are the present and anticipated needs?)
- **Criteria** for the solution.
- **Analysis of options** (with pros and cons for each option).
- **Sources used** (what you did to investigate the problem; who you talked to; what the literature says).
- **Conclusions and recommendations** detailing who should do what—and when, where, and why they should do it.

EXAMPLE: AN INEFFECTIVE INVESTIGATIVE MEMO REPORT

MEMORANDUM

TO: Jan Singh
FROM: Richard Winter
DATE: January 26, 2013
SUBJECT: Digital Scanners

Two different digital scanners were investigated to determine which would be best to suit our needs. According to three companies that have purchased the Ace system, it breaks down fairly frequently. However, the technician usually arrives shortly after the service call has been placed and usually manages to get the machine working again fairly quickly. The alternative is the Top-Notch system, which usually functions reliably for the three companies where I inquired. But when the Top-Notch machine does break down, the service representative has been slow to arrive and the machine was often out of order for several days. Apparently the Top-Notch technicians often have a lot of trouble locating the problem and don't seem to have replacement parts in stock, resulting in extended downtime. This conclusion was supported by an online search. I therefore recommend the Ace system.

EXAMPLE: AN EFFECTIVE INVESTIGATIVE MEMO REPORT

MEMORANDUM

TO: Jan Singh
FROM: Richard Winter
DATE: January 26, 2013
SUBJECT: Evaluation of the Ace and Top-Notch Digital Scanners

As you requested, I investigated the relative merits of two digital scanners to see which would be our best buy in terms of reliability, maintenance, and repair. Specifically, I compared the Ace and Top-Notch systems.

Ace system

The Ace system, according to representatives of three companies that have used it, has frequent minor breakdowns. Customer service technicians from Ace usually arrive quickly and have nearly always managed to get the system working again in short order. As a result, the three companies using the Ace system have had little downtime. In addition, an online search of evaluations and comments posted by Ace users indicates that they are generally satisfied, providing an average rating of 4.5 out of 5.

Top-Notch system

The YY digital scanner, on the other hand, usually functions reliably in the three companies where I inquired. However, representatives of all three stated that the occasional breakdowns that did happen were invariably followed by long delays in operation. In at least two cases it seems that the technicians were never able to locate the trouble. In other cases the parts needed to correct the trouble had to be ordered, resulting in long delays. In addition, an online search of evaluations and comments posted by Top-Notch users confirms the problems with delays in restoring service and produced an average rating of 3.9 out of 5.

Conclusion

I conclude that the Ace system would cause us considerably less downtime than the Top-Notch system. I therefore recommend the Ace system.

Progress and Periodic Reports

Progress reports inform the reader (usually a supervisor or funding body) about the status of a project. The reader wants to know, as quickly as possible, the answer to the question: "How is the work going?"

Here's a typical format for a progress report on a project:

- **Summary,** including a succinct statement on the following:

  Time period covered
  Status of the project (is the project on schedule? ahead
       of schedule? behind schedule?)
  Budget (have there been cost overruns? cost savings?)
  Forecast (will the project be done on time?)

- **Details** in which you explain and justify what you have said in the summary by discussing:

  Work completed
  Work in progress as you write the report
  Work still to be done
  Problems encountered or anticipated at each of these
       stages

- **Revised plan** in which you forecast what will happen during the next reporting period

Periodic reports discuss the achievements and problems occurring during regular time periods—monthly, quarterly, annually. Monthly reports are written to inform supervisors of work accomplished. You will be expected to provide certain routine information, sometimes using a standard form. However, you can make the report more useful if, in addition to providing the required routine information, you highlight the nonroutine event. Mention the success of an innovation or a special program.

Annual reports are a type of periodic report, but they differ from routine monthly reports in three important ways: they are formal reports, they are written for an external audience, and their purpose is public relations. The purpose of the annual report is to highlight, for trustees and the library's public, how well the library is using resources to satisfy objectives.

9.6.2. Formal Reports

As you would expect, formal reports share many characteristics of informal reports, differing in being longer and more elaborate.

Parts of a Formal Report

- **Cover.**
- **Letter of transmittal.** Very formal reports include a letter, either attached to or bound into the report, which serves to document the transfer of the report from one person to another. A letter of transmittal looks like a cover letter. It is usually short and essentially states: "I am attaching the report you asked for."
- **Title page.** Include the full title of the report, the name of the person or organization receiving the report, the author's name and position (Head of Technical Services), the place, and the date of the report. Titles should be specific enough to indicate clearly the purpose and scope of the report.
- **Abstract.** By condensing the essentials of the report to about 150 words, the abstract allows readers to decide whether or not they need to see the report in full.
- **Table of contents.** List in order all parts of the report together with page numbers, except for the title page and the table of contents. Include all the headings and

---

Did You Know? ?

The most common problems with formal reports are:

- lack of an executive summary;
- text that is too detailed or too dense, without section headings;
- charts and graphs that lack labels or are otherwise unintelligible;
- cheesy formatting and design choices; and
- poor copyediting (4.12) as betrayed by typographical errors and mistakes in spelling and grammar.

(See Parker, 2006, for advice on business reports.)

subheadings of the body of the report to help readers go directly to particular sections.

- **Summary.** Explain in a page or two the following: (1) Why was the report written? (2) What were the procedures used to gather the evidence? and (3) What are the major findings or recommendations? You write the summary last, although it appears first in the report. In business reports, this part of the report, called the "executive summary," may be all that busy managers will read.

- **Introduction or background.** Provide readers with information they need in order to orient themselves to the report. The introduction should state the purpose of the report (to investigate the feasibility of digitizing rare maps and photographs in the Regional Collection), explain the history of the topic or problem, indicate the scope (aspect of the topic covered, time period covered, etc.), and briefly summarize the main finding(s) or recommendation(s).

- **Body.** This is the longest part of the report and is usually subdivided into sections with headings like Methods of Investigation, Findings, Present Needs, Predicted Needs, Factors Affecting X, Alternatives, and so forth.

- **Conclusions and recommendations**. This is the payoff of the report—the place where you pull together the results of your study. Don't scatter your recommendations (putting one on page 9, another on page 14, another on page 17), but pull them all together in a numbered list so that the reader can't miss them.

- **Bibliography.** Include an alphabetical list of sources consulted (see 9.16.2).

- **Appendix or appendixes.** If readers do not need to read something in order to understand the report but may want to consult it, put this material into the appendix. Good candidates for the appendix include supplementary tables, copies of a questionnaire, copies of policy statements, lists of authorities whose advice was solicited, and the like.

- **Glossary.** This contains definitions of specialized terms that you have used in your report.

Parts of a Report

Front Matter
The front matter is made up of all the prefatory material that must be provided before the real reporting can begin. In various forms, the front matter provides the reader with condensed indications of what the report is about. Normally the pages of front matter are numbered with roman numerals (iv, v, vi, etc.). While formal reports may do without some of these elements, all should have a title page and a table of contents.

Middle
The heart of the formal report includes the same elements that go into the informal report but often in longer and more complex form.

Back Matter
Back matter contains material that is not essential and won't appear in all formal reports, but it may be helpful.

9.7. Instructions

You may find yourself writing instructions for the public (how to borrow e-books, how to find government information) or for staff members (how to sign up a new cardholder, how to use the digital scanner). Instructions explain how to do something and they differ from procedures, which refer to policies, duties, or protocols that the institution expects employees to follow (see also 9.8 on writing procedures).

Often you will give instructions face-to-face, a method that allows you to demonstrate the way to do the thing. However, there are times when written instructions are useful, either used alone or accompanying spoken instructions:

- When the steps to be taken are complex and hard to remember (In such cases, you may want to provide both a demonstration and written instructions that can be consulted later to refresh the memory.)
- When people need help and nobody is available to help them
- When a lot of different people need help at different times with the same thing
- When it is useful to provide a document for the sake of continuity when new staff are hired

The quality, clarity, accuracy, and completeness of instructions are important because safety may be at stake. In some cases, poorly written, unclear instructions may lead to serious injury, accidents, and potential lawsuits. Less worrying but still a concern is that written instructions too often evoke in their readers responses of either frustration or laughter. Sometimes it seems as if writers of instructions are translating from a foreign language (as, e.g., this sign in a hotel room: "In case of fire, do your utmost to alarm the hall porter"). Here are some suggestions for avoiding common pitfalls and for making your written instructions more helpful.

Getting Ready

- **Analyze the audience** (see 4.1) for whom the instructions are written. How much do these readers already know about the process? What gaps do they have in their understanding? What will your readers need to be told? If your readers are beginners at, say, searching indexes in an online database, you will have to explain everything from the very beginning, perhaps including where to find the "On" button.

- **Analyze the steps** to be taken. Break the process down into its constituent parts. Consider the time sequence. What must be done first, before something else can be done?
- **Distinguish necessary steps** from those that are merely recommended. Ask yourself particularly: What is crucial for the reader to know (e.g., don't do X because doing X will cause an explosion)?

Writing the Instructions

- **Provide a *you* emphasis.** Use a second-person construction to highlight what the reader has to do. Say "Turn the printer off" rather than the ambiguous "The printer should be turned off."
- **Use parallel structure.** In most cases, it works best to start off each step with a verb that indicates the action that the reader should take. For example:

  1. Turn the printer off.
  2. Remove the cover.
  3. Set the release lever.
  4. Grasp . . .
  5. Lift . . .
  6. Place . . .

- **Arrange the steps** in chronological order—the order in which the steps must be done—and number them. Use numbers rather than bullets for sequenced steps.
- **Anticipate problems and questions** that the reader might have. For example, warn the reader that, after being turned on, the overhead projector takes ten seconds to warm up before you see the image on the screen. Explain that a background hum is normal and does not indicate a problem.
- **Explain the reasons.** Say why the optional steps are recommended. Explain why the required steps must always

---

Exercise 🔧

Writing Instructions
(Note: Do not choose a dangerous process for this exercise!)
Write instructions for some process such as changing paper in the photocopy machine (or charging out a library book, or sending a fax). Ask a partner to carry out the instructions *exactly* as you have written them. Suggest that the partner does a "speak-aloud" as she follows the instructions, saying aloud what is going on in her head as she attempts to follow the steps (e.g., "Hmmm. It says X. Does that mean that I should?"). Ask for feedback.

be followed. People are more apt to follow instructions when they understand the reasons.

- **Use plain, everyday language** (4.4). Say "shake" rather than "agitate"; "start" rather than "initiate" or "commence."
- **Use common sense.** Don't warn people not to do things that no one would ever be likely to do (i.e., the do-not-grind-armadillo-armor-in this-mill instruction—see Dobrin, 1985).
- **Cut out all unnecessary words.** Consider the difference between these two headings:

IMPORTANT!

IMPORTANT INSTRUCTIONS TO READ BEFORE OPERATING THE EQUIPMENT!

The instructions can be printed, but they should also be available online. If you want both print and online versions of your instructions, consider how similar or different the structures will be. Duncan Kent (2006) advises that as you plan the print material, imagine how it will appear online.

Formatting

Here are some suggestions for formatting the instructions:

- **Highlight crucial information** and put it first: Never do X. (If you delay your warning, the reader may do the proscribed thing before reading the warning.) You can give further emphasis by using a typographic device like red ink, bold type, or a box to draw attention to crucial information:

Do not do X.

- **Use headings** to cluster together related steps. People cannot easily take in any more than seven unrelated units at once—seven digits in a telephone number, seven unrelated words in a list, seven steps in a process. So if you want readers to assimilate 20 steps you can help by organizing these steps under three or four headings that correspond to major subdivisions of the process. In this example, the reader has four units to keep in mind, not 14:

Before you begin	Operating the machine
–1	–8
–2	–9
–3	–10
	–11
	–12

Setting the adjustments	Putting everything away
–4	–13
–5	–14
–6	
–7	

- **Use diagrams** to illustrate concepts difficult to explain in words. Label parts of your diagram clearly. If you use lines to point to parts of the diagram, don't let the lines cross over each other. Place the diagrams on the page so that they are close to the text that they are intended to illustrate.
- **Leave white space.** Instructions that are crowded are hard to read and intimidating.

Checking the Instructions

- **Scrutinize** for possible problems. When you have finished writing the instructions, read them over carefully, looking for ambiguities or omissions. Have you used any words/sentences/constructions that could possibly be misunderstood? Don't take anything for granted. If there's a way of misreading the instructions, then some reader will do it. Have you left out any important steps in the instructions?
- **Field test** your instructions. Ask a colleague unfamiliar with the task at hand to try to do the task by following your instructions. Watch for areas of uncertainty, difficulty, or error. Afterward, ask your colleague for feedback: What did she find hard to understand? Which part of the instructions

did she find unnecessary? What would she like explained more fully?

- **Revise** and field test again, if necessary.

9.8. Policy and Procedure Manuals

An effective organization usually has two kinds of administrative manuals: policy and procedure. Although some organizations combine policies and procedures into one manual, the distinction between the two is important. A policy is a statement intended to guide long-range decision making and usually reflects the basic responsibilities and principles of an organization. Because a policy usually has legal implications and requires the approval of a governing body (library board or management committee), production of a policy manual differs from production of a procedure manual. The most frequent users of the policy manual are managers or supervisors, board members, and sometimes the public.

On the other hand, procedure manuals are most often used by frontline workers. A procedure is a set of steps, or a series of actions or operations, that must be carried out to achieve a specific result. It explains how to do a work-related task in a particular institution. Writing procedures is a special case of the more general activity of writing instructions just discussed, and the same considerations apply (see 9.7). Organizations may also have a third kind of administrative manual: the organization manual, which includes descriptions of organizational structure, lines of authority, and job descriptions. All three types of manuals are very useful for orientation and training of new staff.

Some General Considerations for Producing Administrative Manuals

- **Consider the needs of the reader.** Who will use this manual? For what purpose? Under what circumstances? Will the reader understand the manual? What could the consequences be if the reader misinterprets or fails to understand the policy or procedure?
- **Organize** the manual clearly, logically, and simply. Choose from a variety of standard numbering systems, according

to the length and complexity of the manual. Numbered sections and subsections can be efficiently cross-referenced by number rather than by section name and page number. For a complex manual, you might need a system of arabic numerals with one or two decimal places or dashes (e.g., 2-23.1). In a smaller organization, you might opt for a simple alphabetic arrangement (A, B, and C). The system should be no more complex than necessary. Every section and subsection should also have a brief descriptive title or heading.

- **Index** the manual. People using a manual want to know about something in particular and want to find it quickly. A manual that lacks an index is frustrating and hard to navigate, especially if the topic of interest is considered in more than one section. Both electronic and printed versions of manuals need an index as well as a table of contents. Indexing keywords and topics by section number also makes it easier when you revise the manual. Remember that automated indexing may look easy to do, but the resulting index almost always requires editing for clarity and consistency. In addition to an index for each manual, consider merging the indexes into a global index if you have more than a few manuals.

- **Cross-reference** the manual. Provide enough cross-references that readers will easily be able to find related sections or manuals, but avoid cross-references that are too detailed or too general. You can help the reader by using headings as well as the section number (e.g., "See also filing procedures, 2.5" rather than "See also 2.5").

- **Use hyperlinks.** Whenever your policy manual refers to other parts of the manual or to other documents (such as the American Library Association's "Library Bill of Rights" or "Code of Ethics"), save readers a step by using links to lead users directly to the documents.

- **Keep the layout simple.** Use lots of white space. Avoid cluttering the manual with logos, lines, and any bit of type or image that does not convey information (see formatting in 4.10).

- **Update the manual** regularly, and put the date on it prominently. An outdated manual may be misleading. Periodically request department heads to submit revisions.

Exercise 🔧

Policy: Specific or Not?
Find several examples of written policies about materials selection. Pick from the different policies the sections that deal with the same issue (e.g., censorship), and compare them for readability, clarity, and specificity. For what reasons might a policy *not* be very specific? Why might the specificity of a policy differ from the high-specificity needed for a procedure? (See the books by Hoffman and Wood [2005, 2007] for discussion of specificity in policies.)

If the manual is printed, use a loose-leaf format to accommodate revisions, and include issue dates for each revision. Most libraries now make their manuals accessible online as web documents or as PDFs. Latest revision dates should be noted on the webpage. (See Kent, 2006, for details on preparing revisable manuals.)

- **Ask for feedback.** In business and industry, user reviews are an important part of manual production. Ask staff to evaluate the accuracy, completeness, and readability of your manuals and to suggest changes if necessary.

One Way to Write Procedures

If a procedure has never been written down, begin by observing an experienced staff member performing the procedure. Ask him to describe what he is doing step by step as he does it and as you take notes. Be alert to routine activities that need to be described in more detail. For example:

> "First, I do the mail."
> "How exactly do you do that? Tell me a step at a time. What do you do first?"
> "Well, first I go to the main office at ten o'clock, and ask for the mail for Technical Services. Then I . . ."

Reformulate this procedure as a directive: "Each working day at 10 a.m., go to the Administration Office and ask for the mail for Technical Services. . . ." After you have a complete draft of the procedure, test it by asking someone (preferably an inexperienced person) to follow the procedure exactly as you have written it. Problems, omissions, and redundancy become clear immediately. Revise the steps, and repeat the test until the procedure is clearly and completely described.

Tips for Writing Procedure Manuals

- Put warnings first. Placing safety instructions at the end can be dangerous. Put this type of instruction first: "If the red light goes on, stop immediately and unplug the machine."
- Tell readers how to do something, not just what to do.
- Speak directly to the reader. Use the imperative mood ("Stack the books on the truck") not the indicative mood

Exercise ⚒

Writing Style for Manuals
Choose a procedure from one of the ARL (Association of Research Libraries) Spec Kits (a complete list is available at http://www.arl.org/resources/pubs/spec/complete.shtml) or from some other accessible procedure manual. Critically examine the way this procedure was written. What specifically has been done well? What could be improved? Revise the procedure to make it better.

("The worker first stacks the books on the truck"). Use the active, not the passive voice. Avoid "X should be done" or "X should be done by Y" constructions.

- Be clear and specific. For example, "File the report within four days" is better than "as soon as possible," but does it mean four working days or four calendar days?

- Use simple words and terms. A procedure manual should require no more than tenth grade reading skills (see 4.2 on readability).

- Use parallel constructions for your headings within the same topic. If the first heading is "Selecting Periodicals," the next heading should be "Reviewing Selection Decisions," not "A Review of Selection Decisions" or "Methods of Reviewing Selection Decisions."

- Be consistent. Procedure manuals should not differ greatly in style from department to department. Centralize the editing and production.

9.9. Staff Newsletters

When an organization gets so big that its members don't regularly see each other face-to-face, then it may be time to develop other channels of communication. A staff newsletter is one way. It can be useful for maintaining morale and for making people feel part of a community. A staff newsletter is a good way to inform people about the following: news items about staff members ("Congratulations to Carol on the safe birth of twin daughters Margo and Marsha"); job openings within the system; progress reports ("Architect promises that the new Whiteoaks branch will open on schedule June 1"); news items of professional interest; and announcements ("Anyone interested in forming a bowling league should come for an organizational meeting . . ."). A newsletter provides an informal channel for a community of people to share information with each other.

However, there are some things to think about before launching into the production of a newsletter:

- Can you give the necessary commitment of time, energy, and resources? Whether printed on paper or distributed electronically, producing a newsletter requires an ongoing effort at newsgathering, copywriting, editing, and layout, not to mention the more routine job of keyboarding. Time spent producing a newsletter is time taken away from other activities and service.

- Who has editorial control? Will the newsletter be perceived as a tool of the administration for downward-flowing messages or as a channel of communication for all kinds of news and messages—downward, upward, sideways?
- How will it be produced and distributed? In hard copy? Electronically through e-mail or on an internally available website or intranet?

The same questions apply to newsletters for the public (see 9.13.2). If you do decide to produce a staff newsletter, consult the sources listed in the Annotated Bibliography (9.17) to ensure that it looks professional and achieves its purpose.

9.10. Forms

Your library probably uses a number of forms that are accessible to users and/or staff. Users should be able to access and submit needed forms online. Examples include virtual reference question forms, forms requesting room bookings, or interlibrary loan request forms. These should also be accessible in printable PDF format so that users can submit them to you by fax, as e-mail attachments, or in person. Forms for staff members, such as cover letters for faxes, should be available as printable PDFs.

The job of writing useful forms requires the combination of a number of writing and questioning skills—especially writing briefly (4.4), formatting the page (4.10), asking appropriate questions (3.4), and giving instructions (3.12). Libraries design their own forms, and you can find hundreds of examples on library websites (such as the University of California incident reporting form noted in 9.6.1). Also worth checking out is the Internet Public Library's excellent ask-a-librarian form (http://www.ipl.org/div/askus/).

A Quick Tip 🕐

Create and Store Forms
You can search Google for "form templates" to find links to free downloadable business-related forms. A form library is a convenient way to store your forms in one location so that they can be shared and tracked. See, for example, http://office.microsoft.com/en-us/windows-sharepoint-services-help/create-a-form-library-HA010092914.aspx.

9.11. Written Communications for Committees

One of the reasons that people work face-to-face in committees and other groups is to communicate with each other more directly than they could through writing to each other (7.1). But written communication can often support or enhance group activities by saving time, providing structure to a discussion, and recording the group's actions or decisions. Virtual groups (7.6) also need the types of written communication discussed in this section. Some functions served by written group communication include:

- giving direction or advance notice (agendas, notices of motions),
- creating a permanent record of group activity (minutes),
- saving the time of the group (background papers, handouts),
- communicating with people who did not attend the group (minutes, background papers), and
- structuring the group's activities (outlines, agendas, handouts).

Use written communication to perform functions that cannot, or should not, be performed by individuals speaking to each other. For example, background papers and written committee reports save the time of group members, who would waste valuable time were they to read the report during the meeting or listen to someone present the report verbatim. Written communications for groups should follow the general rule that writing be clear and concise (4.4) and addressed to the needs of the reader (4.1). The following tips relate to additional considerations for writing the documents commonly used in groups. Read these tips in conjunction with Chapter 7 on working in groups.

Tips for Writing Agendas

- In the first lines, include the name of the group or committee and then the date and time (in bold) and the location of the meeting.

- Consult a standard guide to conducting meetings for the order of business (see also 7.5.4 on the formal meeting).
- If a notice of motion was made at the last meeting, include the wording of the motion.
- Estimate the time of adjournment to let participants plan their day.
- Provide the name and telephone number of a person to contact about attendance at the meeting.
- Don't forget to enclose or attach the background material that attendees are expected to read before the meeting.

Tips for Taking Minutes

- Sit where you can see everyone.
- Have a list of participants' names. Make yourself a "seating diagram."
- Don't be afraid to ask someone to repeat the wording of a motion or to restate the decision as they wish it recorded.
- Don't attempt to record everything that goes on. Report the essential accomplishments of the meeting, not all the process and every pro and con. Keep the report as brief as possible without sacrificing necessary detail about what was achieved.
- Don't use judgmental or emotional words. Summarize two hours of bitter argument in neutral terms: "After lengthy discussion, the group decided to disband."
- Edit or transcribe your notes immediately, before you forget what you meant by "nxt Jn."

See Keeping a Record in 7.5.4 for general guidelines on minutes in formal meetings. For taking formal minutes, also consult a standard meeting manual, such as *Robert's Rules of Order.*

9.12. Signs

Signs are a good way to communicate with the public. They can be produced in-house or by design firms. They can be a permanent physical installation or displayed on screens. Consider using signs for the following purposes:

Exercise 🔧

Record of the Event

1. Examine the minutes of a library board or management committee meeting. What information about this group's activities seems to be missing? What was included that seems unnecessary?
2. Listen to a recording of a short problem-solving meeting. Take notes and prepare a record of the meeting.

- To orient the public to the layout of a building (you can use a floor plan with an arrow and the message "You are here") and to provide directions, with arrows, to destinations such as the circulation desk, information desk, periodical reading rooms, special collections, regional history, washrooms, and exits
- To identify these destinations so that people recognize them when they come to them
- To provide instructions (e.g., how to use catalogs or other equipment)
- To explain regulations (e.g., restrictions on food or beverages)
- To provide up-to-date information such as changes in opening hours

Used in a library context, the term *signage* refers to a system of informational graphics created to help the public understand the library's physical layout and how to use its services. Too many libraries take the higgledy-piggledy approach, producing signs as needed on an ad hoc basis.

General Principles of Good Signage

Planning is necessary to produce an integrated totality that provides the needed information in a graphically consistent form. Designing a coherent signage policy involves two activities: (1) deciding what questions users have about the library that can be best answered by signs and (2) choosing suitable, consistent design elements, including lettering, graphics, color, and the shape and placement of the sign. Remember that following good graphic design principles helps library users concentrate on the message, not strain for readability.

To decide what signs are necessary, here are some suggestions:

1. Analyze your audience into its constituent user groups. Who are you making your signs for—general adult users, children, students, people whose first language is not English? What special needs must be taken into account (e.g., Braille signs for the visually impaired)?
2. Ask yourself, for each of these constituent groups: What is a typical destination for members of this group? What do they need to know as they move along

their route? What signs are needed to give directions? For identification? To provide instructions?

3. Try entering your library and walking through it as if you were a first-time visitor. What information do you need to help you find your way around? (Notice that at the entry point you need only a broad overview of the whole. As you get closer to your destination, you need more specific details.)

4. Look up a title in the catalog and try to find the shelf location. What signage is needed to help you match the catalog number to the physical place in the library where the item can be found?

5. Monitor the questions library users ask about the locations of things and use of services. What do these questions tell you about the problems people are having finding their way around the library and using its services?

6. Consider what kinds of up-to-the-minute, changing information you might put on digital signs to help users.

Once you decide what signs are needed, you need to consider the following design elements:

- **Words and graphics.** What are you going to put on the sign? Graphic symbols are efficient and can be understood by people who don't speak English (internationally recognized symbols used to indicate male and female washrooms, facilities for wheelchair users, lost and found, telephones, parking, etc.). If you are using words, be brief, clear, and specific. Cut out all unnecessary words. Avoid unfamiliar words or library-system jargon. Keep it simple. Signs are minimalist forms.
- **Consistency.** How are you going to ensure consistency in all the design elements of your signage? Consider such elements as graphics, fonts, color, size, sign placement, and choice of terminology. Don't use the term *reference desk* on one sign and *information desk* on another.
- **Tone.** Make the tone as inviting and as positive as possible (see 4.2 on tone). Instead of "No food allowed except in lounge," you could try "Food is allowed only in lounge."

A Quick Tip

Looking for Examples?
Check out examples of signs and symbols. Well-respected texts to consult include works by Dreyfuss (1984) and Modley and Myers (1990). You can also find many examples of graphic symbols on the Internet (search "Symbol libraries" on Google). See, for example, the *Online Encyclopedia of Western Signs and Ideograms* (http://www.symbols.com/index/wordindex-a.html).

- **Lettering.** A sans serif font such as Arial has a clarity that works well for display lettering. (Serifs and tapered strokes make it easier to read long texts but are not so legible at a distance—see 4.10 on formatting for more on typefaces). Avoid all capitals. In general, lowercase letters are easier to read than all-capital lettering because the ascenders and descenders on lowercase letters provide additional clues for the reader.

- **Color.** The greater the contrast in brightness between the print and the background, the easier to see at a distance. Good contrast improves legibility. Therefore, you should use a combination of colors that enhances legibility, such as black on white, black on yellow, green on white. Black on white is much easier to read than type printed in reverse lettering (white on black). Remember that green and red look similar to people who are color deficient or color blind (5 to 9 percent of viewers). Most color-deficient people can distinguish blue from other colors.

- **Size.** Figure out how far away from the sign most readers will stand, and make sure that the sign is big enough to be read from that distance. For example, one-inch lettering can be read without strain at eight feet by people with good vision, but four-inch lettering is needed for signs intended to be read at 30 feet. The sign's heading should be even larger—those who can't read the body text at these distances will at least know what the sign is about and can move closer to read the body text. Make your sign big enough that you can leave margins of white space around your text.

- **Placement.** Your sign should make information available where users are likely to look for it—at the entrances and along the major traffic routes (but don't put your signs in places where people reading the signs will block traffic). Place the sign where it will be seen—not too high, not too low, not obstructed by a post. Don't put up signs in the first 20 to 25 feet from the entrance doors. In this threshold where people make the transition from outside to inside, they are not yet looking at signs. Be consistent so that people learn where to look. Don't make some signs free-standing, hang others from the ceiling, and attach others to walls. However, signs that need to be seen from a distance should hang from the ceiling.

A Quick Tip ⏱

Be Consistent
Aim for continuity in graphics design. If signs use similar design elements and follow an established format, people learn where to look for important information. Develop design guidelines and templates to help sign designers achieve consistency over time.

Exercise 🔧

Positive Messages
Make a list of all the messages on signs you can think of that convey a negative tone. For example:

No loud talking.
Do not remove.
Students are not allowed to use this machine.

Rewrite the messages so that the meaning is still clear but the tone is more positive.

Did You Know? ?

Studies have ranked color combinations used on signs in descending order of readability as follows (Pollett and Haskell, 1979: 238-239):

black on yellow
black on white
yellow on black
white on blue
yellow on blue
green on white
blue on yellow
white on green

- **Documentation.** When you have installed your sign system, document it in a sign manual. Record how the signs were designed and made so that all new signs can be made identical in style to the old ones. The sign manual should include the following information: rules governing the choice of wording; design specifications (panel size, layout, lettering, arrows, symbols, colors); placement (height from the floor or ceiling, distance from door frames); and specifications (materials, mounting details).

Digital Signage

Digital signage is the display of electronic information on screens in public areas. Content may take the form of slides that combine text and image, but it may also include video or animation. For the library, digital signage has the advantage that new messages can easily be added, older messages updated, and a changing sequence of slides displayed. Therefore, it can be especially useful to convey time-sensitive information such as emergency alerts, changes in library hours, or notices of upcoming events. It can also display a welcoming greeting to visitors. Digital signage may be as simple as a loop through a sequence of PowerPoint slides or as complex as a screen divided into a number of zones of varying sizes and purposes: for example, the institution name and logo and the weather in one area, a message running in a banner along the bottom, a static frame with unchanging information in one corner, and another larger frame with a sequence of changing slides.

Many of the design elements for digital signage are the same as for traditional signage. There is the same need for brevity of text, a positive tone, consistency of design, legibility, appropriate placement, and the like. The new element that must be taken into account is movement. Unlike the permanent lettering of traditional signs, digital signage displays messages that change at a regular interval, with the result that there will be noticeable changes to the screen. Because the human eye has evolved to attend to movement, the changing digital sign will attract eyes. Therefore, the digital signs should be located where attracting eyes is an advantage, not a source of irritating distraction.

Before designing the slide, you still need to ask yourself, "What do I want the reader to do or understand as a result of reading this message?" If you are announcing an event, for example, think beyond time and place to what you want the reader to *do*: sign up for an event. So you may say, "Sign up now for free tickets to hear [famous author] read from her bestselling new book [title]."

Here are some tips for creating slides for digital signage:

- Consider the target audience when choosing design elements such as colors, images, and font sizes.
- Put the most important information first. You could start with a short title or a question.
- Follow the 3 × 5 Rule. Use no more than 3 lines of text with 5 words each—or 5 lines of text with 3 words each.
- Keep the slides uncluttered, with legible sans serif fonts large enough to read at the expected distance. Choose graphics, if any, that are specifically related to the text. Avoid generic, noninformative images.
- Choose simple backgrounds that enhance the readability of the slide, providing a sharp color contrast with the color of the type.

> **A Quick Tip** 🕐
>
> **Background Matters!**
> Make the background complement the message as well as the typeface. Don't use a somber background to announce a Books for Babies program or a light pastel to announce a tragedy.

9.13. PR, Publicity, and Promotion

PR, or public relations, is the ongoing communication between your organization and the public—it's about how people perceive your services, staff, and organization. Public relations is not something you choose to have—you just have it, good or bad. Your formally designated "public relations staff" use specific skills to enhance the positive image of the library. But everybody in the organization is a PR person, whether or not that person realizes it. A positive or negative impression of your library may be created instantly by a particularly helpful janitor (or by an especially surly librarian). Public relations extends beyond the formal communication channels of the library. A satisfied user can be your best advertisement; a disgruntled employee can be your worst. Although the library's image is generally positive, most people (including funders) do not have a complete picture of what libraries can do for them. And they may not think of the library as relevant to their own personal lives—this is where publicity and promotion come in.

Publicity is what results when public attention is directed to some aspect of the library. That publicity may be positive or negative. We can influence the kind of publicity we get. For example, we may notify the newspaper of a new service to create public awareness of that service. If the editor throws away our notice, we get no publicity. If a reporter writes a story about the service, we get publicity. If we achieve our objectives through this publicity, the publicity is positive. If not (imagine that public demand exceeds the library's ability to deliver the new service or that the new service isn't available after all), negative publicity results. Communication accidents are just as apt to happen with mass communication as with one-to-one communication. The trick is to recover from them and, if possible, to turn them to advantage.

Promotion is a deliberate, controlled effort to draw attention to the organization in order to increase positive public response. Much of what is called "public relations" or "publicity" is really promotion. The difference between publicity and promotion lies in the amount of control exercised over the resulting effect. Promotion includes such communication methods as media advisories, public service announcements, media releases, newsletters, blogs, websites, podcasts, wikis, signage, and advertising. It also includes special events designed to increase the library's profile and informal, but planned, efforts whose primary purpose is to enhance the library's image and/or enhance public awareness of specific services or events. We recommend the *Communications Handbook for Libraries* published by the American Library Association (2004) as a good starting place for learning about media communications.

Finally, remember that publicity and promotional tools must be part of a larger, planned program of public relations that includes everything from market surveys to training staff in public communication skills. Many excellent articles and books have been written on public relations programs for different types of libraries. In what follows, we provide only a general introduction to common promotional formats and offer some practical tips.

9.13.1. Attracting Media Attention

Developing a brief but thorough media communications plan is the essential first step to gaining publicity for a particular story or event. The plan should take into account your goals, target audience, existing resources, strategies, timing, and budget (American Library Association, 2004). Start by defining two or three goals for a simple campaign. Then analyze your audience. Who are the people you are trying to

---

Did You Know?   **?**

For more information on designing a media communications plan, you can check out the American Library Association (2004: 5-11). See also Lisa Wolfe (2005: 31-33, 53-54, and 305-315) for sample communication plans for different types of libraries.

reach? What media channels do they use to get information (e.g., radio, television, print or online papers, social media, webpages?). Look at readership or audience surveys to learn more about the media use patterns of your target audience.

Next focus on crafting a simple and consistent message. Ask yourself, "What message would I like my intended audience to understand?" You should be able to state the overarching concept in one clear sentence. If the message isn't clear to you, it won't be to anyone else.

What resources do you have available to carry out your campaign? Don't forget that people resources include not only library staff members but also library well-wishers such as your volunteers, Friends of the Library, library trustees, and enthusiastic users.

Next plan your strategy. Decide which individuals or groups to approach and how to approach them. Possibilities include:

- community groups;
- opinion leaders, elected officials, and volunteers, approached through one-to-one contact; and
- the media.

A key piece in this communication plan is to create written materials appropriate for distribution to the particular groups you plan to reach. The rest of this section is about creating interesting and usable materials in the following formats:

> Library Backgrounder and Fact Sheet
> Media Advisory or Media Alert
> News Releases
> Public Service Announcements (PSAs)
> Letters to the Editor
> Advertising

Library Backgrounder and Fact Sheet

The library backgrounder and fact sheet are documents you create in advance so that they are ready to put into journalists' hands when they are working on a story or when you are trying to encourage them to write a particular story. Backgrounders and fact sheets also serve as reference documents for you (be sure to keep them up-to-date).

A Quick Tip 🕐

Online Pressroom
Make it easy for journalists to write about the library by creating an online pressroom and keeping it up-to-date. An online pressroom is a place where journalists can find electronic copies of all of your press kit materials. On the online pressroom make available contact information for the library's media spokesperson, recent and archived press releases, a downloadable version of your library's logo, photos that the media can use, a list of library staff and their expertise, and links to recent coverage of your library and of libraries in the national news. See Wolfe (2005: 146-155) for advice, tips, and examples of online pressrooms.

The two-page *backgrounder* should immediately identify the library (e.g., Lindsey Public Library—Backgrounder), followed by an overview statement that says something interesting and unique about the library itself and includes the library's mission and a short history of the library. For an academic or school library, briefly describe the parent institution and the role of the library in relation to the overall mission of the larger unit. Following the overview, provide a listing of programs and services introduced with a brief statement of guiding principles. Bullet points work best for listing the individual services, each with a one-sentence description and a web link if available. The description of programs and services that you develop for the backgrounder becomes the basis for how you talk about these services in all of your press materials. After the programs and services list, provide a list of facilities with street addresses together with the names and titles of the library's leadership. Conclude with PR contact information.

The one-page *fact sheet* identifies the library followed by the mission statement and a listing of locations, the address of the central library, the names and titles of library leaders, website, phone numbers, and PR contact information. See Wolfe (2005: 120–122) for more information and templates of these documents.

Media Advisories

A media advisory, or media alert, is meant to attract the attention of assignment editors or reporters, who may then contact you to do a story. It is a brief message that contains concise and essential information on upcoming events or developments.

Unlike a public service announcement, a media advisory is not usually read or printed exactly as it has been received, although this sometimes happens. If you have fast-breaking news, telephone or e-mail the assignment editor of the newspaper, radio station, and television station. Then fax or e-mail the media advisory. For routine releases, use fax or e-mail. Use media advisories for:

- a good news item—your budget has been approved; a new director has been hired; you are providing free Wi-Fi at all your library branches; you have just lent your millionth e-book;
- a human interest story—someone returned *The Art of Memory* and it was 16 years overdue;

- news that can be supplemented with an interview or photograph of an interesting visitor—a famous author, politician, or a public figure opens your new branch; and
- issues and problems of public interest—new legislation that has implications for book budgets.

The basic rules are: be clear, be concise, and be brief. Use the five Ws (Who, What, Why, Where, When). If you feel it's necessary or desirable to provide more details (biographical information on a visiting bigwig or specifications of your new online system), include this as a one- or two-page enclosure but make sure that the media release can stand alone.

Always give the name of a contact person. For policy and issue-oriented news, one of these contact people should be at the highest administrative level—the information they give out must be authoritative. A general rule is to give the name of the person who knows the most about the item and who is the one you want quoted or interviewed. Make sure this person is available and informed before you send the release (see 8.7 for tips on the media interview). For a sample advisory, see American Library Association (2004: 22–23) and Wolfe (2005: 137).

News Releases

A news release has a different purpose than a media advisory and is written differently. It is intended as ready-made copy that small papers might print as is and that larger outlets could use as the basis for generating their own print or broadcast news story. A news release should follow the conventions for writing a news story. This means the news release should include a short headline that summarizes the story in a catchy way, preferably geared to the interests of the intended audience; an attention-getting first paragraph; an inverted pyramid style that puts the most important information first; and lively quotations and accurate figures and facts to support the story. (See 4.5 on organizing for more on organizing by order of importance to the reader.) Because the whole point of the news release is to promote the library, make sure that you include the name of your library prominently at the beginning, preferably in the subhead to the article. The final paragraph can be brief summary information about your library—material that can be cut if necessary but is there and available, just in case.

You can use a news release whenever you want to convey a new policy, program, or service; a special event; an announcement of, for example, a new children's coordinator; or any other news. Keep your news release short, concise, and focused on a single story. If you have three news items, write three separate short releases and send them to the specific reporters likely to use them (Wolfe, 2005: 128). Make sure that you include at the top of the news release these important details: (1) the date after which news organizations are free to use the material in the release and (2) one contact name (include title, e-mail address, and a phone number) for follow-up information.

Did you know that the way to indicate the end of a release is with "###"? If not, check out details for formatting the news release in American Library Association's (2004: 25) *Communications Handbook for Libraries*.

Public Service Announcements

A public service announcement (PSA) or media spot is a brief, written announcement intended to be printed by a newspaper or read aloud by a radio or television announcer. Most PSAs are 40 to 75 words long and take 15 or 30 seconds to read aloud. Public service announcements are free—most national broadcasting regulations require television and radio stations to donate time for community service announcements. On the other hand, because you pay nothing, you can't specify when, or if, the announcement will be run. Well-written radio announcements that take the fancy of the announcer may get prime time and an ad-libbed endorsement. Poorly written, dull announcements may never get aired. Use public service announcements to inform the public of new services, library locations, changes in hours, or similar information—but not news or feature items. Public service announcements aren't just for public libraries, either. Academic libraries can use campus newspapers or radio stations. Special libraries can use staff publications or other channels.

Lisa Wolfe (2005: 141) recommends that you contact your target media outlet to discover their preferences before writing a public service announcement: "Some radio and television reporters prefer to take your regular news release and adapt it for their use." And she notes that in some cases they may prefer to receive a prerecorded or videotaped version of the public service announcement, which they can broadcast. Send your announcements well in advance. Check with the newspaper or station for schedules. Deadlines can be two weeks

Did You Know? **?**

Local radio stations will sometimes air prerecorded public service announcements. Lisa Wolfe (2005: 142-143) suggests that for a special message, you could ask a local celebrity (mayor, athlete, author, etc.) to record it.

ahead of airdates. After the announcement has aired, evaluate. Ask your staff and the public if they have heard or seen the announcement and how it came across.

TIPS FOR WRITING PUBLIC SERVICE ANNOUNCEMENTS

- Begin with a short sentence or question to attract attention. For example, "Do you live in the Whiteoaks area?"
- Give the essential facts (what, where, and when). For example, "The XPL bookmobile now stops at the Whiteoaks Park gates every Tuesday afternoon from 2 p.m. to 4 p.m."
- Finally, add or repeat important details, ending with your library's name. For example, "That's the bookmobile stop at Whiteoaks Park gates every Tuesday from 2 to 4 p.m.— a service of the XPL" (46 words in the Whiteoaks PSA).

Letters to the Editor

Letters to the editor are a form of publicity or promotion that can be sent in reaction to an article in the paper or to a political issue in the community. Use them sparingly to correct errors and misquotes or to expand coverage of an event. Follow the newspaper's guidelines for submitting letters, keeping within the word limit of 250 words, or whatever the paper specifies, and signing the letters with a name and the library affiliation. Usually the letters can be submitted by e-mail for a timely response to a recent article.

Letters to the editor have a better chance of being published if they are interesting, written on a provocative subject, and don't require much editing or a follow-up phone call (Wolfe, 2005: 139–140). Although anyone can send a letter to an editor, one signed by the library board chair or library director will have more impact. If you are not the director, you can expedite matters by drafting the letter as long as you get approval before sending it to the newspaper under the person's name. For a sample letter to the editor, see American Library Association (2004: 27–28).

Advertising

Advertising is promotion you pay for. It attracts publicity that you can largely control. You may never have to buy advertising space if you have a good promotional program that includes effective public service announcements, in-house promotional brochures, and good

---

A Quick Tip 🕐

Spot Length

The public service announcement is an exercise in brevity—aim at 40 to 75 words for a spot length of 15 to 30 seconds. Count each digit in a phone number as a word (American Library Association, 2004: 28). Test the length of a public service announcement by reading it aloud.

Did You Know? ❓

Searching the American Library Association's website (http://www.ala.org/) turns up many public service announcements that you can customize, print, or download. Simply type "PSA" into its search window. For additional tips, ask your local newspaper, radio, and cable or television stations. They often have free pamphlets (print or online) that give advice on how to write an effective public service announcement.

contacts with local media representatives and people who regularly communicate with your public. Advertising in a daily newspaper or on any radio or television station can be very expensive, even with an institutional discount. Unless you pay top rates, a paid ad does not guarantee that your message will appear when and where you want it to. Furthermore, once you start paying for advertising, you may give the impression that you're able and willing to pay for what should be public service time.

However, there are occasions when a paid advertisement is the only effective way to get a message to your intended audience. You might want to ensure that a message gets out about a specific program, or you might want to promote a political message (bond issues, for example). You can use your advertising budget for high-profile ads in special editions of newspaper supplements and advertising outside the regular media channels (special publications, calendars, or shopping bags).

TIPS FOR NEWSPAPER ADVERTISING

- Seek advice from the advertising sales department on layout and placement.
- Avoid an overcrowded, cramped appearance. Don't try to cram in too much text.
- Leave white space and use large type to catch attention.
- Specify everything you can—border, size of print, desired location.
- Proofread everything (including page proofs) three times.

9.13.2. Newsletters for the Public

If you're considering a regular newsletter for the public, do your homework. You may need to conduct a market survey. You certainly need a long-term plan for production and distribution. Before you launch into your first issue, you should make a realistic assessment of how much copy you can consistently produce and at what frequency. Czarnecki (2011) advises, "The most basic newsletter should have a few lead stories, shorter news items, and a message from your leader. A more developed publication might include features, departments, columns, an editorial, cartoon, in-house news, news tidbits, regional round-ups, etc." You should produce written guidelines for your writers to cut down on the editing required to make their copy usable. And you need in-house expertise in writing, editing, graphics, and layout, geared to the chosen distribution format, whether print or web based.

Electronic newsletters save on printing and distribution costs and allow you to reach a wider audience. You can mount a web newsletter with full graphics on your library's website and then send e-mails to recipients with the link (Wolfe, 2005: 156–157). The advantage of the web version is that you can archive it and make previous newsletters available on the site. But remember that at least some members of your intended audience prefer print—you may want to continue to print some copies of the newsletter for distribution in the library as well as providing an electronic version.

Newsletter software is available that can lighten the production load, but producing a newsletter is still a long-term commitment. It will involve more staff time and expense than you might imagine—if it's going to be effective. Like any other written material, a good newsletter has to catch people's attention, contain useful information, and be easily available. See the advice on staff newsletters (9.9), much of which applies equally to newsletters for the public.

Public libraries are not the only ones that need the promotional and informational channels that a newsletter can provide. But a newsletter is generally a bigger undertaking for a public library than for a special or academic library where the "public" is more specifically defined and where distribution channels are usually already in place. In any type of library, it's essential to involve staff, management, and probably board members in preliminary discussions. Remember that your newsletter may be a formal public relations vehicle, but the proof of the public relations pudding lies in the individual responses of your public. You can say wonderful things about your organization in the newsletter, but if your staff are not informed or not responsive, you've done more harm than good. The reality must match the image you present. Having said that, we recommend that you consult some of the excellent books available on writing newsletters and general promotion for libraries (see the Annotated Bibliography in 4.14 as well as the one in this chapter, 9.17).

Tips on Producing Newsletters

- As always, writing should be clear, concise, jargon-free, and lively. Graphics should be informative and related to content. The format should be clean and uncluttered.

Did You Know? ?

According to Roger C. Parker, five of the most common design problems in desktop publishing are rivers of white space (running vertically or diagonally through right-justified text), trapped white spaces ("holes" that interrupt the flow), inappropriate column spacing, claustrophobic borders and boxes, and underlining. For other problems, see Parker (2006: 236-255).

A Quick Tip ⏱

Tell Them Again

Sharon Baker and Karen Wallace (2002: 178) remind us that users "may not always take note of the messages a library sends, particularly if they do not immediately need the information. Therefore librarians need to check their beliefs that 'everyone knows that' and publish basic information regularly."

- When telling the story, give it the slant that answers the readers' questions: "So what?" "How does that affect me?"
- Negotiate topic, length, treatment, and deadline with each writer before assigning an article. Include important sources and the key questions that the story will address.
- Offer feature writers a byline and an author's note. List all your writers in an acknowledgment box.
- For an electronic newsletter, put a table of contents near the top and use links to connect to the full text of each article. (Adapted from Czarnecki, 2011; Groundwire.com, 2011)

9.13.3. Handouts, Flyers, and Brochures

Once upon a time, the cheapest, fastest way of promoting library services was to produce a handout—flyers, brochures, pathfinders, bookmarks, and booklists are some examples. Today online distribution is probably faster and cheaper, but the main advantage of a printed handout is its portability and durability. People can take it away, use it as a reminder, read it at leisure, or, if it's a bookmark, use it for years. Downloading the cost of printing onto the user may save the library money but is no bargain if users never print the item. Its promotional value may be less than that of the handout picked up while visiting the library. You are probably best advised to print these materials *and* include them on the library's website.

Handouts should never look homemade, no matter how casual an image you wish to convey. If you don't have the resources to do a professional-looking job, get it done by a company or freelancer who specializes. If you can't do that, don't do it at all.

Handouts may be primarily instructional (pathfinders) or primarily promotional (program announcements), but they always have a promotional element in that they make readers aware of a service, policy, or event and encourage them to use it. Every handout that a library distributes is a promotional piece that should communicate a positive image of the library.

For more on particular kinds of handouts, see discussions of newsletters for the public (9.13.2) and booklists (9.15.1).

Some Quick Tips for Handouts

- Develop a design and style for families of handouts, such as bookmarks or pathfinders, and use it consistently. Aim for

> **Exercise** 🔧
>
> **Promotional Brochures**
> Look at the prize-winning promotional brochures in the John Cotton Dana awards. What common characteristics do they have? Pick a few for closer study. What special features does each have? (For links to the annual awards, see http://www.ebscohost.com/academic/john-cotton-dana.)

a consistent overall look that readers come to identify with the library.

- Always include your logo or at least the library's name, address, telephone number, and e-mail and website addresses in a prominent place.
- Don't try to say too much in one handout. Consider instead a series of one-page handouts in the same format, using different colors.
- Say it in different ways. Reinforce your message with brochures, bookmarks, posters, and public service announcements.
- Keep it readable. Don't use dark colored paper for anything that requires close reading (no matter how pretty "raspberry" is).

> **Exercise** ⚒
>
> **Creating Handouts**
> In pairs, write the copy and prepare a layout for (1) a bookmark to announce new library hours for the library or (2) a brochure describing a storyhour program for toddlers (agree on the basic details before you start to write). You and your partner should do the first draft independently. Then trade drafts. Together, revise the handout into a single document, using the best ideas from each draft.

9.13.4. Using Websites for Promotion

The Internet has opened up a rich space for promotion. Libraries promote their services through various messaging media, such as e-mail alerts, Facebook (9.3.4), blogs (9.3.6), and Twitter. They use wiki software and create webcasts and RSS feeds. In this section we focus on the website itself, which is the gateway to these other Internet-based communication channels. As with all promotional activities, you need a deliberate, global plan for promoting the library on the Internet so that the library website itself is part of an overall strategy. Your library's website allows you to reach out to a broader public who might never set foot in the buildings. Users can connect to library materials and online services, ask questions, communicate with each other, and link to other websites.

Many sources are available to help with the technical aspects of creating webpages, but here we are concerned with writing. The focus is on the communication effects of well-designed, well-written webpages. The key principle is to put your reader first (4.13). Make the needs of your web readers your primary concern, not your own desire to impart particular facts. You may say that you care about users, but readers may doubt it if your homepage is all about "we" and "us" rather than "you" (e.g., the XPL was founded in 1887; *our* mission statement is A, B, and C; *we* believe in principles X and Y). Instead put your emphasis on what the visitor to your site wants to know and what the site allows the visitor to do.

There are a lot of services that your library can promote on its website. Here are a few suggestions adapted from Ohio Library Council (2008). Help users understand what is offered by augmenting the title and link with a concise description of what the service does, for example, "If you enjoy discussing books or want ideas for what to read next, check out our RA blog."

- Readers' advisory blog
- Ask-a-librarian reference services or e-mail reference
- Online catalog, renewals, personal accounts, overdue notices by e-mail
- E-books
- E-newsletters
- Mailing lists
- Virtual tours
- Children's story podcasts
- Online pathfinders
- Opinion polls, feedback, and comment forms
- Purchase suggestion forms
- Community bulletin boards
- RSS feeds for rapidly changing content
- Links to your blogs and Facebook page

Exercise 🔧

Describe a Service

Choose two of the services listed above (the list of some services that can be offered on a website). Write a one- or two-line description that will promote each service. Ask someone not connected to the library to explain the service based on your description. How did you do?

Because the Internet is accessible to so many people with different interests, it's hard to target a specific audience. Still, you should have a clear purpose in creating each webpage and especially the homepage. That purpose could be based on the kind of help that your readers are likely to want from your homepage. How can you tell? Think of the questions that people most often ask you. For example, they may want instructions for searching your catalog, for renewing borrowed books, or for borrowing e-books. They may want to find out about locations and hours of opening. They may want to ask reference questions, to find out about adaptive equipment to help people with disabilities (6.6.1), to find links to other libraries, or to learn about upcoming programs, events, exhibitions, and concerts. Anticipate these common questions, and answer them by providing a well-organized, information-rich, uncluttered homepage.

When readers arrive at your site, they want to know where they are and how to find their way around. Remember that a browser may bring visitors, not to your homepage but to some other page deep in your site. Therefore, every page should contain links that show how the site is organized and how to move around. Visitors to the site should see the name of the library prominently displayed, with links to the homepage and to major services, no matter which page they arrive at first. Create links to the services and place the links near the top of the page. Make it easy for readers to move back and forth within your document and between links, and make it easy to get back to your homepage. To give users a choice of ways to communicate with you, provide an e-mail address, phone number, and fax number. Don't forget to include the full postal and street address—some people still want to write letters, and others may simply want to know where the library is located (Ohio Library Council, 2008; Wolfe, 2005: 156).

Writing for a Website

You won't be surprised when we say that all the principles for good writing discussed in Chapter 4 apply to writing for the web. You still have to analyze your audience, understand your purpose in writing, adopt an appropriate tone, write clearly, correctly, and briefly, and use plain, jargon-free language. You still need to provide a hook for the reader—a question, a quotation, an unusual or surprising fact—that captures attention. Also check out the general suggestions on writing digitally (see 4.11). Here we focus on special considerations for writing for a website.

First consider how readers read webpages. They don't read consecutively, and they don't read every word. They skim and scan. Reading on a desktop screen can be up to 25 percent slower than reading a printed version, despite improvements in screen technology (Redshaw, 2003). Reading on a mobile device puts even more of a premium on brevity and making information easy to find. A web researcher who conducts web usability studies, Jakob Nielsen (2007) recommends that you take the comparable print version and cut the word length in half for a webpage. Because web readers make quick decisions about whether to stay with a page or click through, make your pages easy to scan by using these devices:

- Inverted pyramid structure (4.5) that puts the most important information first
- Two or three word headings and subheadings
- Short paragraphs
- White space between paragraphs
- Narrow columns
- Bulleted and numbered lists
- Arabic numbers rather than words (23 not twenty-three)
- Tables, graphs, and charts to summarize information
- Clearly defined links that name and describe the linked page: "For details on the library expansion plan, see the XPL Annual Report (.pdf, 148 Kb)" is more informative than "Click here" (De Castro, 2009: 35; Nielsen, 2007; Redshaw, 2003)

Second, consider the way that visitors navigate websites. A print reader does not necessarily start at the beginning and read straight through to the end but could do so if desired. However, web readers, if they start with the homepage, are offered a constellation of nodes that they can explore in any order and to any depth. Because you can't know what else a reader may have read first, each page must be self-contained, able to stand on its own.

De Castro (2009: 35) recommends that you sort out basic essential textual and graphical information and distinguish it from supplementary information that can be linked to the text and made available to readers with an exceptional interest in the topic. This subordination of supplementary material streamlines the main page and lets the reader decide whether or not to look at more detailed information. It is helpful to think of each topic in terms of levels that are linked. A mildly interested reader can note that a certain service is provided

---

Exercise

Homepage Comparison
Pick three large public libraries (e.g., New York PL, Toronto PL, Boston PL, Seattle PL, Chicago PL, Edinburgh City Libraries, etc.) plus your local public library. Examine the homepages of the four chosen libraries and compare them. How easy is it to find out what services are offered? How is the information organized? What features on any homepage did you find most helpful? What features did you find unhelpful or distracting or unwelcoming?

Exercise

"'Shut up,' he explained."
Jakob Nielsen (2007) recommends that on webpages you use half the word count or less compared with print writing. Find a paragraph of 200 words or so in a print document written for your library users. Revise it for the web by cutting it to 100 words or fewer.

Experienced web users tend to scan for information rather than reading word-by-word, and they ignore any text or picture that doesn't seem immediately useful or relevant.

without clicking on any links. More interested readers can follow the links down several additional levels, each level providing more detailed and fine-grained information.

- **Level 1** (homepage) displays the link, a description of the link, and perhaps a blurb to tell the reader what to expect. For example, the Toronto Public Library's homepage has a link entitled "eBook help" accompanied with this description, "New to library eBooks? Start here!"
- **Level 2** presents the topic, using the devices described earlier that foster scanning. If you click on "eBook help" on the TPL site, you get a screen, "Getting Started with Library eBooks," that provides an overview of all the various elements of the process, many with links to level 3 pages.
- **Level 3** provides even more finely grained and detailed information. In the "eBook help" example, level 3 provides links to printable "device guides" on how to download e-books to various Wi-Fi-enabled devices as well as a link on how to get or renew a library card.

Finally, consider that you want to make it as easy as possible for visitors to engage with your site. Here are some of the things that visitors might want to do. Make it easy for them by providing clear links from your homepage: Search for Books or Multimedia; Download E-books; Get a Library Card; Renew Borrowed Books; Download Music; Ask a Reference Question; Sign Up for a Library-Sponsored Event.

Exercise: Cut to the Chase

Rewrite and reformat this text about the summer reading program to make it friendly to web readers. As a first step, identify the intended audience and write with that audience in mind.

Write two versions:

1. No more than 15–20 words that could go on a homepage
2. No more than 100 words that could go on a linked page

Library Offering Youth a Summer Reading Program
Celebrating its 55th year of offering summer reading

programs, the Muntown Public Library has encouraged thousands of children over the years to let their imaginations soar. It's almost summer again, which means that the Muntown Public Library has a new summer reading program!!!

The goals of our summer reading program are to encourage and strengthen the habit of reading for pleasure, to create lifelong learners, to increase children's reading skills, and to help reduce the learning loss that happens over the summer holidays. Research suggests that students who participate in public library summer reading programs score higher in reading achievement in the next school year than did their peers who were not participants.

The love of reading for pleasure is one of the most important gifts that you can give to your child. Children will build their literacy skills by attending weekly drop-in programs, sharing stories, using their imaginations, winning prizes, and having fun with special guests! The program is free and is open to any child currently in grades 1 to 5. The program starts on July 5 and runs until August 2. Sign up early to avoid disappointment. To register, call the library at xxx-xxx-xxxx or check out our website at www.muntownsummerreading. (211 words)

> **A Quick Tip**
>
> **Avoid the Bells and Whistles!** Don't be tempted to use all the capabilities of webpage creation software. Too many graphics or animated bells and whistles are as distracting in virtual space as they are in print and have the additional drawback of making your page slow to load. Choose only features that contribute directly to good, clean design.

9.14. Proposals

Proposals are, above all, rhetorical. That is, their main function is to persuade. You want to get the reader to do something: to approve a project, to approve the purchase of equipment, to give you money to carry out research, and so on. Your proposal is competing for attention and scarce resources against other proposals. Therefore, to be successful, your proposal must convince readers that:

- your proposal is worth reading in the first place;
- you have a doable project that is manageable and realistic;
- your project is worth doing (where "worth doing" is defined in terms of the goals of the assessors of the proposal); and
- you are capable of doing it.

Here are some suggestions for writing a winning proposal.

Before You Start Writing

Analyze your audience (see 4.1). Ask these questions about the assessors of your proposal: What types of projects does this group of reviewers (or this funding agency) want to encourage? Does your proposed project fit its criteria? How can you make clear the relevance of your project to the funding agency's goals?

Assess the project that you are proposing. Has this project already been done before by someone else? (If so, you may not need to do it at all. Or perhaps you can build on this previous work for your own project.) Before you can convince others of the value of the project, you must be clear in your own mind about the following points: Why is this project worth doing? What difference will it make? Who, specifically, will benefit from its completion? How will they benefit? You should aim to provide a statement about your project such that nobody, after hearing it, can say "So what?" (Here's a statement that doesn't pass the so-what test: "This project will result in a bibliography of over 2,000 entries." "So what?")

Think through your methodology carefully. Be detailed and concrete. What, specifically, do you want to do? How do you plan to do it? It's not enough to say that your research project involves surveying public library users to find out their information needs. You have to know specific answers to such questions as these: How do you define "library users" and "information needs"? What research questions are you trying to answer? How will you choose your sample, and how many people do you need in the sample? What survey method will you use—self-administered questionnaire? online survey? structured interview? unstructured interview? When will the survey be conducted? Who will conduct the survey? (If you plan to hire others to conduct the survey, how will you train them?) What specific questions will you put on your questionnaire or interview schedule? How do you plan to pretest your survey instrument? How do you plan to tabulate and analyze the answers? How will the responses given by your subjects help you answer your original research questions? How much will the project cost? In what form will you report your findings?

Be very clear about the *whats*, the *hows*, and the *whens* of your project in order to persuade assessors of your competence. Vagueness about details is taken as a sign that you don't know what you're doing. A carefully worked-out project of limited scope is more impressive than a grandiose project that skimps on concrete detail.

Look, if possible, at other people's successful proposals to see how they did it. Examine published work that has dealt with similar problems or issues.

When You Write

Having clarified for yourself the proposal's precise objectives and expected benefits, you have to write a proposal that communicates these points to others. Your writing style should be clear and precise (see 4.2 to 4.4). Use active verbs. Your tone should be confident but not inflated or grandiose. Whenever possible, avoid jargon and technical language. Make your proposal understandable to the nonspecialist by beginning with a general statement explaining the overall point of the project before getting into specific details.

The organization to which you are applying may provide a printed proposal form or guidelines to follow. If no format is suggested, set up your proposal to include the following elements:

- **Project title.** This should be a short descriptive title that accurately conveys the nature and scope of the proposed project.
- **Nontechnical summary.** This is like the executive summary in a report—a short, intelligible, nontechnical statement of what you plan to do and why. Write the summary last.
- **Statement of purpose or problem (broadly defined).** In the case of a research project, the problem is the research question that your project is designed to answer. In the case of a nonresearch project, it is the situation that the project is designed to address.
- **Context.** Put your project in a framework. Describe how the proposal fits into the field. What historical background led up to it? What will happen, as a result of the project, when the work is over? Don't assume that assessors will already know the context. Spell it out. If you are doing a research project, the context should include a discussion of the related literature (which you can put into a separate section, labeled Review of Related Research, although it's often better not to).
- **Specific objectives.** Explain clearly what you are proposing to do. In the case of a research proposal, state your

hypothesis to be tested or the questions you are trying to answer.

- **Procedure.** Explain, in precise terms, the whos, whats, hows, and whens of your project. In a research proposal, this methodology section is written for other researchers and peer reviewers and may use specialized technical language. You would talk about the assumptions underlying the research, the research design, methods of data collection, and the treatment of the data. If you are using subjects or participants, you should discuss ethical issues, including how you will ensure confidentiality.
- **Institutional resources.** Mention institutional resources that are available to support the proposed project, such as office space, computer facilities, library resources, release time for personnel, and so forth.
- **Budget.** Provide detailed and justified estimates of costs: personnel (including employee benefits), space, travel (justify the travel; don't just list), office supplies, project materials, support services such as photocopying, equipment.
- **Significance.** You have to demonstrate that your project has social or scholarly benefits sufficient to justify the cost. Again, don't assume that the project's significance is self-evident to everybody, just because it is obvious to you. Spell it out.
- **Qualifications of personnel.** In the case of a research proposal, you append a curriculum vitae, reworked to highlight your credentials that qualify you to undertake the project. If you don't have all the necessary qualifications yourself, you may want to pool strengths by collaborating with another colleague or a group of colleagues.

After You Have Written the First Draft

Proofread for spelling mistakes and grammatical errors. Ask colleagues to read your proposal with a view to identifying vague statements, inflated statements, obscurities, and omissions. Ask the most critical people, and tell them that you really do want negative as well as positive feedback (3.15). If the colleague gives it back with nothing written on it, saying, "It's great," don't ask him or her again. At least one of your readers should be someone who is not particularly familiar with the area: if this nonexpert can understand the proposal, then it will probably be clear to the assessors.

Checklist for evaluating your own proposal:

- ☐ Does the proposal conform to the guidelines of the funding or approving agency?
- ☐ Is the proposal complete?
- ☐ Has the need for the project been clearly stated and convincingly documented?
- ☐ Has the project been placed in a framework or context? Are the objectives clear?
- ☐ Is the methodology clear? Is it appropriate?
- ☐ Is the budget realistic? Are expenditures justified?
- ☐ Have you been concise? Have you stayed within the suggested guidelines for length?
- ☐ Have you made it hard for a reviewer to dismiss your proposal with a "So what?"

Quick Tips for Writing Proposals

If you don't have any experience or publications in the field of your proposed project, it is better to start with a small project. It's like applying for credit: you have to establish your credit rating by being successful in paying back a small loan before you're entrusted with a large loan.

Break up a large project into smaller stages, each of which is self-contained and results in a usable product. Toward the end of stage 1 (to allow for continuous funding), you write another proposal for stage 2, and so on.

Be realistic in what you say you will do, how soon you can do it, and how much it will cost. Remember that everything always takes longer than you think it will, and take this into account in your timetable. Don't be extravagant in your cost estimates, but don't be unrealistically penny-pinching either.

9.15. Writing about Books

When we use the term *books* in this section it should be understood as shorthand to mean books, yes, but also other formats that libraries collect such as audiobooks, film, and video games. In writing about

A Quick Tip 🕐

Be Selective

Don't put too many items on your list. Instead of a booklist of 100 titles, try a shorter annotated list of 15 books to narrow the field for the reader and help her choose. You can alert the reader to the existence of other items by saying, "These books are only a selection of those available on topic X. Ask us about finding others."

A Quick Tip 🕐

Ready-Made Lists

You can compile your own materials lists or adapt lists that someone else has created. You can find such lists online on the websites of other libraries, at genre sites, in the archives of electronic mailing lists like Fiction_L, and in various library journals (e.g., *The Unabashed Librarian*). Baker and Wallace (2002: 281-282) recommend adding short annotations when these lists are not already annotated.

materials in these formats—providing lists, annotations, or reviews—you are helping readers make choices. We know that for many library users the problem of "overload" is daunting, as they are faced with thousands and thousands of choices. Library users welcome help in narrowing choices so that they can more easily find items that they will enjoy or learn from.

9.15.1. Booklists

The booklist provides a way of overcoming the problem that books can be put on library shelves in only one order—Dewey, Library of Congress, alphabetical by author, or whatever. But readers often want books and other materials brought together in other orders. For example, they want mysteries (or historical romances or horror stories or vampire stories). Or they want everything related to Arthurian legends—myths, recent fiction based on the legends, accounts of the staging of Camelot, historical maps of Wales, literary criticism of Thomas Malory. Or perhaps they want fiction and nonfiction materials brought together that provide help in particular situations (e.g., in coming to terms with cancer or getting back into the workforce or going on a pilgrimage).

Lists are much more useful when they are specific and narrowly focused. Don't draw up a list called Good Books You Might Like. Think of topics in demand in your library where the materials are scattered and hard to find. For example:

- Recent books on climate change
- Fiction books with a focus on Hispanic Americans
- Travel books dealing with a specific type of destination
- Local writers
- Books offering financial advice
- Fiction and nonfiction materials to help a reader cope with divorce/illness/job loss
- Materials on coping skills for the new parent
- Material related to a current event

9.15.2. Annotations

Good annotations provide information that can help readers decide whether or not a book is worth their time. An annotation answers questions like: Is this book on a topic that I would be interested in? Does it address the problems I'm concerned about? Is it written at a level appropriate to me?

A short annotation can be done in one sentence. Fiction books in particular lend themselves to a short annotation of the sort intended to whet the reader's interest in the book:

> [Gothic Romance] When Sarah arrives as a governess in Holyrood House, she is enchanted by her new situation—until she begins to suspect that someone is trying to kill her. (28 words)
>
> *Dear Life*. Alice Munro's collection of award-winning short stories explores with unusual sensitivity the "pain of human contact." (16 words)

Longer annotations (two to three sentences) are sometimes written for annotated bibliographies. The annotation is meant to inform the reader of the relevance, accuracy, and quality of the work. An annotation of a work of nonfiction addresses such questions as the following but does so in a very condensed way:

- What is this book about, and how well does the book deal with its topic?
- What approach does the book take—is it theoretical? practical?
- What are the qualifications of its author(s) to write this book?
- What point of view does the author have on the subject?
- What special features does the book have that might interest the reader—illustrations, practical exercises, an annotated bibliography, appendixes containing useful tables, a companion website?
- Who is the intended audience for this book—a beginner? a specialist? a professional group?

The challenge is to condense a lot of information into just two or three readable sentences.

Did You Know? **?**

In her classic work on book selection, *Living with Books*, Helen Haines (1935: 128) described the writing of annotations as an art demanding concentrated intelligence and expert expression: "Every word must count, every sentence must be compressed to give specific, definite fact; yet at the same time there must be indication or reflection of the color, the texture, the spirit of the book."

Example

Written by [a Professor of English/a skydiver/an ex-prisoner], this [textbook/collection of critical essays/exposé] provides an [introductory treatment/a specialist's analysis] of [topic]. Readers may be willing to overlook [the rather dull opening chapter/the jargon-ridden writing style/the confusing graphics and tables/the lack of an index] because the [strong point of the book] is so valuable. [Plus a sentence on the strong point.]

To pack the most into the fewest words, annotation writers often write sentence fragments: "Fast becoming the standard work in the field." Or they start right in with the verb: "Provides a detailed discussion of X." "Deals with theoretical aspects of Y." "Gives practical information on Z."

Tips for Writing Annotations

- Be brief—one or two sentences. An annotation is not a review.
- Consider your audience. For whom are you writing the annotation? What kinds of information do your readers want from your annotation?
- Consider your purpose. Are you trying to attract the reader's interest to a book on a reading list? Or are you providing a balanced and informative assessment of books in a field for an annotated bibliography?
- Use active verbs rather than passive verbs. Better to say "This practical how-to manual explains how to deal with five tricky situations" than "Five tricky situations are dealt with in this practical how-to manual."
- Let the reader decide. Instead of saying "a poor book," provide the specific grounds for your evaluation (the black-and-white illustrations are muddy) and let your reader decide whether this factor matters.
- Try to get some variety in the annotations by varying the sentence structure and the approach. A list of annotations is often read all together as a group, but you don't want them all to sound the same.

9.15.3. Reviews

Reviews can range from something just slightly longer than an annotation to a review article of a thousand words or so. Which kind you write depends on your audience and where your review will be published. Usually professional journals for librarians favor short, current reviews that quickly provide just enough information to enable a purchasing decision.

Scholarly journals that are discipline oriented are more leisurely in their approach to reviewing, trading off brevity and currency for critical insight and thoroughness of treatment. Because one of their purposes is to provide current awareness to academic readers, these reviews tend to summarize key arguments of the book. Whatever the length, however, the primary purpose of the review is to provide balanced information that the reader can use to make a decision: Is this book worth seeking out and reading? Is it worth borrowing or buying?

Before you write your review, read other reviews published in the outlet in which you expect to publish yours. This will give you an idea of the style expected of you. In any case, stick to the number of words your editor allots you (200 words, 700 words, 1,200 words) and get your review in by the deadline. If you go beyond the limit, your best sentences might be cut by the editor, the review could be returned to you for editing, or it could be rejected outright.

As you are thinking about what to say in your review, it may be useful to think about where you stand on the issue of reviewing. Reviewers can be divided into two ideal types, depending on what they think they are doing when they read books and write reviews. One type thinks of the text as having an objective, autonomous existence apart from any reader. Such reviewers therefore consider it their job to make objectively true statements about the text: the book is about the petroleum industry; it has ten chapters; it has a 30-page index. Evaluative judgments, if provided, are phrased as objective attributes of the text rather than the response of the reviewer: the book is enlightening/dull/disturbing.

The second type of reviewer considers that all reading is a transaction between reader and text in which the reader is actively engaged in making meaning. These reviewers tend to see themselves as offering, not objective statements about the book, but statements about their own response to the book: "I found the book enlightening/dull/disturbing" (with the implication that, if you are like me, you will find it this way too). These reviewers often provide a few brief details

> **A Quick Tip** ⏱
>
> **Why Should You Review?**
> Writing reviews is one of the primary ways you can contribute to the profession because, as Crawford (2003: 42-44) reminds us, reviews help librarians and readers make informed choices. But you also benefit. You hone your writing skills, your writing gets published in a form that is widely read, you broaden your expertise—and you get to keep the books!

about themselves so that readers of the review can judge whether or not their tastes are like the reviewers' ("I usually prefer the British country-house mystery to the hard-boiled San Francisco type. However, I found this hard-boiled mystery thoroughly enjoyable and stylish"). This approach requires tact so that the review doesn't sound like a biography of the reviewer's own reading taste. However, its advantage is that it is based on a theory of reading that takes into account what actually does happen in the review process. Your review evaluates the book. But then your reader evaluates your review to decide if you should be trusted.

What should go into a review? At a minimum, a review should answer the questions that are answered in a good annotation (see 9.15.2): Who is the book for? What is this book about? How well does it do what it sets out to do? What approach does it take? What special features does it have? What are the credentials of the author? Provide factual statements, but go beyond facts to an evaluation. After all, your readers want to know more than that the book is about the petroleum industry. They want to know: How good/accurate/fair-minded/thorough is this treatment of the petroleum industry?

In addition, reviews often do one or more of the following:

- **Comment** generally on the field to which the book belongs. (You could, for example, say that the commonest approach for books on this topic has been to emphasize the social and political factors, so this book's economic emphasis fills a gap.) The focus of discussion could be:

    Genre based (What characteristics of the thriller does this particular thriller exemplify, either well or badly?)

    National or international (What advances have been made in the past decade in, say, intellectual freedom legislation worldwide? How does this particular analysis compare with other work on the same topic published elsewhere?)

    Theoretical (What theoretical controversies divide this field? Where does this book fit in?)

    Methodological (What methodologies are available to investigate questions in this field? How does the research methodology used here measure up?)

- **Relate** the reviewed work to other comparable works in the field. You could say that this new directory supersedes some former standard work in the field. Or that the book, though not comprehensive, is the only available book that treats some particular aspect of the subject. Or that the work is a good popularization of topic X but provides nothing new to readers already familiar with works Y and Z.

- **Compare** the reviewed book to other works by the same author. You might show how this latest book by an author fits into the total canon of the author's work. For example, the book returns to a preoccupation addressed in the author's first book; it shows the maturation of the author's thinking; or it will disappoint readers who want a repeat of the previous bestseller but will delight readers who appreciate risk taking.

- **Discuss** the underlying assumptions of the book, the theoretical stance taken, or the ideology espoused by the book. You could point out that the book has illuminated its topic from the perspective of Marxist materialism/ chaos theory/Jungian psychology/feminism/supply-side economics/phenomenology/postmodernism, and so on.

- **Analyze** specific features important in the type of book it is. You could analyze the style of a literary work, the development of character and plot in a novel, the relation of pictures to text in a graphic novel, the use of primary sources in an historical or biographical work, the use of tables and graphs in a report, the choice of methodology in a research study.

- **Test** aspects of a reference work such as its accuracy, its currency, its ease of use, the balance of its coverage, and so on. Check some index entries. You could read a picture book to a group of children to test its appeal.

Some Tips for Writing a Review

- Read the book thoroughly. Skimming isn't fair to the author or to your readers.
- Don't review a book in a case where there is a conflict of interest (you dislike the author or the author is your best friend; you have spent your lifetime combating the position taken by the book).

Did You Know? ?

The book reader and the professional library book selector each want to know somewhat different things about the book under review.

For a fiction book, the reader wants to know what the main appeal of the book is (fast-paced plot, well-drawn characters, exotic setting, a particular theme) and how this book compares to others by the same author or to others in the same genre. Meanwhile the professional selector of fiction also wants to know how the novel rates among other novels coming out at the same time, what groups of readers will want to read it, whether there are elements in the novel that will limit its readership, and what libraries should buy it.

- In your review, try to convey the flavor, or the "feel," of the book.
- Keep things in proportion. Don't give a disproportionate amount of attention to some minor feature, however irritating you may find it.
- Review the book that was written, not the one you wish had been written. Don't complain that the author didn't do something that she never intended to do.
- Use criteria appropriate for the type of book being reviewed. It's not fair to make a negative evaluation on the grounds that a book on Husserl uses unfamiliar Germanic terminology or that a work of Young Adult realism dwells too much on the downside of adolescent experience. (You can, however, point out such things as features that the reader may wish to know about.)
- For a nonfiction work, summarize the main arguments of the book. But never, never give away the plot of fiction in which suspense is important to the reading experience.

9.16. Contributing to the Professional Literature

Contributing articles and books to the library and information science (LIS) literature is a way to participate more fully in your profession. For librarians with faculty status in college and university libraries, publishing may be a job requirement. But many librarians write because they have something to say or experiences they want to share. You might have conducted research, the results of which you think will be useful to other librarians. You might have noticed that nothing useful has been written on a particular topic and want to fill the gap. You might simply want to challenge some commonly accepted idea. Walt Crawford (2003: 1–3) notes that these are all good reasons to write for publication. You might want to review the suggestions in Chapter 4 on effective writing, all of which apply in spades when writing for publication.

9.16.1. Getting Published

If you have never published anything, you possibly think that it must be very, very difficult to break in. It is, if you want a major publisher to accept your first novel. But getting shorter pieces published is mostly a matter of understanding the needs and requirements of particular publishing outlets and writing to meet those needs. Think of writing as an apprenticeship. Entry-level publishing opportunities include book reviews (see 9.15.3), posting on virtual discussion sites (9.3.5), and blogs (see 9.3.6). You might start with in-house publications, move on to regional publications, and then try for more competitive venues, when you have had some publishing success. Prestigious international peer-reviewed journals receive far more submissions than they can accept and have a high rejection rate. Some international journals reject up to 90 percent of the articles submitted (De Castro, 2009: 38–39). But some small journals and newer journals are always looking for papers. There are lots of possibilities, and the number of print and online journals in the LIS field is growing.

Where to Publish an Article

A good place to start is with the LIS journals that you already read and know. With your article idea in mind, look at these journals' websites to see which ones would be most likely to publish the kind of piece you want to write. Clearly subject matter is a key consideration. Some journals have a broad eclectic scope, while others focus on specific facets of LIS (e.g., reference, cataloging, information storage and retrieval systems, youth services, collections). Some specialize in different kinds of libraries (e.g., academic libraries, public libraries, archives, law libraries, children's libraries).

However, a more fundamental difference is the distinction between scholarly academic journals, which publish research-based articles, and professional journals, which publish articles directly applicable to the work of professional librarians. Scholarly journal articles typically include some or all of the following elements: a statement of the research problem to be addressed; a review of the relevant literature; an account of the research method(s) used; a report of findings; and a discussion of their significance and possible applications. The professional journals accept articles that are less formal and have more popular, general appeal.

Be clear in your own mind what kind of article you intend to write. When you have narrowed down the field of potential journals for your article, scan through many issues of each journal. Read the comments from the editor and the instructions to authors, sample some articles,

A Quick Tip

Don't Start Alone
If you're hesitant to write that first article yourself, team up with a colleague. Co-authoring is accepted practice and gives you experience with the publication process.

A Quick Tip

Which Journal?
Before choosing a journal to submit to, check out its website. Here you should find information on the journal's aims, scope, and readership, as well as such practical details as publisher name, ISSN, names of members of the editorial board, frequency, impact factor (if any), inclusion in databases, online availability, subscription price, and copyright policy. Most also include guidelines for authors (De Castro, 2009: 37-38).

and get a feel for the style, content, and format expected. This process will help you weed out unsuitable candidates.

The most common mistake beginning writers make is to submit something to a publisher with no previous history of publishing the kind of thing submitted. You might think that a journal packed with articles full of quantitative data would be pleased to balance things out a bit with your qualitative, ethnographic study—but you would be wrong. Submitting your work to an inappropriate journal or book publisher wastes their time and yours.

As LIS professionals, you have a big advantage when it comes to choosing an appropriate journal because you already know a lot that's relevant to making the final choice, such as:

- Journals are ranked in a hierarchy of prestige that is determined for scholarly journals by impact factors and for professional journals by the size of readership and the authority of the publisher.
- An article published in a journal that is covered by indexing and abstracting services has a greatly enhanced chance of being found by others and read. Hence you want your article to appear in an outlet that is well indexed.
- The more prestigious the journal, the more articles it receives and the higher its rejection rate of submitted articles. Therefore, you need to make a realistic assessment about the likely competitiveness of your article. Aim for a journal not too low in rank but also not too high.
- You cannot submit an article to more than one journal at a time, but if the article is rejected you can, and should, resubmit to another journal. If timely publication is important to your career advancement or if the content of the article is time sensitive, you might think twice about submitting it first to a journal known to be very slow in making a decision.
- The time required for the evaluation process for accepting or rejecting articles varies a lot among different journals, depending on whether the decision is made internally by the editor (a faster process) or by a process of peer review (which can take six months or even longer).
- Scholarly journals use a peer-review process of sending an article out for evaluation to three or more arm's-length referees who recommend outright acceptance/resubmission

A Quick Tip

Tell Me Something Good
Walt Crawford (2003: 27) writes that if "tell me something new" is shorthand for scholarly journals, the key for informal articles is "tell me something good." Tell your readers something they haven't heard before "either because of your sources, your approach, or your ability to bring in outside issues and make them real. Something that they find interesting enough to read."

following revisions/or rejection. Many professional LIS journals are not peer reviewed, with the result that your work, if accepted, will appear in them more quickly.

- Articles in online journals are usually published more quickly than those in print journals, and readers, in turn, may find them more quickly using browsers. Print journals still have a bit more prestige than online journals, but that is likely to change over time.
- Generally the time between when the article was first submitted and when it was published is shorter in the case of online journals partly because online journals are less likely to have a large backlog of accepted but as yet unpublished articles.
- Open access journals can be a good option (for a directory of open access journals, see http://www.doaj.org/).

Before you write the first word of your article, know where you plan to send it. Write the article to the specifications of the chosen journal—or choose another journal that is a better fit for your subject matter and approach. Each journal's website will provide you with author instructions, including information on which style manual to use as well as details on manuscript length, fonts, margins, indents, and figures. Follow to the letter the editor's requirements for word length, format, and citation form. You will save yourself a lot of revising work that would otherwise be needed if you write the article first and then try to match the journal's specifications.

Be aware that you may be asked for revisions by the journal editor who responds to your submission. Take the advice and resubmit. Sometimes an editor who is unable to accept your article offers ideas for improving the article and sometimes suggests other journals that might be interested in it. If so, don't put the article in a drawer for two years. Make the suggested revisions and resubmit right away to another journal. Don't give up.

Publishing a Book

To get a sense of the scale involved, think of writing an annotation; then a review; then a journal article; then a book. As you go from an annotation to a review, there is at least a tenfold increase in work involved. As you go from a review to an article, there is another tenfold increase or more in work involved. Ditto the move from

Did You Know? ?

Art Plotnik (1985: 82), former editor of *American Libraries*, holds out the encouragement that "although a so-so article has only a 10 percent chance of being published, an original and readable article smashes like a comet through the curve of probability and has virtually a 100 percent chance of seeing print."

A Quick Tip 🕐

Get Advice

Contact an editor at the publishing house before you get too fully immersed in writing your book. Editors can tell you if there's any likelihood of interest in your idea and, if the answer is yes, will be aware that your proposal is coming. Meet editors at conferences and book exhibits. Editors attend these events to make contacts with potential authors—don't hesitate to speak to them. If they aren't likely to publish the book you want to write, they will often make good suggestions about where you might submit your work.

journal article to book. Writing a book is a large commitment, which is best energized by your own deep interest in and your knowledge about your topic. (In this section, we are concerned with books that contribute to the professional literature of LIS, not with the various other kinds of fiction, nonfiction, poetry, children's books, etc. that librarians in fact often do write.)

The advice for finding a book publisher is the counterpart to the advice given earlier on finding a place to send your journal article. A good starting point is with the LIS publishers whose names you recognize and whose books you have read. Look at books you admire and note who published them. Draw up a list of books published on the subject you intend to write about and identify their publishers. Ask your colleagues who have already published for suggestions. Check out the websites of likely publishers to find out their publishing aims, scope, and guidelines, just as you would for a journal article.

A key element in selling a book to a publisher is writing a winning proposal. All publishers require a book proposal (even if they have asked you to write a book). Some publishers also want a sample chapter or two—check the requirements of the specific publisher you have chosen. Your proposal should minimally include the following elements: a clear, brief statement about what the book is about; a description of the intended audience; an analysis of what books have already been published on your topic (the competition); a description of the unique features your book offers and why your book will interest the intended audience; a statement about the approach you intend to take; and possibly something about the structure and organization of the book and your timeline for completing the project.

Publishers looking at proposals by first-time authors will want evidence that you can write, have something to say, and will finish the project. When you submit your proposal, you should also include a brief cover letter highlighting your qualifications to write the type of book you propose (e.g., previous publications, background experience that qualifies you to write about your topic).

In his book *First Have Something to Say: Writing for the Library Profession*, Walt Crawford (2003) provides wise advice on getting published. Here are some of his tips.

Walt Crawford's Suggestions for Writing a Book Proposal

Before writing a book proposal, ask yourself the following questions:

- What is this book about (in one sentence)?

- What makes it a book? Or should it just be a long article?
- Why is this book needed? How will the book serve the library field?
- What else is out there? What is the competition?
- Why are you the right writer? Will you do this alone?
- What's the schedule and length? Can you meet the schedule?

Crawford (2003: 84–87) advises that once you have answered these questions, you will have the material you need to write the proposal. Include the working title, a brief (no more than one paragraph) description, an outline, and answers to all of the listed questions.

9.16.2. Citation Form

To be fair to other authors, you must indicate sources from which you have quoted or borrowed. Correct and consistent citation form also increases the credibility of reports, articles, and any document in which you cite the work of others. Many classic manuals are available, both in print and online, for consultation on the correct form for references and bibliographies. If your editor does not specify a particular style, choose one that is appropriate to your purpose. At the very least, be consistent in the style you use.

We cite the work of others in order to give credit where credit is due. But a related purpose of providing citations is to help readers track down the work to examine it themselves. To serve this purpose, we use a standard format that helps the reader know what each element in the citation represents. For example, the requirement to follow the book title with (*place of publication: publisher name*) helps the reader find the exact book that was used, something that is particularly helpful with out-of-copyright books that may be published by several publishers. Accuracy is obviously important. Misspelling the author's name or getting wrong a journal's volume or issue number wastes the reader's time. Moreover, such errors seem to live forever in print or online indexes and in bibliographies, causing problems for years to come. Providing accurate and complete citations in a consistent manner makes an intellectual contribution to the record of what has been published and used.

The standards for citing electronic sources are not yet universal, but, as in the case of print sources, the most important thing to remember is to give information that is complete and accurate

---

A Quick Tip

Why Index?
We believe that a nonfiction book without an index is useless. Indexing is an intellectual endeavor that adds value to the text. Don't rely on the indexing capabilities offered in your word processing software; you will have to check every entry in any event. Because the index is created after the page proofs have been created, the paging will be different from the paging of your manuscript. Your publisher can recommend an indexer who will charge you at some rate—per indexed term or for the whole project. Alternatively, you can index your book yourself. Because you know the content better than anyone, you can make sure that the concepts (and not just the words) are represented in the index. For annotated lists of books on indexing see http://www.anindexer.com/about/book/bookindex.html.

A Quick Tip

Preparing Bibliographies
It's a good idea to review the how-to-do-it rules from time to time. For a quick overview, see the Reference and User Services Association's (2008) *Guidelines for the Preparation of a Bibliography*.

enough for someone else to retrieve it easily. Citations of electronic sources should also be consistent within any given bibliography or set of endnotes.

The issue of copyright of electronic sources is not entirely clear. If you are citing or quoting from a personal e-mail or including a lengthy quote from a website, you should not only provide the address of the source but also ask the original writer for permission, if only as a courtesy. Be sure to state the purpose for which you want to use the quote.

Basic Components of a Reference Citation

Looking at various manuals, you will see that they are quite consistent in defining the basic elements of citations. Often the only difference is the order of items and the punctuation. Here are the basics:

- **Elements for books:** Author or editor's last name, first name, date of publication, title of book (in italics), place, publisher. Different style manuals might indicate variations in terms of placement of the date (it can come at the end), placement of edition number (if there is more than one edition), the treatment of multiple authors, and how citations to chapters in books should be handled. Punctuation within citations can vary as well.
- **Elements for journal articles (or newsletters and other serials):** Author's last name, first name, title of article (in quotation marks), title of journal (in italics), volume and issue number of journal, paging. As with citations to books, the manuals have different options for placement of date (before paging), multiple authors, special issues, and so on.
- **Elements for citations to electronic sources:** If the electronic source is a book or a journal article, the elements remain the same as those listed above, with the addition of the URL and (if required) the date accessed. Citations to websites and other electronic sources should conform as much as possible to the pattern for print materials. Are you citing a page on a website? Then it's like a journal article. Are you citing a complete website? Then it's like a book. Place the URL at the end of the citation, with the date accessed if required. Guides to citing electronic sources are listed in the Annotated Bibliography (9.17).

9.17. Annotated Bibliography

Writing: General Texts

Blicq, Ron S. 2005. *Communicating at Work: Creating Messages That Get Results*. 4th ed. Toronto: Prentice Hall Canada. This comprehensive guide to written business communication contains excellent guidelines for writing many sorts of print and electronic documents. It also includes an extensive section of exercises for each chapter.

De Castro, Paola. 2009. *Librarians of Babel: A Toolkit for Effective Communication*. London: Chandos. This book includes brief chapters on writing journal articles, conference papers, books, reports, chapters, and leaflets. It also covers the use of illustrations and citing others.

Ellis, Richard. 2009. *Communication Skills: Stepladders to Success for the Professional*. Chicago: University of Chicago Press. This is an excellent compact guide. Chapters 13, 14, and 15 cover effective writing, the process of writing, and specific types of writing (including reports, letters, e-mailing, and writing for journals and the web).

Harty, Kevin J., ed. 2011. *Strategies for Business and Technical Writing*. 7th ed. Boston: Pearson/Longman. This anthology contains good advice on all types of work-related writing, including reports and proposals, résumés, good news and bad news letters, memos, and e-mail.

Kolin, Philip C. 2012. *Successful Writing at Work*. 3rd ed. Boston: Wadsworth/Cengage Learning. This popular textbook covers all aspects of work-related writing.

Lamb, Sandra E. 2011. *How to Write It: A Complete Guide to Everything You'll Ever Write*. 3rd ed. New York: Ten Speed Press/Random House. This guide covers all kinds of employment-related communications, with chapters on proposals and reports, inquiries, requests and responses, problems and resolutions, media relations, and electronic communication.

Nankivell, Clare, and Michael Shoolbred. 1995. *Presenting Information*. Library Training Guide. London: Library Association. This work examines writing skills and oral presentations in a library context.

Northey, Margot, and Joan McKibbin. 2011. *Impact: A Guide to Business Communication*. 8th ed. Toronto: Pearson Education Canada. This sensible, concise guide to business writing and speaking provides specific strategies for common business problems, such as bad news correspondence, informal and formal reports, and proposals.

Parker, Roger C. 2006. *Looking Good in Print: A Guide to Basic Design for Desktop Publishing*. 6th ed. Phoenix, AZ: Paraglyph Press. This helpful handbook includes evaluation checklists for preparation of all types of documents. Chapter 9 covers brochures and other sales materials, and Chapter 20 covers business communication, letterheads, business cards, and fax cover sheets. It provides lots of examples and a list of common design pitfalls. Includes a section on creating documents, newsletters, and forms for use on the web. See also Parker's website NewEntrepreneur.com for "Create the Perfect Business or Organization Newsletter" (2000) at http://www .newentrepreneur.com/Resources/Articles/12_Step_Newsletter/12_ step_newsletter.html.

Plotnik, Arthur. 2006. *The Elements of Expression: Putting Thoughts into Words*. New York: Barnes and Noble. Highly recommended and frequently reprinted, this text is written with wit and humor for people who care about language and want to write and speak effectively and expressively.

Rentz, Kathryn, Marie Flatley, and Paula Lentz. 2011. *Lesikar's Business Communication: Connecting in a Digital World*. 12th ed. New York: McGraw-Hill. This frequently revised text covers the main forms of business communication with several chapters on writing and many examples and checklists. Appendixes contain useful templates for letters, memos, and reports; a grading checklist for reports; and bibliographical style for electronic communication.

See also the Annotated Bibliography in Chapter 4.

Writing Digitally

Angell, David, and Brent Heslop. 1994. *The Elements of E-mail Style: Communicate Effectively via Electronic Mail*. Reading, MA: Addison-Wesley. The authors deal with e-mail etiquette, cultural awareness for international e-mail, structuring messages for impact, flame control, and adding punch through formatting. They also include warnings about when *not* to use e-mail.

Barr, Chris, and editors of Yahoo! 2010. *YAHOO! Style Guide: Writing, Editing and Creating Content for the Digital World*. New York: St. Martin's Griffin. This guide covers all aspects of editing and writing for websites. A related website provides additional and updated information: http://styleguide.yahoo.com/.

Canavor, Natalie. 2010. *The Truth about the New Rules of Business Writing*. Upper Saddle River, NJ: FT Press. This book is recommended for its advice on writing effectively using e-mail, chat, text messaging, blogs, e-newsletters, and the like.

Carroll, John. 2010. *Writing for Digital Media*. New York: Routledge. This useful textbook teaches how to write effectively for online audiences. It covers writing for all kinds of digital platforms, including websites and blogs, and has a companion website. Chapter 20 covers online business communication.

Fernandez, Peter. 2009. "Balancing Outreach and Privacy in Facebook: Five Guiding Decision Points." *Library Hi Tech News* 26, no. 3/4: 10–12. See also a response to this article by blogger A. Rivera on *The Gypsy Librarian* (blog), July 10, at http://gypsylibrarian.blogspot .ca/2009/07/article-note-on-libraries-deciding-to.html.

Fong, Jennifer. 2011. "7 Essential Steps for Writing Engaging Facebook Page Updates." *Jennifer Fong: Social Media Success Strategies for Direct Sellers* (blog), January 26. http://www.jenfongspeaks.com/7-essential -steps-for-writing-engaging-facebook-page-updates/. This is one of many blogs that provide tips for Facebook postings.

Freeman, John. 2009. *The Tyranny of E-mail: The Four Thousand-Year Journey to Your Inbox*. New York: Scribner. This text considers e-mail in the context of different technologies for correspondence.

Gaertner-Johnson, Lynn. 2010. "Tips for Efficient Instant Messaging at Work." Business Writing. Syntax Training. http://www. businesswritingblog.com/business_writing/2010/10/tips-for-efficient -instant-messaging-at-work-.html. The Syntax Training website is a great resource for improving your professional writing skills.

Gerolimos, Michalis. 2011. "Academic Libraries on Facebook: An Analysis of Users' Comments." *D-Lib Magazine* 17, no. 11/12 (November/December). http://www.dlib.org/dlib/november11/ gerolimos/11gerolimos.html. This article examines users' comments on Facebook pages of 20 American academic libraries.

Jacobson, Terra B. 2011. "Facebook as a Library Tool: Perceived vs. Actual Use." *College and Research Libraries* 72, no. 1: 79–90. http://crl .acrl.org/content/72/1/79.full.pdf. This article reports on findings of research comparing librarians' perceptions of use of Facebook pages with actual use at 12 colleges and universities of various sizes.

Landis, Cliff. 2010. *A Social Networking Primer for Librarians*. New York: Neal-Schuman. This is a good introduction to social networking.

Nielsen, Jakob. 2007. "Show Numbers as Numerals When Writing for Online Readers." *Alertbox* (blog). April 16. http://www.useit.com/ alertbox/writing-numbers.html. This work, based on eye-tracking research, makes various recommendations regarding use of numbers when writing for the web.

Quan-Haase, Anabel, Joseph Cothrel, and Barry Wellman. 2005. "Instant Messaging for Collaboration: A Case Study of a High-Tech Firm." *Journal of Computer-Mediated Communication* 10(4), article 13. http://jcmc.indiana.edu/vol10/issue4/quan-haase.html. This article illustrates how knowledge workers use IM.

Quan-Haase, Anabel, and Alyson Young. 2010. "Uses and Gratifications of Social Media: A Comparison of Facebook and Instant Messaging." *Bulletin of Science, Technology and Society* 30, no. 5: 350–361. This article focuses on how young people use Facebook and IM.

Redshaw, Kerry. 2003. "Web Writing: Writing for a New Medium." *KerryR. net*. http://www.kerryr.net/webwriting/index.htm. This excellent site provides guidelines on content, structure, metadata, and hypertext. It includes suggestions on writing, FAQs, repurposing print documents for the web, and grammar, punctuation, and word usage.

Shipley, David, and Will Schwalbe, 2007. "The Elements of Email Style." National Public Radio. April 10. http://www.npr.org/templates/story/story.php?storyId=9495170. This useful article is excerpted from their book *Send: The Essential Guide to Email for Office and Home* (New York: Knopf, 2007). This book is praised as an essential primer to help avoid the "bad things" that often happen when using e-mail.

Song, Yuwu. 2003. *Building Better Websites: A How-To-Do-It Manual for Librarians*. New York: Neal-Schuman. A step-by-step guide to building websites from scratch, this is also a good resource to use to improve existing websites.

Thimm, Caja. 2010. "Technically-Mediated Interpersonal Communication." In *APA Handbook of Interpersonal Communication*, edited by David Matsumoto, 57–76. Washington, DC: American Psychological Association. This is an insightful scholarly article.

See also the Annotated Bibliography in Chapter 4.

Writing Reports and Proposals

Blicq, Ron S., and Lisa A. Moretto. 2001. *Writing Reports to Get Results: Quick, Effective Results Using the Pyramid Method*. 3rd ed. New York: John Wiley for IEEE. This is an excellent guide to all kinds of reports (formal and semiformal) and proposals.

Carpenter, Julie. 2008. *Library Project Funding: A Guide to Planning and Writing Proposals*. New York: Neal-Schuman. This text is a practical guide to writing funding applications.

Hall, Mary, and Susan Howlett. 2003. *Getting Funded: A Complete Guide to Writing Grant Proposals*. 4th ed. Portland, OR: Portland State University Press. This guide provides a stepwise approach to proposal writing, with useful examples. See especially the "Proposal Development Checklist."

MacKellar, Pamela H. 2001. *Writing Successful Technology Grant Proposals: A LITA Guide*. New York: Neal-Schuman. In addition to how to write and submit grant proposals, this book covers planning and designing technology projects and finding specific sources and resources for technology grants.

Paxson, William C. 1985. *Write It Now! A Timesaving Guide to Writing Better*. Reading, MA: Addison-Wesley. Section 2, "How to Prepare Ten Typical Documents," discusses major reports, trip reports, and progress reports. The book provides very helpful model outlines, which we have drawn upon here for our own discussion of such reports.

Writing Policy, Procedures, and Instructions

Dobrin, David. 1985. "Do Not Grind Armadillo Armor in This Mill." *IEEE Transactions on Professional Communication* PC-28, 4 (December): 30–37. This much-cited article uses J. R. Searle's Speech Act theory as a basis for arguing that written instructions should respect the reader's common sense.

Hartley, James. 2005. "Designing Instructional and Informational Text." In *Handbook of Research for Educational Communications and Technology*, 2nd ed., edited by David H. Jonassen, 917–947. Mahwah, NJ: Lawrence Erlbaum. Also available at http://www.aect.org/edtech/34.pdf. An excellent consolidation of research, this chapter covers all aspects of presenting information in texts, including typographical considerations in designing text, navigating text (how to make it accessible), making text easier to understand, measuring text difficulty, and designing text for readers with special needs.

Hoffman, Frank W., and Richard J. Wood. 2005. *Library Collection Development Policies: Academic, Public and Special Libraries*. Lanham, MD: Scarecrow. Primarily a guide to writing collection development policies, this text is organized by the component parts of policies, with many examples. See also their 2007 companion volume on school library policies.

Kent, Duncan. 2006. *Writing Revisable Manuals: A Guidebook for Business and Government*. Vancouver, BC: Duncan Kent and Associates.

http://www.techcommunicators.com/emanuals/wrm/index.htm. This work is full of excellent information on preparing print and online manuals.

Larson, Jeanette, and Herman L. Totten. 2008. *The Public Library Policy Writer: A Guidebook with Model Policies on CD-ROM*. New York: Neal-Schuman. The authors discuss traditional and more recent policy topics. The CD-ROM includes model policies for more than 65 policy areas.

Nelson, Sandra, and June Garcia for the Public Library Association. 2003. *Creating Policies for Results: From Chaos to Clarity*. Chicago: ALA Editions. This text provides guidelines for evaluating existing policies and creating new ones.

Price, Jonathan, and Henry Korman. 1993. *How to Communicate Technical Information: A Handbook of Software and Hardware Documentation*. Redwood City, CA: Benjamin Cummings. This guidebook is still considered a good basic reference manual for writing technically. It is full of sensible advice for writing procedures, getting feedback, and testing.

Signs and Symbols

Beneicke, Alice, Jack Biesek, and Kelley Brandon. 2003. "Wayfinding and Signage in Library Design." Libris Design Project. http://www.librisdesign.org/docs/WayfindingSignage.pdf. The authors cover the principles of wayfinding, the design process, and working with a design consultant.

Dreyfuss, Henry, ed. 1984. *Symbol Sourcebook: An Authoritative Guide to International Graphic Symbols*. New York: Van Nostrand Reinhold. This classic graphic design resource by a renowned industrial designer is still a valued guide to standard international symbols.

LibrarySupportStaff.com. 2009. "Library Signs and Displays." http://librarysupportstaff.com/libsigns.html. This useful site provides links to a wide variety of resources (publications, guidelines, presentations, signage vendors, clipart, etc.). When accessed on January 4, 2013, the site was still undergoing revision; see http://librarysupportstaff.com/.

Modley, Rudolf, assisted by William R. Myers. 1990. *Handbook of Pictorial Symbols: 3,250 Examples from International Sources*. Magnolia, MA: Peter Smith. This large comprehensive dictionary of symbols was originally published in 1976 (New York: Dover).

Pollett, Dorothy, and Peter C. Haskell, eds. and comps. 1979. *Sign Systems for Libraries: Solving the Wayfinding Problem*. New York: Bowker. This provides a comprehensive introduction to sign systems.

White, Leah L. 2010. "Signage: Better None Than Bad." On My Mind. *American Libraries* 41, no. 9 (August): 23. See also the online discussion following this column at http://americanlibrariesmagazine .org/columns/my-mind/signage-better-none-bad.

Designing Newsletters, Publicity, and Promotion

American Library Association. 2004. *Communications Handbook for Libraries*. Chicago: American Library Association. http:// www.ala.org/ala/issuesadvocacy/advleg/advocacyuniversity/ advclearinghouse/commhandbook.pdf. This brief (39-page) handbook includes helpful advice on the written work needed for media communications (media advisories, news releases, public service announcements, etc.).

Arth, Marvin, Helen Ashmore, and Elaine Floyd. 1995. *The Newsletter Editor's Desk Book*. 4th rev. ed. Saint Louis, MO: Newsletter Resources. This text contains useful sections on headlines, formats, makeup, and production. It also includes guidelines for writing some basic kinds of stories: personnel items, meetings, speeches, reports, notices, and controversies.

Baker, Sharon L., and Karen Wallace. 2002. *The Responsive Public Library Collection: How to Develop It and Market It*. 2nd ed. Englewood, CO: Libraries Unlimited. See Chapter 10, "Marketing-Based Promotional Policies and Practices."

Bivins, Thomas. 2010. *Public Relations Writing: The Essentials of Style and Format*. 7th ed. New York: McGraw-Hill. This book covers everything you need to know about developing and writing public relations material in all areas of PR, including social media. The earlier title was *Handbook for Public Relations Writing*.

Blake, Barbara Radke, and Barbara L. Stein. 1992. *Creating Newsletters, Brochures, and Pamphlets: A How-To-Do-It Manual for School and Public Librarians*. New York: Neal-Schuman. This manual includes chapters on organization, design, graphics, and basic writing tips. Examples of forms and fliers are provided in the appendixes. Although these materials are now usually distributed electronically, the design principles remain the same.

Czarnecki, Al. 2011. "Newsletters—15 Tips on Editing and Writing Newsletters." Al Czarnecki Communications. http://www.topstory.ca/newsletters.html. This brief list of tips provides sound advice.

Gould, Mark, ed. 2009. *The Library PR Handbook*. Chicago: ALA Editions. An instruction manual designed to help maximize the impact of public awareness programs, it includes 14 essays by communication experts.

Groundwire.com. 2011. "Writing E-mail Newsletters: Best Practices." http://groundwire.org/resources/articles/writing-newsletters-best-practices. This work briefly explains eight things to consider when crafting an e-mail newsletter.

Heath, Robert L., and Timothy Coombs. 2005. *Today's Public Relations: An Introduction*. Thousand Oaks, CA: Sage. This text contains case studies and guidelines.

Karp, Rashelle S., ed. 2002. *Powerful Public Relations: A How-To Guide for Libraries*. 2nd ed. Chicago: ALA Editions. In addition to providing instructions for creating news releases, public service announcements, newsletters, brochures, and such, this edition succinctly covers how to create web-based PR strategies, develop multimedia promotion programs, and use desktop technology to create PR material.

Maxymuk, John. 1997. *Using Desktop Publishing to Create Newsletters, Handouts, and Web Pages: A How-To-Do-It Manual*. New York: Neal-Schuman. This is a step-by-step guide to creating desktop publications that read well and command attention.

Newsom, Doug, and Jim Haynes. 2010. *Public Relation Writing: Form and Style*. 9th ed. Belmont, CA: Wadsworth. This book covers all aspects of public relations writing in print and online.

Ohio Library Council. 2008. "Marketing the Library." http://www.olc.org/marketing/index.html. This training website is a good place to teach yourself about library promotion techniques. See especially the web marketing module.

Walters, Suzanne. 2004. *Library Marketing That Works*. New York: Neal-Schuman. Part II explores techniques librarians can use, including marketing using websites.

Wolfe, Lisa A. 2005. *Library Public Relations, Promotion, and Communications: A How-To-Do-It Manual*. 2nd ed. New York: Neal-Schuman. Wolfe discusses positioning the library and planning and evaluating PR campaigns. She includes strategies and methods for attracting media attention, using technology as a PR tool, and preparing print communications materials, with much good advice, lots of tips, and many examples and samples. The appendix contains public relations/communications plans for various types of libraries.

Writing Booklists and Annotations

Baker, Sharon L. 1993. "Book Lists: What We Know, What We Need to Know." *RQ* 33, no. 2: 177–180. To help readers choose books, Baker recommends that librarians learn to write informative and entertaining booklist annotations and provides several examples.

Chelton, Mary K. 1993. "Read Any Good Books Lately? Helping Patrons Find What They Want." *Library Journal* 118, no. 8 (May 1): 33–37. This article gives seven tips for writing readers' annotations.

Haines, Helen. 1935. "The Art of Annotation." In *Living with Books: The Art of Book Selection*, 125–144. New York: Columbia University Press. The chapter on annotation writing contains much wise advice that is still relevant. The entire book is a much-loved classic well worth revisiting.

Harner, James L. 2000. *On Compiling an Annotated Bibliography*. New York: Modern Language Association. Harner offers information on planning and organizing an annotated bibliography and covers how to evaluate works, compile entries, and write the annotations. Although focused on a literary bibliography of a single author, the procedures and techniques apply to selective and subject bibliographies (and booklists) in any discipline.

Saricks, Joyce G., and Nancy Brown. 2005. *Readers' Advisory Service in the Public Library*. 3rd ed. Chicago: American Library Association. See their advice on creating bookmarks and targeted annotated booklists.

Writing Reviews and Publishing Professionally

Alley, Brian, and Jennifer Cargill. 1986. *Librarian in Search of a Publisher*. Phoenix, AZ: Oryx Press. Although somewhat dated, this work still provides useful advice.

Bluh, Pamela, ed. 1997. "Special Section: So You Want to Be a Writer?" *Library Administration and Management* 11, no. 1 (Winter): 11–25. This work includes three articles that are still helpful: "Becoming a Published Author: Eight Simple Steps for Librarians" by Mary E. Jackson (pp. 11–13); "Steps Toward Writing a Sure Thing" by Gloriana St. Clair (pp. 15–16); and "From Book Idea to Contract" by Patricia Glass Schuman and Charles Harmon (pp. 19–25).

Crawford, Walt. 2003. *First Have Something to Say: Writing for the Library Profession*. Chicago: American Library Association. This book is full of good advice, anecdotes, and details of the publishing process, all delivered in an entertaining style.

DeCandido, GraceAnn Andreassi. 1998. "How to Write a Decent Book Review." http://www.well.com/user/ladyhawk/bookrevs.html. The author provides ten tips on writing a good book review.

Dew, Stephen H. 2008. "An Editor's Tips on Publishing in Library Literature." The University of North Carolina at Greensboro. http://libres.uncg.edu/ir/listing.aspx?id=334. In addition to reviewing publications that offer advice to aspiring writers, Dew provides a useful list of tips.

Gordon, Rachel Singer. 2004. *The Librarian's Guide to Writing for Publication*. Lanham, MD: Scarecrow Press. This book includes chapters on getting started, submitting your work, proposals, writing and editing, networking and collaboration, writing a book, marketing and promotion, the electronic environment, and more.

Hinchliffe, Lisa Janicke, and Jennifer Dorner, eds. 2006. *How to Get Published in LIS Journals: A Practical Guide*. Elsevier Library Connect Pamphlet #2. San Diego: Elsevier. http://libraryconnect.elsevier.com/sites/default/files/lcp0202.pdf. This pamphlet includes short articles by authors, editors, and journal publishers and provides a list of additional resources.

Labaree, Robert V. 2004. "Tips for Getting Published in Scholarly Journals." *College and Research Libraries News* 65, no 3: 137–139. This article offers practical advice.

Plotnik, Arthur. 1985. "Secrets of Writing for the Professional Literature without Losing Your Self-Esteem." In *Librarian/Author: A Practical Guide on How to Get Published*, edited by Betty-Carol Sellen, 79–90. New York: Neal-Schuman. See also other chapters in this book.

Putnam, Laurie L. 2009. "Professional Writing and Publishing: Resources for Librarians." *C&RL News* 70, no. 4. http://libguides.fiu.edu/content.php?pid=162808&sid=1657221. This helpful listing of resources is a good starting point for librarians who want to get into professional writing.

Warren, Thomas L. 1992. *Words into Type*. 4th ed. Englewood Cliffs, NJ: Prentice-Hall. This useful guide for writers, editors, and publishers also includes sections on preparing the manuscript, copyediting, grammar, and the choice of words.

Citing Print and Electronic Sources

The Chicago Manual of Style: The Essential Guide for Writers, Editors, and Publishers. 2010. 16th ed. Chicago: University of Chicago Press. This basic guide emphasizes bibliographic form but covers many other aspects of preparing manuscripts as well. It is also available online by subscription as *Chicago Manual of Style Online* at http://www .chicagomanualofstyle.org/home.html.

Hacker, Diana, and Barbara Fister. 2010. *Research and Documentation in the Electronic Age.* 5th ed. Boston: Bedford/St. Martin's. This text provides models of documentation for paper and electronic sources, including blogs, podcasts, and online videos, in various documentation styles, including MLA, APA, and Chicago. A related website is *Research and Documentation Online* at http://bcs .bedfordstmartins.com/resdoc5e/.

Hensley, Merinda Kaye. 2011. "Citation Management Software: Features and Futures." *Reference and User Services Quarterly* 50, no. 3: 204–208. This article examines four of the most popular citation managers from the perspectives of both the user and the librarian who must choose and teach software use. See also the *Wikipedia* article "Comparison of Reference Management Software" at http:// en.wikipedia.org/wiki/Comparison_of_reference_management_ software.

Li, Xia, and Nancy Crane. 2000. *Electronic Styles: A Handbook for Citing Electronic Information.* 2nd ed. Medford, NJ: Information Today. Reprint of the 1996 edition. This guide is based on both the APA and MLA styles.

Reference and User Services Association. 2008. *Guidelines for the Preparation of a Bibliography.* http://www.ala.org/rusa/resources/ guidelines/guidelinespreparation. These guidelines briefly cover purpose, scope, methodology, organization, annotations, and other aspects of preparing enumerative bibliographies.

See also the many guidelines for citing electronic sources available on the Internet. Use your browser to search for a single searchable unit such as "Chicago Manual" combined with [AND] "style" or "citation." Don't try "Chicago" and "style" or you'll end up with pizzas. University and college writing centers usually have helpful materials readily accessible on their websites. For example, see Purdue University's Online Writing Lab for a site that provides good suggestions and links to guidelines at http://owl.english.purdue.edu/owl/.

Videos

Library Video Network. 2008. *Wikis, Podcasts, and Blogs, Oh My!* 28 min.
11106W (DVD) or 11092W (VHS). http://www.lvn.org/store/index
.html. This program highlights blogs, wikis, podcasts, RSS feeds,
social networking websites, and video-sharing websites. It shows how
libraries use these technologies to reach out to new customers and
improve their services.

Training Others in Communication Skills

10

10.1. How to Use This Book for Training

Allen E. Ivey, who developed the microcounseling model for interpersonal skills training, identified four levels of skill mastery: (1) identification, where the learner can recognize both the skill and its effect; (2) basic mastery, where the learner is able to use the skill in a training setting; (3) active mastery, where the learner is able to use the skill on the job; and (4) teaching mastery, where the learner is able to teach the skill to others. This chapter is for those who have reached the fourth level and are beginning to train others. How you use this book as a training resource depends on the type of training program you are planning, the needs of participants, and your own level of expertise as a trainer.

What do we mean by the term *training*? Although the terms *training* and *education* are sometimes used interchangeably, *education* usually refers to a more broadly based process that includes general principles. *Training* is more narrowly focused on specific skills appropriate for a particular situation or a particular job. The teaching of communication skills is appropriate at all stages of the education/training spectrum: preprofessional education; continuing education; in-service training; conferences and workshops; coaching and mentoring; and informal learning opportunities that occur on the job. We cannot assume that most people naturally pick up these skills on their own without a systematic program any more than we would assume that most people naturally pick up how to play the piano. Library schools and paraprofessional programs should certainly teach communication skills as part of the preparation for library and information work. But because learning is a lifelong process, practitioners on the job will also benefit from opportunities to update or enhance their basic skills.

How do you know when people need training in communication skills? In the area of continuing education, the need for training in communication skills often presents itself as an interest in signing up for sessions on, for example, "Handling Problematic Situations" or "How to Present Your Budget." In libraries and information centers, training needs often arise as a result of changes, small or large—for example, the arrival of a new staff member or the introduction of a new telecommunications system. Sometimes the triggering event is a major organizational change such as the development of a new public service or the restructuring of the lines of authority. Sometimes in-service training programs are designed in response to problems such as complaints from the public or evidence of poor staff morale. In fact, the first clue to unmet training needs is usually a gap between expected and actual performance of an employee.

For all of these settings, the first step in training is to assess the need for training. Before launching into a training program to resolve some problem, you should ask: Is this problem really one that can be solved with training, or is it some other kind of problem altogether? If training is needed, you should strive to understand how the need arose, how your staff or students perceive the need, and how training can help meet it. Whenever possible, trainees should be fully involved in the needs assessment and planning process. The next steps in planning training are:

- identifying the focus: the skills that should be taught;
- selecting appropriate training methods;
- developing the training programs or formats; and
- developing the means of evaluating the success of the training.

These steps are not described in detail here because there are already many excellent publications on the training process (see the Annotated Bibliography, 10.11). The rest of this chapter focuses instead on how to use *Communicating Professionally* as a training resource.

If you are an experienced trainer looking for new approaches, exercises, or suggestions for reading, you will already know how best to incorporate the ideas in this book into your own programs. Others of you will be planning training sessions for the first time and may be looking for a recipe. We have no magic answers or guaranteed formats for training, but there's no reason why you can't begin simply by reading this book and using selected sections almost verbatim with your trainees. The one proviso is that you practice active listening and solicit feedback so that you can adapt these materials to the needs of your participants. Here are some other suggestions:

1. **Ask trainees to read and discuss specific sections.** The discussion might include sharing opinions about the applicability of specific skills to the job or ways for adapting these skills to unique situations that arise in your library. Use the tips provided in Chapter 7 on discussion techniques to generate a productive exchange of ideas and reactions. You can use this approach in the classroom or in regular staff meetings, when the last half hour could be reserved for discussion.

2. **Teach one microskill at a time.** For a more formal training program, select the microskills that will be most useful to your trainees. Follow the sequence that occurs within each section in Chapters 1–4 on individual skills: explanation of the skill and how it functions; recognition of examples; demonstration through exercises; and practice with suggestions for follow-up. Use the applications chapters (6–10) to provide examples and exercises.

3. **Begin with problem situations.** Often, it's more appropriate to begin with a discussion of the situation that has generated communication problems (e.g., conducting the reference interview, giving booktalks, or dealing with problematic situations) and then proceed to teaching single skills that will help trainees deal with these situations. Use Chapters 6–10 as an outline that you can expand by introducing individual skills from Chapters 1–4 at the appropriate points.

4. **Teach at the point of need.** Sometimes an impromptu training session can help to resolve an employee's communication accident. It takes only a few minutes to teach a skill such as acknowledgment by following the microskills principle: describe the skill and its function; give an example; model the skill; ask the

trainee to demonstrate it; and then ask the trainee to use it on the job and let you know what happened. (See also the following discussion of coaching.)

5. **Train for improved performance.** Individual training sessions can also be useful after performance evaluations. You may have used the DESC technique (see 3.13) to let the employee know that some of her communication skills need improvement, let's say attentiveness to library users. But people find it easier to accept requests for improvement if they have some concrete idea of how to fix the problem. Therefore, it may help the employee to work through the sections of this book on eye contact (1.2), active listening (2.2), or acknowledgment (3.2)—sections that provide manageable steps for changing the dysfunctional behavior.

6. **Use this book to heighten awareness.** Orientation of new employees provides another opportunity for individual or group training in communication skills. Some sections of this book—the reference interview, writing reports, and handling complaints—may be especially useful in sensitizing new employees to the range of situations that they will encounter on the job and in helping them understand that it's not only necessary but also possible to achieve high standards of personal performance. An important message for employees is that there are many ways to interact with others, some more effective than others, and that skills training gives them tools for choosing and using the more effective ways.

Coaching

For most of this chapter, we talk about training as if it were always provided to groups. However, sometimes individual coaching is a better option than providing group training. Coaching can be used when there is a new hire who needs to be brought up to speed or when a single individual shows the need for improvement in an area. Many of the suggestions for training provided in the rest of this chapter can be adapted for the one-to-one process of coaching.

Ruth Metz (2011: 2) defines coaching as "the purposeful and skillful effort by one individual to help another achieve specific performance goals." To coach, you need to observe and assess the other person's performance, provide specific feedback, offer instruction, and track improvements. In coaching, as in any other area of adult learning, the basic principles of fostering adult learning apply (see 10.2 on teaching adults). Here are some additional suggestions from Ruth Metz (2011: 22–23) for successful coaching:

- Be purposeful. "Purposefulness involves assessing a potential coaching situation and planning for the coaching interaction before launching into it . . . and tracking the [individual's] progress and evaluating the process."
- Pay full attention to the person you are coaching.
- Observe body language—silence, posture, and facial expression are indicators of the frame of mind and receptivity of the person being coached.

10.2. Teaching Adults

Adults learn differently from the way in which children learn. Therefore, staff trainers and college faculty should know something about andragogy, the study of how adults learn (see Knowles, Holton, and Swanson, 2011). Andragogy takes into account the learner's maturity and how life experience affects learning patterns. Adults learn best when they are involved in planning, implementing, and evaluating their own learning experiences. Bringing a wealth of complex experiences, attitudes, and beliefs to the learning process, adults can readily see when training programs are irrelevant or inappropriate to their needs. They want to be able to apply what they have learned immediately. Learners and learning situations differ from one to another, with variations introduced by differences in individual cognitive style and in the subject matter being learned (Laird, 2003: 142–143). However, certain core assumptions of andragogy and adult learning priorities generally apply:

1. Adults learn best when the learning environment encourages the learner's active participation and when the learner herself understands the need for the new learning. Adults need to know *why* they need to learn it, *what* they need to learn, *how* they can learn it, and what the payoff will be.

> **Did You Know?** ?
>
> Hargie (2006: 555) identifies three distinct phases of communication skills training: (1) preparation or identifying the skills needed, (2) implementation, and (3) evaluation. In the implementation phase, trainees identify and label communication skills through readings, seminars, videos, and the like, followed by practice and feedback of recorded practice. The evaluation phase involves ascertaining the attitude of the trainees to the program and charting changes in the behavior of trainees. Trainers should also evaluate their programs informally, seeking feedback from trainees, colleagues, and users. This feedback can guide future training approaches.

2. Their readiness for learning is life related. When adults feel a need to cope with a life situation or perform a task more effectively, they are motivated to learn.

3. Adults learn best when the learning environment is collaborative, problem centered, and contextual and puts the emphasis on experiential activities. Environments that are content centered and based on authority are not as good at fostering learning.

4. Most adults feel uncomfortable (and therefore not receptive to learning) when placed in situations where they have little control or where they feel challenged because of their lack of knowledge.

5. Adults learn best when the learning environment encourages them to introduce past experiences as a way of reexamining and reflecting on that experience. Adults' past experiences can be converted into new knowledge and understanding, reframed within appropriate learning structures.

6. Planning and evaluation are more conducive to learning when they are done collaboratively between learner and instructor. (Adapted from Laird, 2003: 139, 143–144; Jurow, 2001: 7)

10.3. Planning the Training Program

Training people in communication skills involves two basic activities common to any training program: (1) setting objectives and (2) deciding on the appropriate format. The following section also includes planning suggestions and tips for trainers.

Setting Training Objectives

To ensure that your communication skills training program is systematic and not hit-or-miss, you will want to set objectives that address the areas where improvement is desired. Your objectives should be:

- concrete,
- realistic,
- time bound, and
- measurable.

A Quick Tip 🕐

Accommodate Different Learning Styles

Trainers tend to assume that everyone learns the same way they do. They run training sessions that suit their own preferred learning style. Hence a hands-on experiential learner will include lots of practical activities but may spend too little time on theory and leave little time for reflection. Be aware of your own preferred learning style and take conscious steps to meet the differing learning needs of the whole spectrum of learners (Allan, 2003: 35).

These are examples of manageable program objectives for communication skills training:

> To conduct a two-hour orientation session for each new staff member in the circulation department within that person's first month of service
>
> To provide each permanent staff member on the information desk with three hours of continuing education annually
>
> To conduct for interested staff members a session on using Facebook for library purposes by October 31

Then, for each program, write specific learning objectives. For example:

> By the end of this program on effective questioning, participants will be able to:
>
> 1. Recognize the difference between an open and closed question.
>
> 2. Demonstrate use of open questions in a role-played interview.
>
> 3. Use open questions on the job.
>
> 4. Teach another staff member how to use open questions.

For this example, you could measure the extent to which the objectives were met through an exercise, through observation, or through self-report. Although objectives should be measurable, it is more important for them to be specific and realistic.

Formats for Training

Training should vary in format according to the needs of participants and according to program objectives. Even within one session you can use several training formats. You might want to start with a short lecture to explain a skill, go on to role-playing or a demonstration, follow with a group discussion, and finally recommend some reading for independent study. Such variation in format provides a change of pace for participants and is compatible with training objectives. The lecture on its own doesn't usually work very well for teaching people new communication skills. Consider alternatives to the lecture. For example:

- Assigned readings
- Minilectures
- Case studies
- Demonstrations, modeling
- Field trips combined with structured observation
- Group exercises such as fishbowls, buzz groups, and games
- Panel discussions
- Role-plays
- Simulation exercises
- Small group discussions
- Web-based instruction

It is not easy for managers to find time or money for staff training. Much time must be spent on technical training, with the result that much staff training (including and maybe even especially communication skills training) has been left to supervisors to do one-to-one or simply doesn't get done at all. However, if it is really impossible to bring people together face-to-face, you can use various technologies to bring people together virtually (7.6). Online discussion sites are good venues for exchanging tips and ideas. Individuals and groups can be brought together in tele- or videoconferences or using web conferencing software. At the very least, you can have a good manual, use a buddy/mentor system, incorporate discussion into performance appraisal, and give people time to read and practice skills with other staff.

Chapter 8 provides an overview of principles and procedures that are basic to all presentations, including training programs. Use handouts, demonstrations, and presentation slides of high quality. Materials should not look homemade (see 8.3.6). Prepare the materials well in advance. When you are the trainer, it is all the more important to demonstrate your skill at program planning and implementation, because trainees are learning from your performance, good or bad.

Some Suggestions for Communication Skills Training

- Make sure trainees have an opportunity to help set the goals for the training session.
- Elicit from trainees real examples of the situation that the workshop is about (e.g., angry users making a complaint). This input of real examples works well as an icebreaker at the beginning of the training session.

- Make use of the experience within the group. Instead of telling people things they already know, give them the chance to tell each other what they know and share solutions that worked for them.

- Prepare written scripts that illustrate two different ways of handling a situation: (1) the typical transaction when the skill (e.g., using open questions [3.4] or the appropriate use of DESC [3.13]) is *not* used; and (2) the same situation when the skills are used effectively. The scripts can be used for modeling skills in training scenarios.

- Give trainees a chance to practice the skill in the workshop. Break the participants into small groups of two or three so that everyone gets a chance.

- Provide printed handouts that can be taken back to the job and used to practice new skills.

- Form trainee support groups to encourage integration of the new skills into the daily routine.

- Refresh the communication skills of previously trained employees by asking them to coach new trainees on the job. (From Race and Smith, 1996: 77; Todaro and Smith, 2006: 47–57; Wehmeyer, 2001: 103)

10.4. Using the Microskills Training Model

The microskills hierarchy, illustrated in Chapter 5, consists of a series of single skills that are progressively more complex, beginning with the basic listening sequence and moving toward the most difficult part of training and learning: skill integration. At the top of the hierarchy is the task of choosing one's own personal style and theory within which to use the microskills approach. With the exception of these two final stages, a cardinal rule in microteaching is to teach one skill at a time. Although good and bad examples of other skills may occur during the training session, focus only on the specific skill being taught.

For each of these single skills, the basic microskills teaching model involves five steps: definition, recognition, reading, practice, and feedback. You have probably noticed that, for the most part, Chapters 1–4 of this book use these same five steps in the presentation of the speaking and writing skills needed in library settings.

Did You Know? ?

Trainees can learn to change their behavior through microskills training. In a controlled experiment, prospective librarians significantly improved their verbal and nonverbal communication skills. Nonverbal skills were learned more easily than verbal skills (Jennerich and Jennerich, 1997).

Here are the five steps that you can use in your own training sessions for teaching microskills:

1. **Warm-up and definition of the skill.** Discuss the value of the skill with examples of library situations in which it could be used, define the skill, and explain how it functions.

2. **Recognition: examples and modeling.** Ivey recommends video, audio, or live demonstrations of the skill. The modeling might involve two trainers role-playing the skill. Alternatively, you could ask two volunteers to read the transcript of a conversation between a librarian and a user. Then ask the other trainees to identify the skill modeled and discuss the effect of its use within the context of the transaction. Another suggestion is to make a pair of recordings or transcripts in which the first example is an exaggerated model of the failure to use the skill well and the second example involves a clearly effective use of the skill. Model only one skill at a time.

3. **Reading.** Ask trainees to read the relevant sections in this book or some other reading that summarizes and provides examples of the skill. Include the citations for a few suggested readings on handouts for participants. Make the readings themselves available electronically to make it easy for participants to read them.

4. **Practice.** The key component in microskills training is practice—the "do" part of "Learn, do, and teach." Trainees should be given an opportunity to demonstrate use of the skill in the training session through supervised exercises or role-plays. (The acknowledgment exercise in 3.2 is a good example of role-plays used to provide supervised practice.)

5. **Self-assessment, feedback, and generalization.** Using the tips for practice (5.7), encourage trainees to practice one skill outside the training session, preferably on the job. Trainees can demonstrate mastery through practice in teaching the skill to someone else. Group discussion or exercises will help the trainee assess the level to which the skill has been mastered. Feedback of

---

Exercise 🔧

Introducing Yourself
Instead of introducing yourself at the beginning of the training session, get participants to interview you about yourself, using only open questions. Warn them in advance that you'll answer "yes" or "no" to closed questions. This is a guaranteed high-interest exercise.

what worked and what didn't will help you assess the need for further training.

10.5. Modeling Good Behavior

One way in which trainees learn communication skills is by watching the trainer's behavior and consciously or unconsciously imitating it. Therefore, the trainer must model the effective use of communication skills in a consistent, intentional, and spontaneous way. Trainees notice how the trainer talks, moves, looks, and behaves in informal contacts as well as in formal training sessions. When there is a discrepancy between the way the trainer communicates and the skills that are taught ("Do as I say, not as I do"), a credibility gap occurs. This incongruity reduces the trainees' confidence in the training sessions and affects their ability to integrate the skills into their own behavior.

Quick Tips for Modeling Good Behavior

- **Examine your own communication behavior.** How well are you able to integrate the skills that you are teaching into your communication with trainees? When you're having lunch with trainees, do you practice the communication behavior that you have been preaching? How often do you use open questions in small talk instead of making assumptions?

- **Consciously practice your skills.** Focus especially on those skills that are hardest or newest for you. You can overcome your own awkwardness by making this explicit: "Now I'm going to ask an open question!" Don't be afraid of communication accidents, but do let trainees see your efforts to repair them: "I just interrupted you, which means I wasn't listening—exactly what I said not to do—so tell me again."

- **Ask your colleagues for feedback.** Other trainers can practice giving feedback by telling you how you're doing. Make sure you get positive feedback as well as negative feedback (see 3.14 and 3.15).

> **Did You Know?** ?
>
> Trainers should think of themselves as performers, on stage. Webb and Powis (2009: 34) say that staff trainers in libraries don't need to become actors, but they do need to understand "voice control, movement, and how the learners perceive the teacher."

Checklist for Trainers: Modeling Nonverbal Skills

❑ What is my posture saying to trainees? Am I showing interest and encouragement? Or am I showing boredom or irritation? Do my crossed arms indicate resistance to what trainees are telling me? Am I controlling my nervous gestures?

❑ What are my good (or bad) speech habits? Can people hear me? Am I speaking slowly (or quickly) enough? When I give instructions, do I make my voice stronger and lean forward?

❑ Do I periodically make eye contact with everyone in my group? How often do I catch myself talking to the floor or the screen?

❑ Am I considering cultural differences between my trainees and me and taking these differences into account?

Checklist for Trainers: Modeling Speaking Skills

❑ How often am I using open questions to encourage trainees to talk? For example, "What problems do you think you might have in using this skill?" NOT, "Do you think you might have problems with this?"

❑ When I want to structure discussion around situations, how often am I using sense-making questions? For example, "Tell me what happened when you practiced this skill." NOT, "Did you have trouble practicing this skill?"

❑ How well am I giving instructions? Do I give explicit instructions and check to make sure they're understood? For example, "Turn to the person beside you and describe one recent situation in which you had trouble understanding a user. Now, just so the exercise is clear, tell me what you are going to do." NOT, "In pairs, discuss typical problems of this type."

❑ What communication accidents am I having? How often do I interrupt trainees unnecessarily? What assumptions am I making about trainees? What am I doing (or not doing) when trainees misunderstand something?

❑ To what extent do I reflect content or paraphrase trainees' remarks? When a trainee says, "I wrote a report that evaluated the success of our chat reference service," am I showing my attentiveness by repeating some of these words?

❑ How accurately am I reflecting feeling? When a trainee says, "I don't think I'm ever going to be able to do this," how do I respond? "You feel it's going to be hard to change your behavior" or "Nonsense, everyone can learn this"?

❑ How well do I model feedback? Am I asking for feedback regularly? Am I listening actively to verbal and nonverbal feedback? How helpful is the feedback I'm getting? What am I doing about it?

Checklist for Trainers: Modeling Writing Skills

❑ When do I communicate with my trainees in writing? Is the written communication necessary? Would personal contact be more effective? Do I use a written description of the training program to supplement the personal contact?

❑ How effective are my training materials—handouts, reading lists, and presentation slides? Am I trying to cram too much on one page or one screen? Is the font easy to read? Are key concepts highlighted? Can people see my visuals from every seat in the room, not just from the front row?

❑ When I send an e-mail message to trainees, is it clear? Brief? Is it written in a style appropriate to the situation and the reader? Can the readers tell from the first sentence what the memo has to do with them?

❑ How good are my written instructions? Are they clear? Are the sentences short and simple? Are the instructions put in a logical order and numbered?

❑ What spelling, grammar, or punctuation errors do I need to guard against? Am I proofreading my written material (including electronic postings) carefully?

10.6. Using Audio- and Videorecordings for Training

An essential feature of microskills training is the opportunity for trainees to observe and evaluate their own behavior. In order to provide a record of this behavior that is both objective (not just based on self-reports) and durable (so that the trainee can use it at leisure), it is useful to make audio- and/or videorecordings of trainees role-playing a skill or reacting to a simulated situation. Using a recording to provide feedback to trainees on their use of skills can be helpful for training in a variety of areas. Here are some scenarios in which trainees could

Did You Know? ?

Video feedback plus practice is the most effective combination of training techniques for enhancing durability of communication skills (Mills and Pace, 1989: 159-176).

role-play the interaction and record it: the use of acknowledgment (3.2) and open questions (3.4) in the reference interview; providing feedback (3.14); the use of DESC (3.13) to change behavior; and the use of reflection of feeling (3.9) when dealing with an angry user. Remember that the focus should be on one skill at a time. When the trainee has completed the recording to his satisfaction, he reviews it himself. He then selects a portion of the recording to show to the group and to get feedback (3.15) from other trainees on the use of the skill.

Why Provide Video Feedback?

Audiorecording is good, but videorecording is even better as a tool for communication skills training, especially those nonverbal skills discussed in Chapter 1. Dutch researchers Fukkink, Trienekens, and Kramer (2011: 46) examined 33 experimental studies of the effects of video feedback on the interaction skills of professionals in a range of contact professions in many countries. Their meta-analysis concluded that the video feedback method is an effective way to "improve key interaction skills among participants, from rank beginners to experienced professionals" (p. 57). One caveat: nonverbal skills "seem more difficult to influence" than verbal skills (p. 56). The best outcomes occurred when feedback sessions were accompanied by a standard evaluation form that helped participants focus on the desired target behavior when they reviewed the video. The authors suggested that "such a form structures the observation, thereby focusing the participants' attention on the aspects of their own behavior that are central to the program" (p. 56). Through this finding, the meta-analysis lends weight to the microtraining approach of focusing on one skill at a time.

Making the Recording

The exercise of making an audio- or videorecording should be productive and not endanger the trainee's self-esteem and motivation. You can avoid some common pitfalls by following these basic procedures:

- Respect the privacy and integrity of the trainee.
- Explain the purpose and value of recording clearly to each individual trainee and to the library administration. State the ways in which the recording will and will *not* be used.

A Quick Tip 🕐

First Learn the Technology
Teach trainees prerecording procedures. Get them to test the volume and clarity by recording and playing back an identification statement such as, "This is the role-play for XPL training program recorded on October 24, 2013." When trainees are familiar with the recording equipment before recording, the recording session itself is less likely to suffer from technical glitches, and the trainee will be able to focus on communication, not on the technology. Label the recording to identify the content and date.

Trainees are sometimes worried that the recordings could wind up as evidence for performance appraisal.

- Recording must be voluntary. No one should be forced to participate. Those not wanting to be recorded should not be required to give a reason and should not be treated differently in any way. Provide an alternative activity.

- Instruct trainees who are recording their interviews with others—friends, family, or other trainees—always to ask for permission. The simple question "Do you mind if I record this?" or "Are you willing to be recorded?" is sufficient but must always be asked.

- Never record real library users or staff members without written permission from the library administration and formal consent, preferably written, from those who are to be recorded.

- Tell trainees that they have the right to delete all or part of their recordings at any time if they feel uncomfortable with the interaction.

- Leave the trainee in control. Assure her that she controls the playing of the recording and selecting the portions to be played.

- State clearly who owns the recording and what will happen to it—a good guideline is to give ownership to the person recorded and to arrange to delete all recordings at the end of the training program. Trainees must be able to feel safe that their digital recording won't end up on YouTube or on any in-house or external websites.

The technical aspects of making the recording can either enhance or distract from the learning experience. Ensure effective technical production. If possible, enlist the aid of a technician who is not part of the training program. If you want your trainees to learn how to operate the equipment, separate the two goals of learning communication skills and learning how to operate equipment. Provide a foolproof instruction sheet that can be consulted at the time of making the recording. Finally, make sure trainees have a comfortable, quiet, and private room for the recording session.

Working with Recordings

Trainees are often anxious about working with their own recordings, and they almost always need guidance in using them effectively to improve their performance. Here are some suggestions:

- Explain the purpose of recording before the recordings are made. Restate the purpose, and then specify the immediate use of the recordings.

    Example: Your recording is your own property. We're going to ask you to listen to/watch it privately and then fill out a checklist (or whatever the task is). Bring the recording with you to the next session, and we will ask for volunteers to share them with the group; if you don't want others to hear your recording, that's okay.

- Tell trainees what to expect when they first see or hear themselves in a recording. Many have already seen and heard themselves, but some have not. Trainees are often initially alarmed by their appearance or the sound of their voice, and the trainer must take time to overcome this reaction.

    Example: When you first listen to yourself, you might think, "Hey, that can't be me. How awful! I sound weird (childish, gruff)." This is a normal reaction. Just listen to the recording all the way through, and then play it again. The second time around, you'll start hearing or seeing the things you do well, and you'll be able to analyze your verbal and nonverbal behavior more objectively. So even if you're horrified at first, promise that you'll play it at least one more time. The more you play it, the more benefit you will get from it.

- In individual or group feedback, focus on what the trainees are doing well, not on what they're doing poorly or not doing. Reinforce the positive. The negative is all too apparent to the trainee and to others. When a recording is made as an exercise in a particular skill, comment only on that skill, not on other skills or behaviors no matter how good, interesting, or unusual they are. Use closure (3.11) to discourage discussion that doesn't focus on the particular exercise.

- Focus on behavioral units, not on personality or on general impressions. Help participants look for the smallest, most concrete evidence of skills. Model good feedback behavior (3.14), and teach the trainees how to give good feedback to each other.

Tips for Discussing Behavior on the Recording

Say: What helpful questions did the librarian ask? What questions did not seem to help? What did the user do or say that communicates his feelings about the service?
Not: How would you rate that interview?

Say: She had no eye contact with the user and looked down at her notebook while the user was speaking.
Not: She doesn't look interested.

Say: He asked four open questions.
Not: He found out what the user wanted to know immediately.

Say: When the user started to explain why he was really mad about the fines notice, the librarian cut him off and started to explain library policy.
Not: The librarian's listening skills need work.

Say: What could you have done to get more information?
Not: You shouldn't have asked a closed question there.

Reducing Anxiety

Some trainees are visibly anxious about their performance as seen or heard on a recording. Even those who seem quite confident and motivated to learn may be inwardly anxious. Do some general discussion and problem solving, as the need occurs. Encourage trainees to express their concerns, no matter how trivial. Ask, "What is your worst fear about recording this role-playing exercise/interview/presentation?" Then listen, and take anxieties seriously. Don't say, "Oh, nonsense, you'll love it. It will be a breeze." Because recording involves risk taking on the part of the trainees and because the process is somewhat intrusive, you need to be especially careful. Build trust by focusing on positive, not negative, performance. Here are some things you can say:

1. We'd like you to try to record yourself because it's a proven training technique and we know you will learn something from it. But if you don't want to do it, you don't have to. And you don't even have to give a reason.
2. Listening to/viewing yourself for the first time is always a shock. Promise to listen/view at least twice.
3. The technical quality of this recording isn't important. This isn't the *Oprah Winfrey Show*. What is important is what you can see/hear about yourself and your use of communication skills.
4. This is your recording. You get to say how we can use it. If you want to erase/delete some or all of it, you can.
5. If you think the recording didn't work out, do it again.
6. Take a dry run through your interview to make sure the equipment is working and you're not distracted by it.
7. Sometimes we can learn more from looking at mistakes than by looking at a perfectly executed presentation.
8. What you say inside this room is confidential. I want to make this a safe place for you to practice and hope you will do the same.

10.7. Technology-Enhanced Training

A wide range of technologies are available to be used for training, including videos, tele- and videoconferences, virtual discussion sites, podcasting, and virtual conferencing sites. Web-based training is an attractive option when it's inconvenient or impossible to get everyone together at one time and in one place. The question is, can online instruction be used effectively for communication skills training? The answer is yes. It has been demonstrated in study after study that learning outcomes in many different subject areas can be as good in virtual environments as in face-to-face environments. The key is to design the online instruction properly in a way that takes into account the bias

---

A Quick Tip

Planning Webinars
Griffiths and Peters (2009) advise, "When determining whether a webinar [web seminar] is the best medium for your needs, consider your audience, the subject matter, and the time you'll need to cover your topic." Webinars should be shorter than face-to-face training sessions—two hours maximum but one hour is more common. Break the curriculum into modules, and teach one skill at a time. Encourage trainees to practice the skill before the next session.

of the medium used. In programs delivered online, people can learn selected skills such as those that support assertiveness, interviewing, small group interaction, and writing. See 7.6 on various technologies that enable group interaction.

You need to find ways to incorporate into the online training the essential components of learning a new communication skill: having the skill defined, reading about the skill, seeing it modeled, practicing it oneself, and getting feedback.

Ways must be found to develop participants' sense of shared knowledge and social connectivity in both synchronous and asynchronous environments. The *synchronous* environment, in which participants are all connected at the same time, is a virtual classroom that can be used for small group training. More convenient for some learners, an *asynchronous* environment allows participants to participate and contribute to discussion at times that suit their schedule. Web-based training may be either synchronous or asynchronous and may be used flexibly along with face-to-face training sessions. Some libraries use social software to advantage. Coleman, Theiss-White, and Fritch (2011: 40) describe using a spectrum of social software applications to enhance communication, to make it easier for staff to find important information, and—the relevant point in this chapter—to deliver training.

> ### A Quick Tip 🕐
>
> **Using Training Videos**
> If you're not ready to make training videos yourself, you might incorporate into your training program portions of recorded training workshops and seminars previously presented at your library or elsewhere. See the video sources listed in Where to Get Help (10.10) and the titles listed at the end of the Annotated Bibliography (10.11). A Google search under "using videos for interpersonal skills training of library staff" leads to many nonprofit and commercial sources of relevant training videos.

10.8. When Trainees Are Resistant

If everyone in your training group is enthusiastic, open, and happy to be there, you are unusually lucky. This ideal scenario hardly ever happens. People are often required to go to training sessions against their own desires. It may turn out that the training session is being held on a day when they'd rather be doing something else. Some people are skeptical about the effectiveness of any kind of training or think their own communication skills are already superb. In a required credit course on communication skills, for example, there are usually some students who are reluctant or even openly hostile.

These are some typical comments from trainees with misgivings:

> This will never work. We're far too busy to smile at everybody. You can't learn these skills. You're either born a good
> communicator or you're not.

I feel silly doing this stuff. If I go "Uh-huh" or "You seem
  frustrated," people will really wonder about me.
Aren't you trying to change people's personalities by teaching
  these skills?
I know all this. I took psychology.
I have been doing all these things for years anyway.
Are we librarians or social workers?

Be prepared to deal with this resistance. Here are some suggestions:

- Consider the extent to which these remarks are expressions
  of real concerns. If staff are indeed overworked in
  unsatisfactory conditions, smiling at every user can't be a
  priority and may indeed seem ridiculous, even to the user.
- Acknowledge the legitimacy of trainees' comments. Then
  ask for a chance to provide a different perspective. For
  example, "You're right. Some people seem to be naturally
  good communicators. But we have pretty good evidence
  that the rest of us can improve our skills, so could you
  reserve your judgment until the end of the session? Let's see
  what we can do here."
- Show that you have attended to their anxieties by reflecting
  feelings: "Many people feel awkward using this skill for the
  first time" or "I understand your concern that these skills
  could be manipulative."
- Handle the "know-it-all" according to the procedures
  outlined in 7.7.2. Acknowledge that this person may have
  been a perfect communicator for years, but suggest that
  everyone focus on the new skills or ideas rather than on
  what they already know. Asking the know-it-all to share his
  or her expertise with the group sometimes works. But it can
  backfire when the know-it-all is also a monopolizer.
- The "librarian/social worker" argument appears in every
  training session sooner or later. An answer along these
  lines seems to satisfy concerns: "It's true that social
  workers get training in basic communication skills to do
  their jobs as counselors. But other helping professions
  need some of these same skills, such as listening accurately
  and asking productive questions. That doesn't make us all
  into social workers. The skills are much the same, but the
  applications are different. We're not trained as counselors

---

Exercise

How Would You Handle This?
Unexpected things can happen in
training sessions. Consider how you
might deal with these situations:

1. Two participants arrive ten
   minutes late.
2. Two participants disagree loudly
   and start an emotional side
   conversation.
3. The session has an hour to run
   and one participant stands up and
   says, "This is dumb, I'm leaving"
   and storms out.

or therapists, and nobody is suggesting that we perform those functions."

Don't ignore resistance. Failure to deal with it promptly will make the group less productive. With a group of people who know each other fairly well and have come to trust you as a leader, you may be able to deal with the problem together by using the skill of confrontation.

When trainees become hostile in a training session, Ivey advises responding without defensiveness—"That's an interesting point"—and not attempting to persuade or argue but looking away from the resistant trainee toward the rest of the group. Do not make eye contact with persistent critics. Instead, you might invite the critic to discuss the problem with you privately after the session.

Group anxieties and resistance are reduced as you, the trainer, develop a reputation for fairness, nonjudgmental behavior, and what psychologists call unconditional positive regard. This means that you like your trainees anyway, no matter what they do or don't do. If you don't like and respect your trainees, don't train. Outside the group, never discuss a trainee's performance with other trainees, their supervisors, or anyone else.

10.9. Evaluation and Follow-Up

When we first began to give our workshops on interview skills, the director of a large public library asked us: "How do we know that our staff have learned anything from your workshop?" At that time, we were using a brief evaluation form that asked participants to rate the workshop as excellent, good, fair, or poor on two dimensions: content and presentation. We pointed out that the workshop had been highly rated. "That's all very well," said the director, "but we still don't know if they learned anything or if they're doing a better job as a result of the workshop." Of course he was absolutely right. From an administrative viewpoint, performance changes as a result of training are a prime concern.

10.9.1. Evaluation

It is important to develop practical methods of evaluating the outcome of training for library workers. There are several good guides

---

Did You Know? ?

If your evaluation shows that the training program has had little or no impact on trainees, you need to do another evaluation. Evaluate the program itself. Consider such questions as these (Allan, 2003: 207–208): Did the right people come? Were the objectives clear? Was the training session structured to help trainees achieve the objectives? Was there a suitable balance between theory, reflection, and practice? Was there enough variety in the format to keep people engaged and awake? Were the written materials/handouts clearly written, useful, and closely related to the skills being taught?

available, and we refer you directly to these for detailed accounts of evaluation methods and tools. Some basic ideas are summarized here.

What's the difference between measurement and evaluation? Measurement is the process of gathering data. Evaluation is the process of making judgments about those data. It's not necessary to measure in order to evaluate, but measurement provides concrete evidence (usually in the form of numbers) to reduce disagreement about the disinterestedness of the judgments and to enable pre-training and post-training comparisons (see Laird, 2003: 235).

What do you want to measure or evaluate? Knowledge? Skills? Native ability? Job performance? Attitudes? Beliefs? Are you measuring change resulting from the training, or are you assessing the extent to which training objectives have been met? Be clear about your goal. A trainee who fills out a form and says she is highly satisfied with a workshop may or may not have changed in any fundamental respect. Kirkpatrick (1994) describes four different levels of measurement:

1. Measuring reactions: the participants' immediate response—what they think or feel about the training immediately afterward
2. Measuring learning: how much the training participants increased their skill and knowledge
3. Measuring behavior: on-the-job behavior of the trainees after the training program as compared to their behavior before the program
4. Measuring the impact of training on the organization

Level 1 and possibly 2 can be measured during or just after the training session. Levels 3 and 4 require pre-training data as well post-training data and need to be evaluated over time. See Massis (2004: 55) and Williamson (1990: 228) for further discussion.

What are the methods of measuring? Depending on what you want to evaluate, there are usually two basic methods of measuring: observation and questioning. Direct observation techniques include activity sampling and watching a trainee's performance at specified times. Indirect observation techniques include self-reports, usually through a diary kept by the trainee or through a record of events related to the employee's behavior, such as the number of complaints about an employee or the number of revisions required in the employee's written work. Questioning includes questionnaires completed by the trainee and interviews either with the trainee or with people who observe the trainee's behavior, including library users. Numerous sample questionnaires, logs, and interview schedules are reproduced in the books listed at the end of this chapter.

Why evaluate? Evaluation benefits the trainer, the trainee, and, in the case of in-service training, the library administration. Evaluation helps to place in context the training program as a long-term rather than a one-off or hit-or-miss project. For a successful evaluation, it is important for the trainees to have a full understanding of the reasons for evaluation. In the case of in-house training programs, trainees can be invited to participate in designing and implementing the evaluation process.

The **Sample Workshop Evaluation Form** is designed to be filled out and handed in by participants at the end of the training session itself, a method that results in a high completion rate. You will note that this instrument measures what Kirkpatrick calls level 1—trainee's reactions (see earlier in the discussion on what you want to measure).

In the **Sample Workshop Evaluation Form**, the question about length of employment provides data that can be used to detect differences in reactions between new and seasoned employees. Participants are asked to rate "helpfulness" rather than "satisfaction" because "satisfaction" is generally too broad for measuring training outcome (e.g., trainees might simply have enjoyed the day off or liked the lunch). Question 3 gets at problems or gaps in the training and may elicit suggestions for future sessions. Asking trainees to rate the extent to which they felt the workshop was worthwhile gives a quantitative measure of success, which should correlate with the final question on whether they would recommend this workshop to someone else. Using the same form for different workshops provides a reliable comparison in a series of training sessions. Results of the questionnaire, including a categorization of open-ended comments, should be reported not only to the trainer and to the administration but also to the participants.

Did You Know? ?

A Maryland study found that the best results from training library staff in reference interview skills came from three factors: (1) a minimum of three days' training with sufficient time for practice; (2) peer coaching several times a week for at least a month after the training; and (3) specific strategies such as the existence of a reference policy or procedure requiring the use of the skills taught (Dyson, 1992, 284-289).

A Quick Tip 🕐

Thank You!
A good way for the library to support the training program is to create channels for feedback from users. Training is reinforced when library staff receive rewards and recognition for good service. Make it easy for library users to thank them. Walters (1994) suggests that you prepare forms that people can use to thank staff for helping them. The forms could be printed and available in the library or directly accessible on the library website.

Sample Workshop Evaluation Form

Please help us to evaluate this workshop by completing this form and handing it in at the end of the workshop.

1. How long have you worked in your current position? Check one:

   ❏ Less than 1 year   ❏ 1-3 years
   ❏ 4-9 years   ❏ More than 9 years

2. What aspects of the workshop were *most helpful* to you?

_____

_____

_____

_____

_____

3. What aspects of the workshop were *least helpful* to you? What kind of help would you have liked instead?

_____

_____

_____

_____

_____

4. Generally speaking, was the workshop a worthwhile experience for you?

1 .... 2 .... 3 .... 4 5

(Not at all worthwhile)   (Very worthwhile)

5. Would you recommend this workshop to a friend or colleague?

❏ Yes   ❏ No

Please use the back of this page for further comments.

10.9.2. Follow-Up

The evaluation process may be conducted immediately after training or at later intervals. Because most evaluation of skills training occurs immediately after training, usually without any measurement of pre-training or baseline performance levels, we know very little about the long-term effects of training. Research into the effects of training counselors suggests that training effects can be very short-lived—that skills can be lost within 24 hours of the training session. But research also shows that trainees are more likely to maintain their new skills if they are able to integrate these skills immediately into their everyday communication behavior. What this means is that the trainer must help trainees follow up on their training experience.

Quick Tips for Follow-Up

- Explain to trainees the importance of practicing immediately.
- Ask trainees to report on results of practicing the new skills and to collect specific examples of their efforts.
- Encourage trainees to share these examples with the group at a follow-up session or clinic or through an electronic discussion group set up for this purpose.
- Make handouts that trainees can tape to their desks to remind themselves to practice.
- Provide time in staff meetings or subsequent training sessions to review the skills previously learned.
- Announce follow-up clinics at the three-week, eight-week, and six-month points. Review skills, analyze examples, and set new objectives.
- Distribute evaluation forms after trainees have had a chance to practice their skills, not at the training session itself.
- Encourage trainees to teach others. Create opportunities for practice teaching of one skill to two or three other people.
- Be available for troubleshooting and to reinforce successful practice attempts.
- Route relevant articles, clippings, or reports to trainees. You might, for example, circulate a news photo that illustrates bad or good nonverbal behavior.

Changing behavior, particularly nonverbal behavior, is not easy and happens in little steps. Allan (2003: 212–213) recommends thinking about behavior change as progress along a continuum. For measuring training effects, we could begin with "aware of proposed skills," advance to "willing to try new skills," then to "prefers the new skills," next to "identifies with new skills," and finally to "incorporates skills into communication behavior" on the job. Learning any new skill is a matter of successive approximations that get closer and closer to the correct performance of the skill. Supervisors and trainees themselves should be encouraged to recognize and celebrate taking the first steps. Remember the Chinese proverb about the thousand-mile journey.

10.10. Where to Get Help

Help in planning and carrying out the training program is available from many sources. We have found the following types of sources particularly helpful:

- **Resource lists and bibliographies.** Many books on training have extensive, annotated bibliographies.
- **Networks and special interest groups.** The American Library Association's Learning Round Table (LearnRT) puts you in touch with other trainers (see http://alalearning. org/). It issues *The Learning Exchange*, a quarterly newsletter (formerly *The CLENE Exchange*), full of practical advice, reviews, and short articles that are well worth the membership fee. Earlier issues are archived and freely available at the LearnRT website (http://www.ala.org/ learnrt/newsletter/). See also the LearnRT's blog at http:// alalearning.org/blog/. The American Library Association's Public Library Association (PLA) online learning site (http://www.ala.org/pla/onlinelearning) has information on webinars (upcoming and archived), links to monthly webinars, and self-directed online workbooks. PLA's sections regularly publish notes on continuing education opportunities in public libraries.
- **Library journals and newsletters.** Many publications have regular columns on continuing education and training. For example, the *Journal of Education for Library and Information Science* (JELIS) publishes research articles and columns on various aspects of education for librarianship.
- **Specialized periodicals.** Use a periodical directory to identify publications for professional trainers. Or look for journals devoted to particular kinds of communication. *The Journal of Business Communication*, for example, is geared largely to the business community but almost always has articles about new techniques for training people to write

and speak more effectively (for tables of contents and some access, see http://job.sagepub.com/).

- **Local organizations.** Your own community includes organizations that focus on training. Look for associations of human resource managers, councils of continuing education agencies, or specialized training groups such as Toastmasters International that focus on public speaking.

- **Courses and resource people.** Many community colleges and other educational agencies offer noncredit courses in leadership skills, public speaking, and other communication topics. Take the course yourself, or, if the leader has a good reputation, recommend it to others. Colleges and universities often offer programs for improving teaching techniques. Look to your nearest college of education for good resource people.

- **Videos.** Library Video Network (http://www.lvn.org/store/page2.html) provides information on videos that are useful for training produced by various libraries and library associations.

- **American Library Association.** The American Library Association (http://www.ala.org/offices/library/alarecommends/recommendedviewing) provides a list of recommended videos. A few individual titles relevant to communications are listed at the end of the Annotated Bibliography in this and several other chapters in this book.

- **The Internet.** There is a wealth of information on training and development from business and education sources. You can also look for specific topics (e.g., public speaking, netiquette, citation style). Specific sites for librarians usually include information on training and development. Here are some library-related sites to get you started:

> American Library Association's *Staff Development* wiki (http://wikis.ala.org/professionaltips/index.php?title=Staff_Development#On_the_Job_Training)
> *Library Success: A Best Practices Wiki*, which includes, among other topics, a webpage on Training and Development for Librarians, with links to "online training resources for librarians," "staff development," and "blogs and websites

to watch" (http://www.libsuccess.org/index
.php?title=Library_Success:_A_Best_Practices_
Wiki)

WebJunction, which describes itself as a learning
community for library staff and provides online
learning opportunities, including access to
archived conferences and webinars (http://www
.webjunction.org/)

Finally, and perhaps most important, **get help from the people you
work with**, including other trainers, administrators, staff, and students. Solicit their ideas and feedback. And listen!

10.11. Annotated Bibliography

General Approaches to Training

Allan, Barbara. 2003. *Training Skills for Library Staff*. Revised and adapted
by Barbara Moran. Lanham, MD: Scarecrow. This excellent resource
provides a discussion of learning styles, the roles and skills of trainers,
various training methods, and plenty of examples, activities, and
techniques for designing, delivering, and assessing training programs.
See also Allan's book *The No-Nonsense Guide to Training in Libraries*
(London: Facet, 2013).

Avery, Elizabeth Fussler, Terry Dahlin, and Deborah Carver. 2001. *Staff
Development: A Practical Guide*. 3rd ed. Chicago: American Library
Association. This practical handbook provides essential how-to
information for staff training, and a resource list. See especially
Chapter 8 by Anne Grodzins Lipow, "How to Get Started: Questions
to Ask," pp. 38–41; and Chapter 19, by Julie Todaro, "Evaluating Your
Program," pp. 155–161. See also the fourth edition, published in 2012.

Brine, Alan, ed. 2009. *Handbook of Library Training Practice and
Development*. Vol. 3. Burlington, VT: Ashgate. This excellent guide to
in-service training includes chapters on various aspects of training.
See especially "Customer Service Training" by Beryl Morris (pp.
145–176), which succinctly covers advantages and appropriateness
of different approaches to and methods of training. Volume 1 (1986)
and Volume 2 (1990), edited by Ray Prytherch, are still useful.

Creth, Sheila D. 1986. *Effective On-the-Job Training: Developing Library Human Resources.* Chicago: American Library Association. This book deals with training objectives (knowledge, skill, attitudes); overcoming resistance to training; learning principles; and public service attitudes.

Jurow, Susan. 2001. "How People Learn: Applying Adult Learning Theory and Learning Styles Models to Training Sessions." In *Staff Development: A Practical Guide*, 3rd ed., edited by Elizabeth Fussler Avery, Terry Dahlin, and Deborah Carver, 6–9. Chicago: American Library Association. This chapter provides the theoretical context for designing a focused and evolving training program.

Knowles, Malcolm S., Elwood F. Holton, and Richard A. Swanson. 2011. *The Adult Learner: The Definitive Classic in Adult Education and Human Resource Development.* 7th ed. Boston: Elsevier. This book covers the basic theory of adult learning as well as the background of andragogy. The first section contains all of Knowles's original chapters from his influential 1970 book on andragogy, *The Modern Practice of Adult Education*, and the remaining two sections cover advances on the theory. The book is useful as background reading.

Laird, Dugan, 2003. *Approaches to Training and Development.* 3rd ed., revised and updated by Sharon S. Naquin and Elwood F. Holton. Cambridge, MA: Perseus Books. This is a resource book for the trainer, with clear explanations of the relationship between learning theory and training practice. The sections on teaching techniques, questioning techniques, and relating to students are particularly practical.

Levy, Philippa. 1993. *Interpersonal Skills.* Library Training Guide. London: Library Association. Although somewhat dated, this text is still useful for discussion of topics such as the challenges of facilitating role-play and other participatory activities, cultural differences in the perception of interpersonal skills, and lack of training skills experience on the part of either trainers or staff.

Teaching Communication Skills

Carver, Deborah A. 2001. "How People Apply What They Learn: Transfer of Training." In *Staff Development: A Practical Guide*, 3rd ed., edited by Elizabeth Fussler Avery, Terry Dahlin, and Deborah Carver, 149–154. Chicago: American Library Association. This chapter provides suggestions for ensuring that participants transfer their learning back to their work.

Dyson, Lillie Seward. 1992. "Improving Reference Services: A Maryland Training Program Brings Positive Results." *Public Libraries* 31, no. 5 (September/October): 284–289. Dyson describes a successful training program that increased librarians' communication skills.

Hargie, Owen. 2006. "Training in Communication Skills: Research, Theory and Practice." In *The Handbook of Communication Skills*, 3rd ed., edited by Owen Hargie, 551–565. New York: Routledge. This thorough discussion of communication skills and training is well worth reading.

Ivey, Allen E., Mary Bradford Ivey, and Carlos P. Zalaquett. 2009. *Intentional Interviewing and Counseling: Facilitating Client Development in a Multicultural Society.* 7th ed. Belmont, CA: Brooks/ Cole, Cengage Learning. Exercises and resources are available on the accompanying CD and online on the publisher's companion website. You can also contact Microtraining Associates (http://www .emicrotraining.com/) for information on training materials. Most of these materials are geared to counselors, but some are sufficiently general to be used with librarians.

Jennerich, Elaine Z., and Edward Jennerich. 1997. *The Reference Interview as a Creative Art.* 2nd ed. Littleton, CO: Libraries Unlimited. This book emphasizes training and development of reference librarians.

Lee, Marta K. 2011. *Mentoring in the Library: Building for the Future.* Chicago: American Library Association. This text covers the kinds of skills the mentor should have, how to establish a mentoring program, and techniques for successful education and training.

Metz, Ruth F. 2011. *Coaching in the Library: A Management Strategy for Achieving Excellence.* 2nd ed. Chicago: American Library Association. This book explains how business principles of coaching to improve employee performance can be used by managers in any library. It covers basic coaching behaviors and includes examples of actual coaching sessions.

Robbins, Stephen P., and Phillip L. Hunsaker. 2006. *Training in Interpersonal Communication Skills: Tips for Managing People at Work.* 4th ed. Upper Saddle River, NJ: Pearson. This book complements more theoretical works. Designed to provide training in interpersonal skills, it includes a self-contained program that allows for actual practice of communication skills, with exercises, checklists, and tests. See also the latest edition, published in 2012.

Stueart, Robert D., and Maureen Sullivan. 2010. *Developing Library Leaders: A How-To-Do-It Manual for Coaching, Team Building, and Mentoring Library Staff.* New York: Neal-Schuman. The chapters on mentoring, coaching, and team building provide a solid introduction to each topic with key concepts and practical tips.

Todaro, Julie, and Mark L. Smith. 2006. *Training Library Staff and Volunteers to Provide Extraordinary Customer Service*. New York: Neal-Schuman. This excellent resource explains how to train library staff and volunteers, taking into consideration the work they do in various types of libraries. The authors propose multiple training methods because individuals have different styles of learning. They outline the steps for providing training modules. Sample scripts and scenarios come with instructions on how to write one for your particular situation.

Turner, Anne M. 2004. *It Comes with the Territory: Handling Problem Situations in Libraries*. 2nd ed. Jefferson, NC: McFarland. This book has an excellent chapter on training staff (pp. 112–121), and each chapter features a special section, "Ten Minutes a Week for Training," with lots of good discussion material on training in communication skills.

Walters, Suzanne. 1994. *Customer Service: A How-To-Do-It Manual for Librarians*. New York: Neal-Schuman. See especially Chapter 6, "Staff Training," pp. 43–47, and Chapter 8, on employee motivation.

Webb, Jo, and Chris Powis. 2009. "Training for Pedagogical Development." In *Handbook of Library Training Practice and Development*, Vol. 3, edited by Alan Brine, 29–47. Burlington, VT: Ashgate. This chapter covers methods of training and means of implementation.

Wehmeyer, Susan. 2001. "How to Train for Building Communication Skills." In *Staff Development: A Practical Guide*, 3rd ed., edited by Elizabeth Fussler Avery, Terry Dahlin, and Deborah Carver, 101–104. Chicago: American Library Association. This chapter outlines steps to follow in developing a communication skills training program.

Practical Tools

Coleman, Jason, Danielle Theiss-White, and Melia Erin Fritch. 2011. "Social Software for Training and Managing Reference Staff." *Indiana Libraries* 30, no. 1: 40–48. This article describes an approach to training and management that combines in-person training sessions and meetings with a variety of online tools and resources accessible anywhere at any time.

Eitington, Julius E. 1996. *The Winning Trainer: Winning Ways to Involve People in Training*. 3rd ed. Houston, TX: Gulf Publishing. This hefty paperback does not focus exclusively on communication skills but has ready-made handouts to copy (e.g., listening self-test), forms such as observation sheets for small groups, guides to role-playing, and exercises to break the ice, energize, or relax trainees.

Fukkink, Ruben Georges, Noortje Trienekens, and Lisa J C Kramer. 2011. "Video Feedback in Education and Training: Putting Learning in the Picture." *Educational Psychology Review* 23, no. 1: 45–63. This meta-analysis of 33 experimental research studies (including studies of microtraining) found a statistically significant effect of video feedback on the interaction skills of professionals in a wide range of contact professions. A good discussion of the research literature on different kinds of training.

Gannon-Leary, Pat, and Michael D. McCarthy. 2010. *Customer Care: A Training Manual for Library Staff.* London: Chandos. The book provides a detailed customer care course suitable for delivery to library staff at all levels. It provides information on training of communication behaviors useful for dealing with all types of customers.

Gordon, Jack, ed. 2004. *Pfeiffer's Classic Activities for Interpersonal Communication: The Most Enduring, Effective, and Valuable Training Activities for Improving Interpersonal Communication.* San Francisco: Pfeiffer. Loose leaf. This text includes problems, exercises, and training.

Griffiths, Kami, and Chris Peters. 2009. "10 Steps for Planning a Successful Webinar." TechSoup, The Technology Place for Nonprofits. http://www.techsoup.org/learningcenter/training/page11252 .cfm?cg=tsblog&sg=webconf. This thorough article includes many practical tips for organizing and producing online seminars. An excellent resource for planning webinars, it is directed at nonprofit organizations and libraries. TechSoup.org itself is worth a visit for accessing how-to articles, worksheets, product comparisons, free webinars, and other learning events.

Massis, Bruce E. 2004. *The Practical Library Trainer.* New York: Haworth Press. This compact book is full of suggestions for administrators who want to develop formal training programs. It includes a case study on blended learning.

Mills, Gordon E., and R. Wayne Pace. 1989. "What Effects Do Practice and Video Feedback Have on the Development of Interpersonal Communication Skills?" *Journal of Business Communication* 26, no. 2 (Spring): 159–176. These researchers found that a combination of both practice and feedback produced the greatest effect on long-term performance scores.

Race, Phil, and Brenda Smith. 1996. *500 Tips for Trainers*. Houston, TX: Gulf Professional Publishing. Race and Smith provide practical suggestions for any type of training. Each chapter consists of two pages of "quick tips" on various topics.

Trotta, Marcia. 2006. *Supervising Staff: A How-To-Do-It Manual for Librarians*. New York: Neal-Schuman. See Chapter 4 (pp. 71–88) on ongoing staff training and Chapter 5 (pp. 89–102) on mentoring and coaching.

Evaluating Training

Kirkpatrick, Donald L. 1994. *Evaluating Training Programs: The Four Levels*. San Francisco: Berrett-Koehler. The author is known as the guru of training evaluation, and his four-level performance evaluation model continues to be the standard. See also his more recent book *Improving Employee Performance through Appraisal and Coaching* (New York: American Management Association, 2006, 2nd ed.).

Phillips, Steven. 1993. *Evaluation*. Library Training Guides. London: Library Association. This guide is a concisely written summary of best principles and practices in evaluating training.

Williamson, Michael G. 1990. "The Evaluation of Training." In *Handbook of Library Training Practice*, Vol. 2, edited by Ray Prytherch, 226–262. Brookfield, VT: Gower. This chapter covers all aspects of evaluation, including the strategies for evaluation from checklists and questionnaires to long-term observation and formal interviews.

Zweizig, Douglas, Debra Wilcox Johnson, and Jane Robbins with Michele Besant, eds. 1996. *The Tell It! Manual: The Complete Program for Evaluating Library Performance*. Chicago: American Library Association. This text includes chapters on adult learning theory and evaluation of training. See especially "Planning Training Activities: A Checklist," by Ruby A. Licona, pp. 50–59.

Videos

Library Video Network. 2002. *Arch Lustberg Communicator Collection.* DVD. The collection includes three videos suitable for seminars on communication techniques: *Face It!* (16 min), *Perfecting Presentations* (37 min), and *Controlling the Confrontation* (44 min).

———. 2010. *Customer Service Basics.* 15 min. Recommended for all library employees. Among the items covered are approachability, effective listening, coping with unhappy customers, and completing transactions successfully.

———. n.d. *The LVN Staff Development Library.* DVD. This is a collection of 11 videos related to staff development.

See the Library Video Network catalog for more titles at http://www.lvn.org/store/page2.html.

Index

Page numbers followed by the letter "s" indicate sidebars.

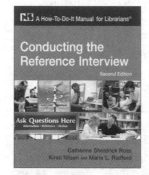